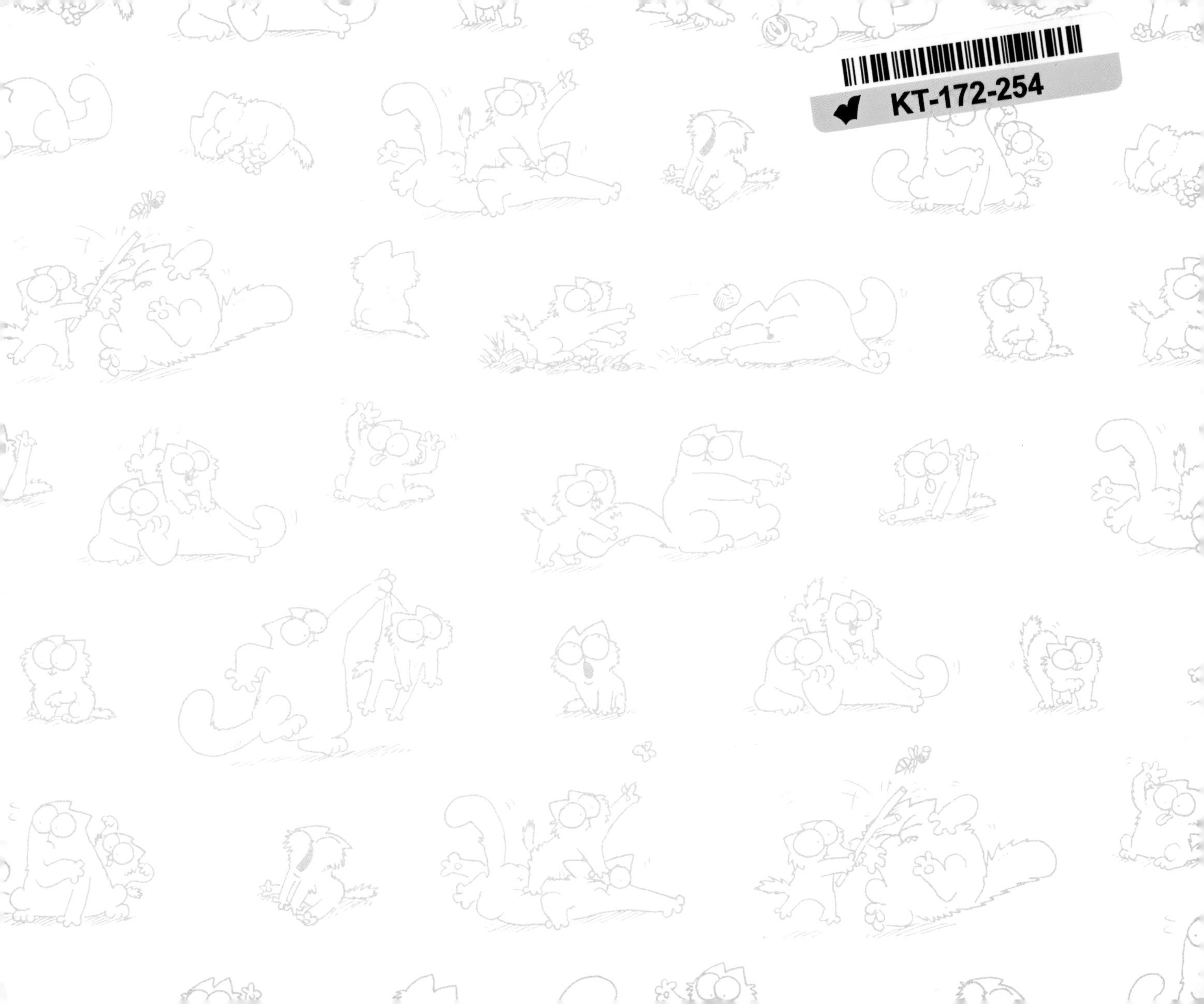

Simon's Cat

Book 3

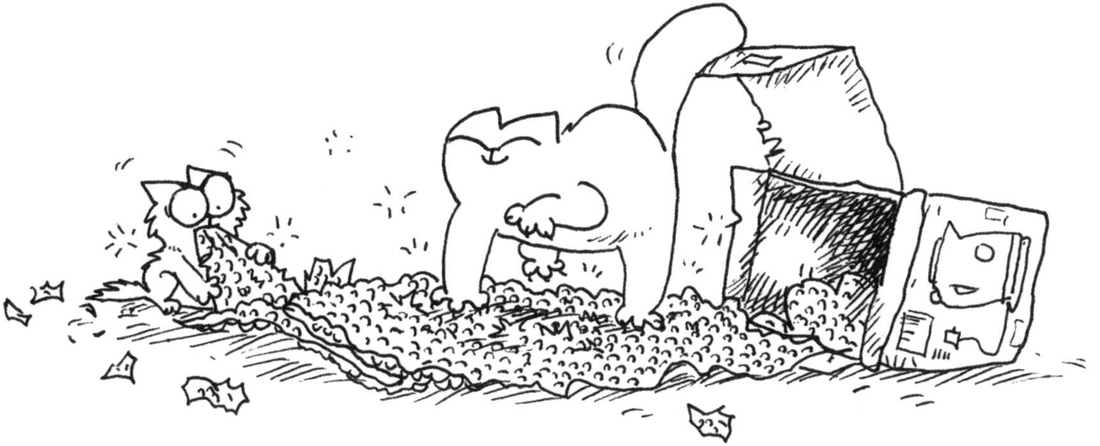

Simon's Cat in Kitten Chaos

by Simon Tofield

CANONGATE

Edinburgh · London · New York · Melbourne

Published in Great Britain in 2011 by Canongate Books Ltd,
14 High Street, Edinburgh EH1 1TE

5

www.canongate.tv

British Library Cataloguing-in-Publication Data
A catalogue record for this book is available on
request from the British Library

ISBN 978 0 85786 078 1

Typeset by Simon's Cat

Printed and bound in Great Britain by Clays Ltd, St Ives plc

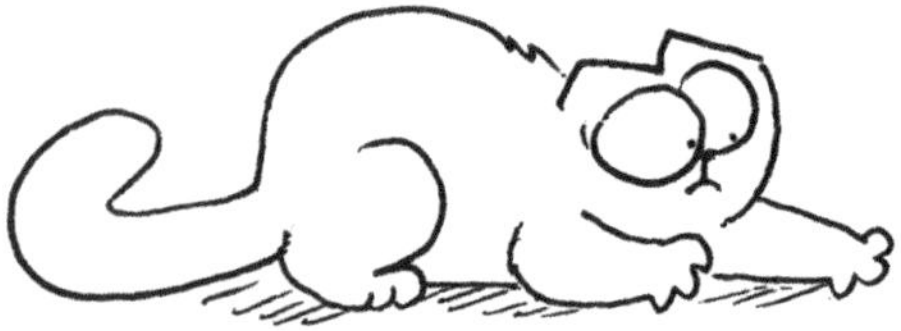

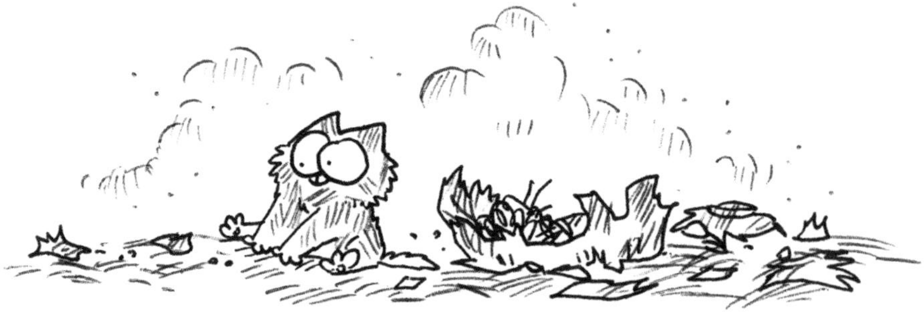

This book is dedicated
to Don Evans

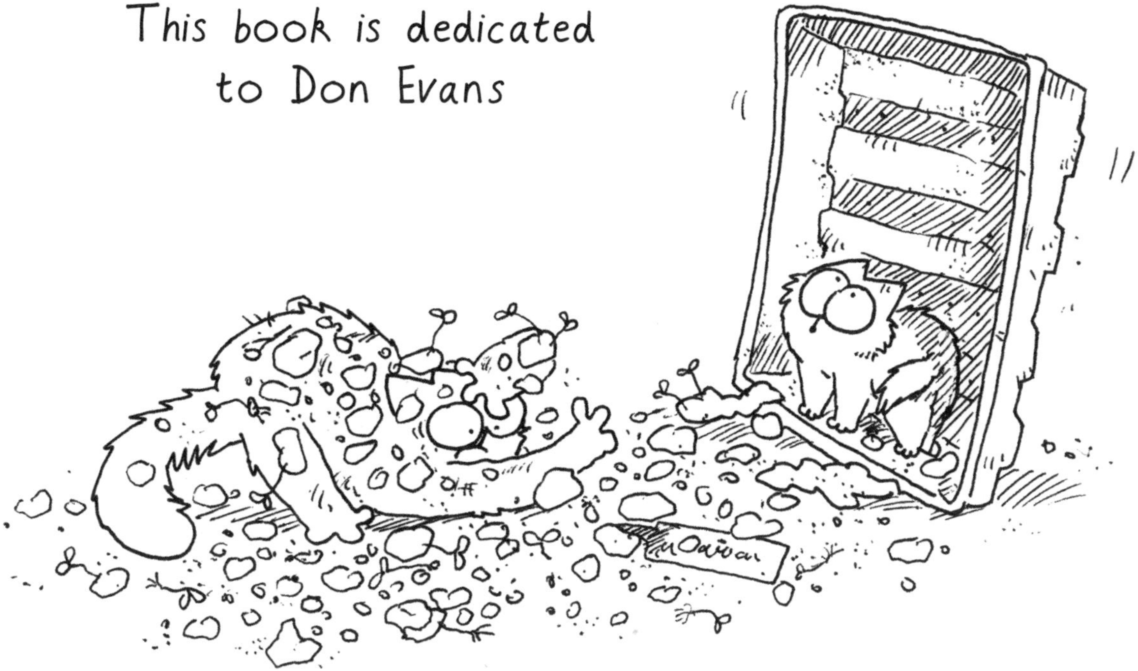

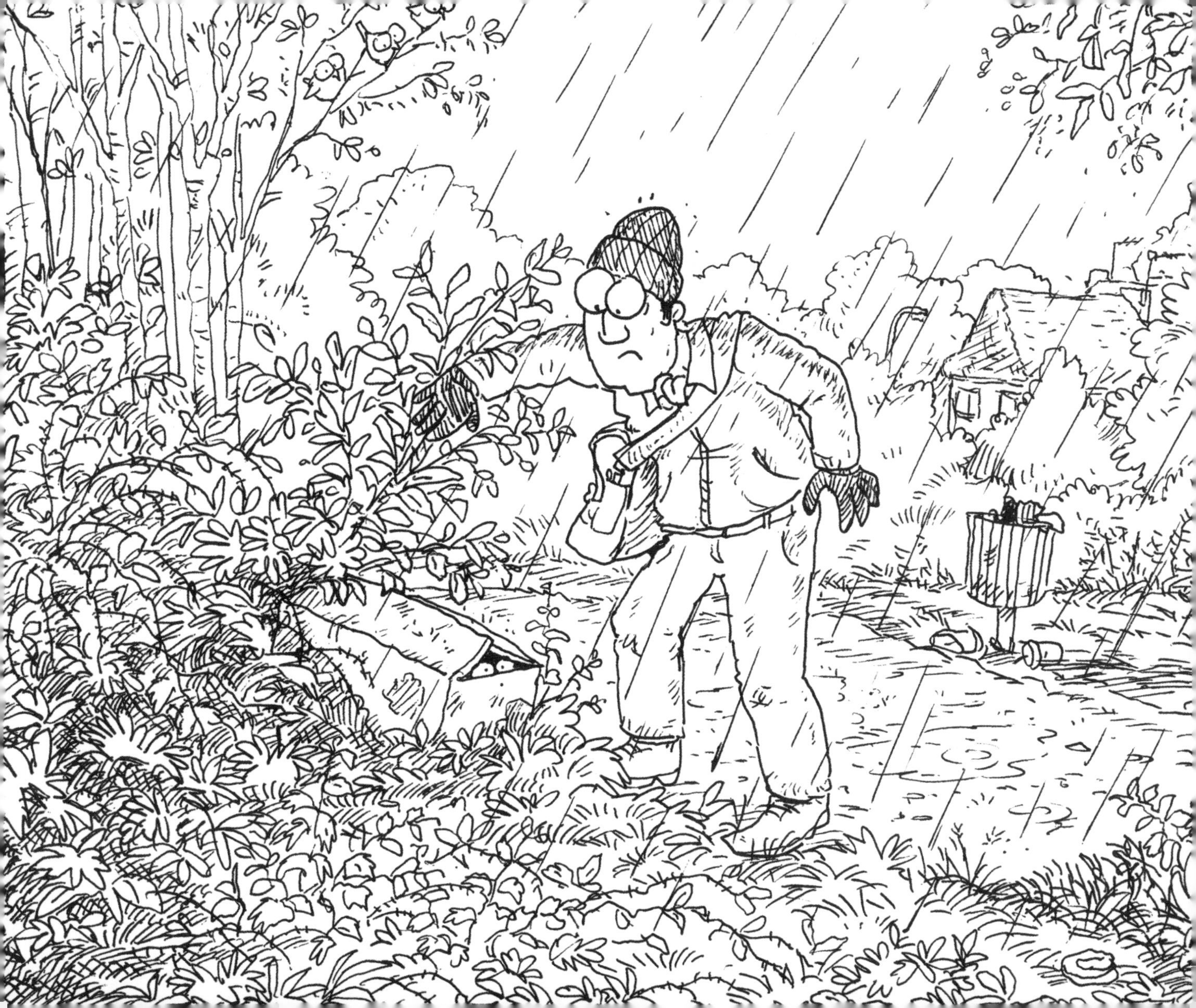

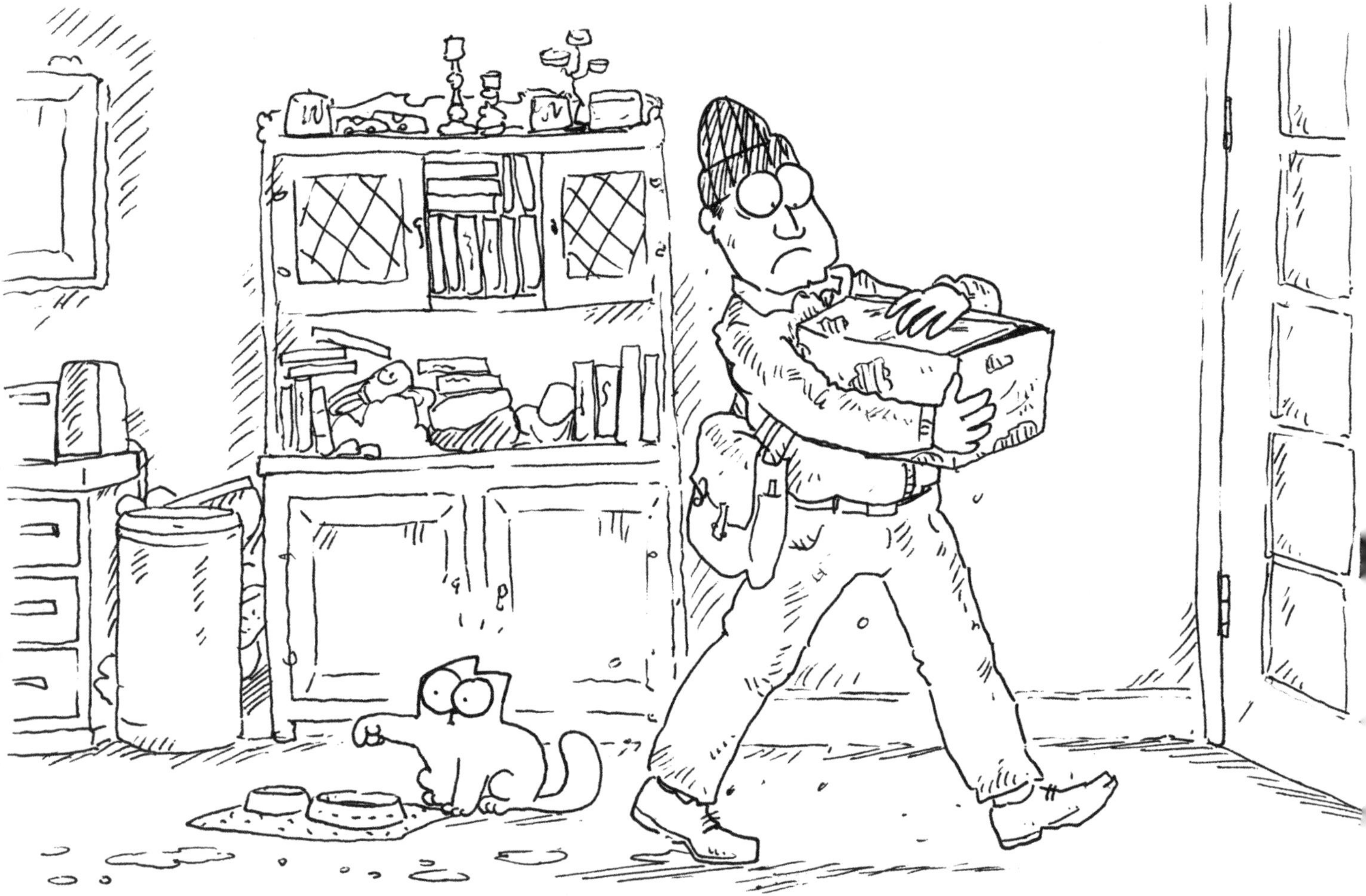

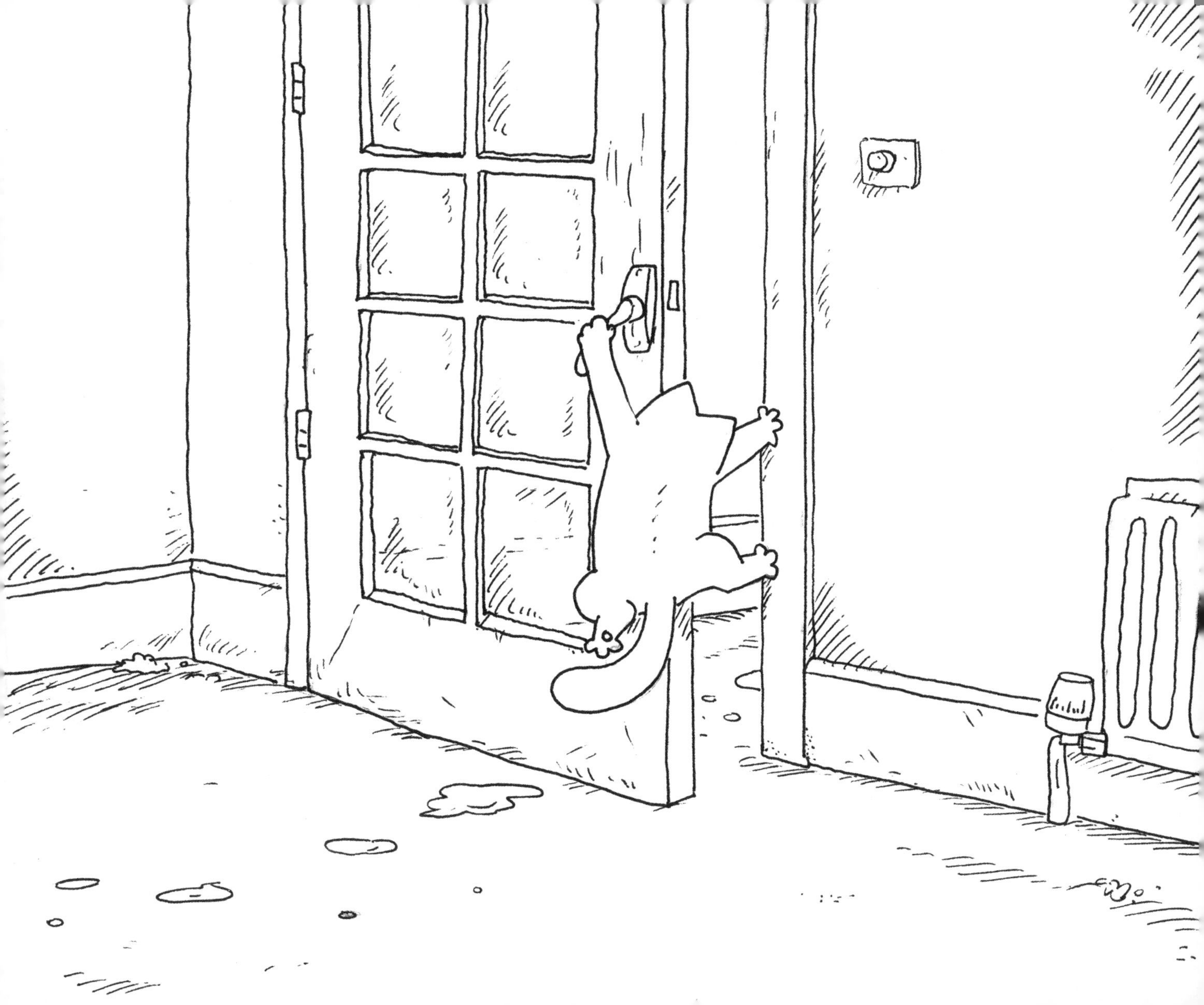

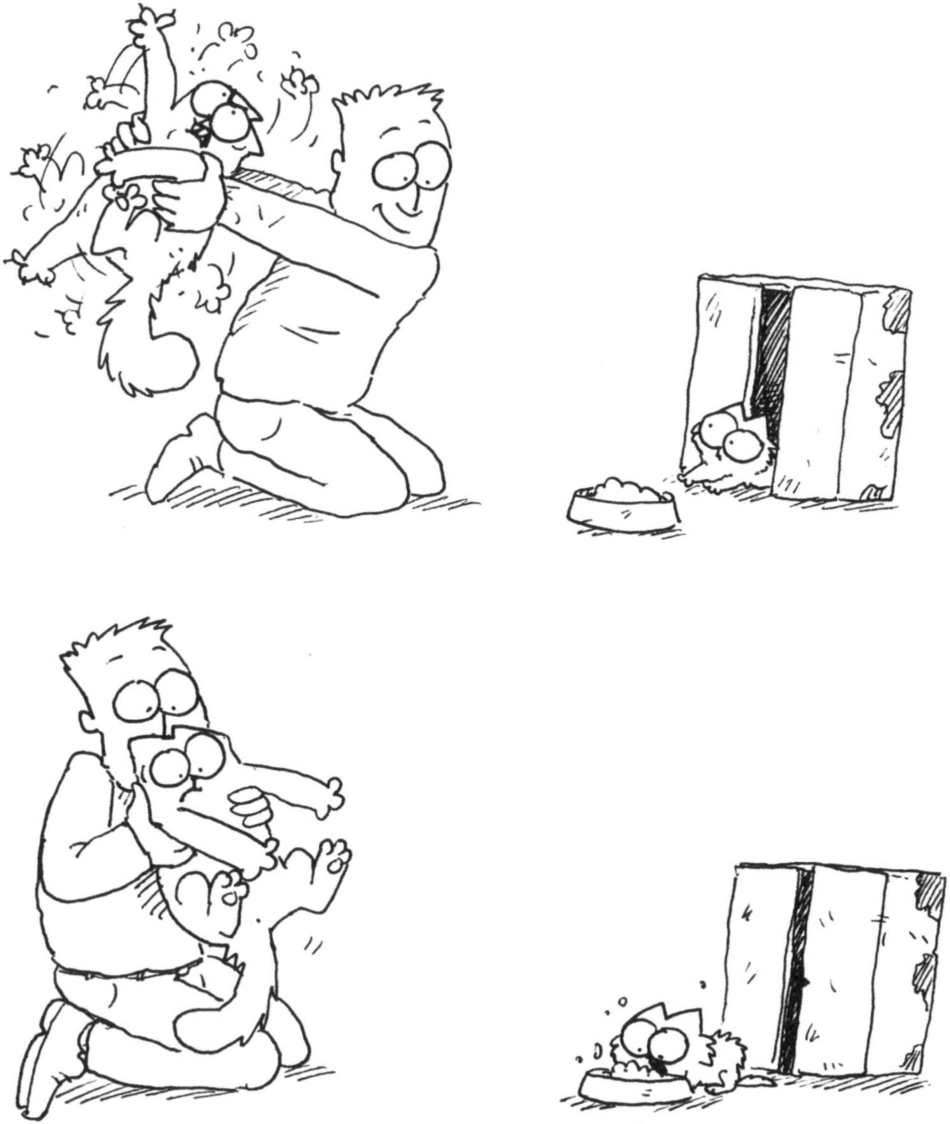

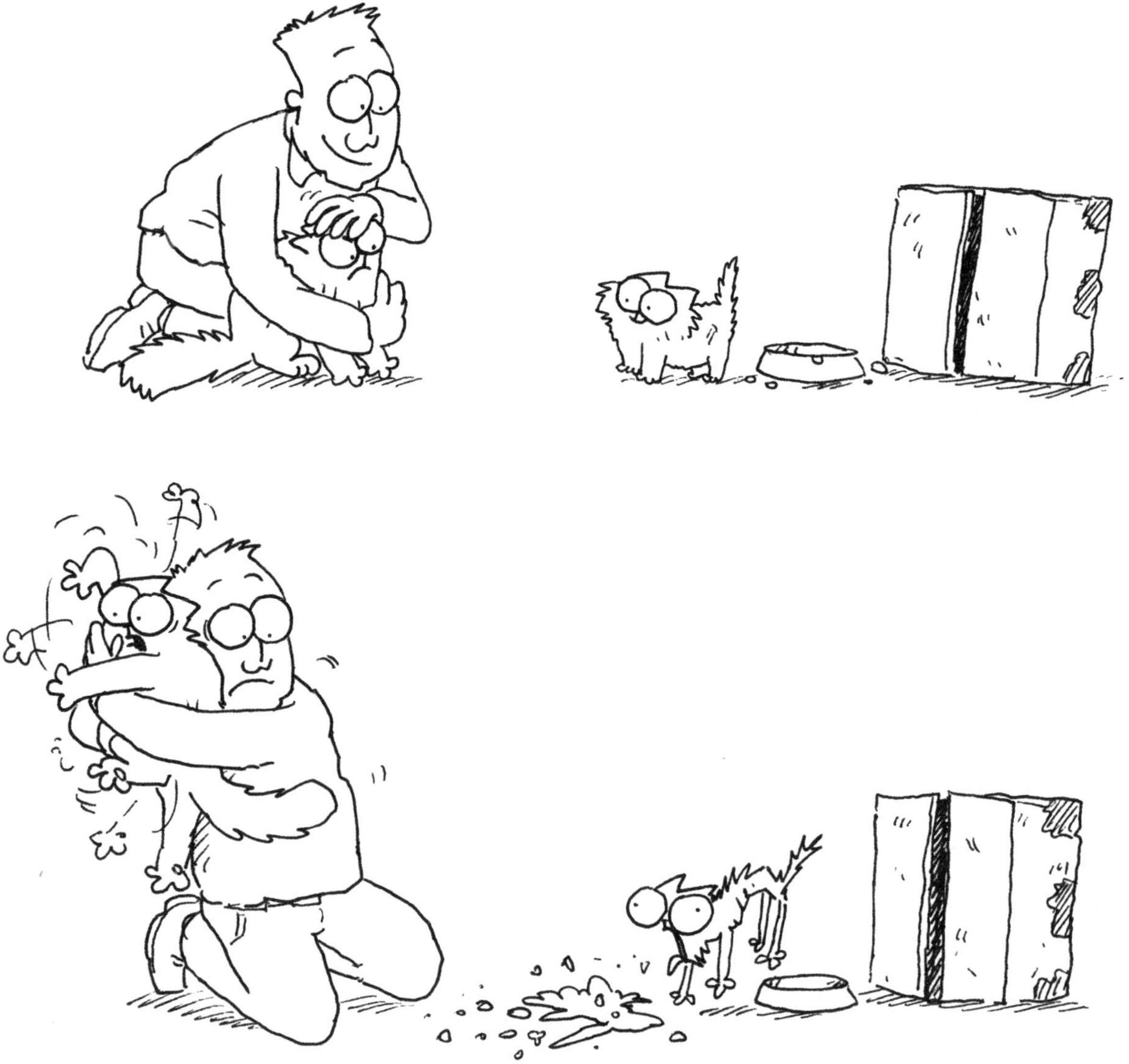

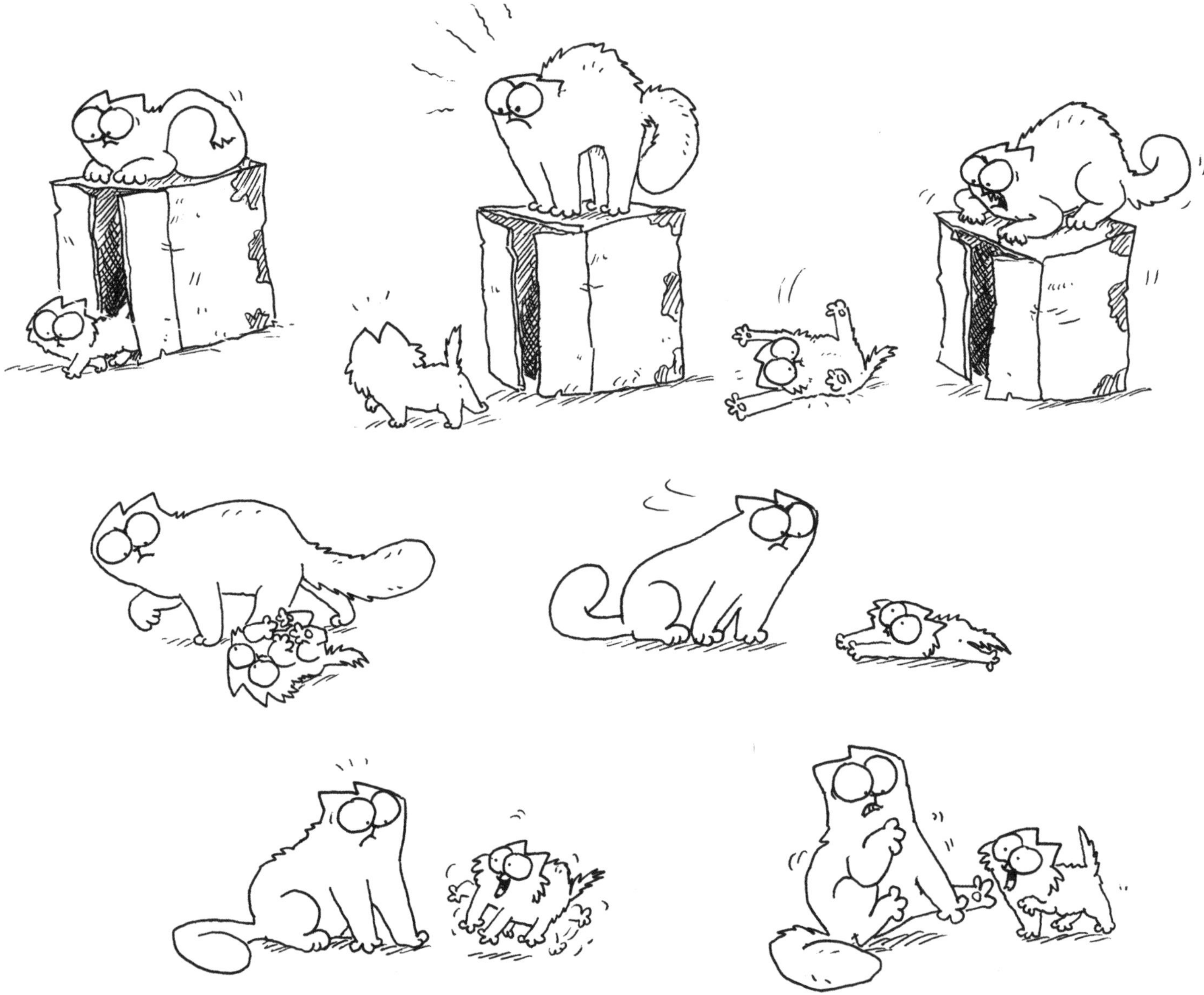

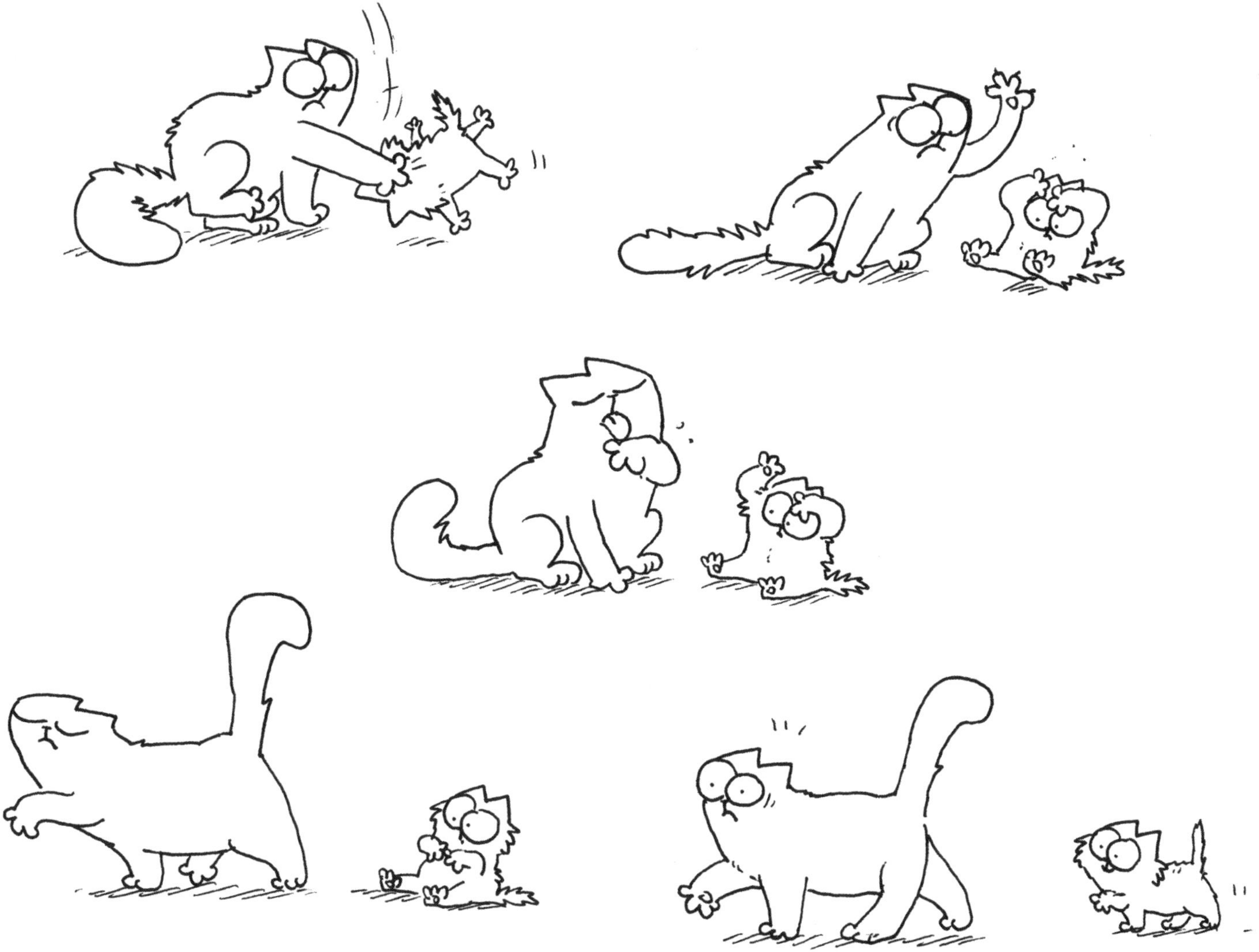

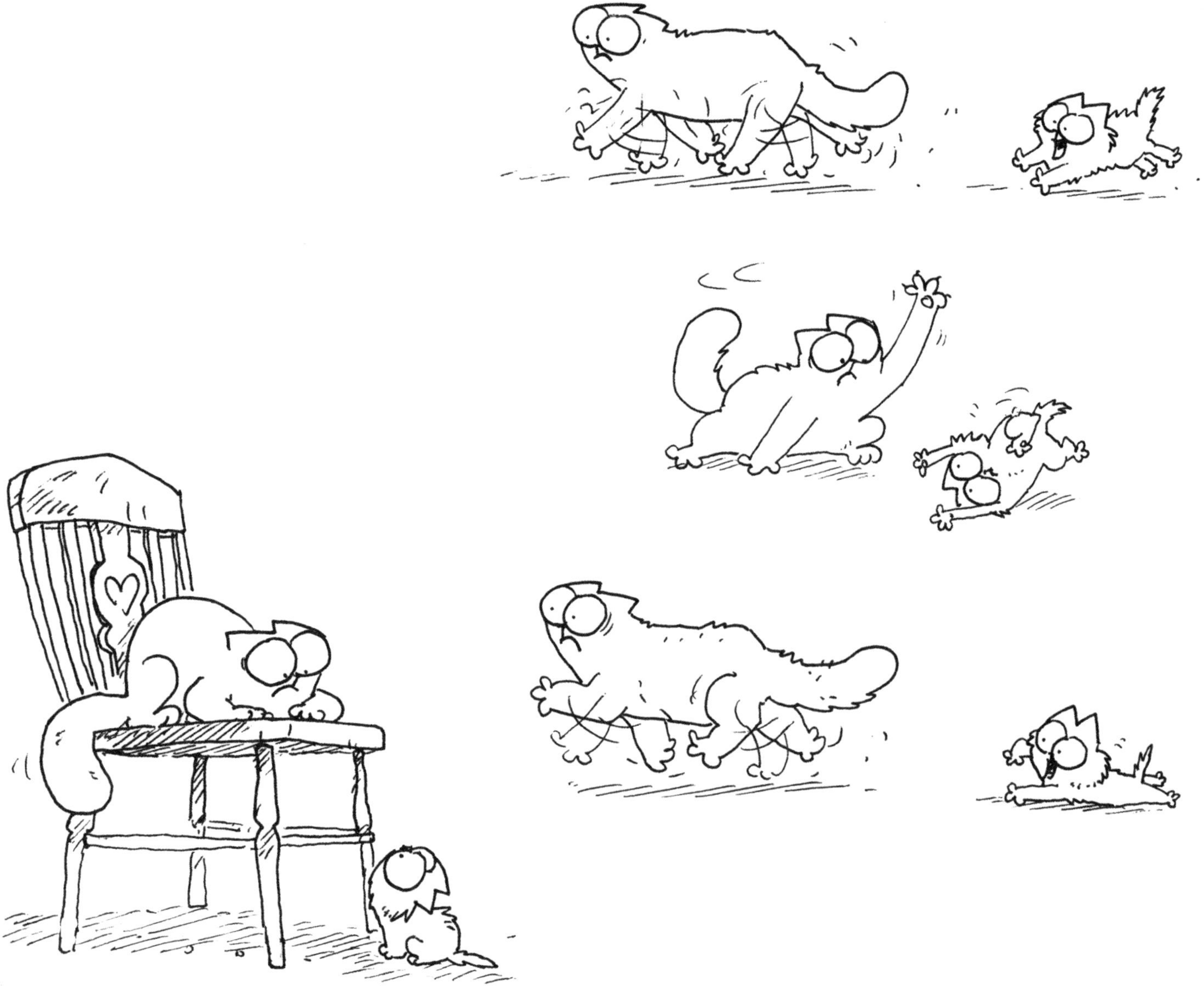

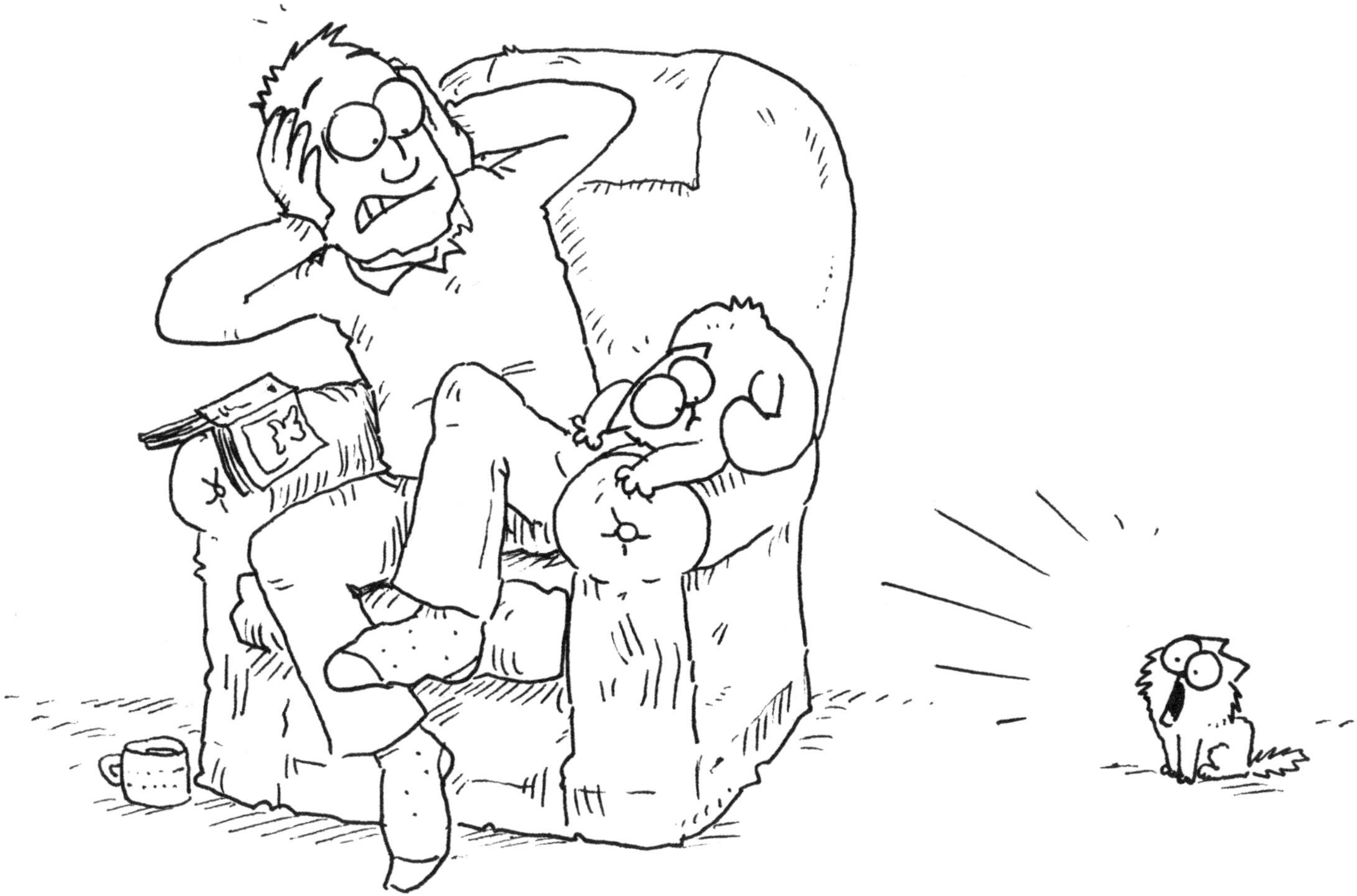

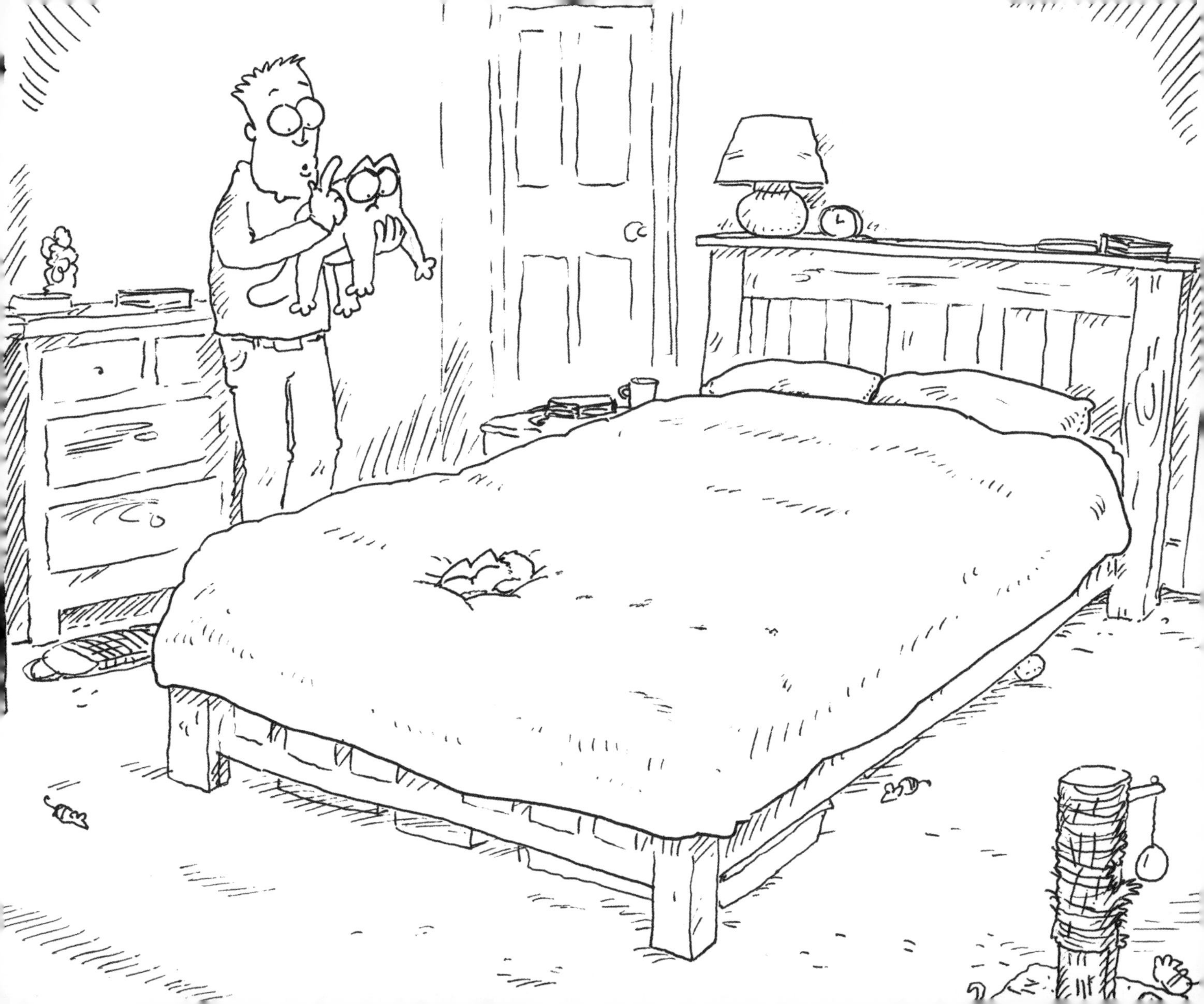

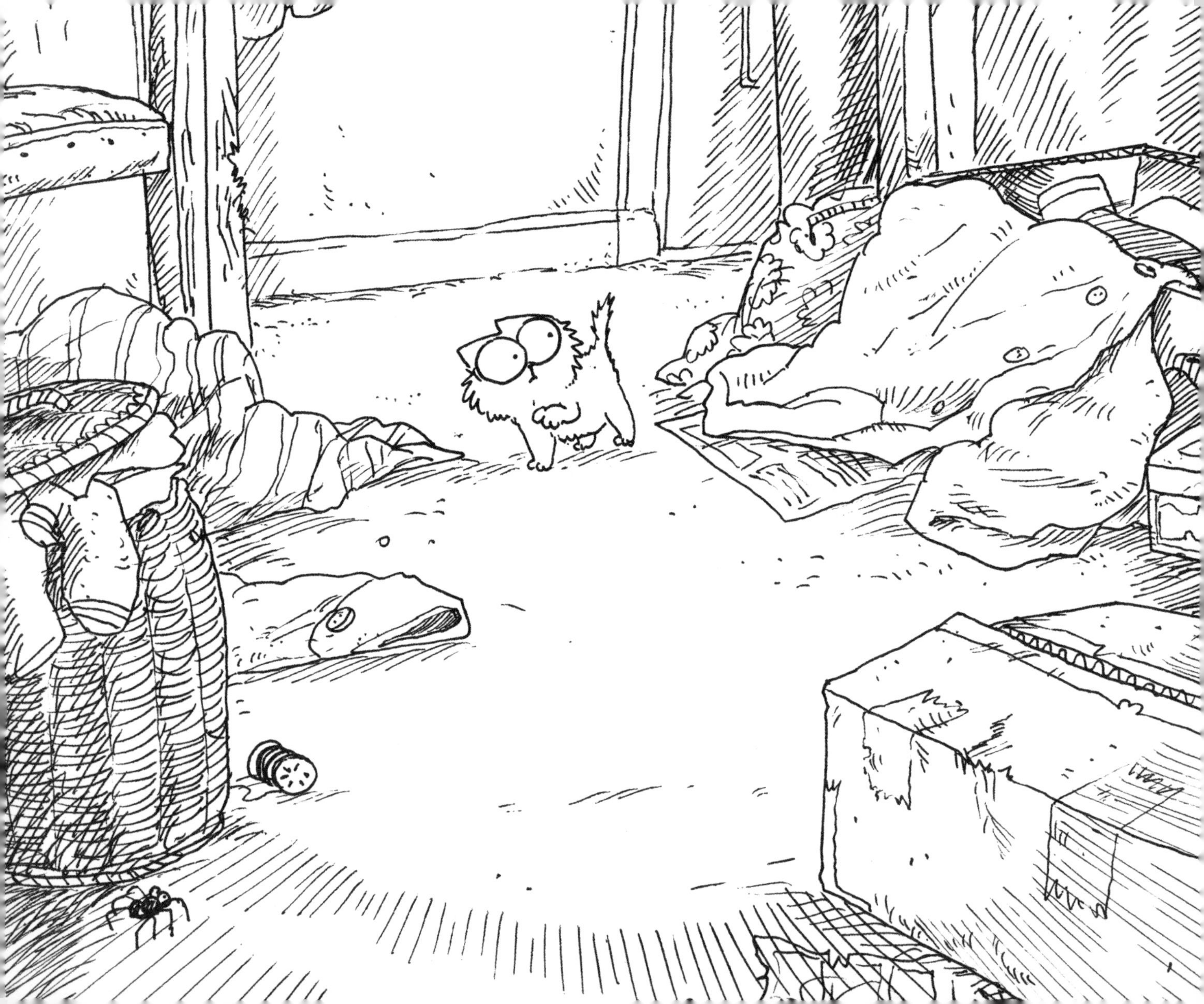

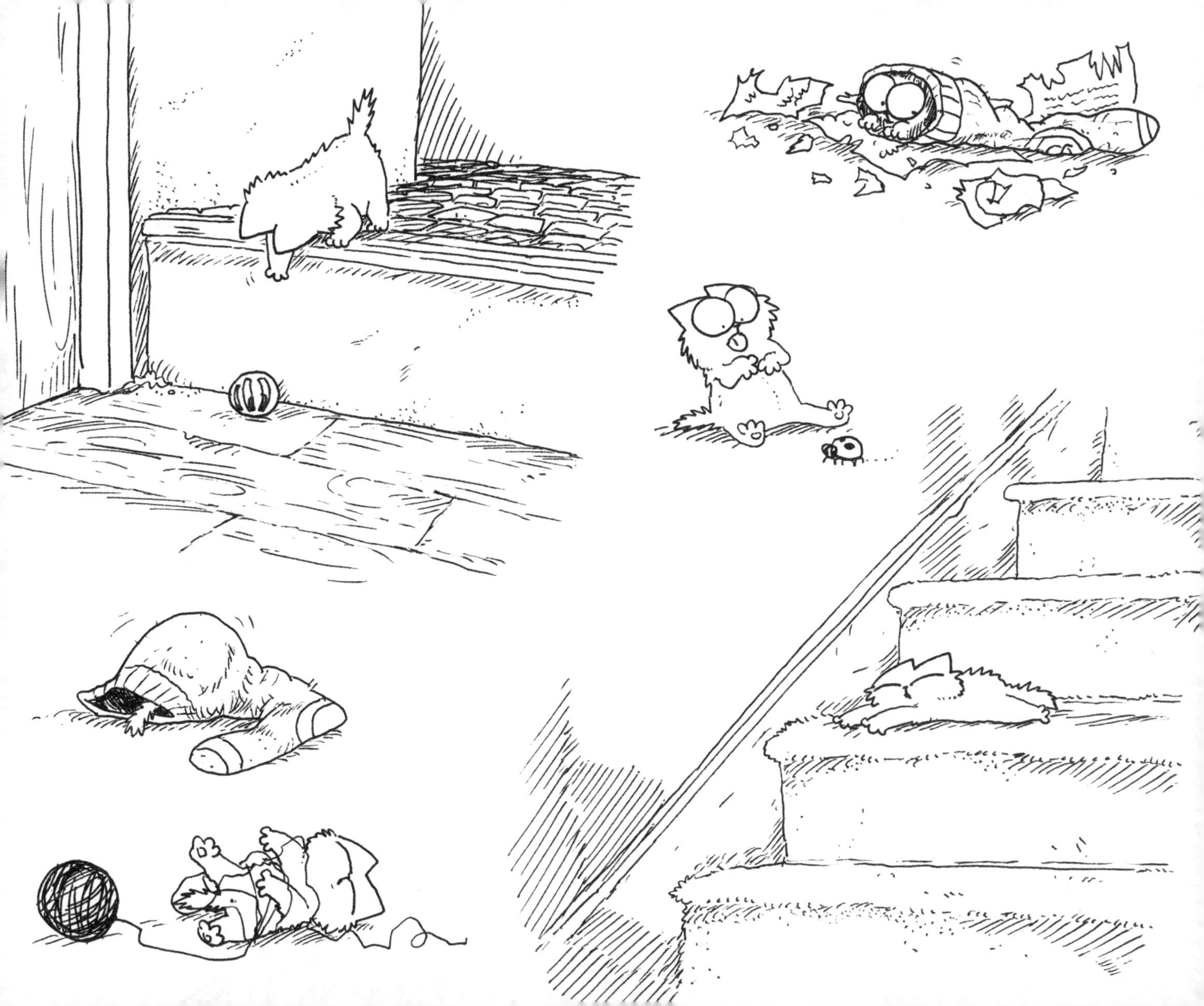

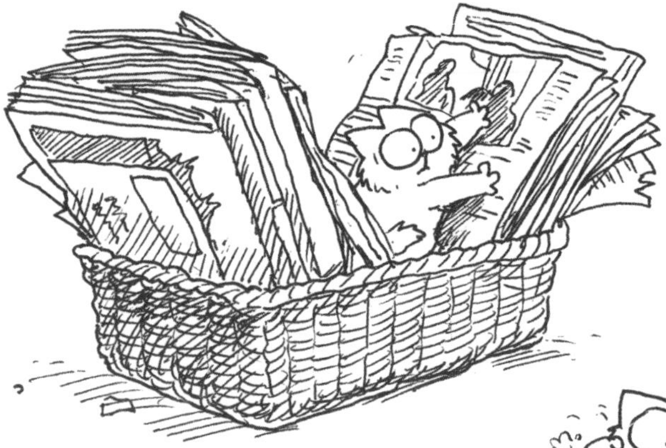
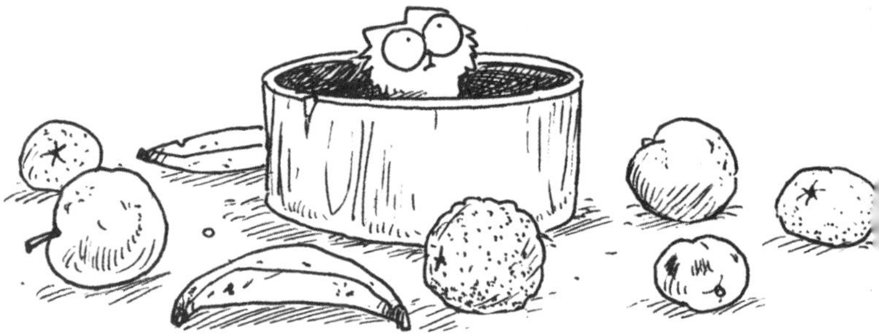
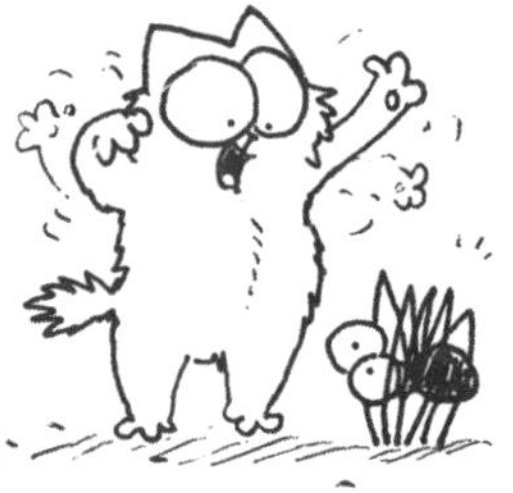
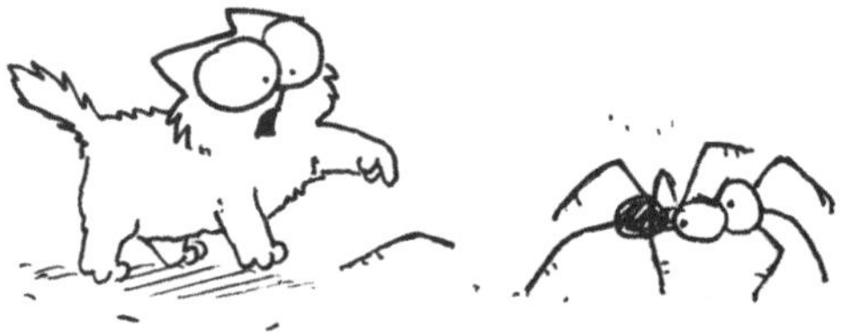
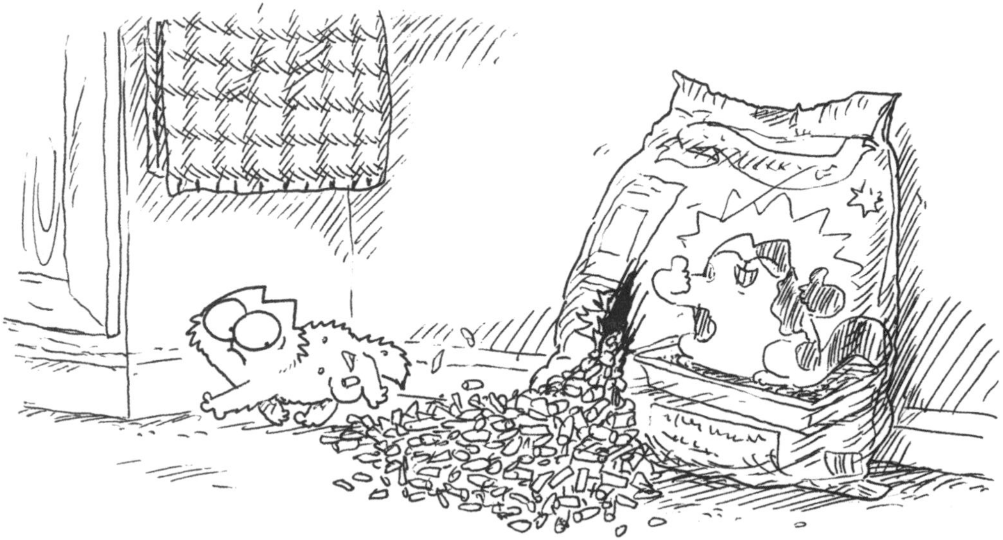
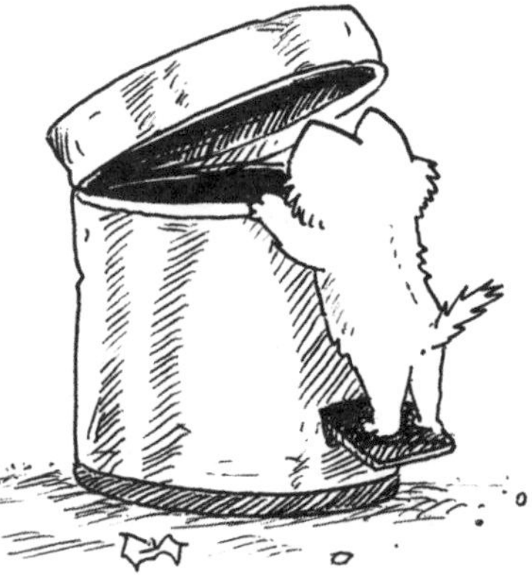

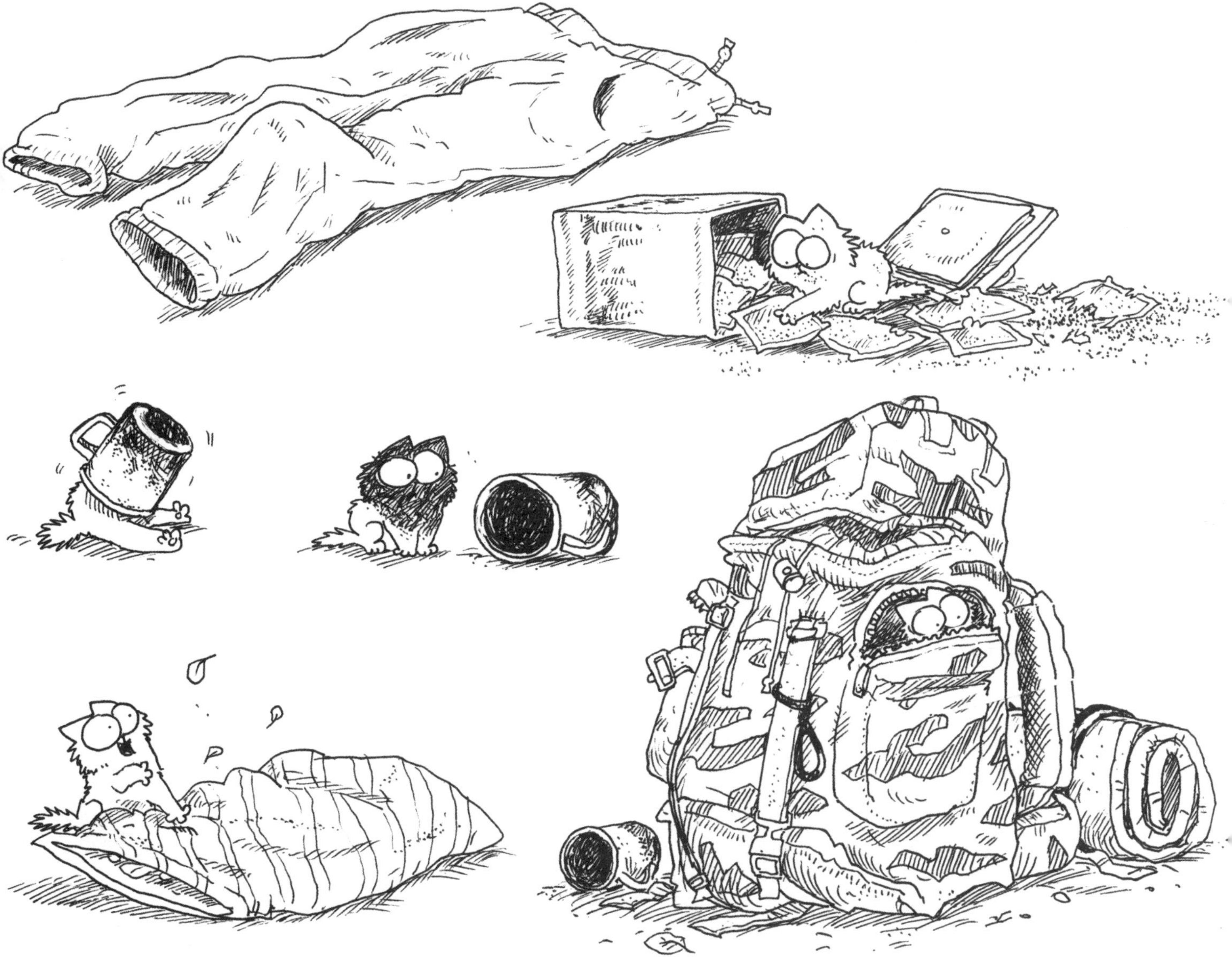

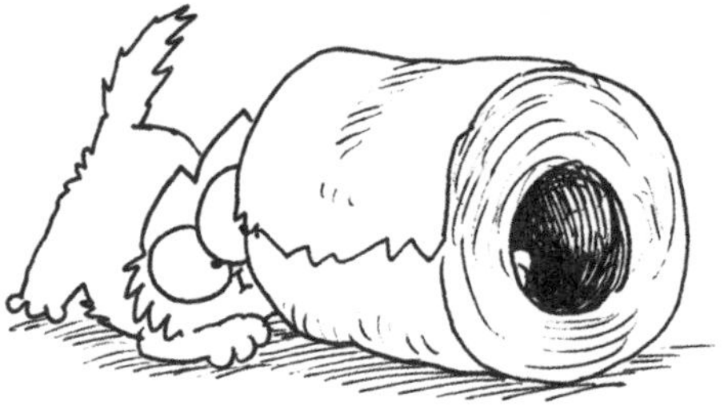

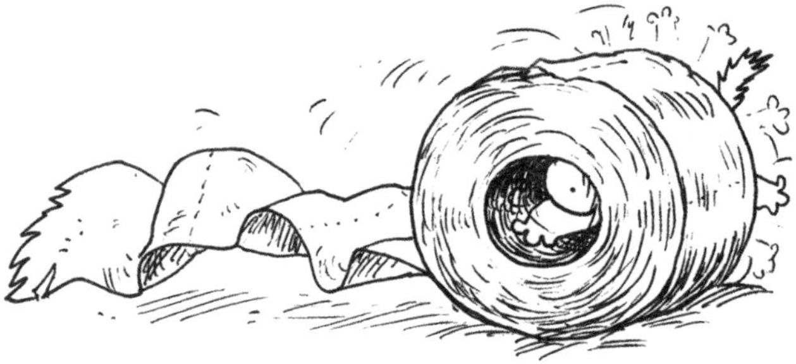

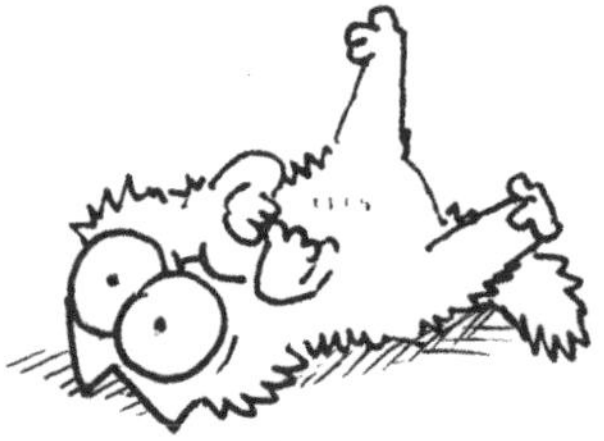

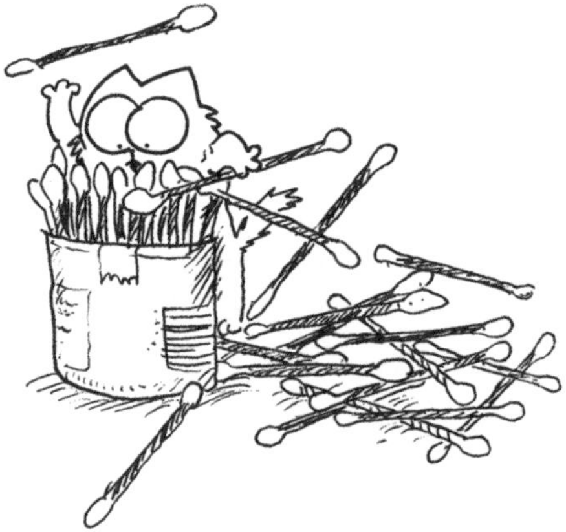

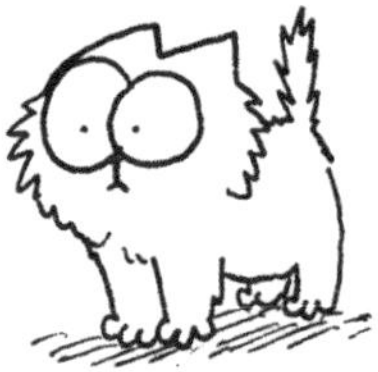

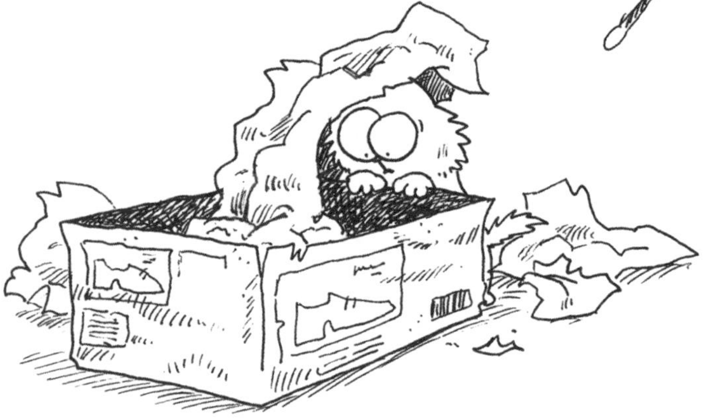

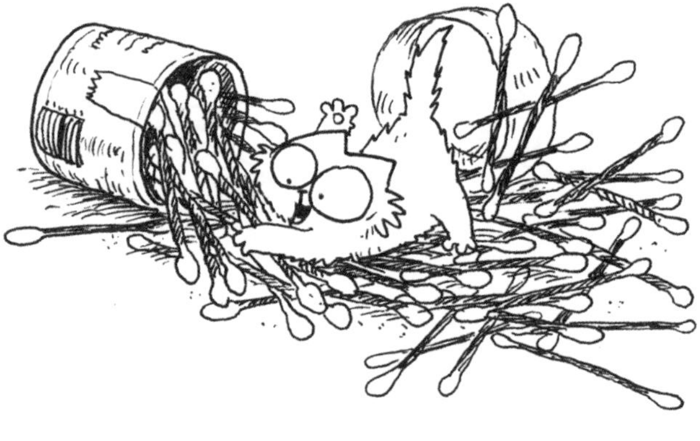

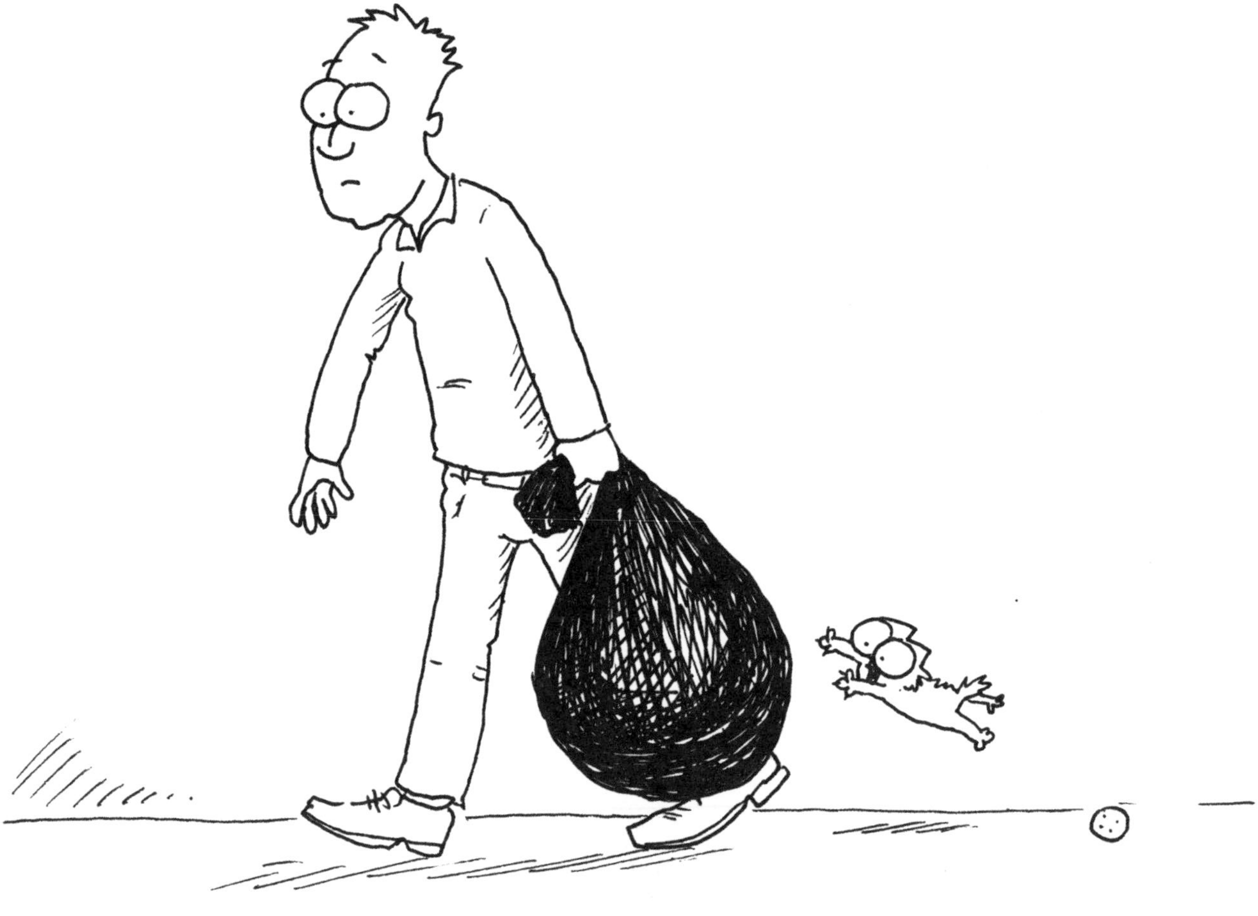

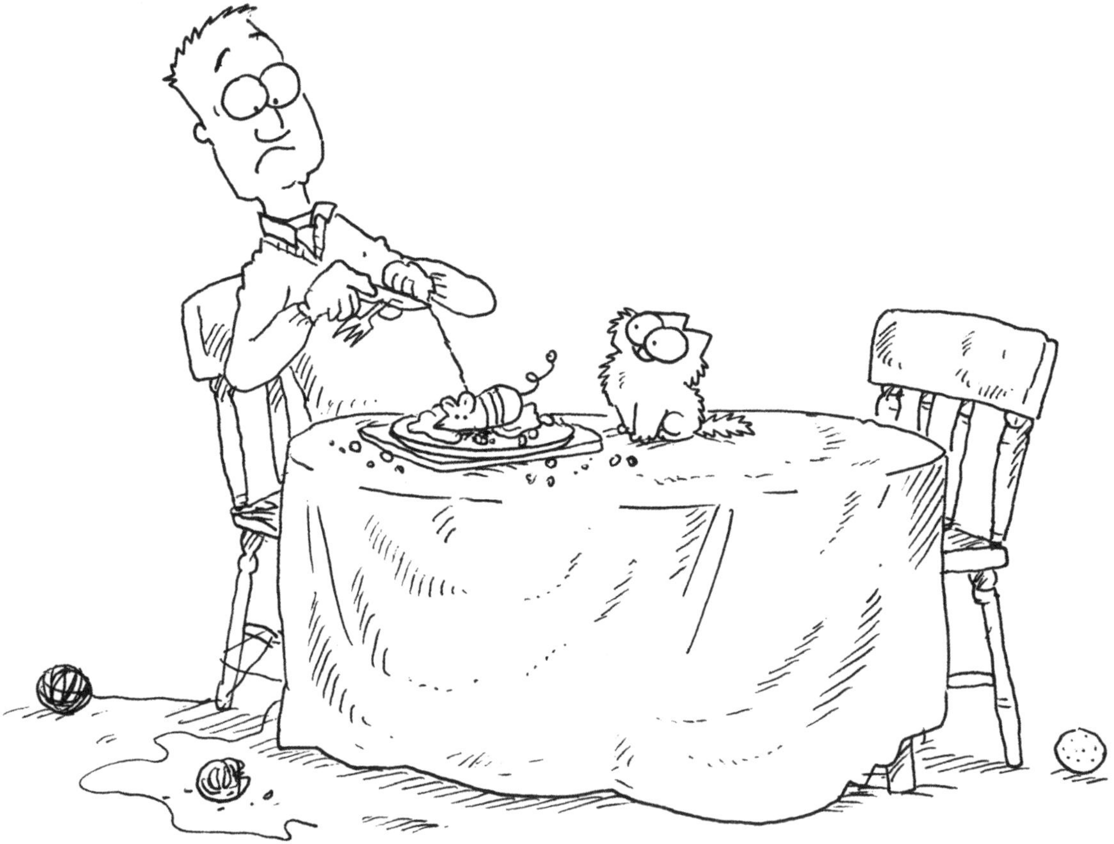

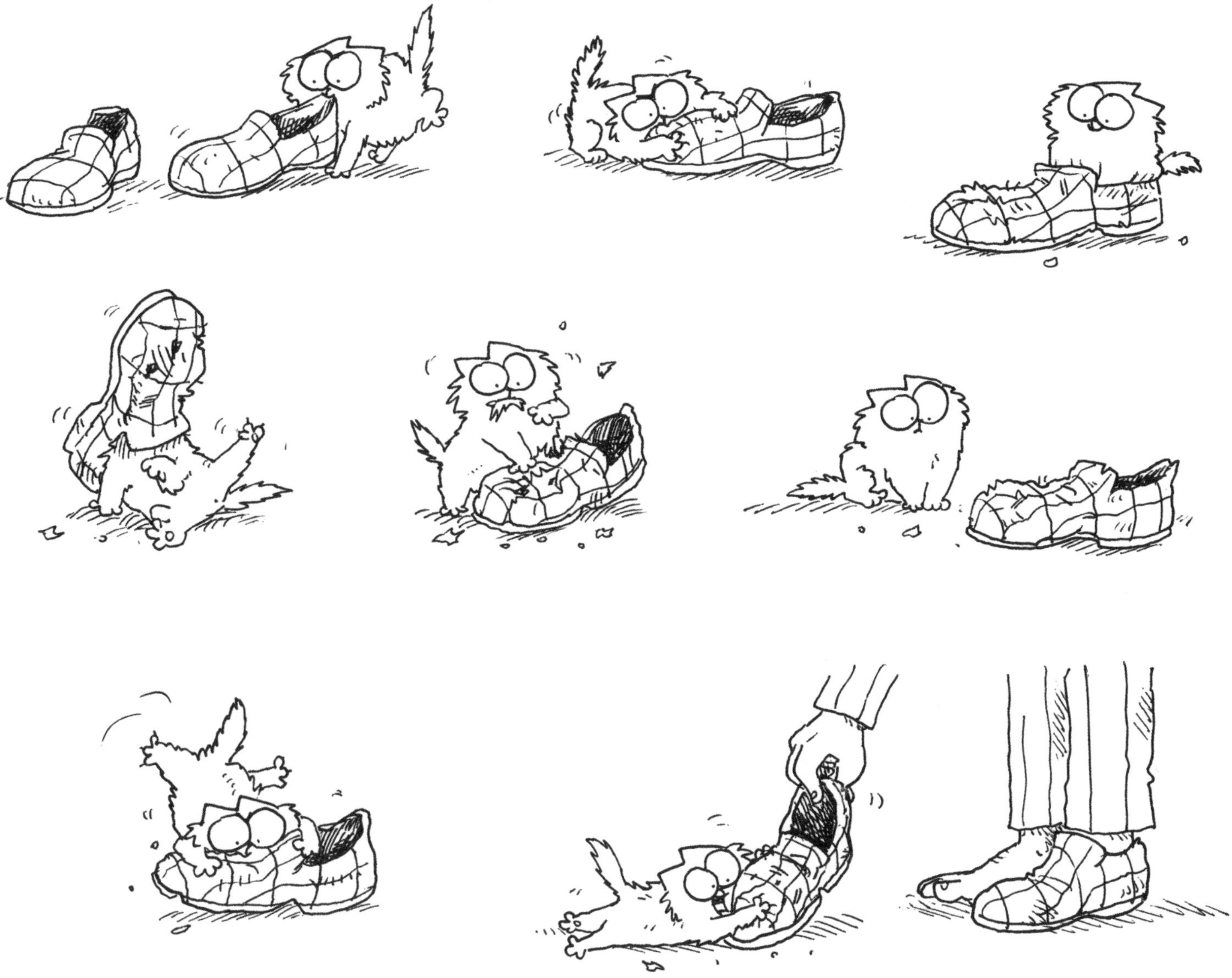

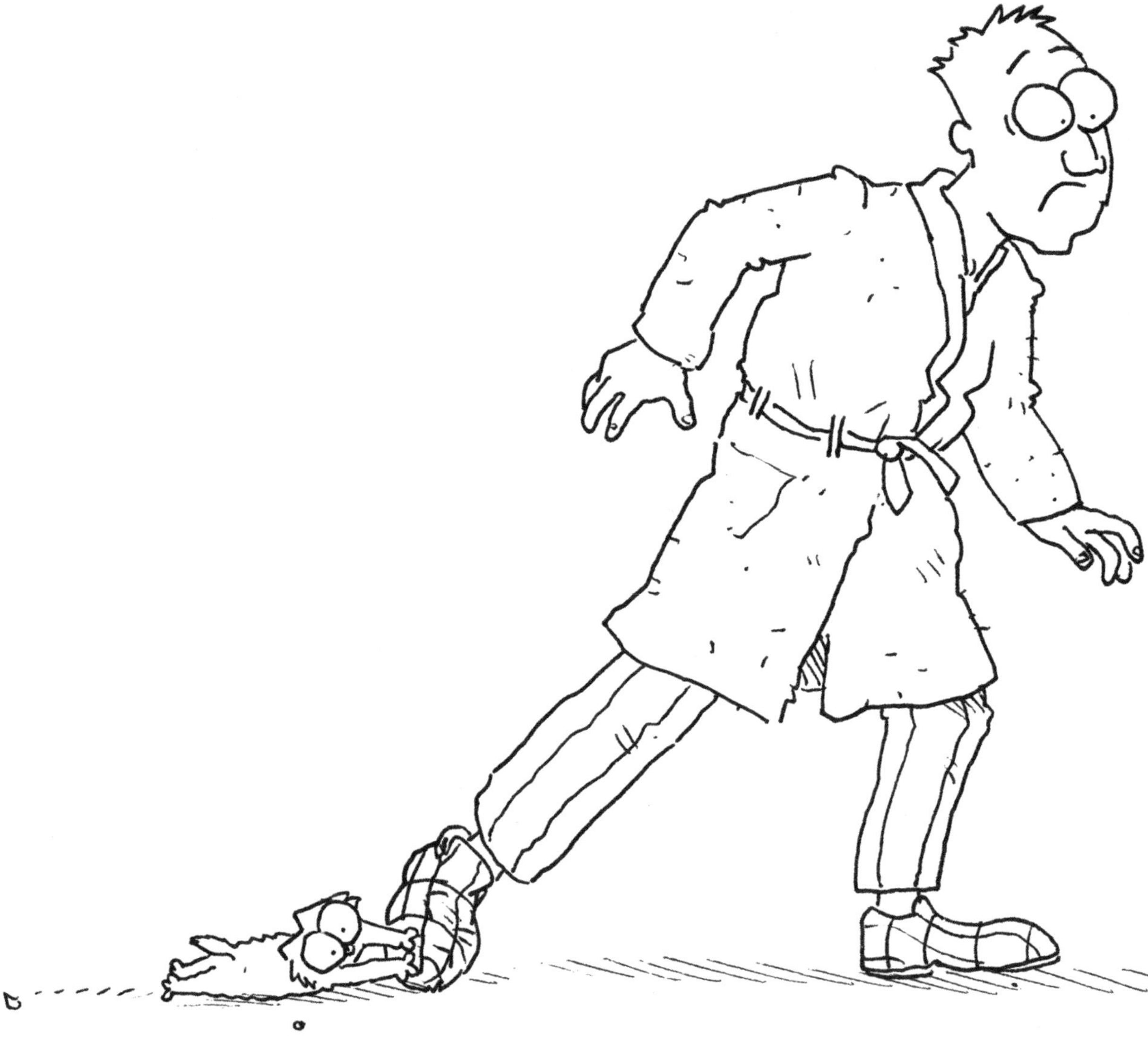

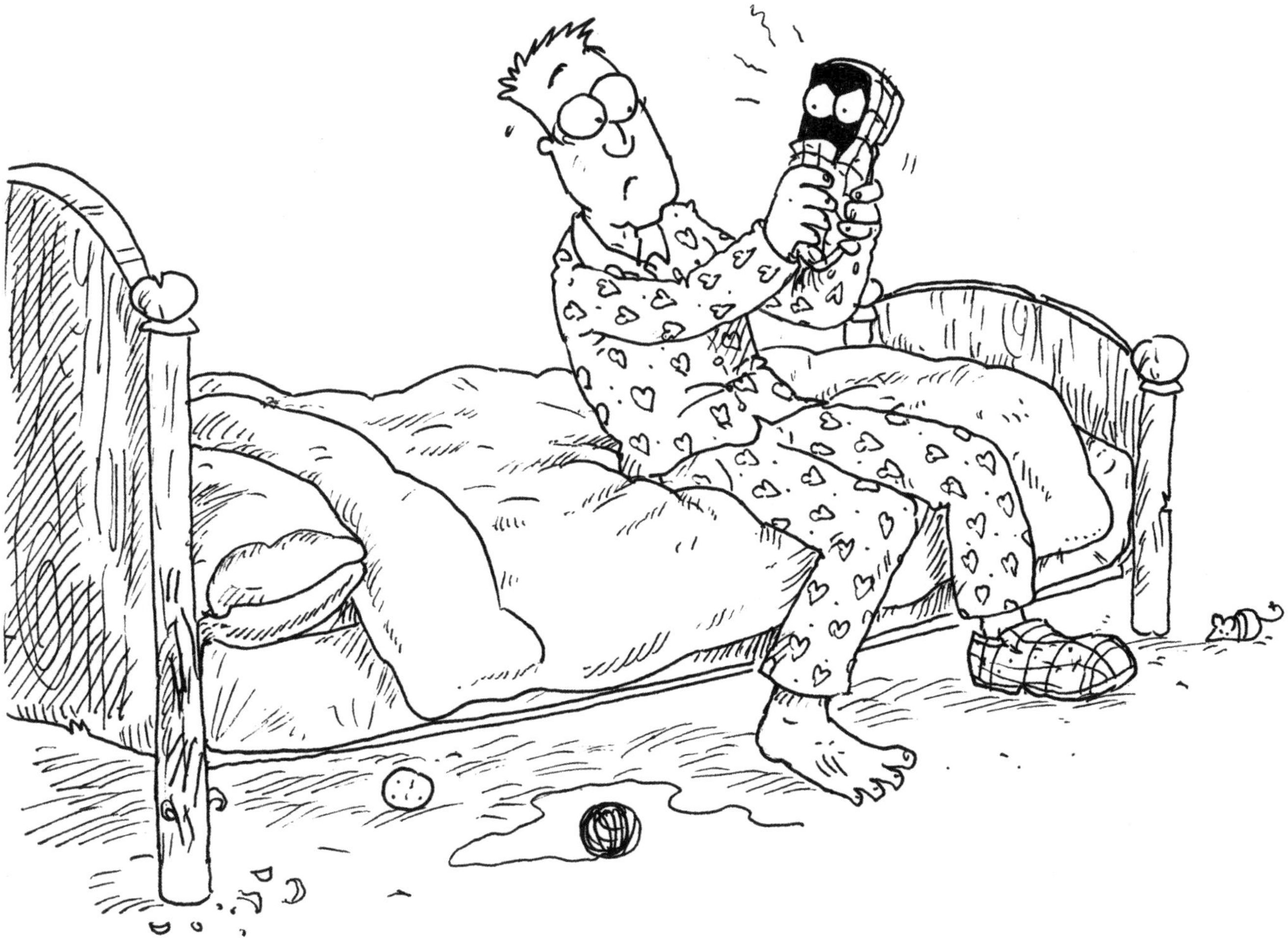

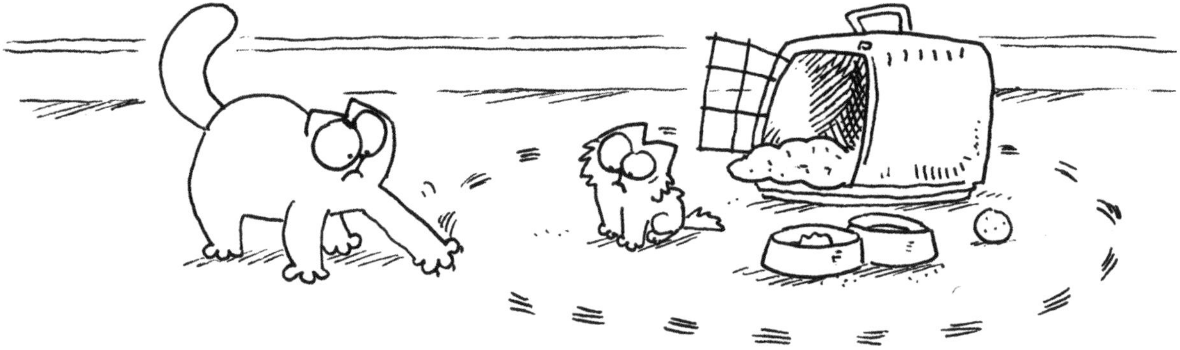

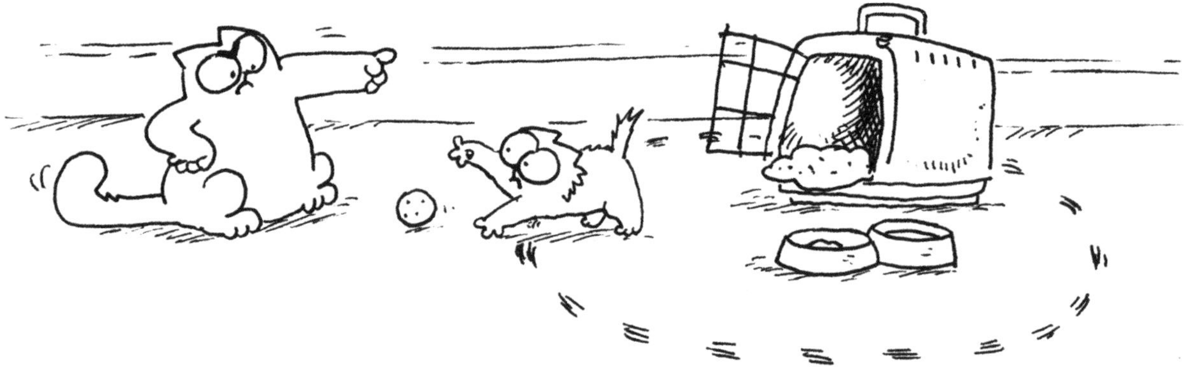

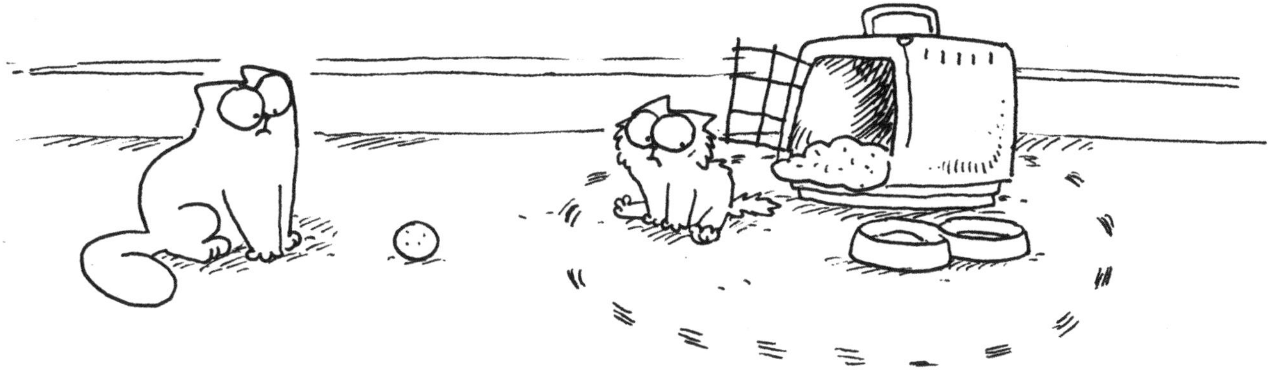

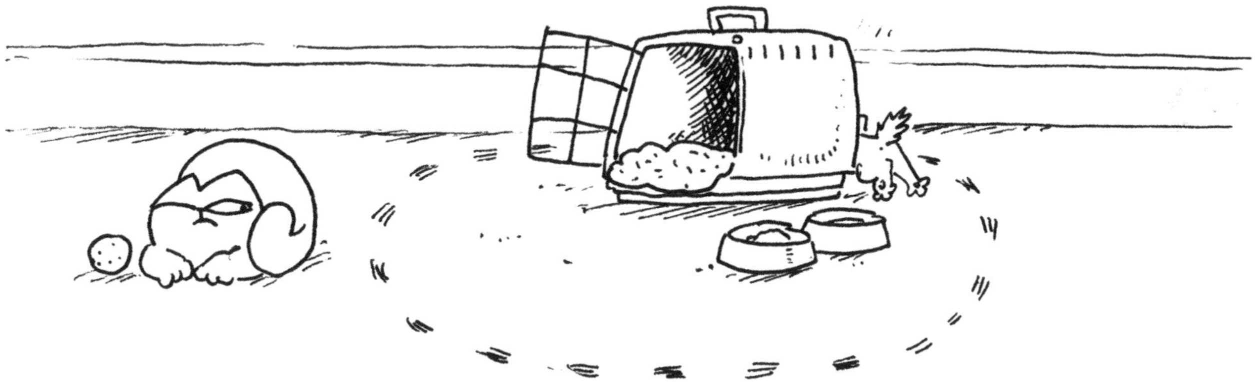

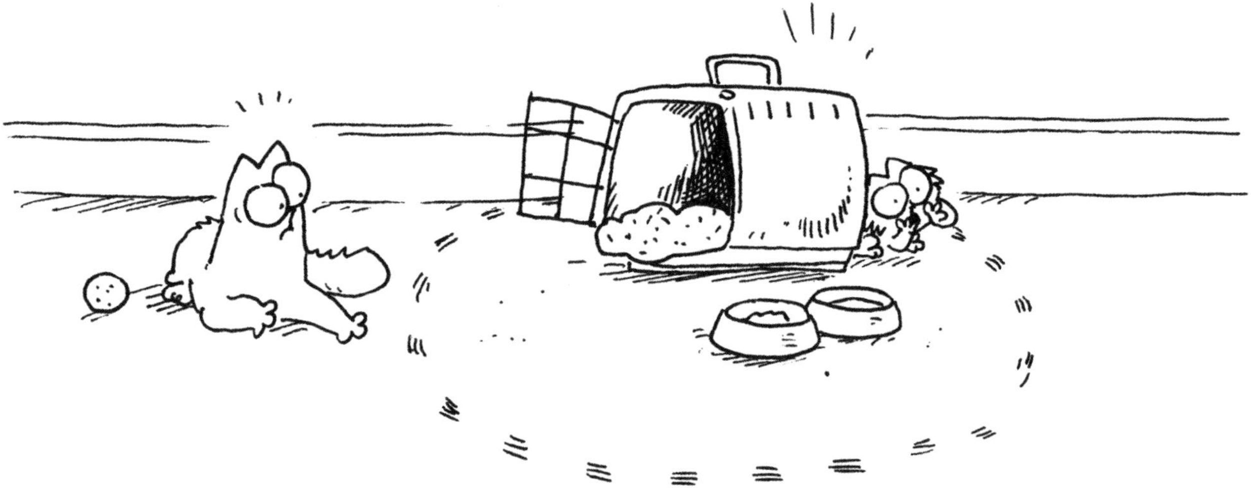

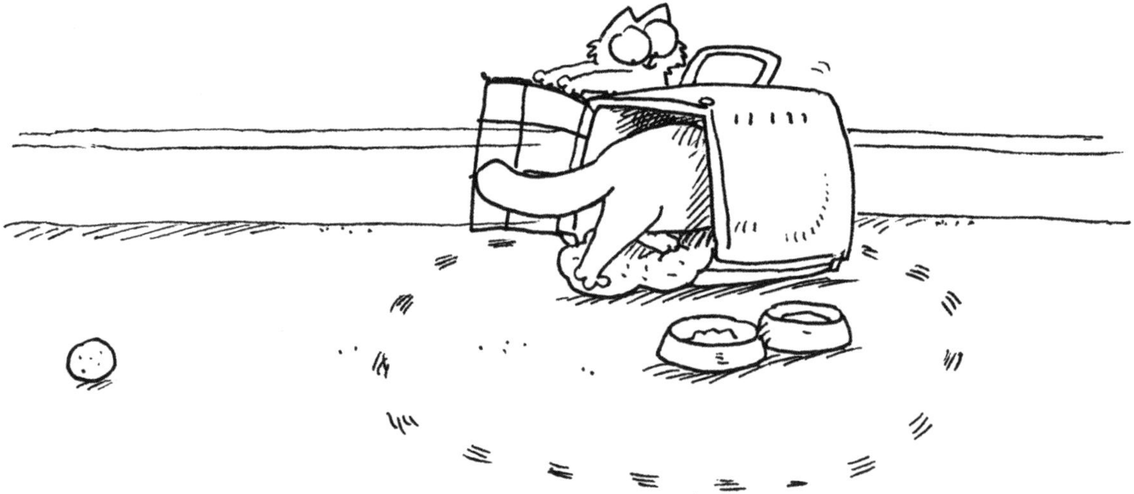

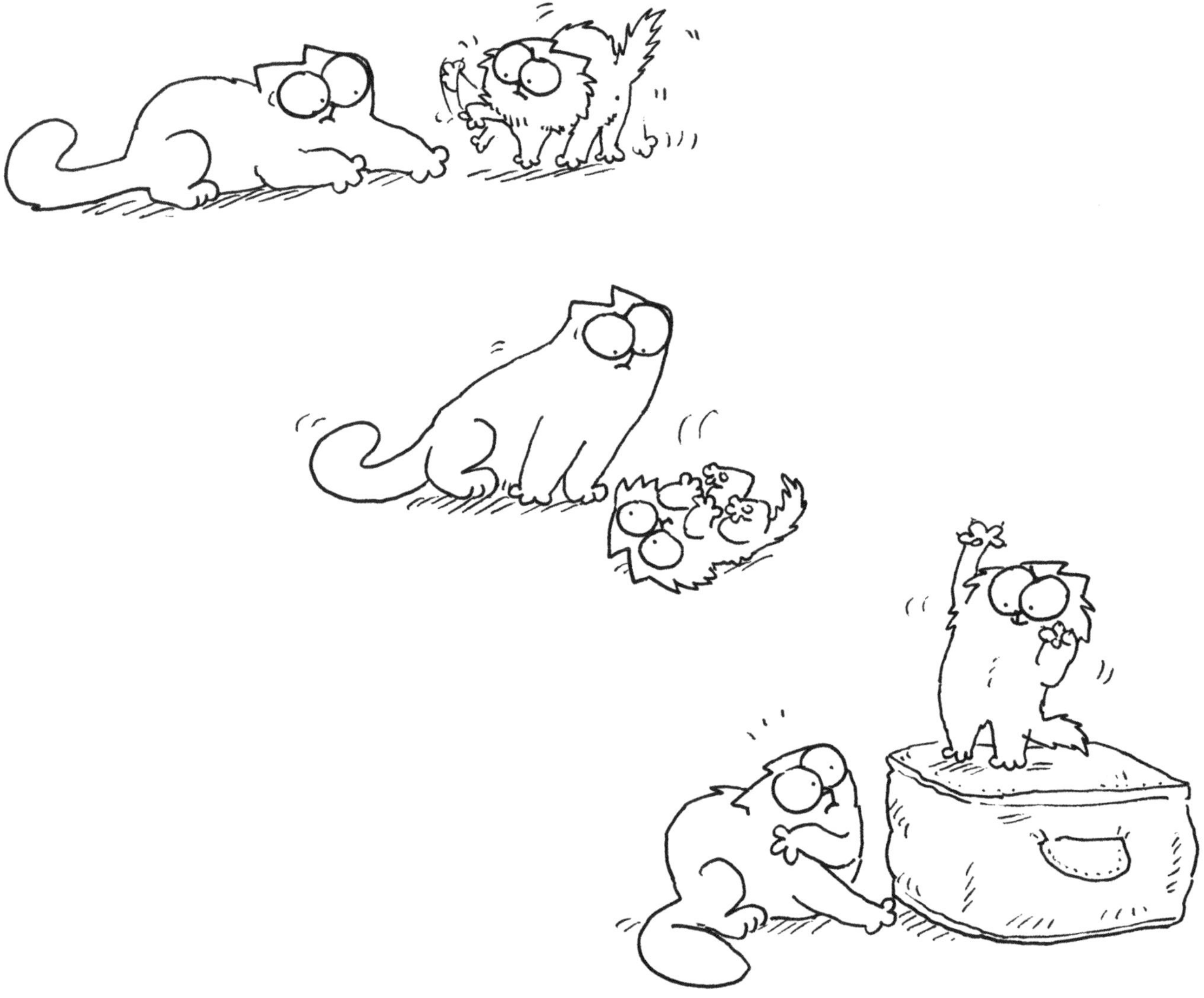

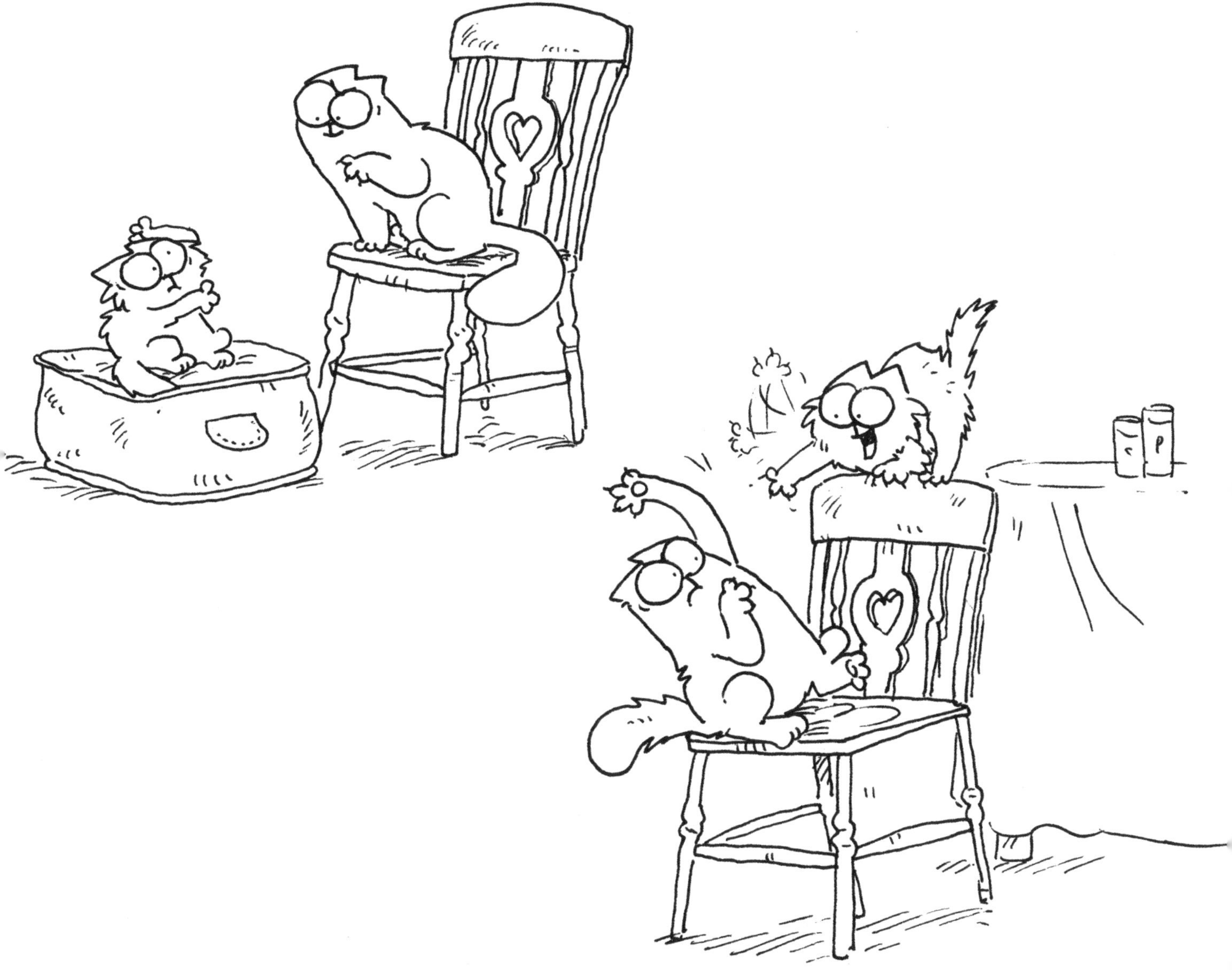
P

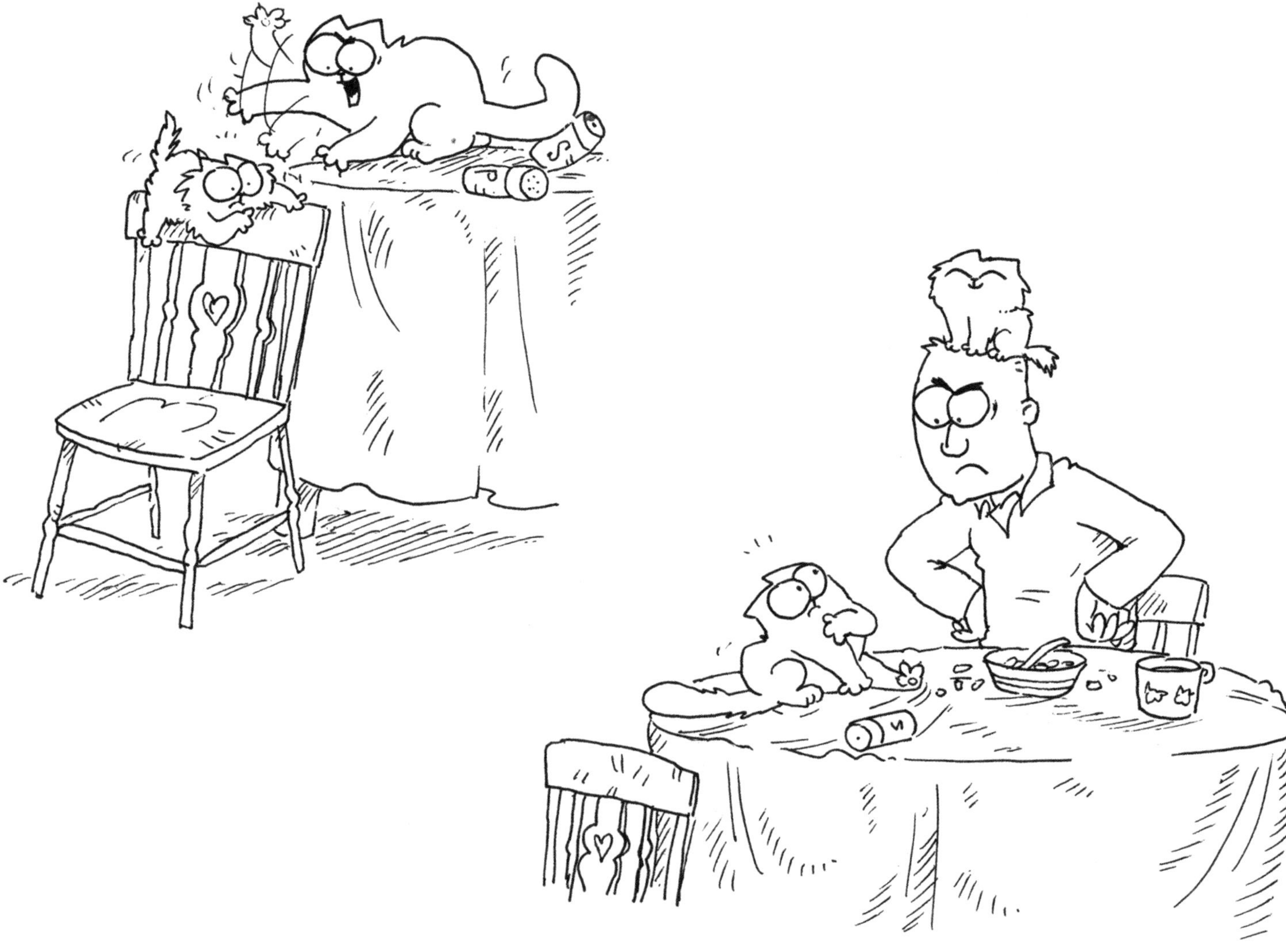

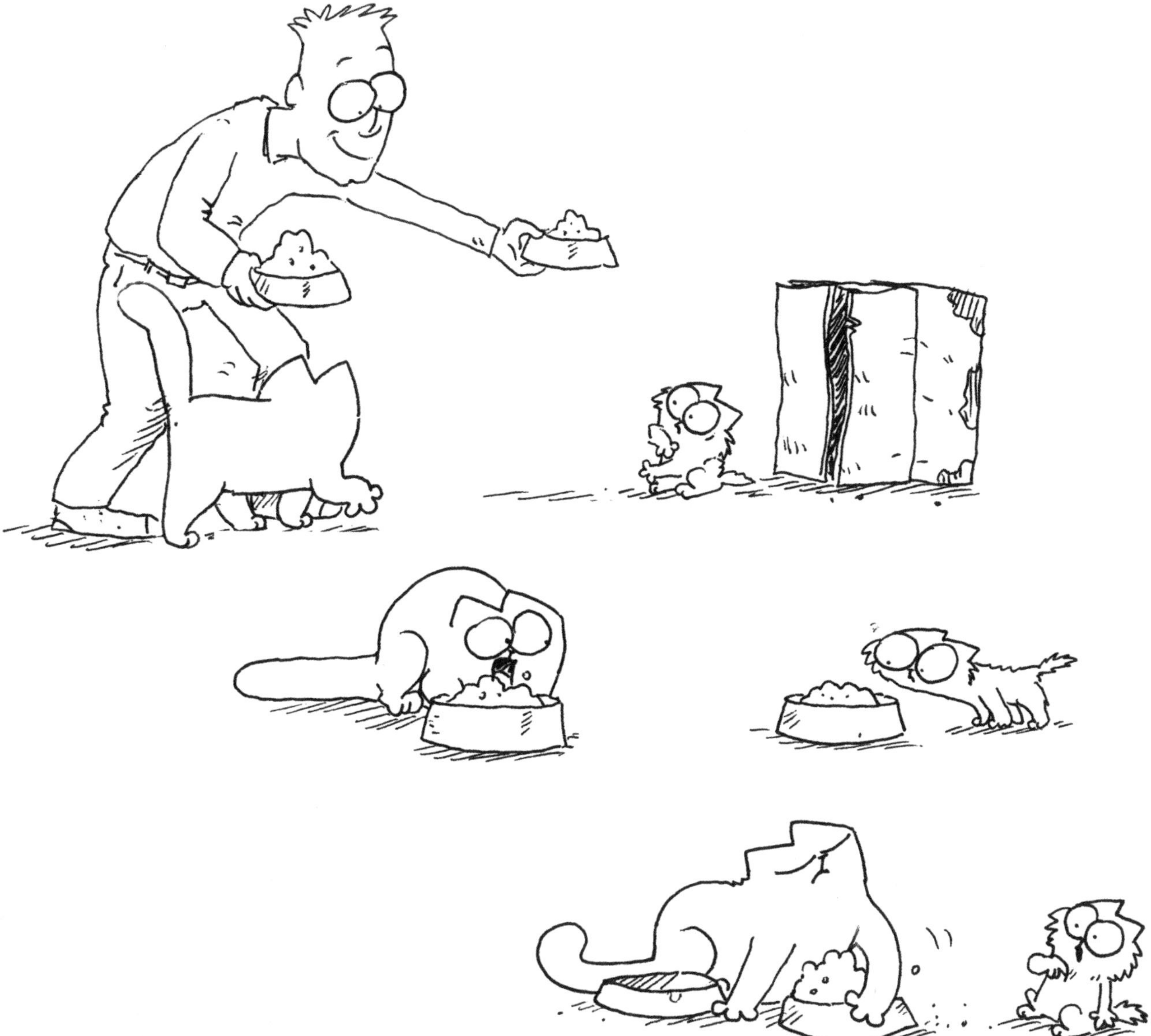

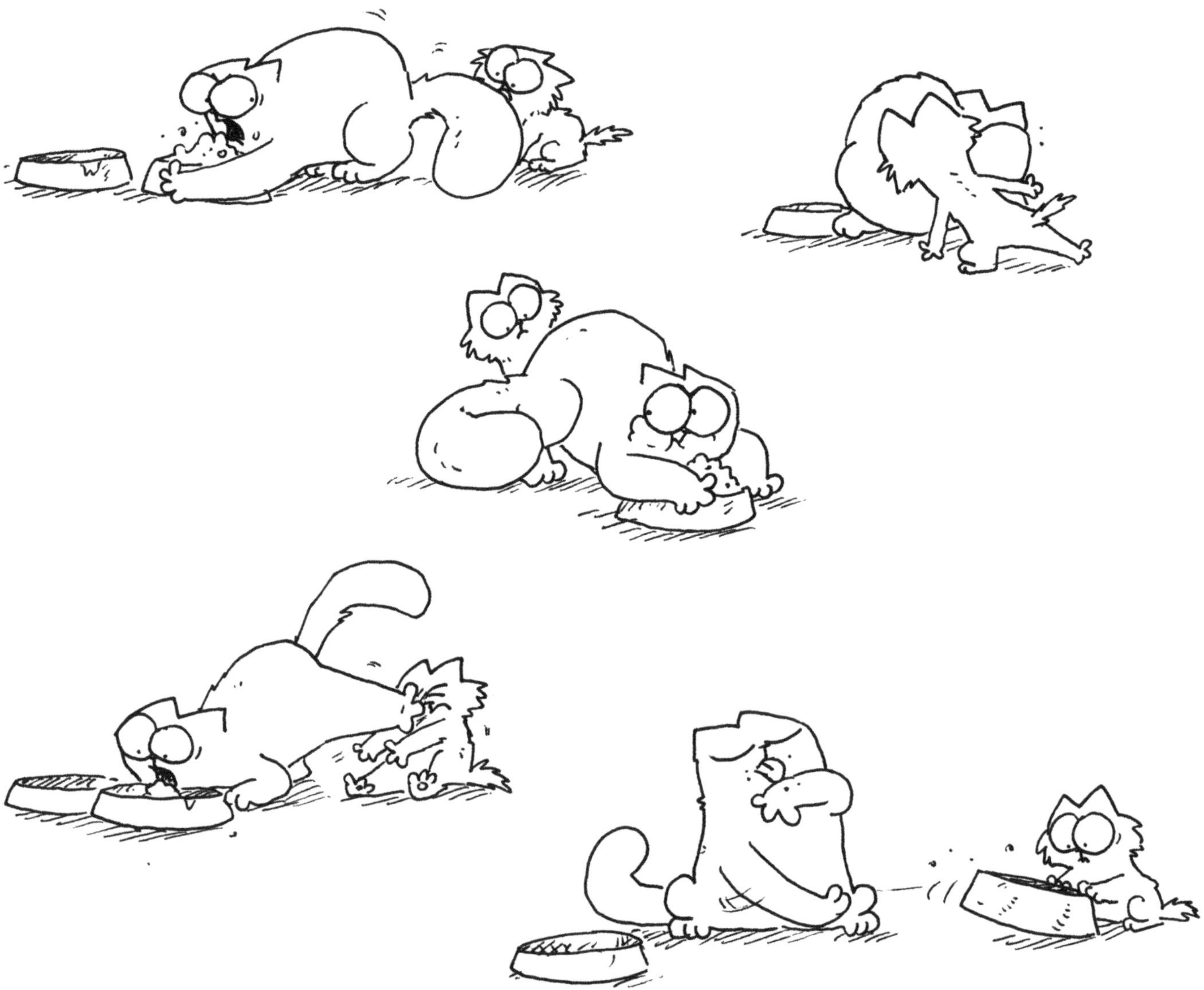

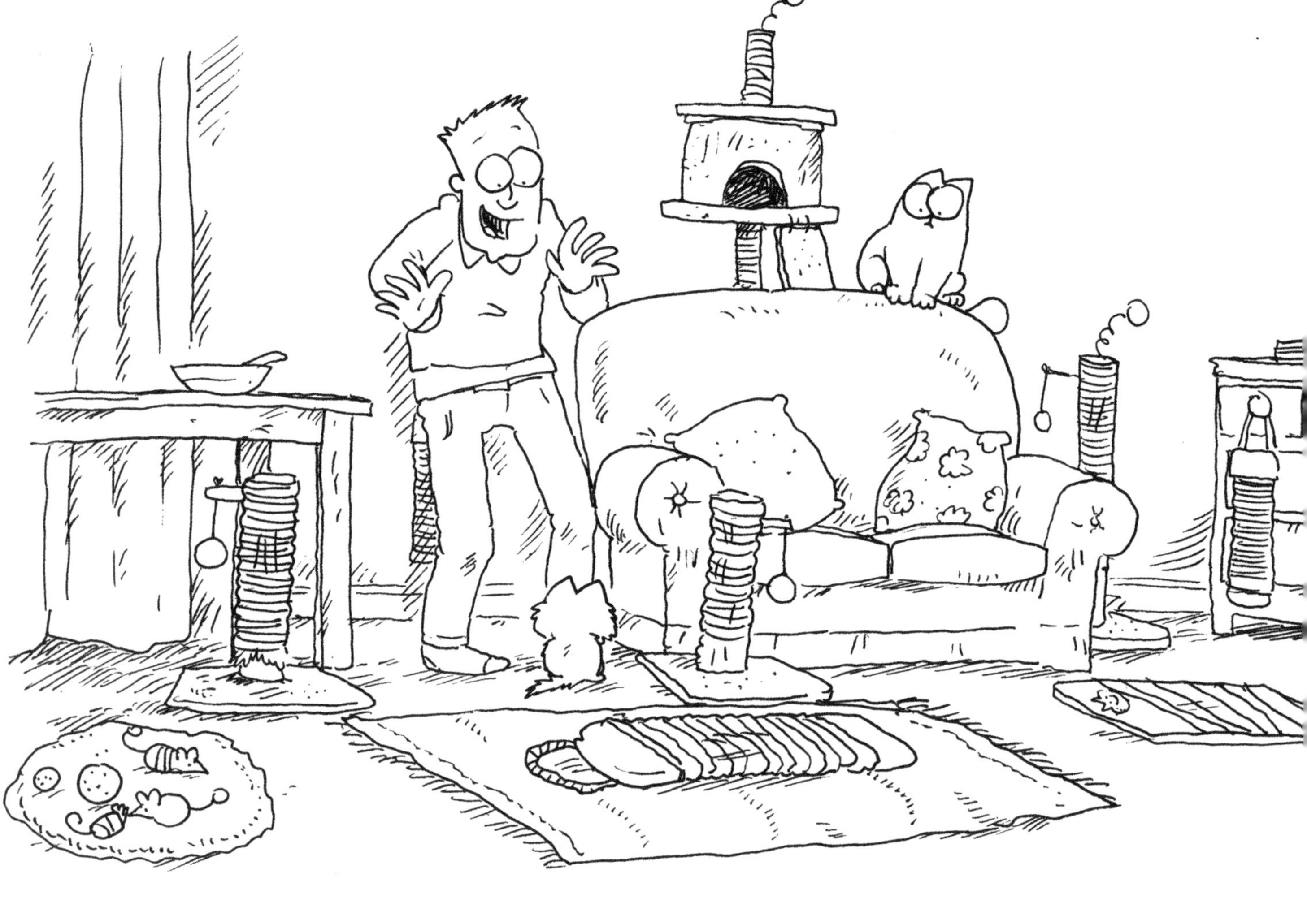

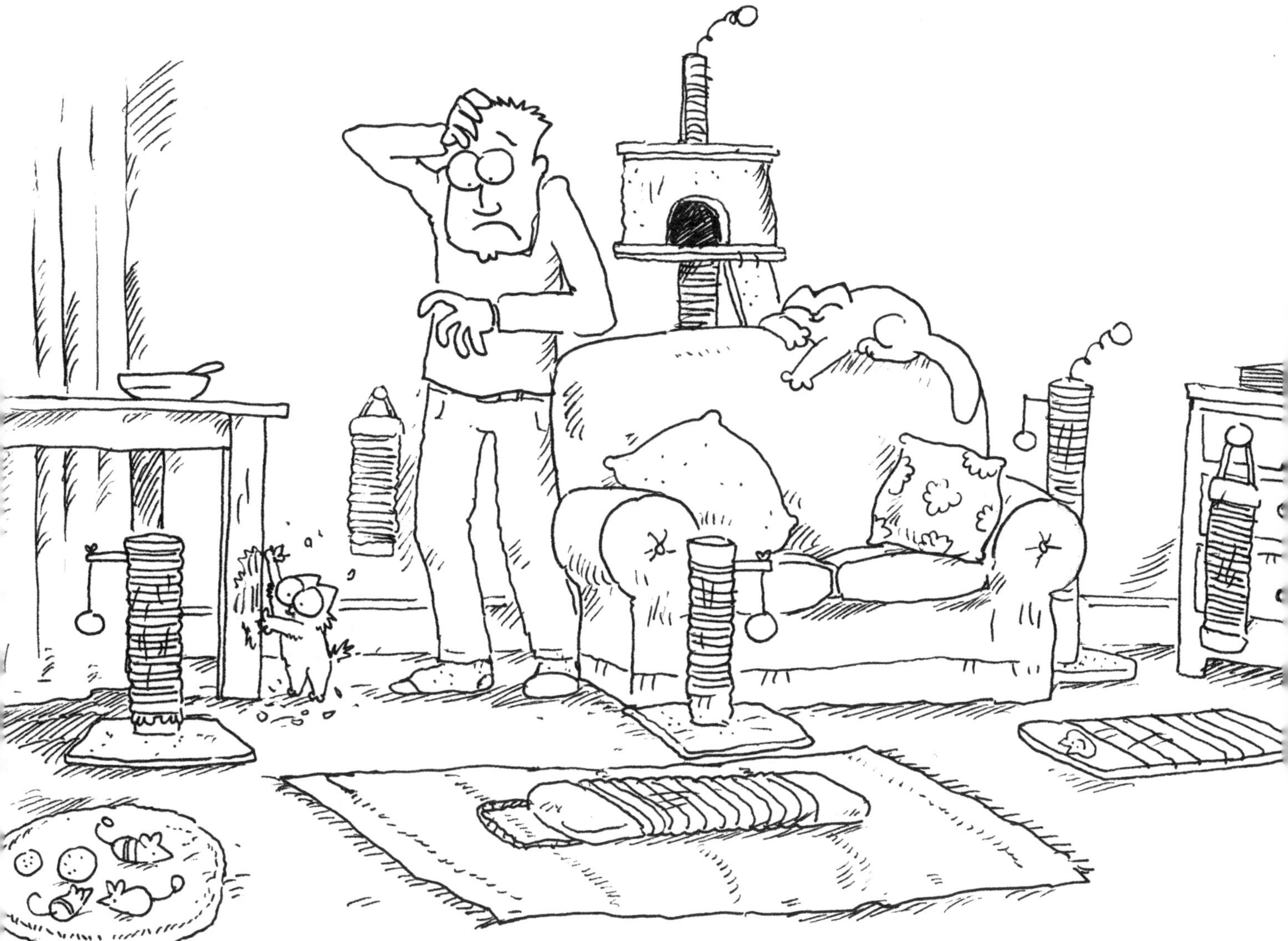

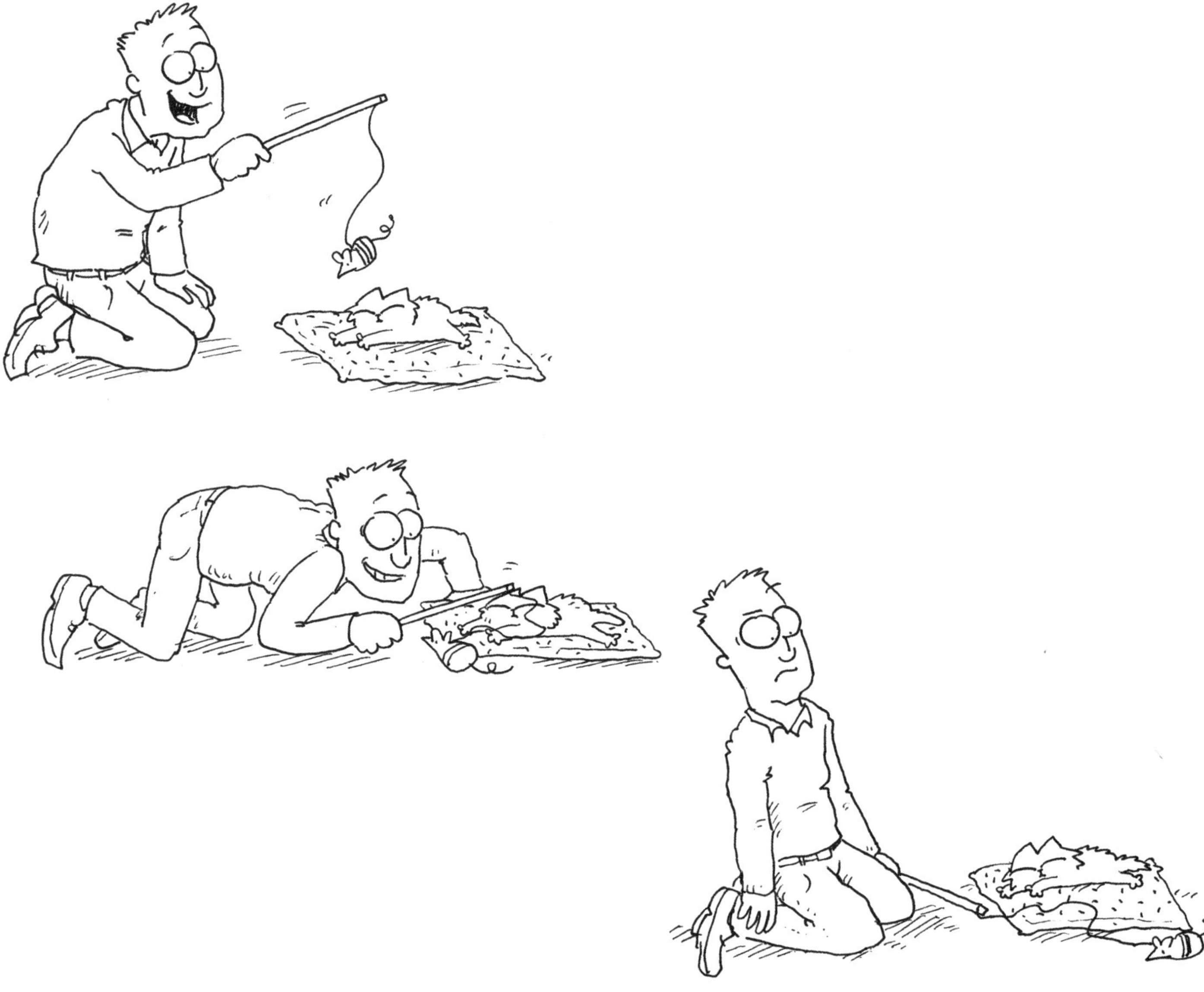

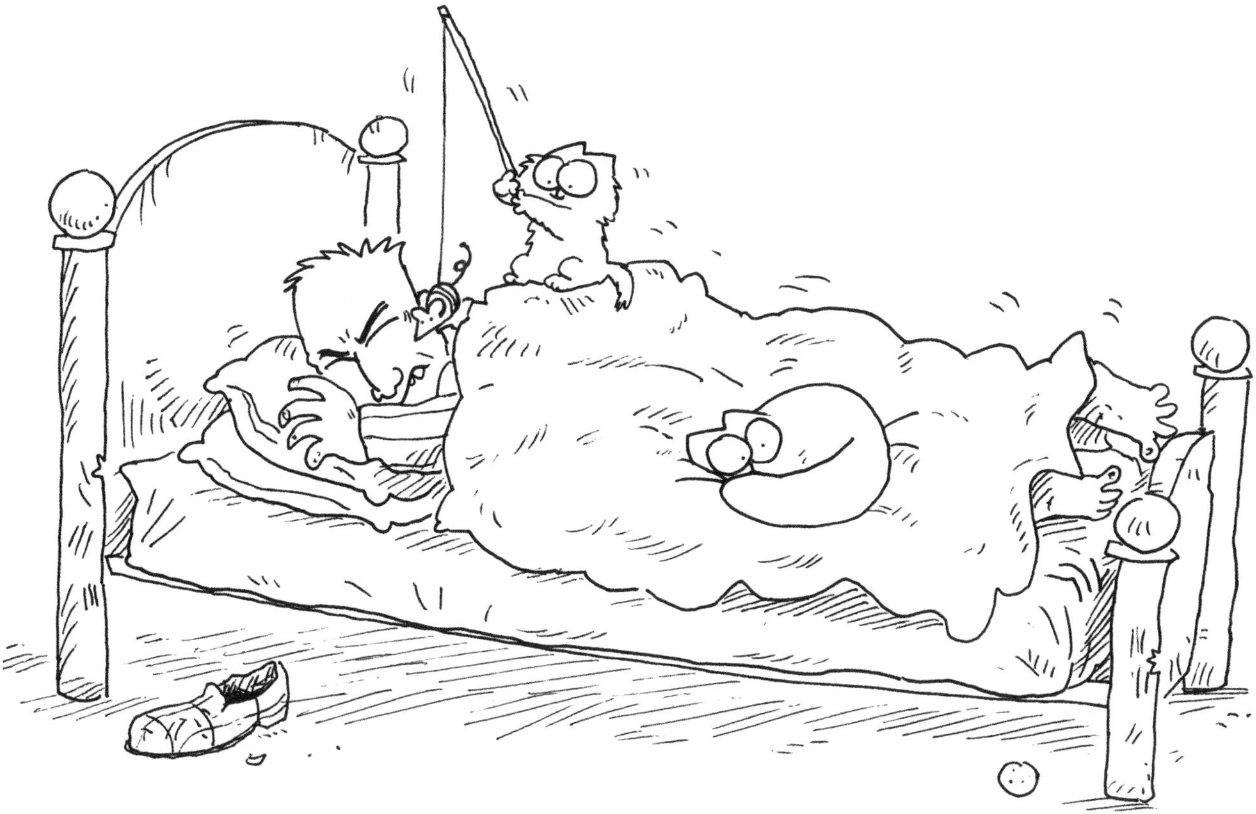

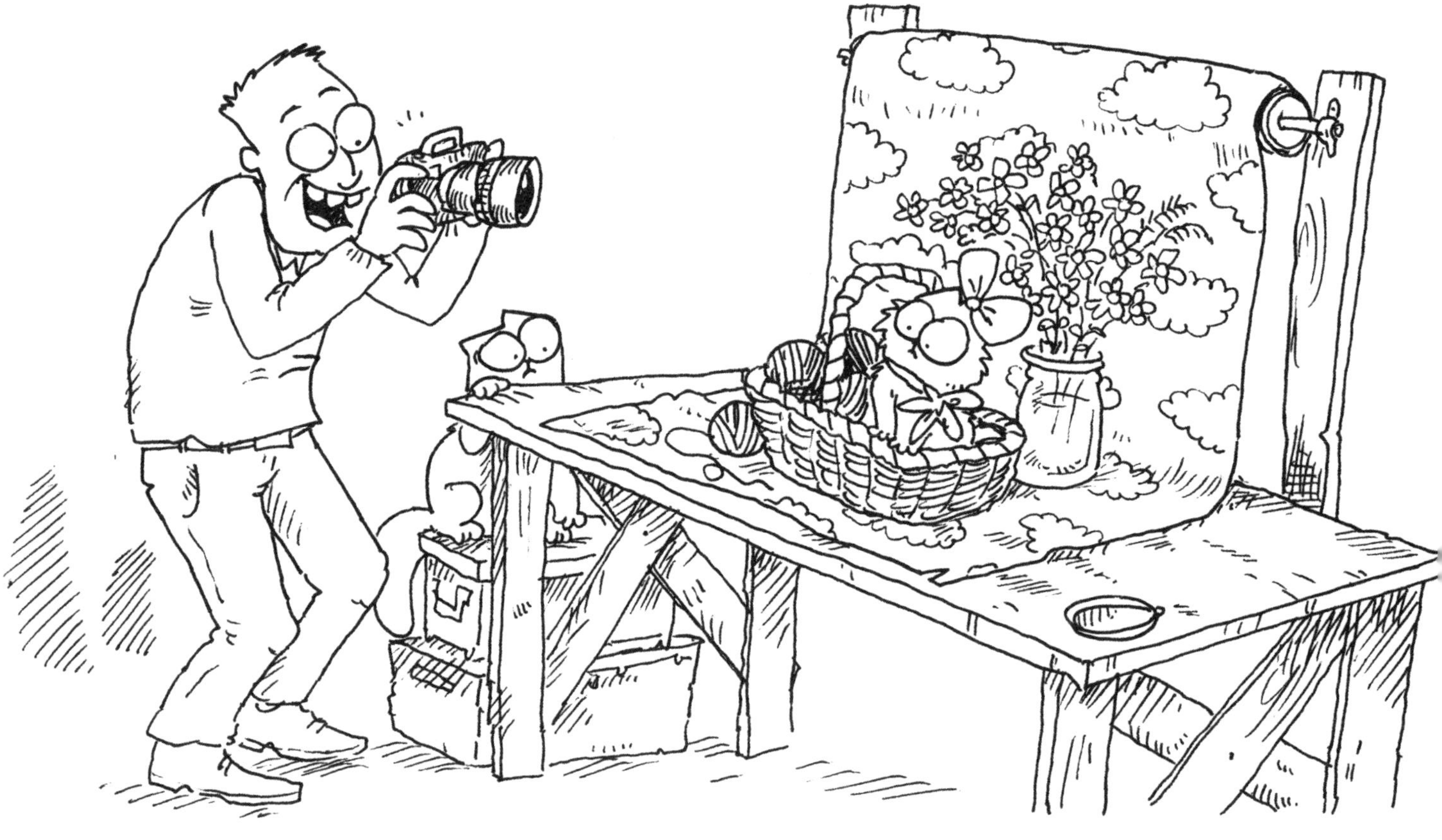

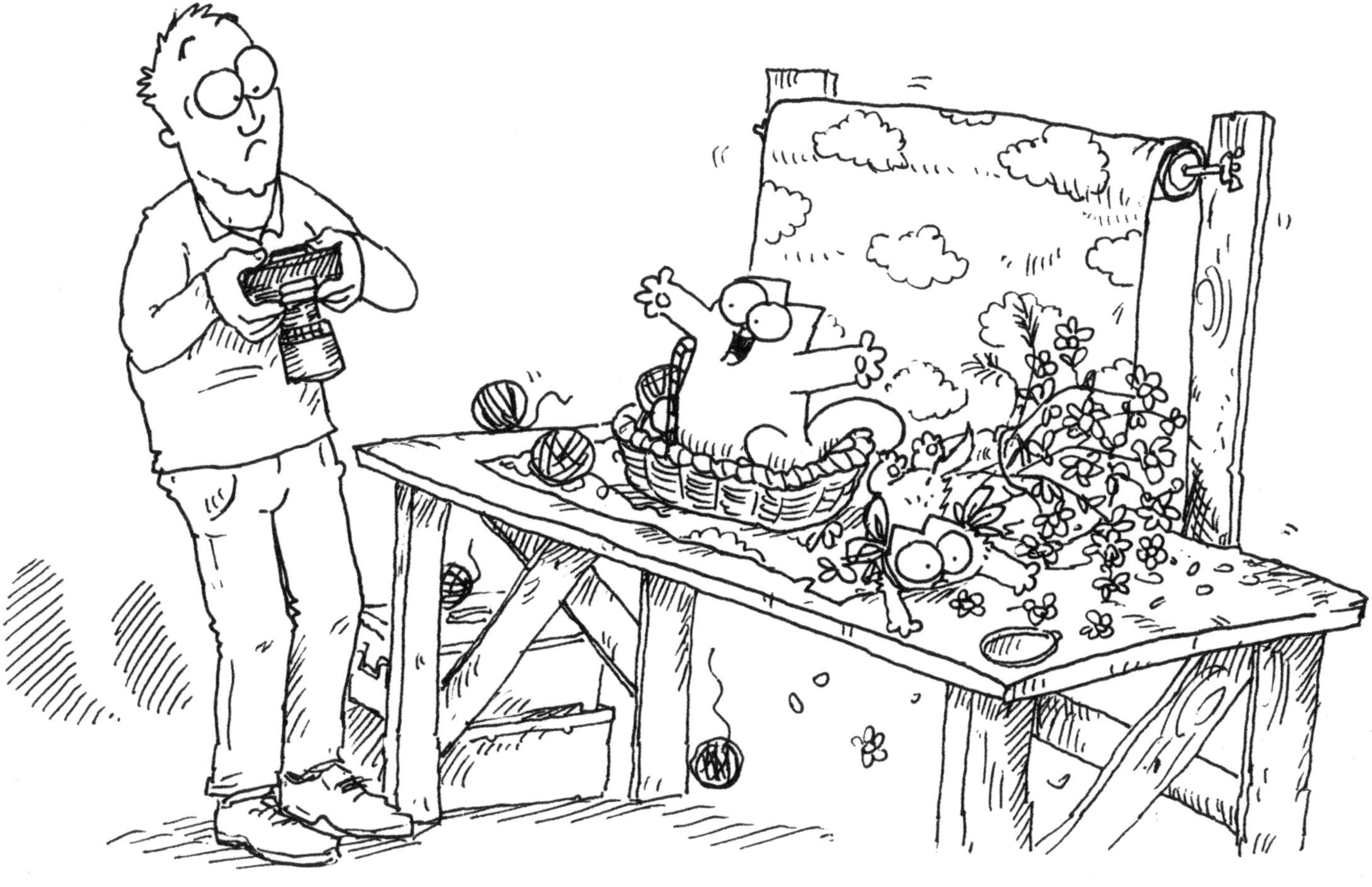

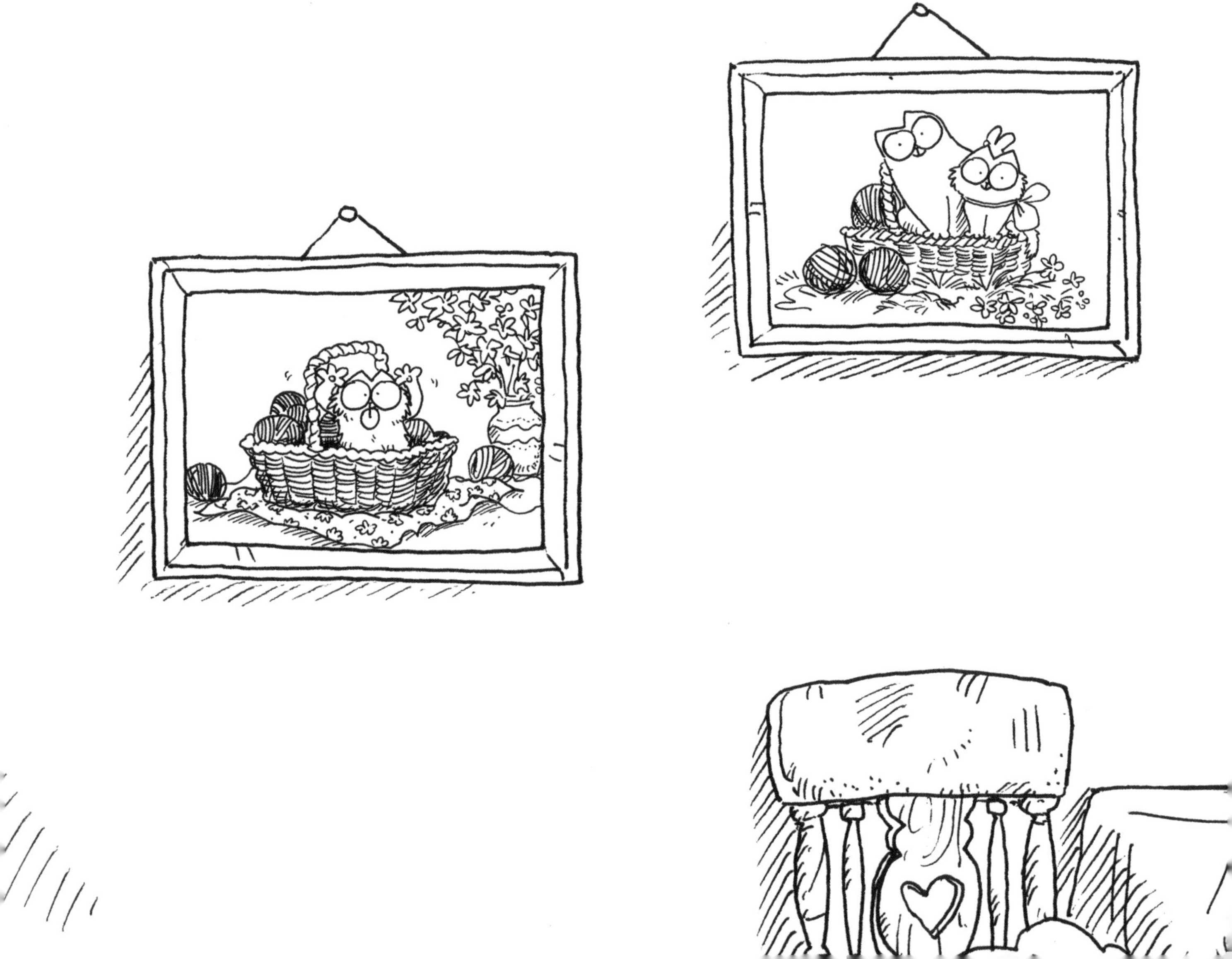

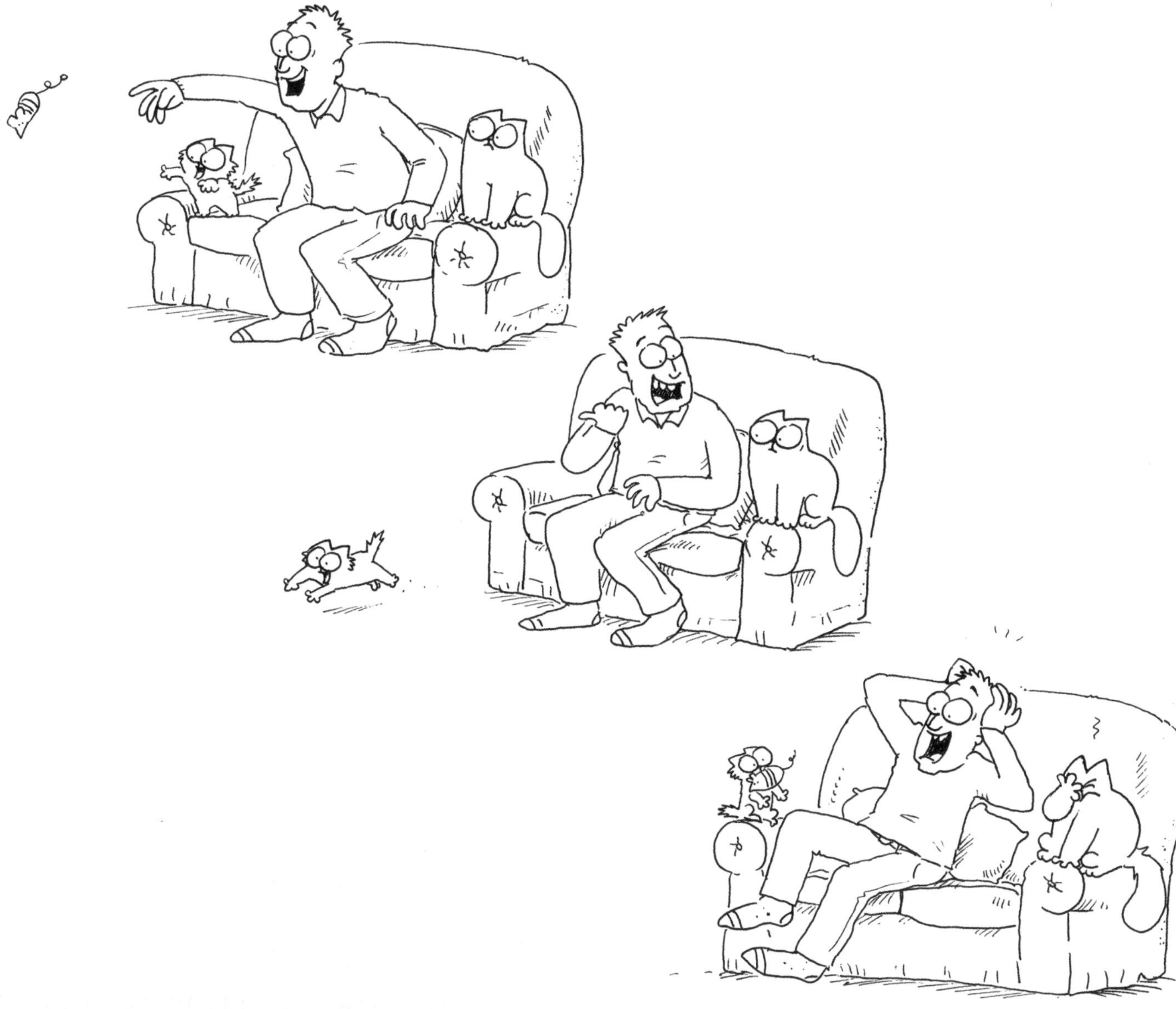

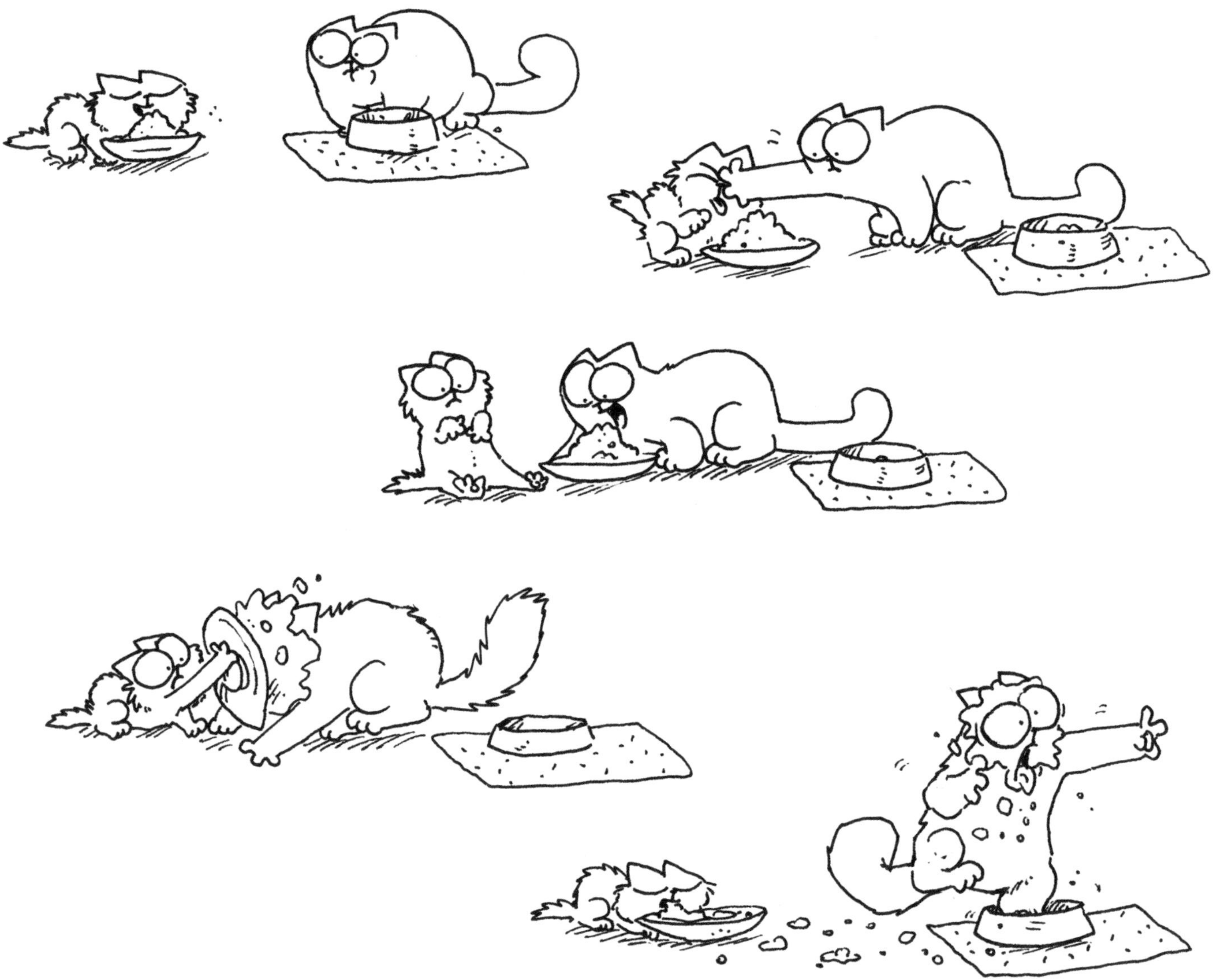

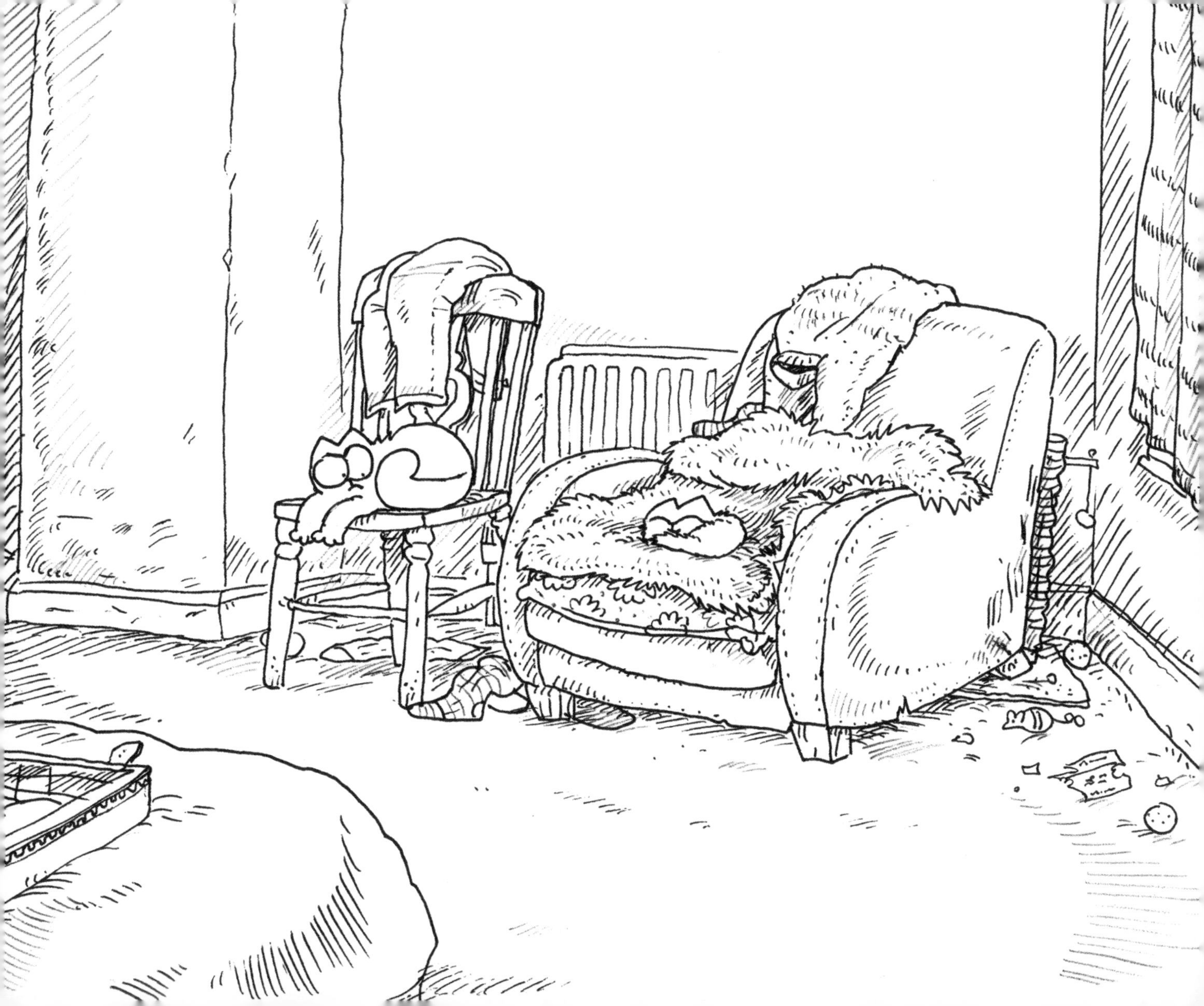

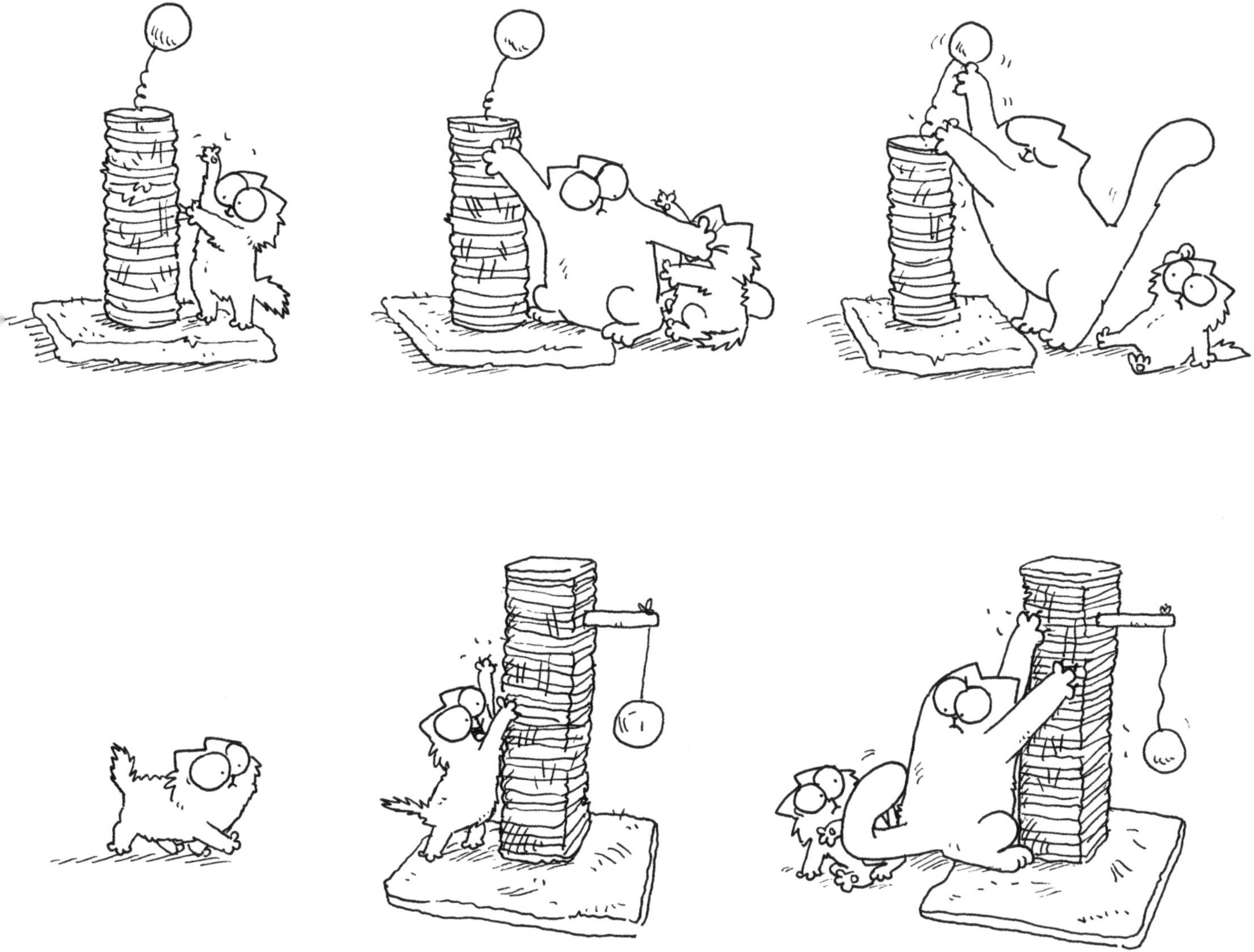

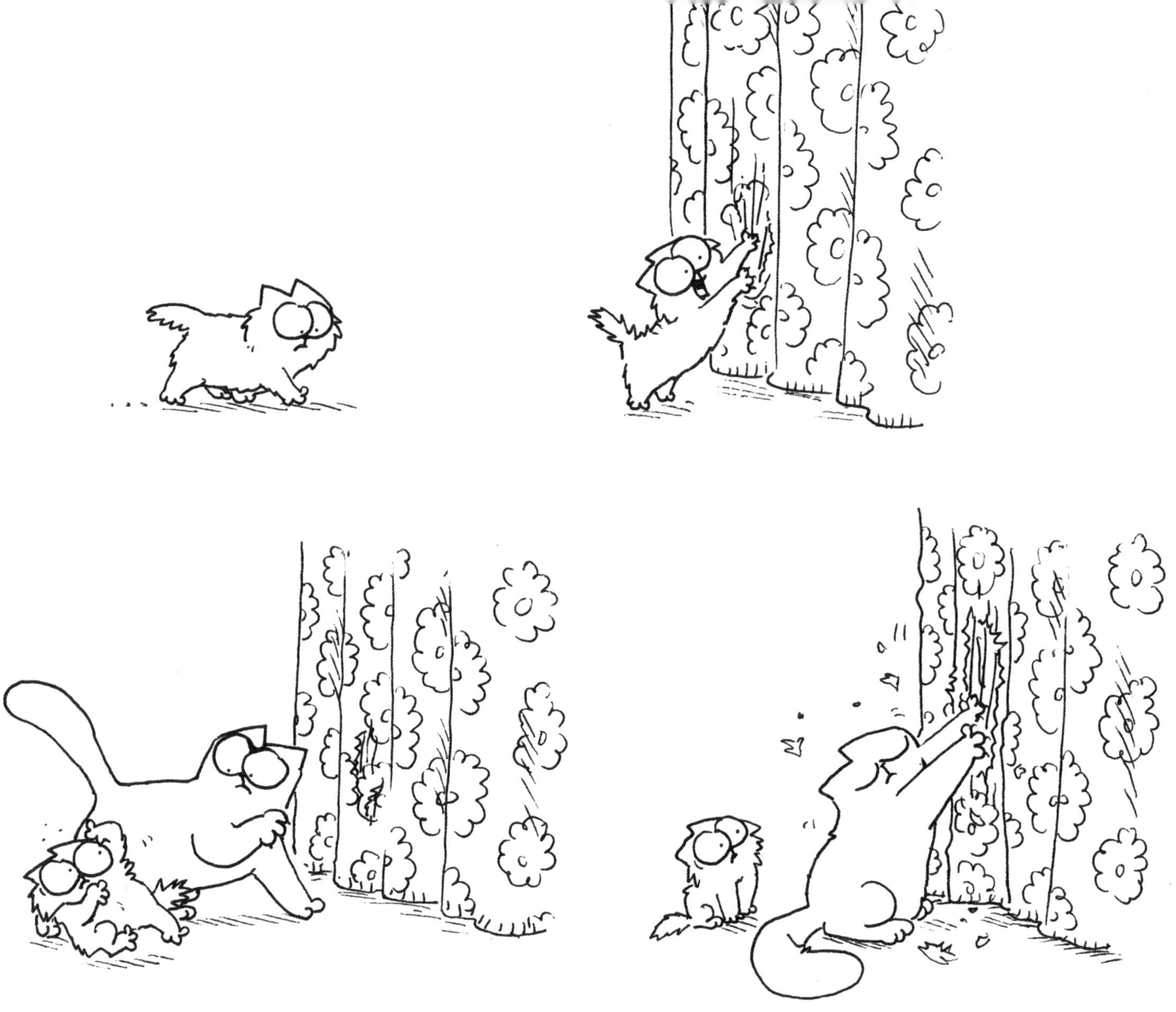

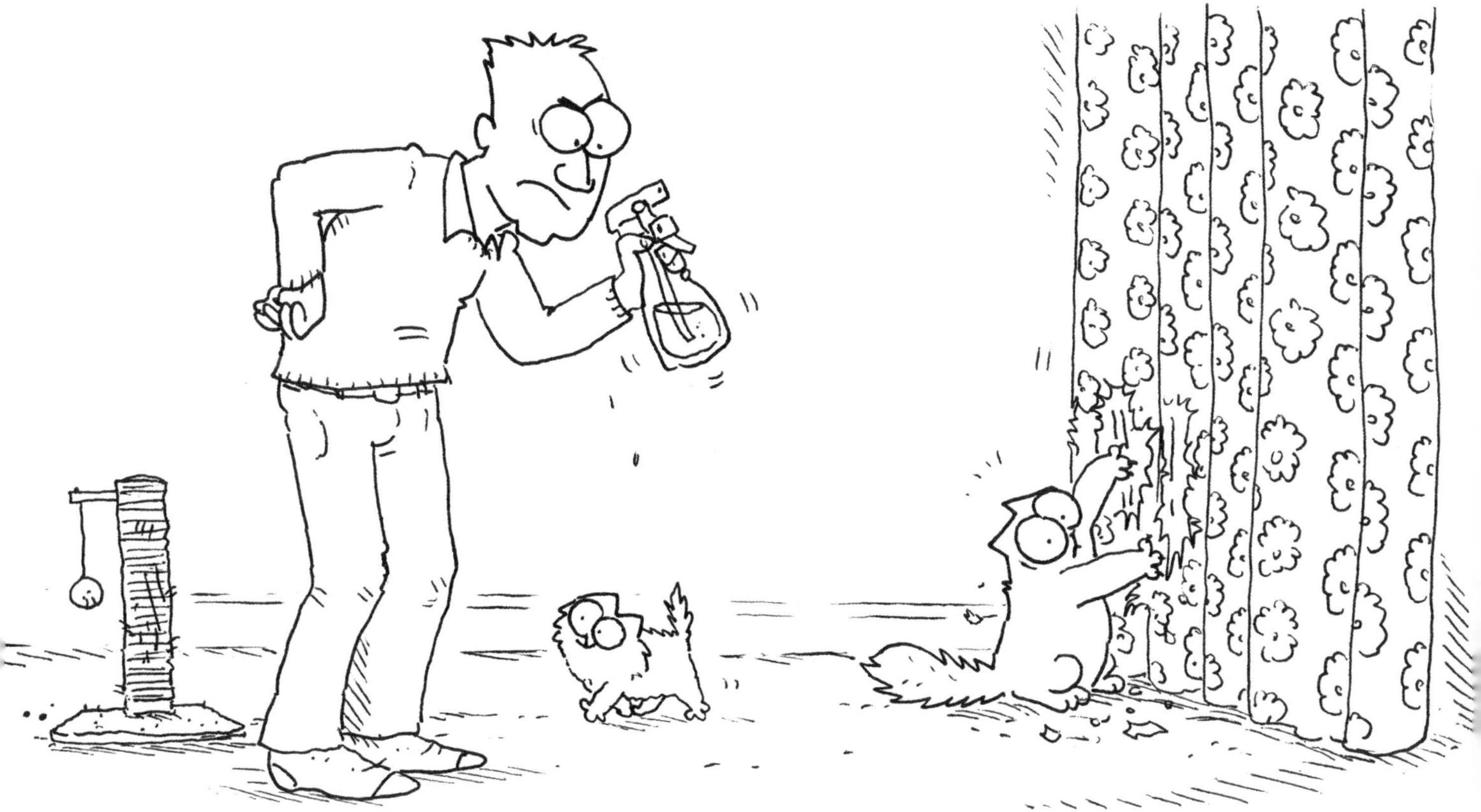

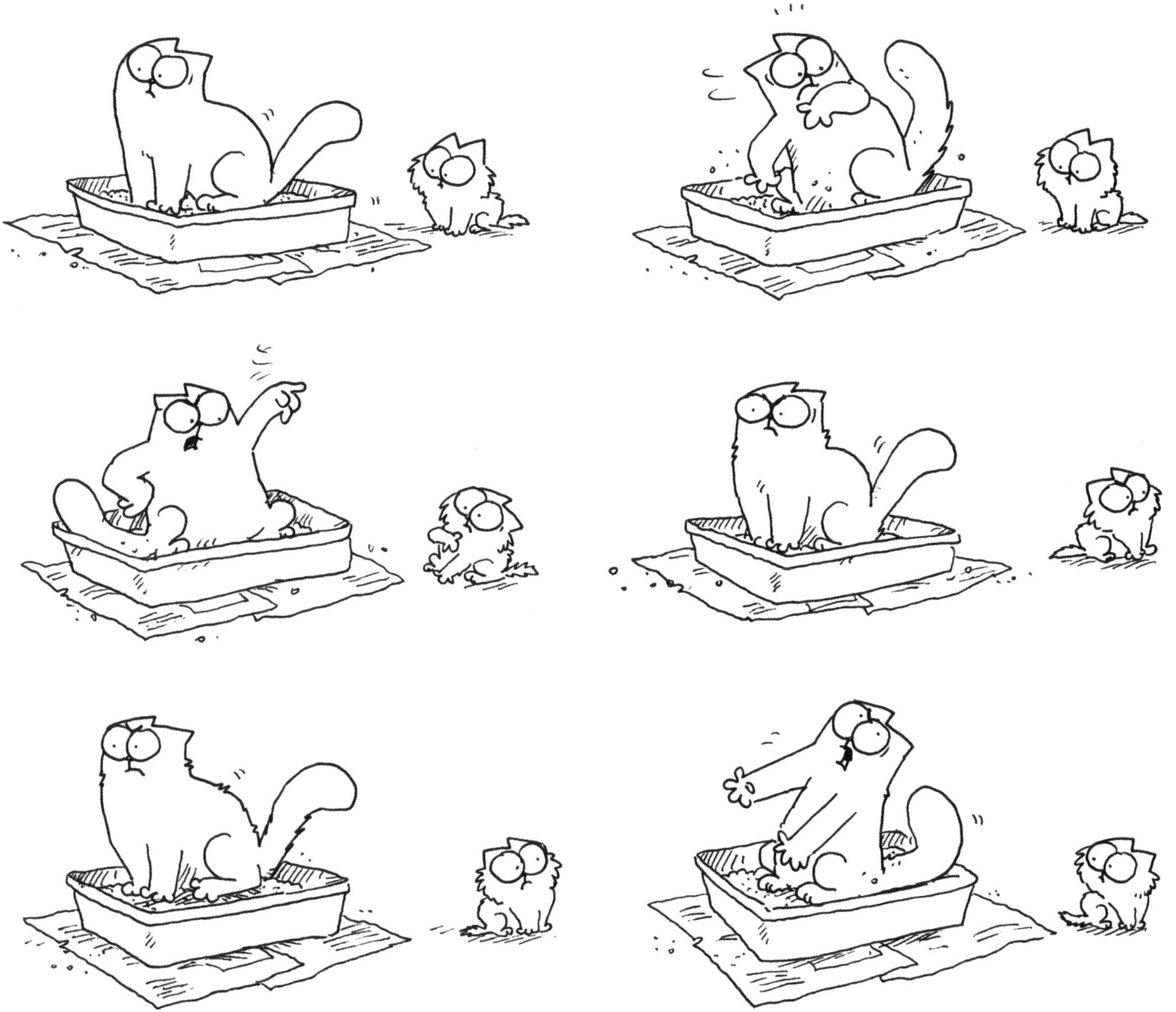

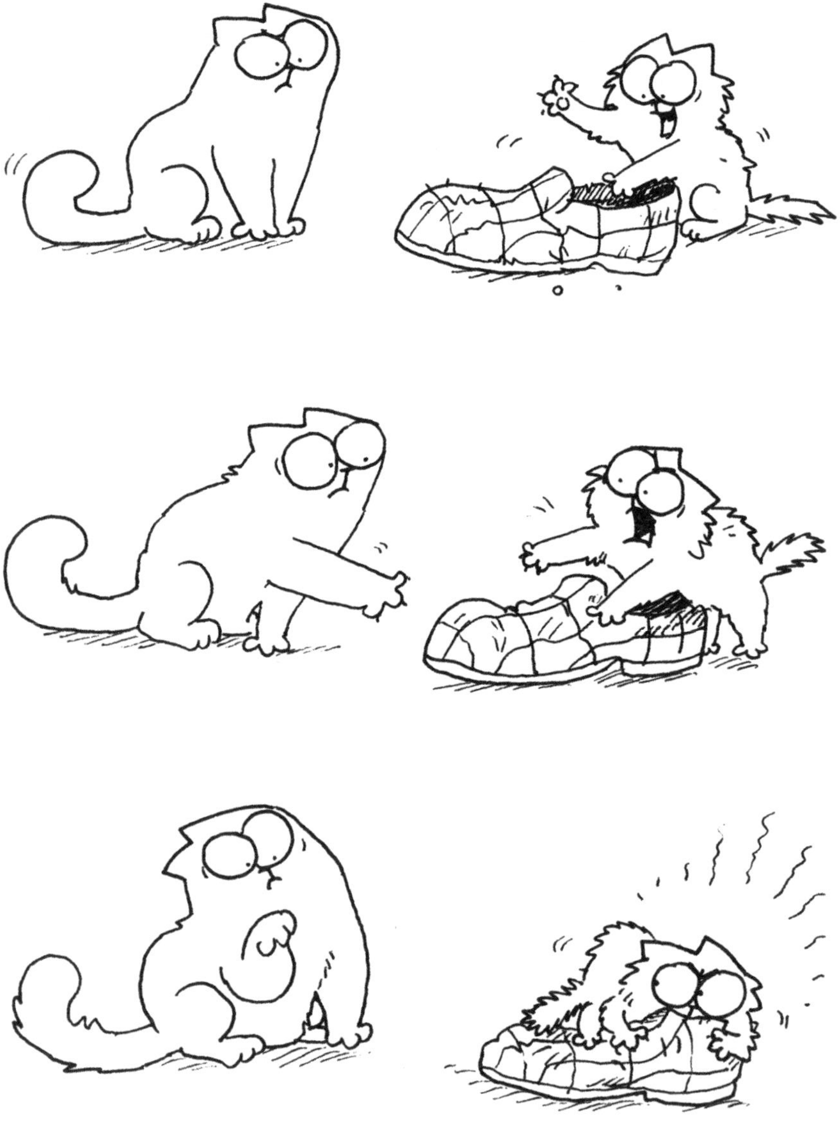

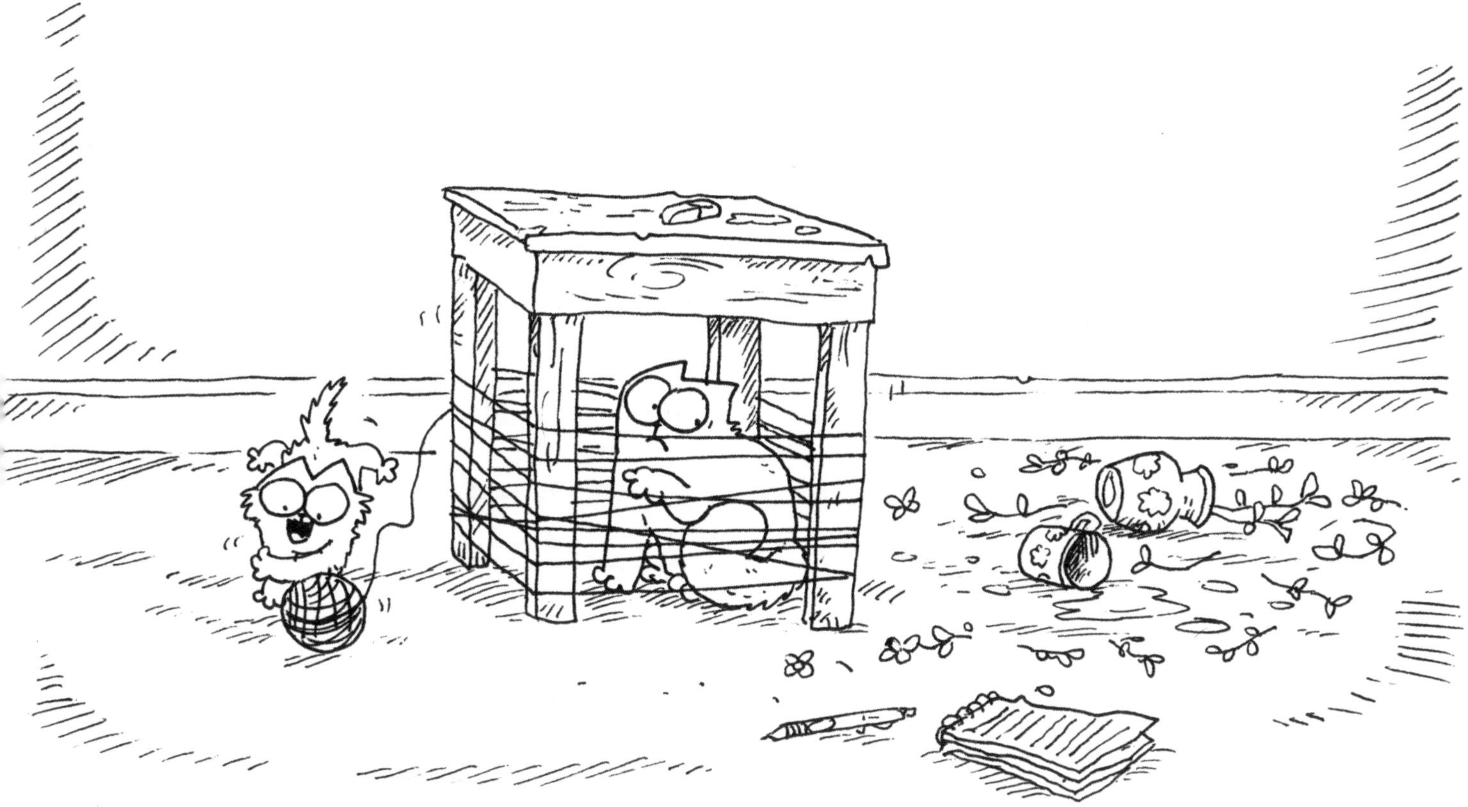

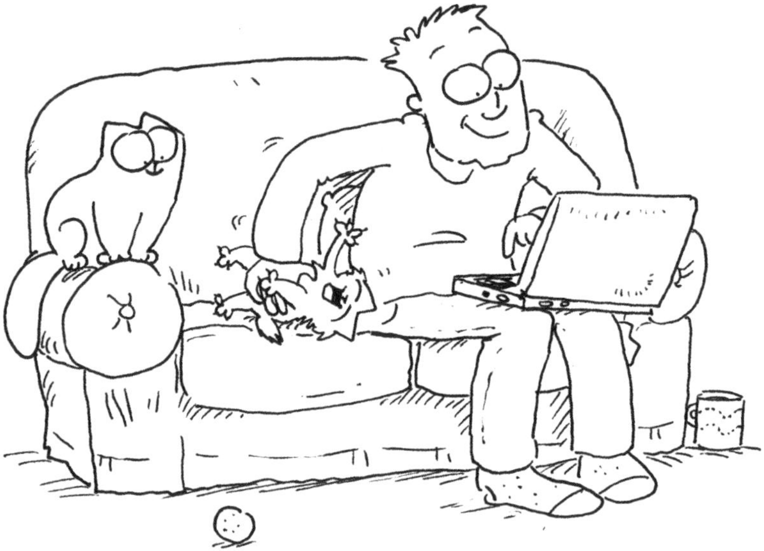

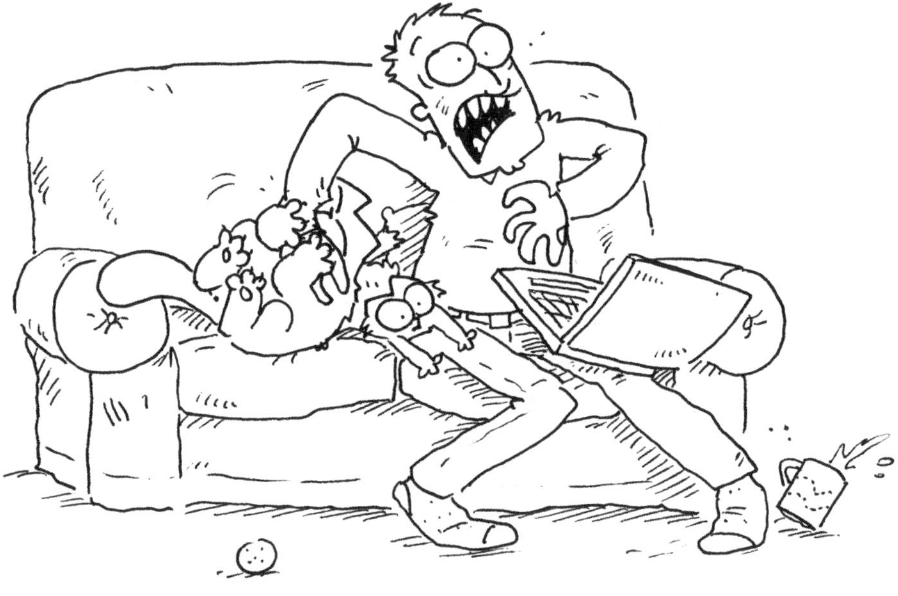

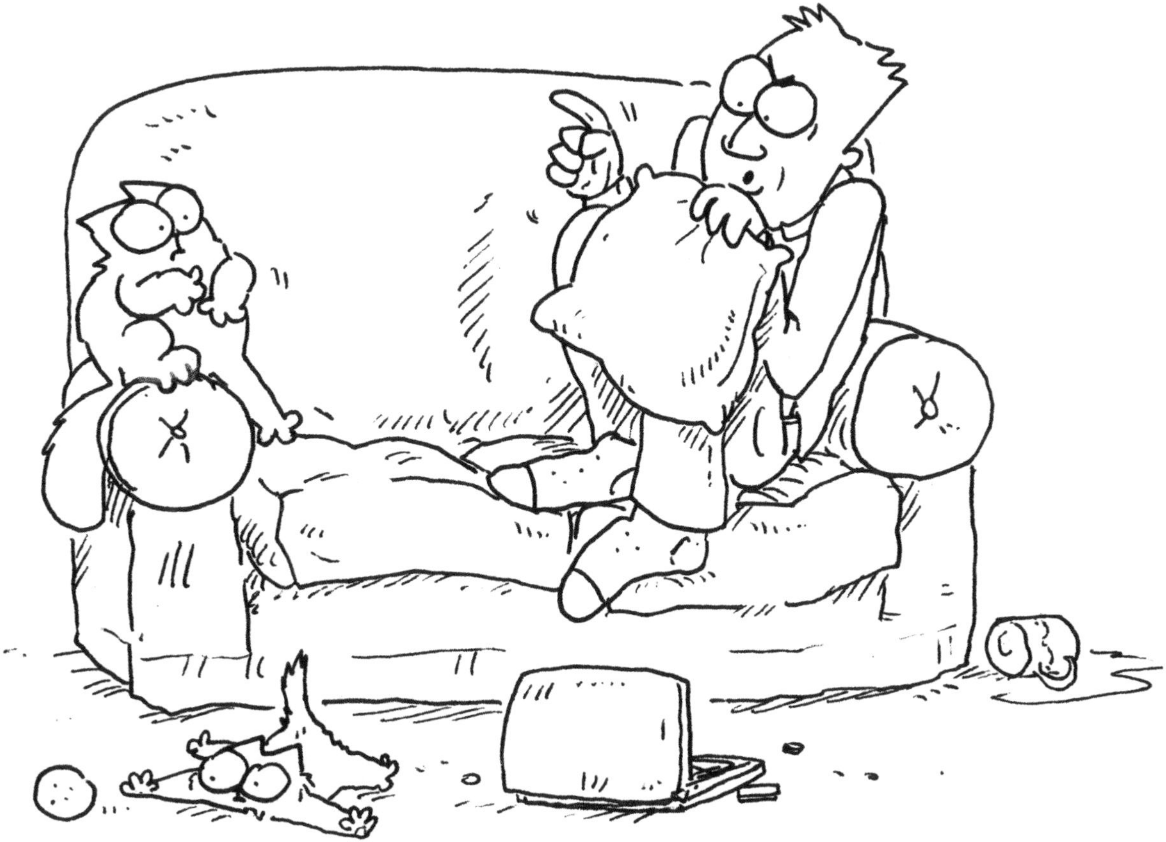

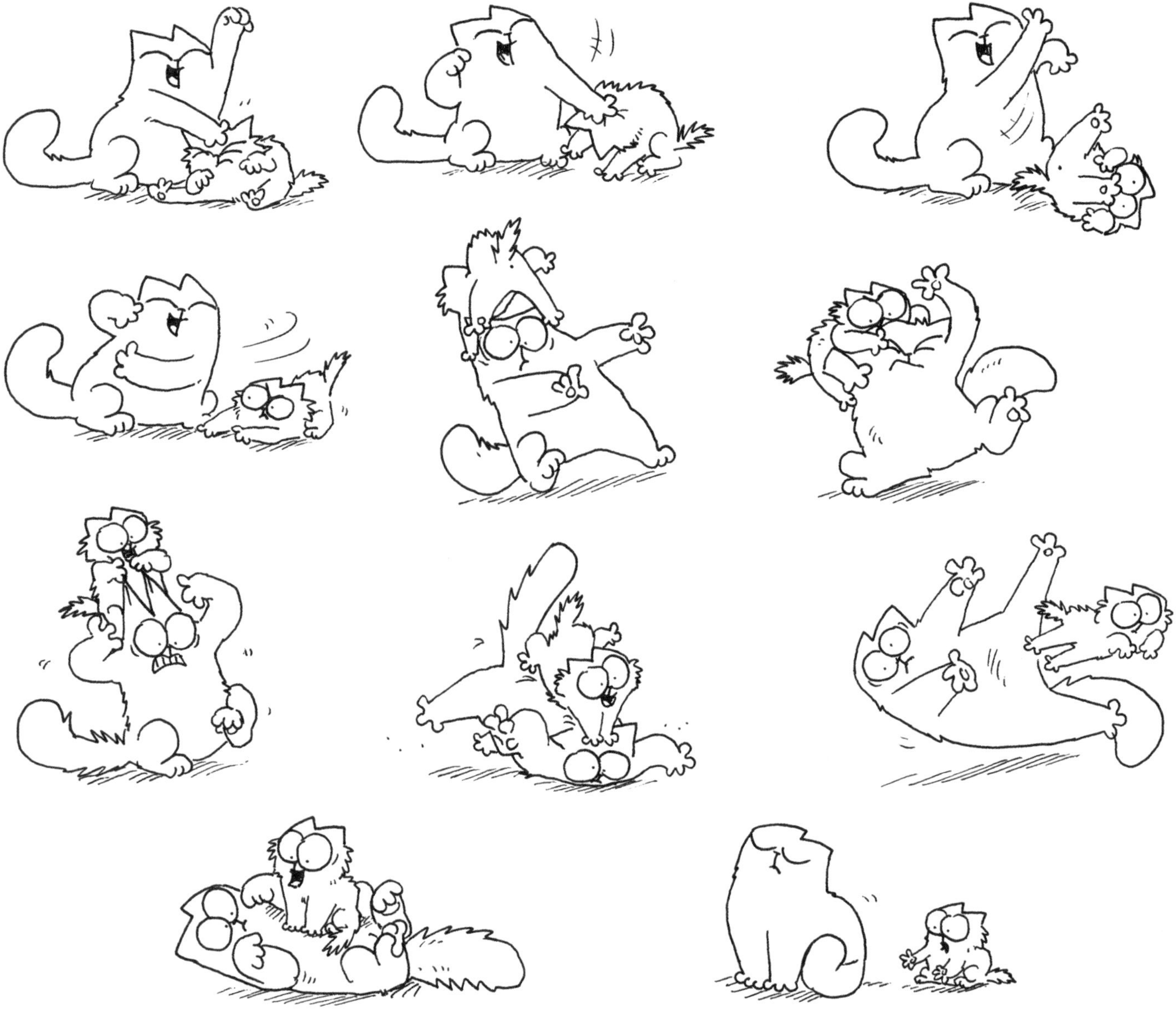

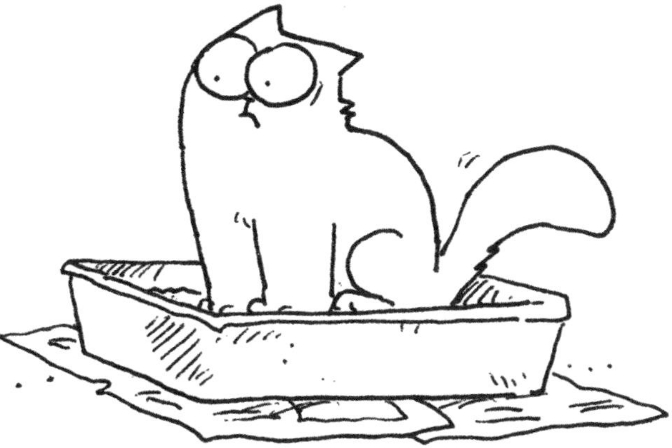

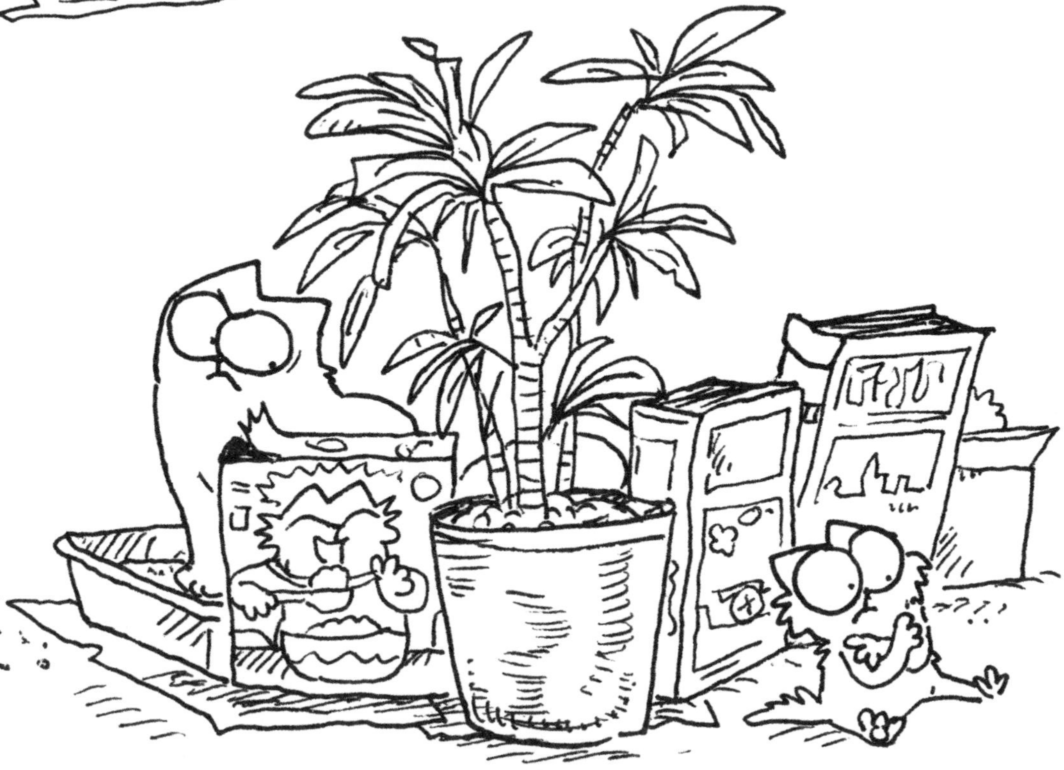

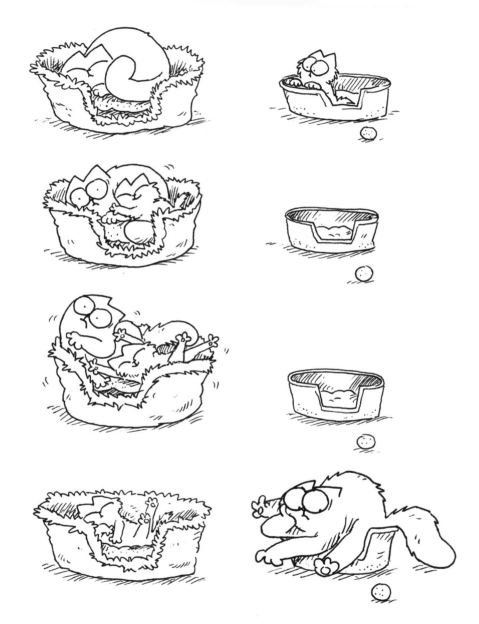

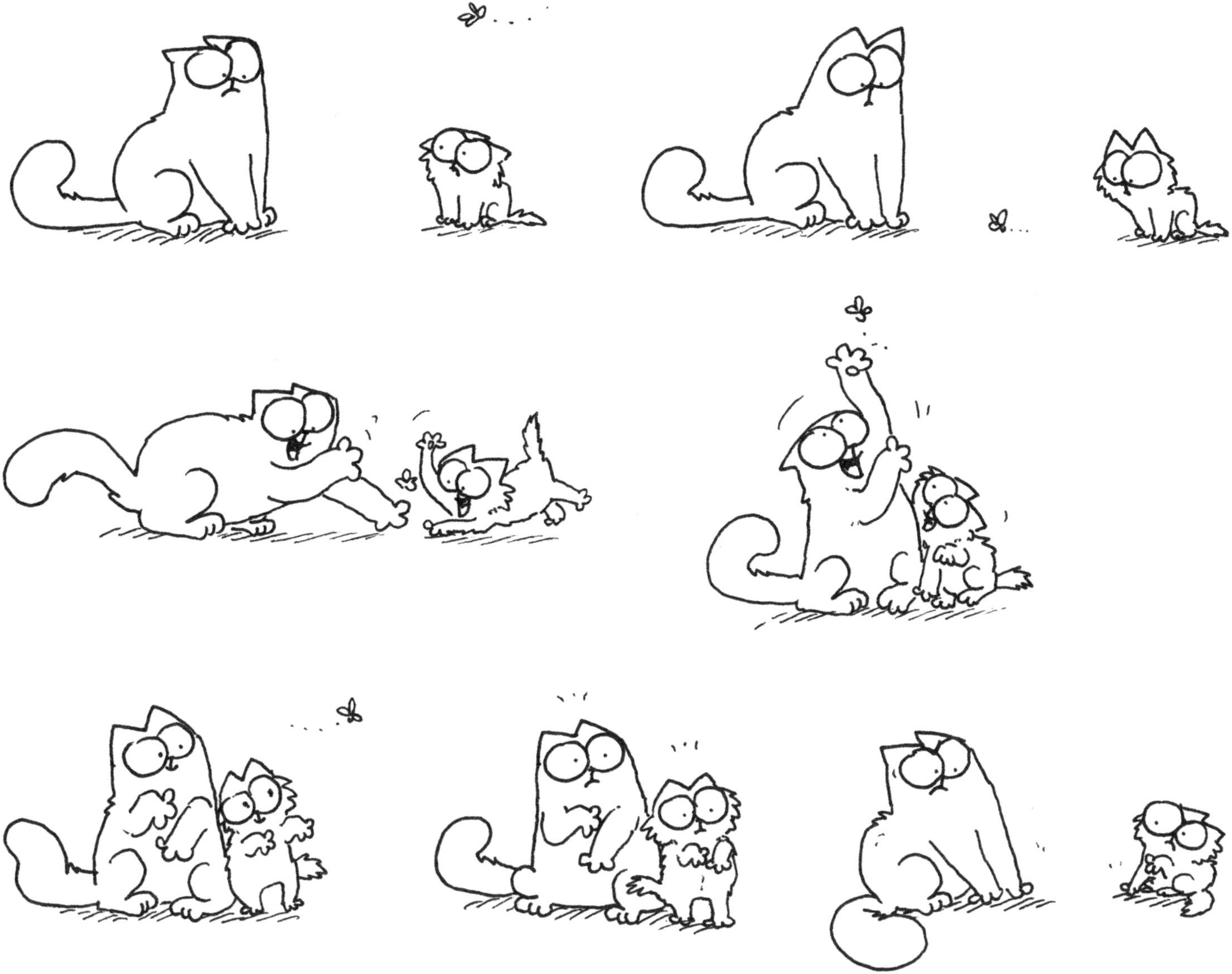

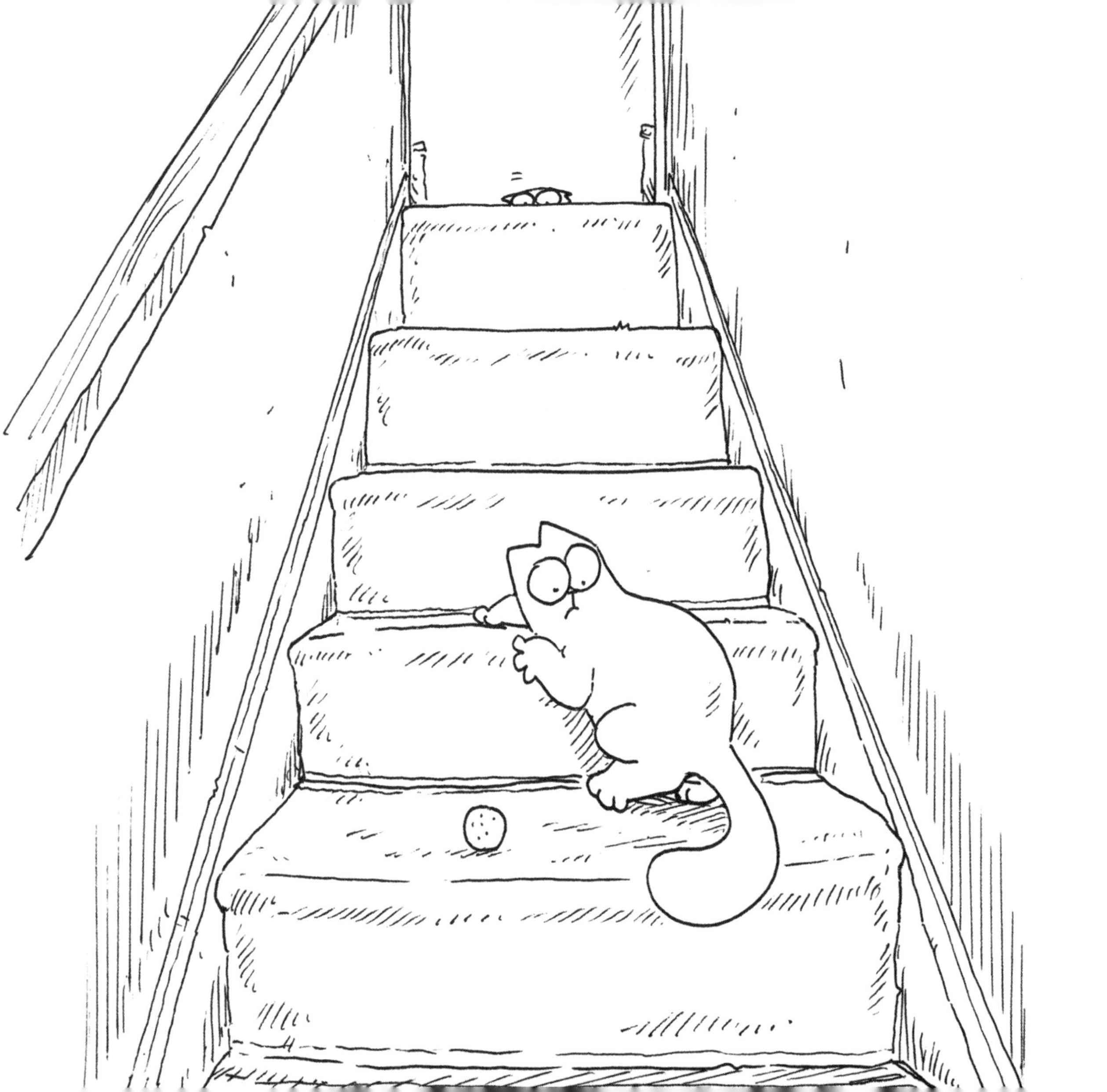

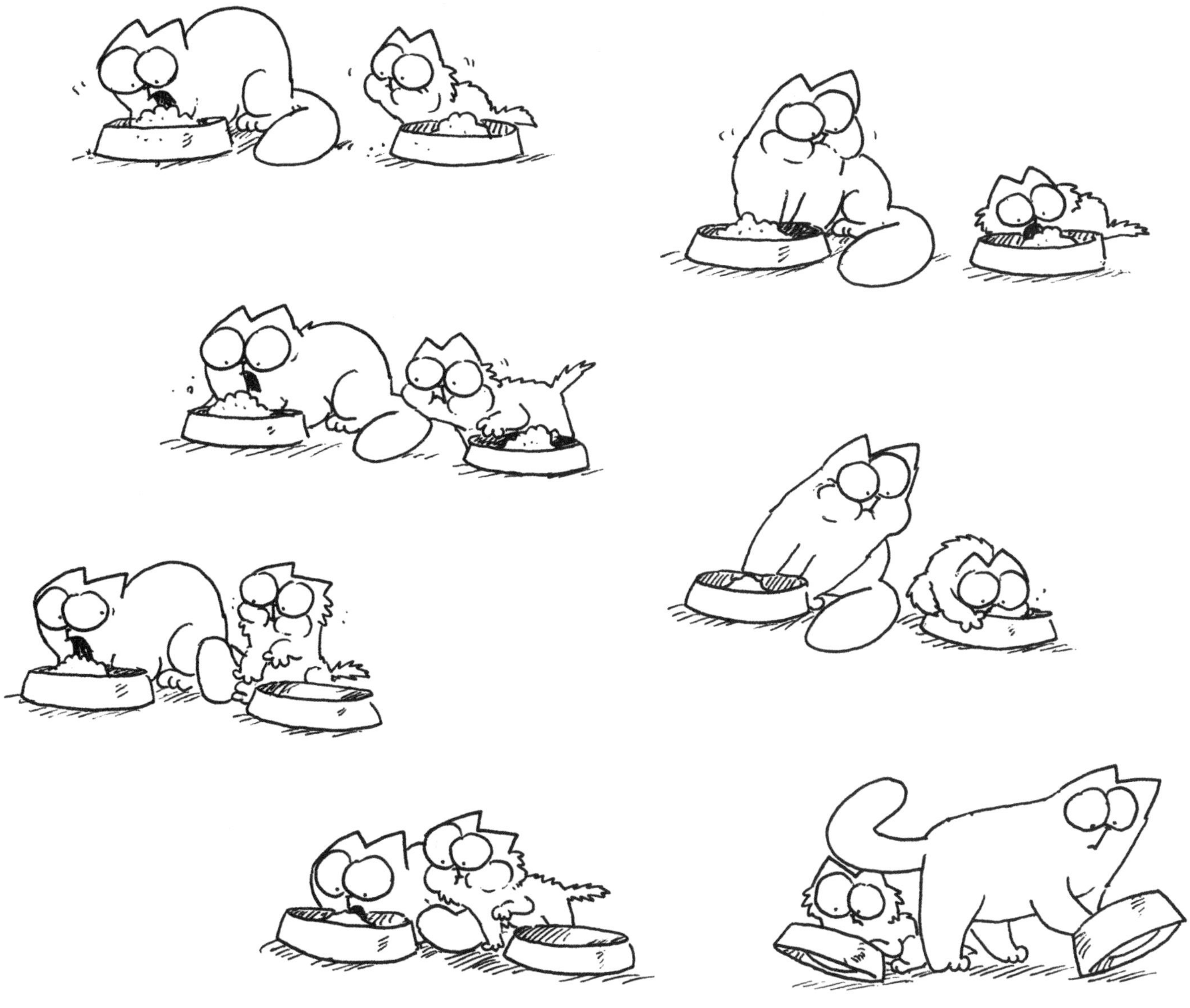

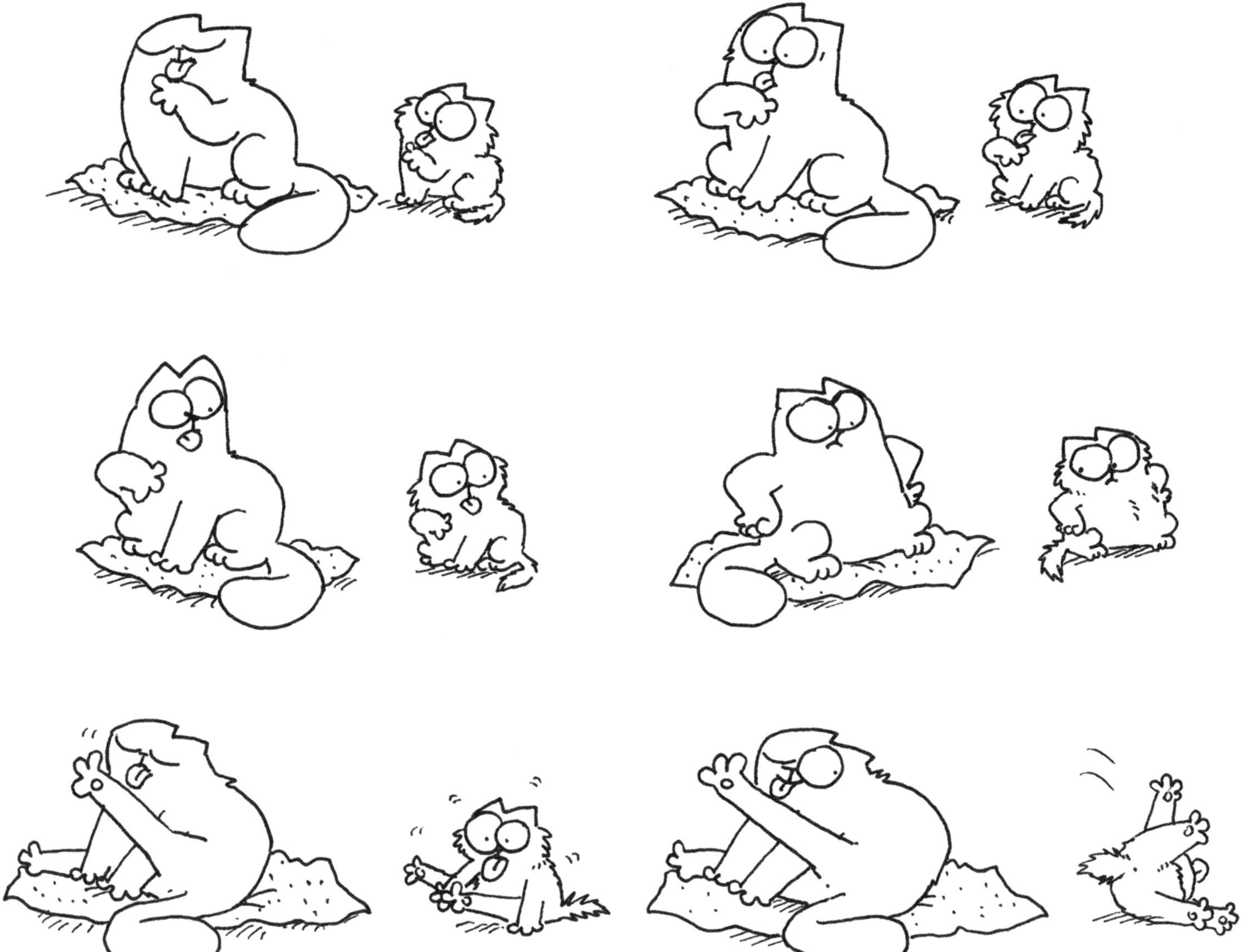

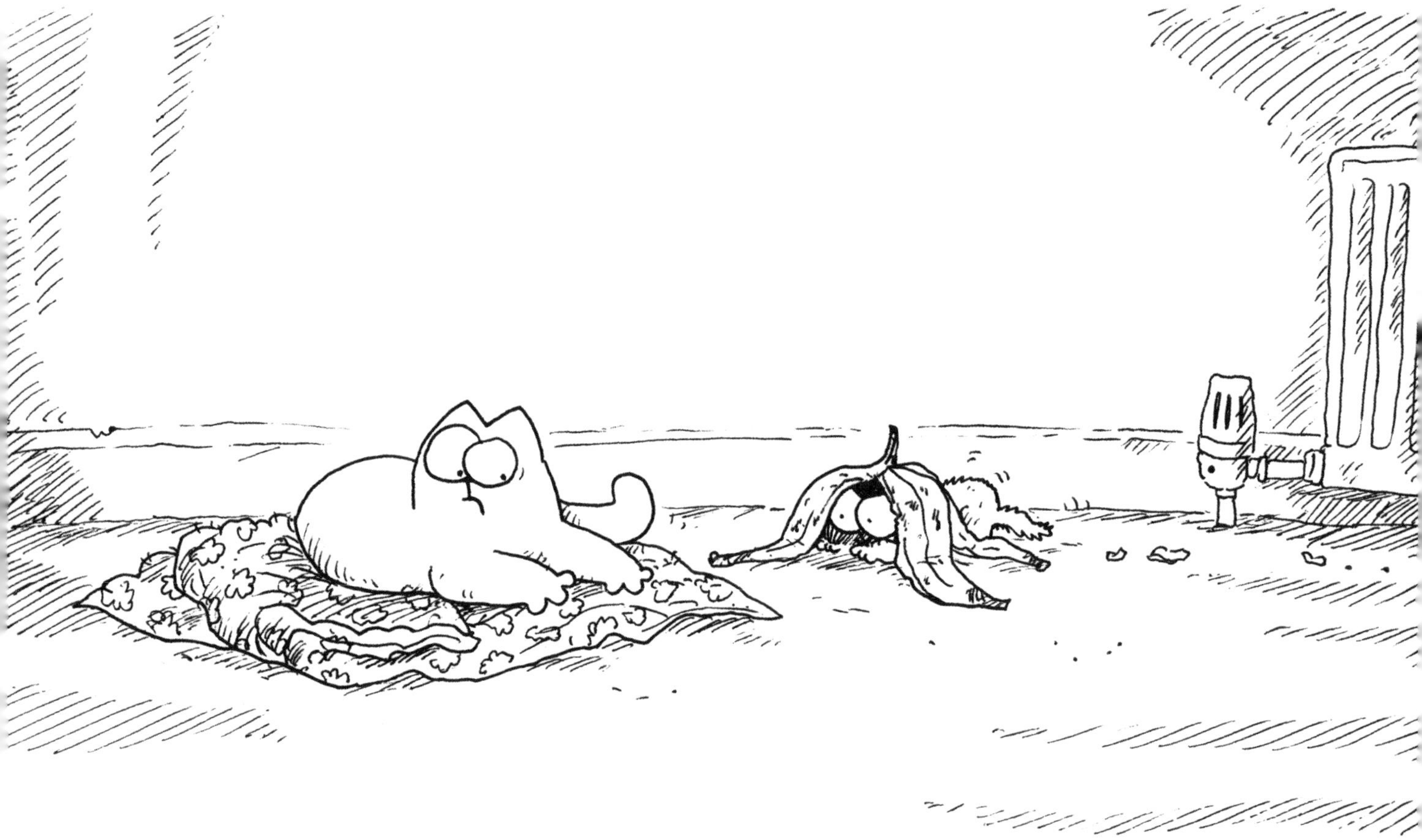

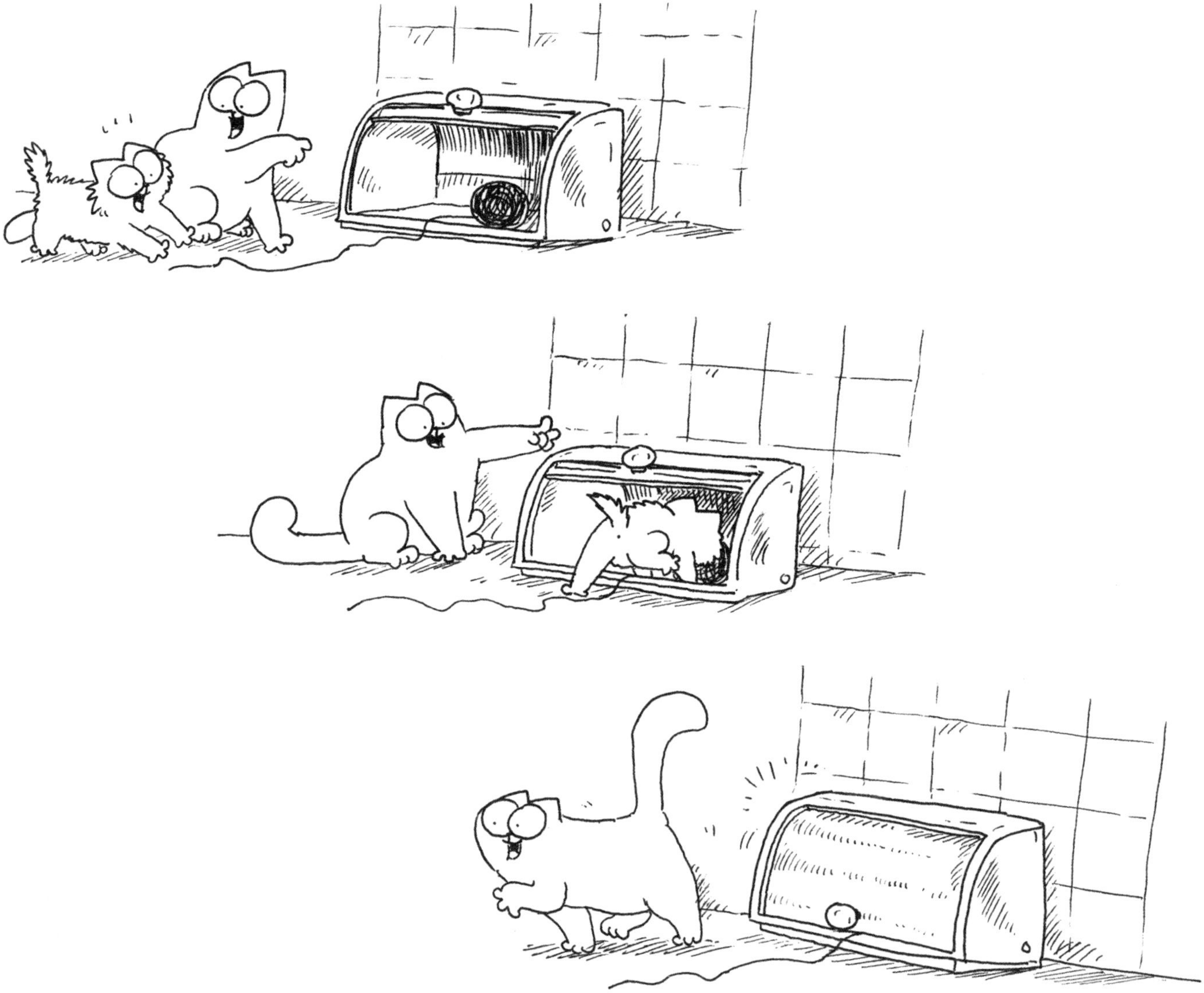

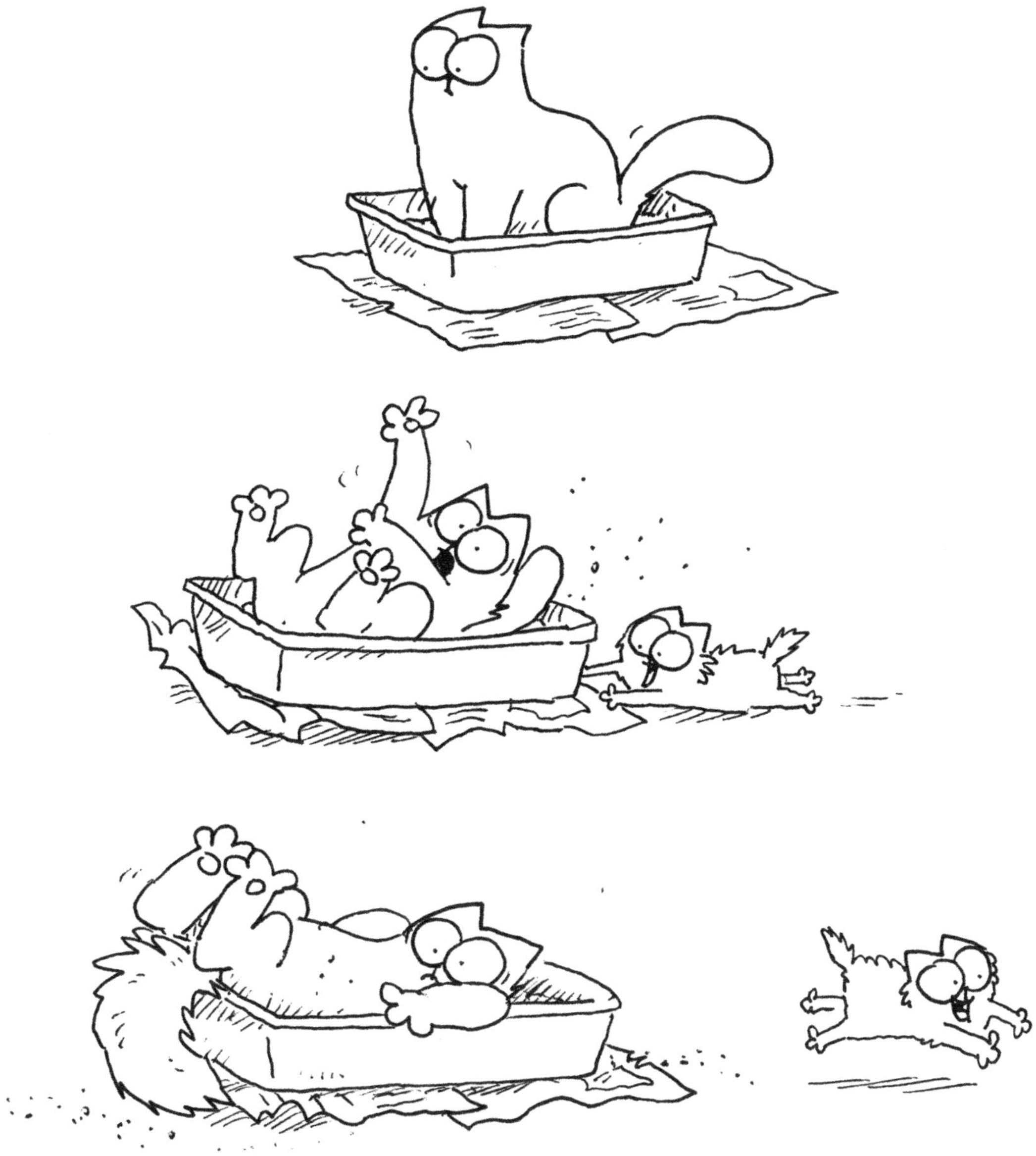

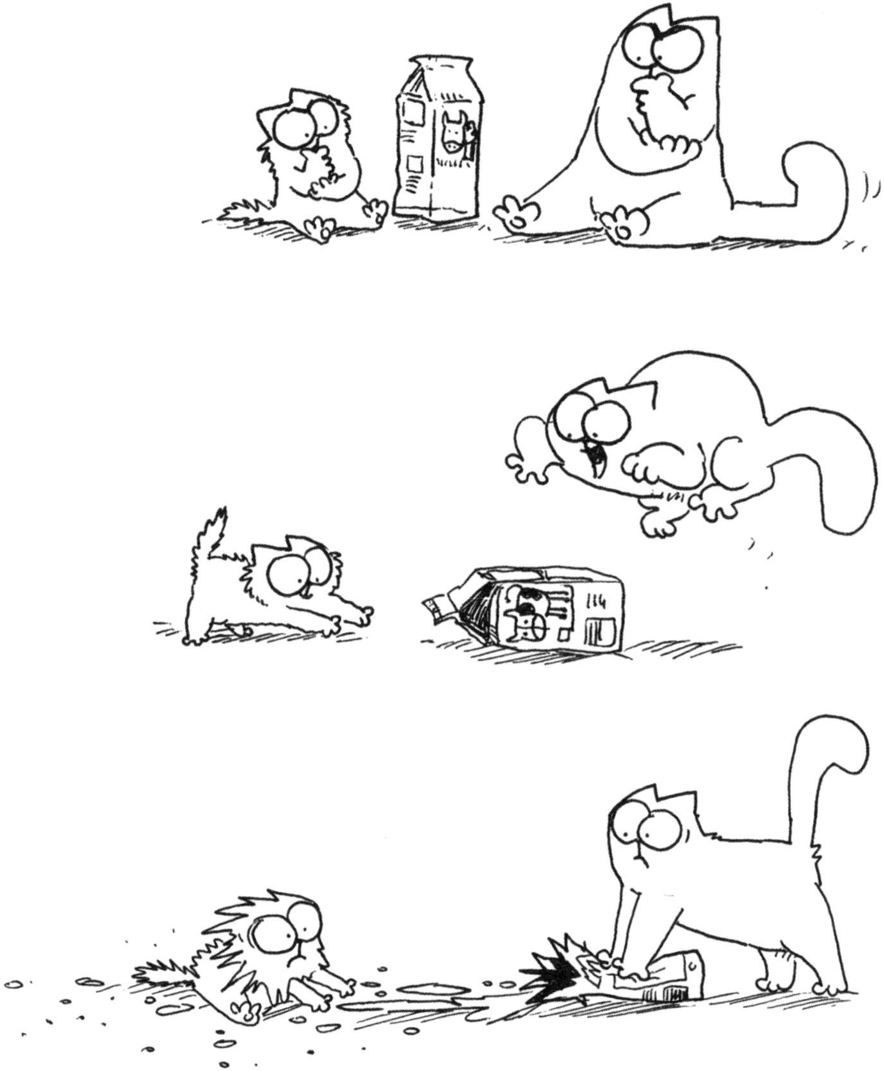

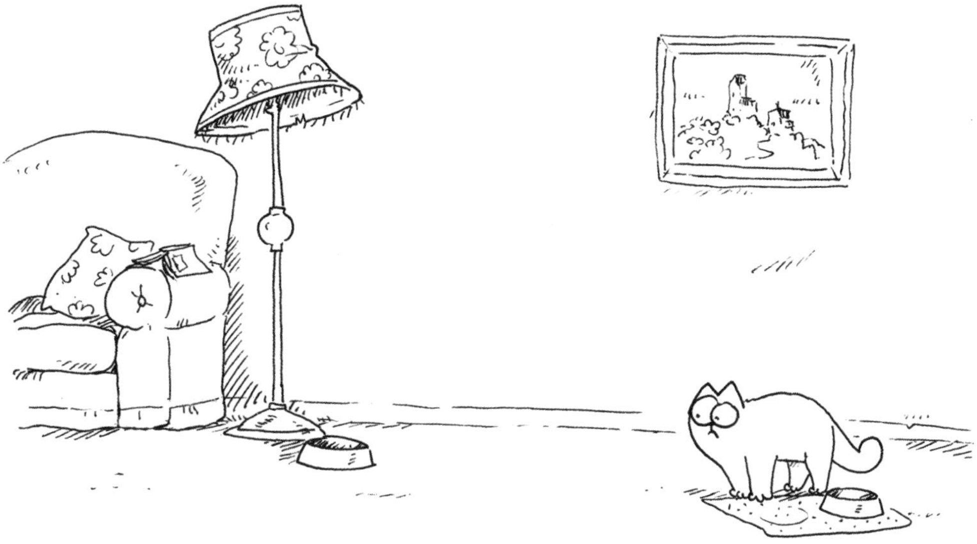

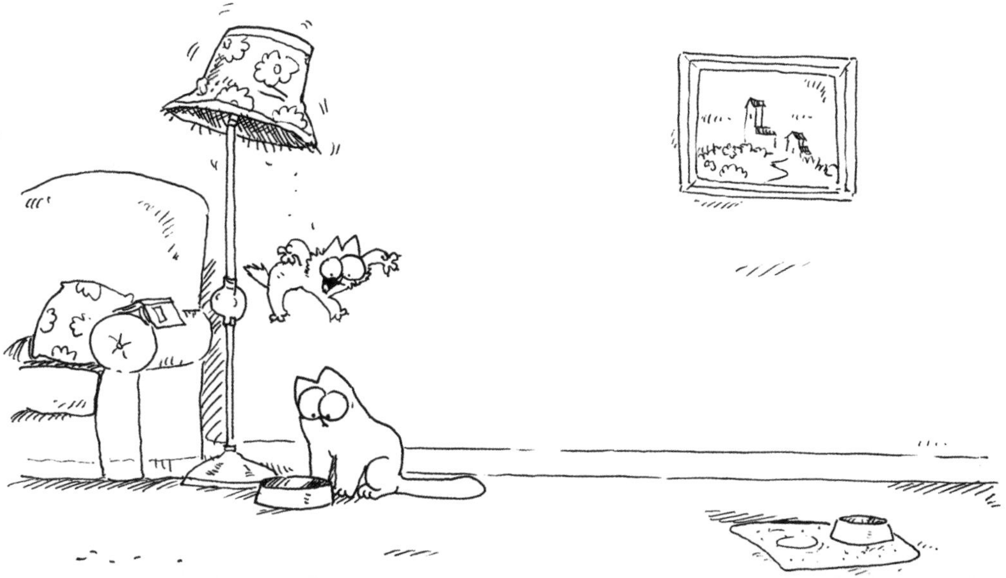

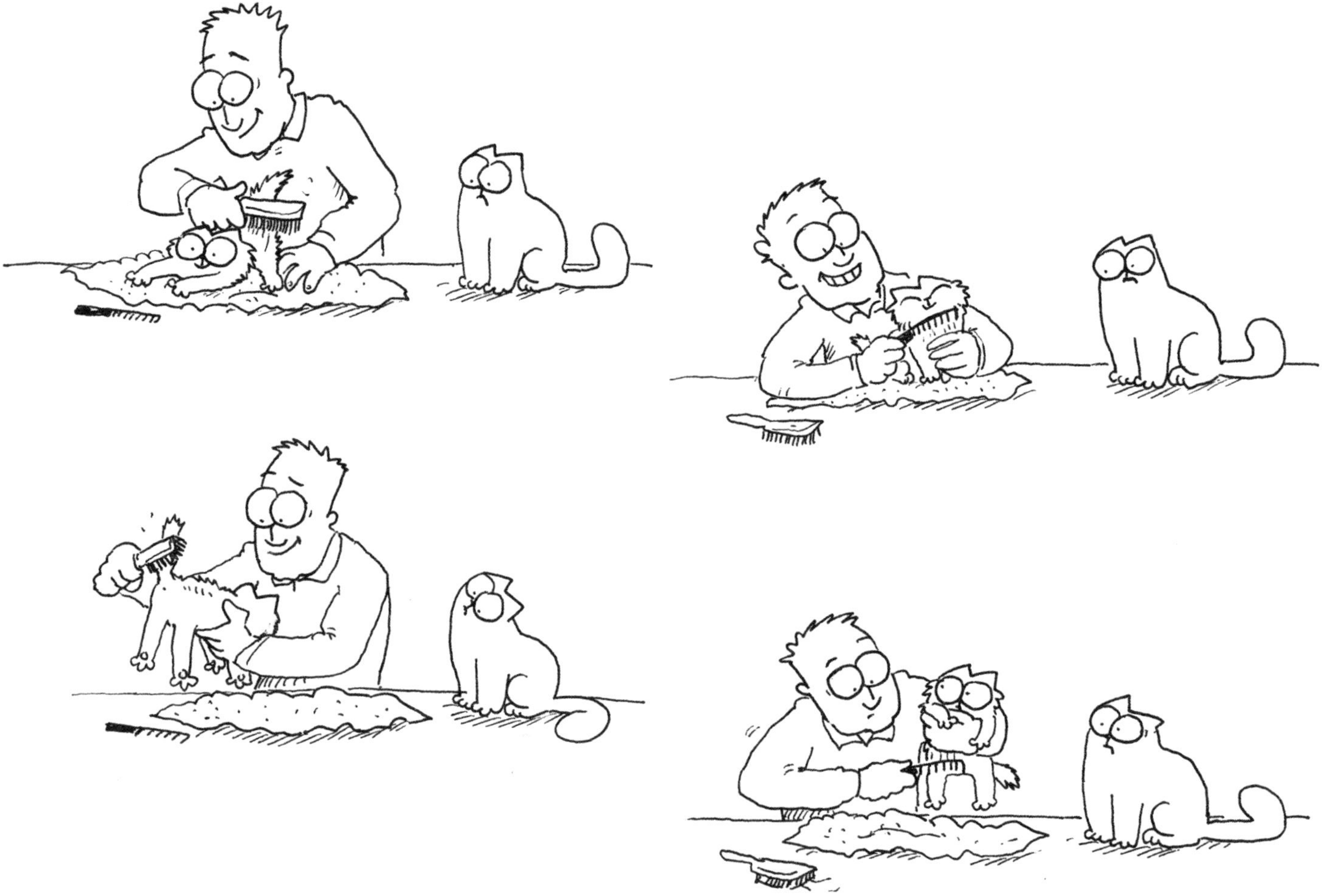

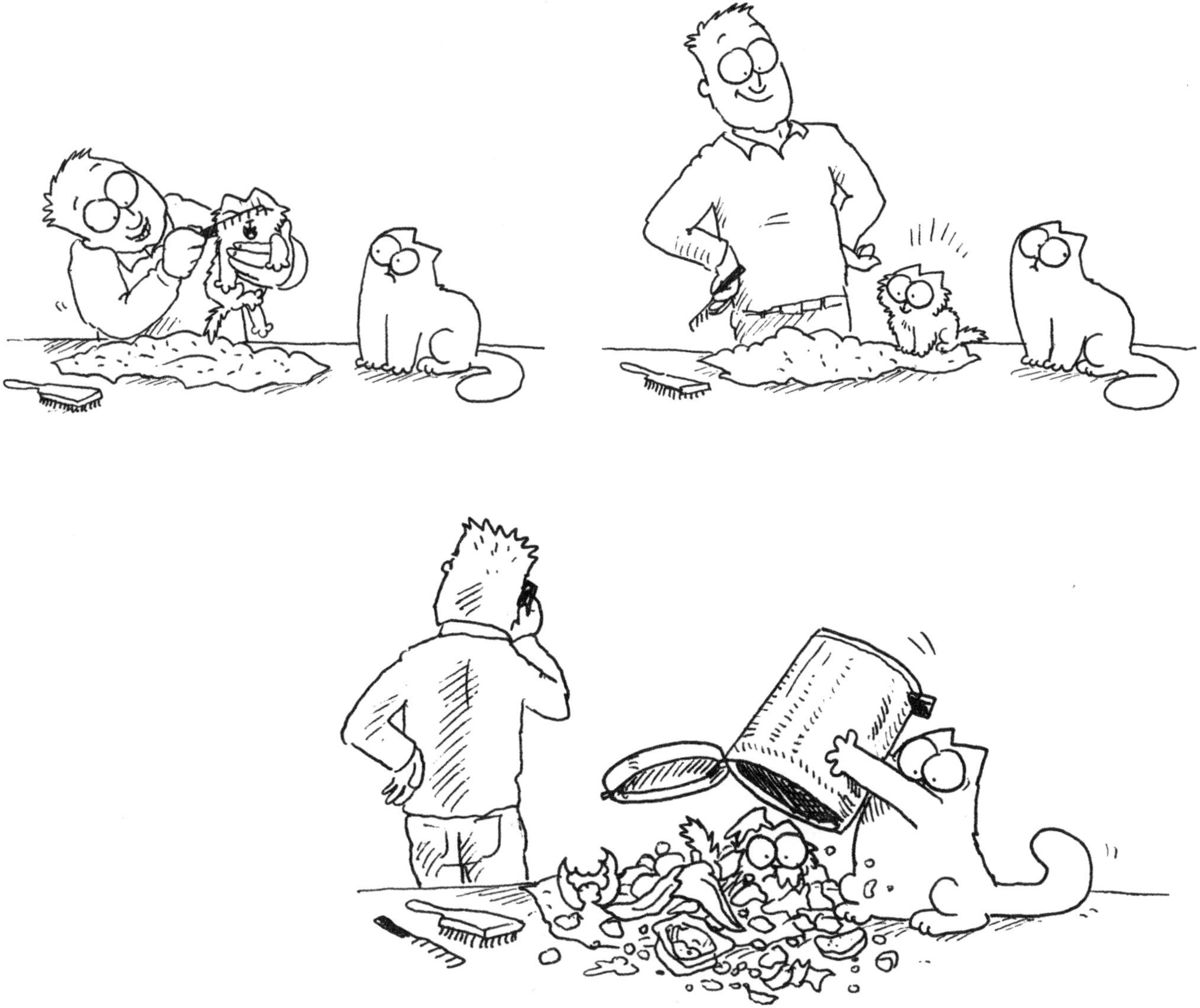

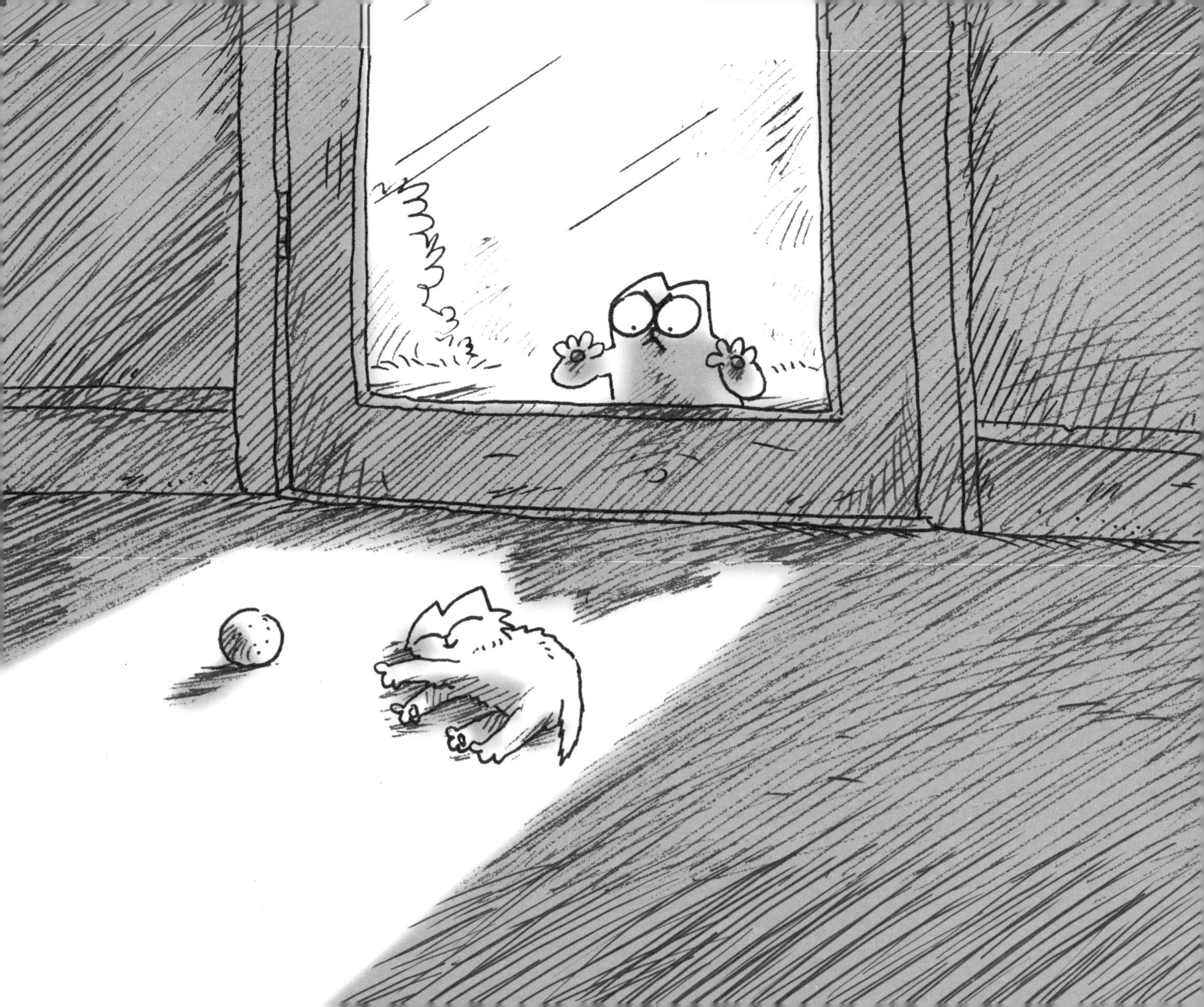

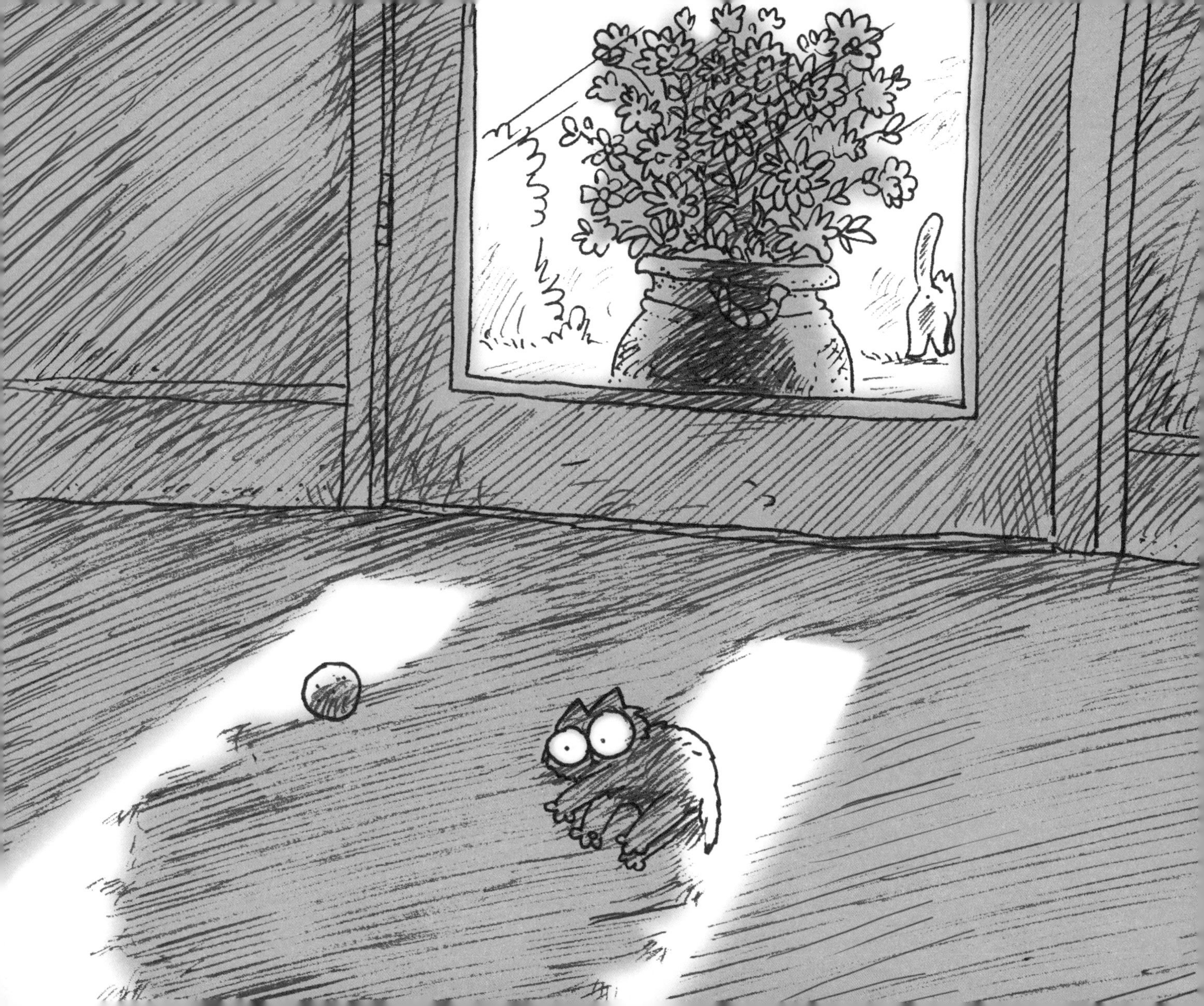

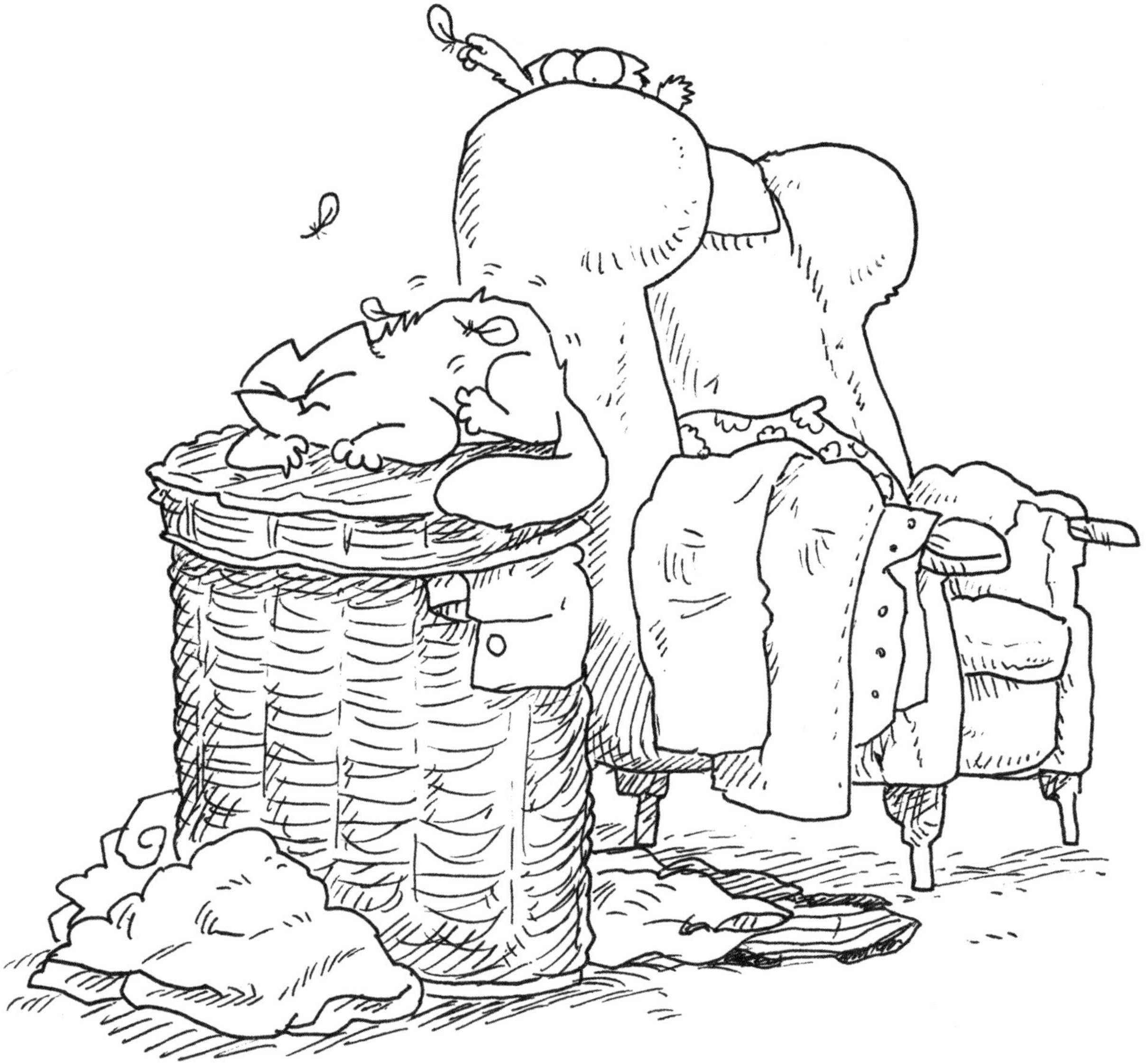

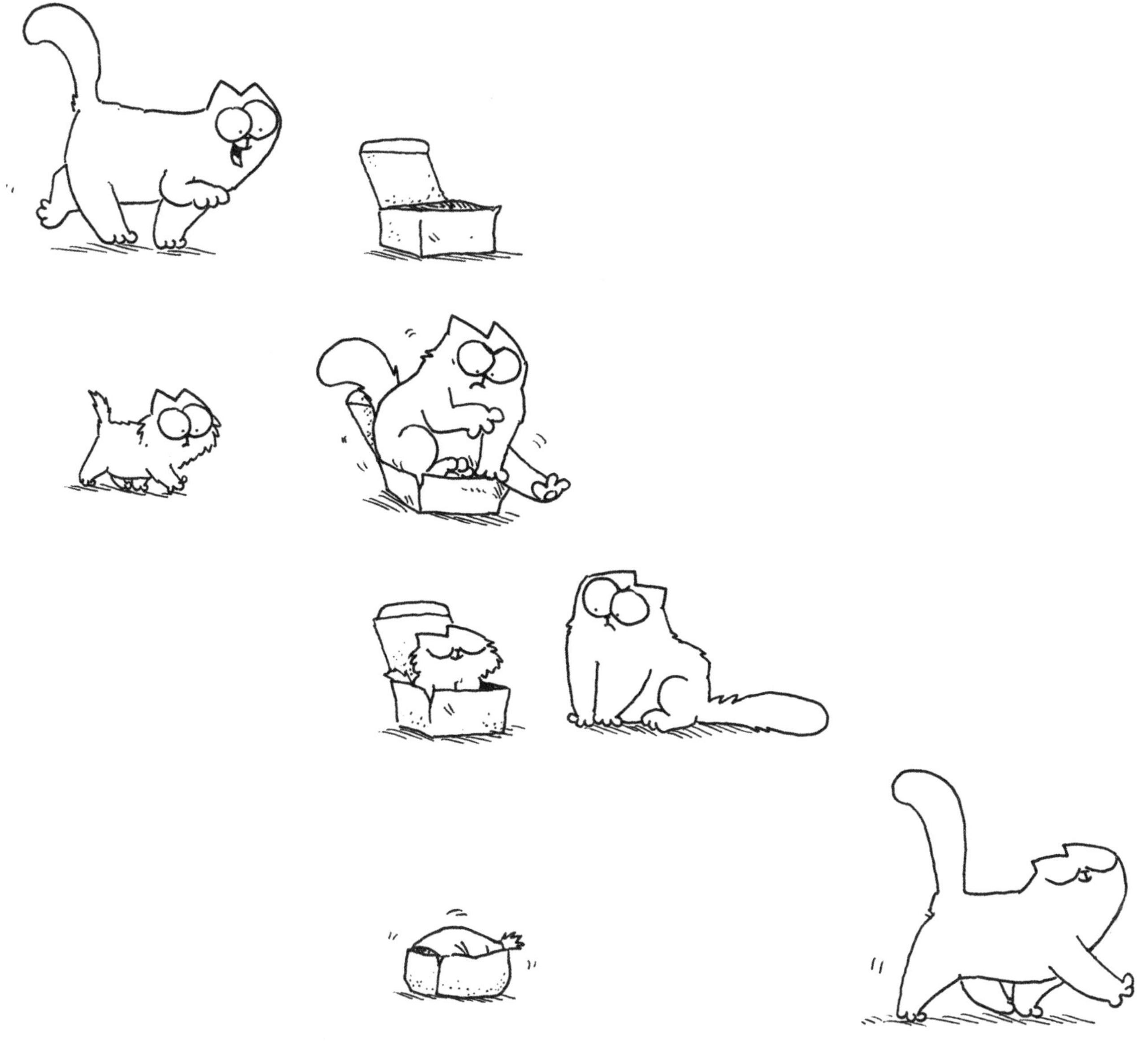

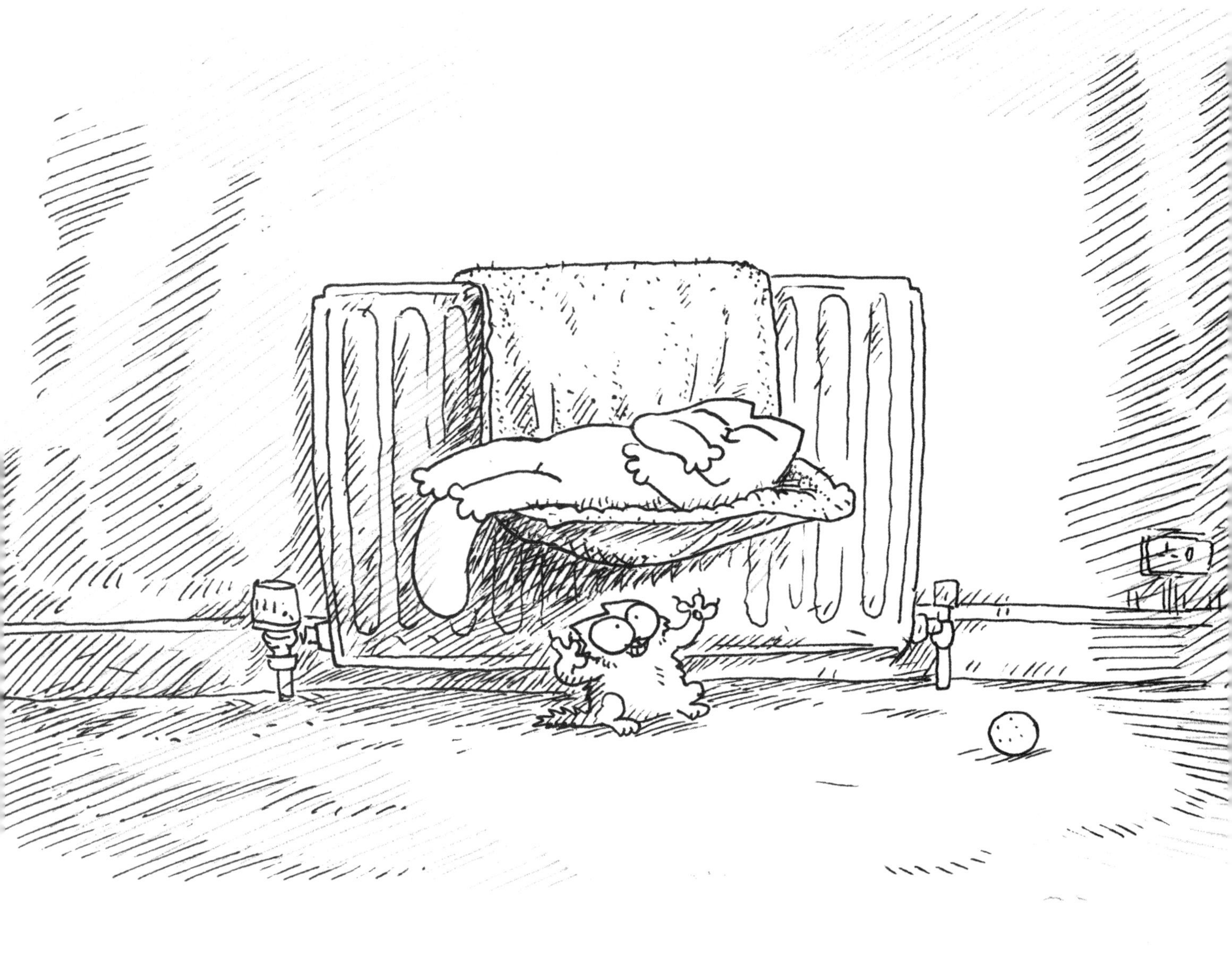

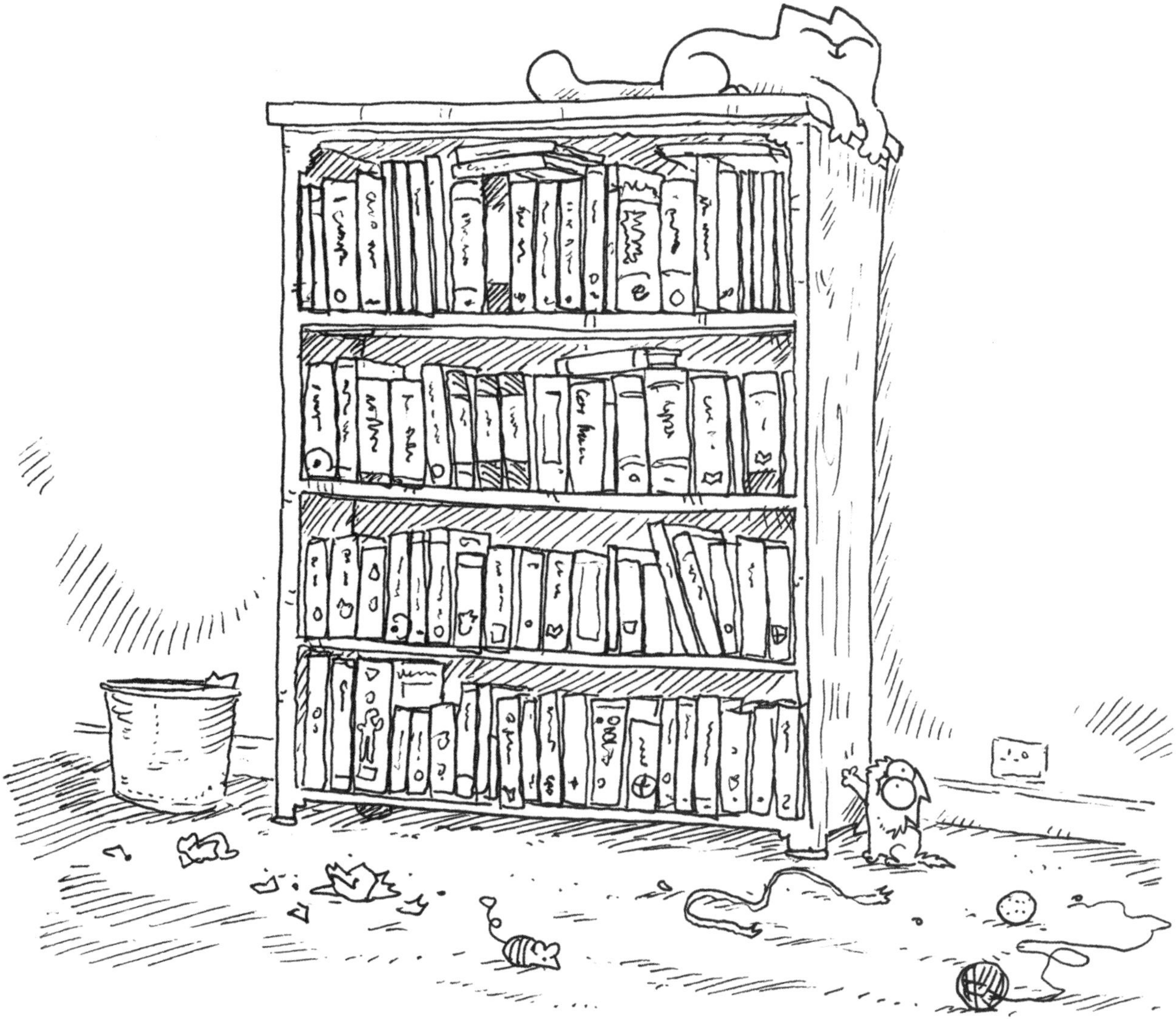

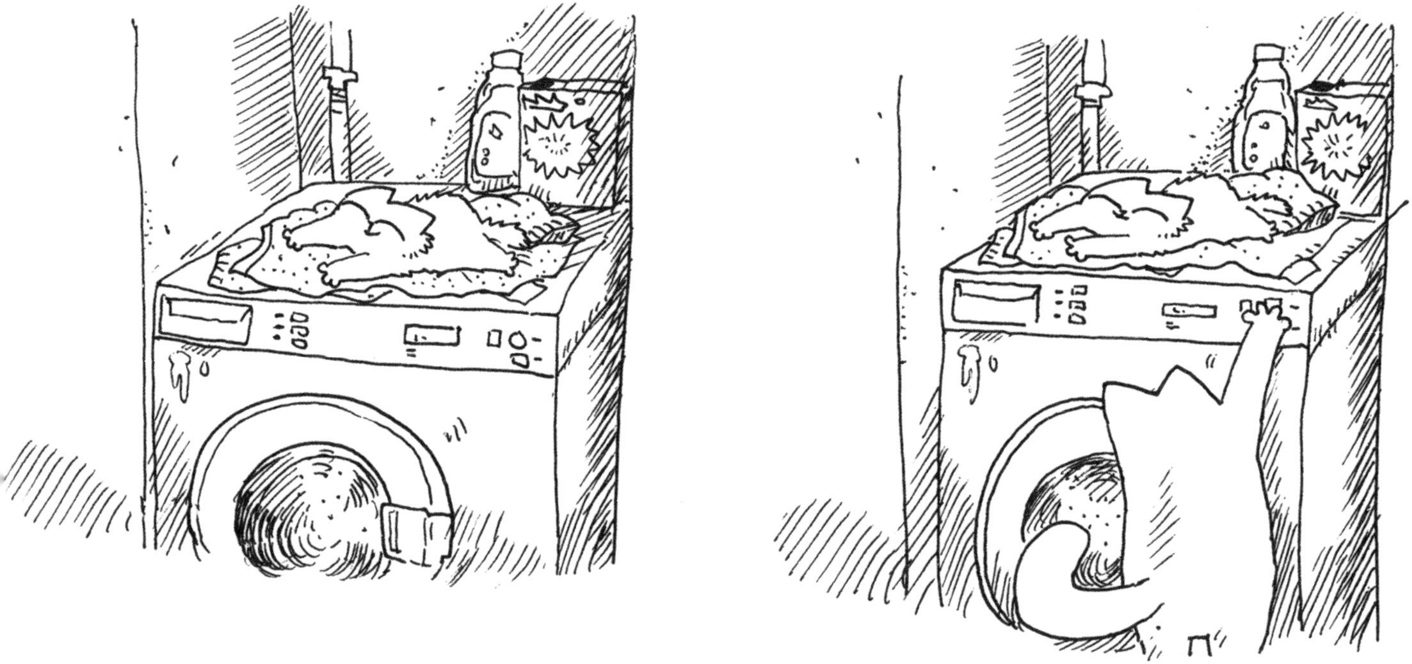

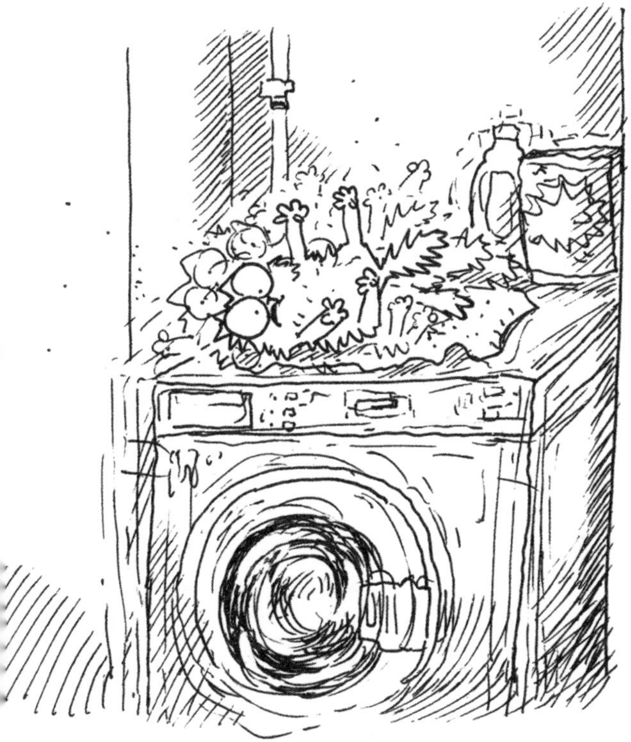

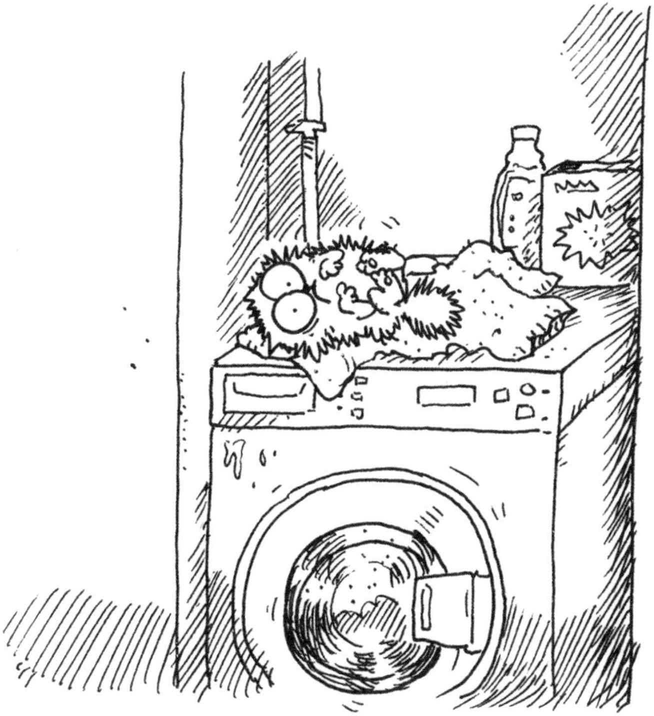

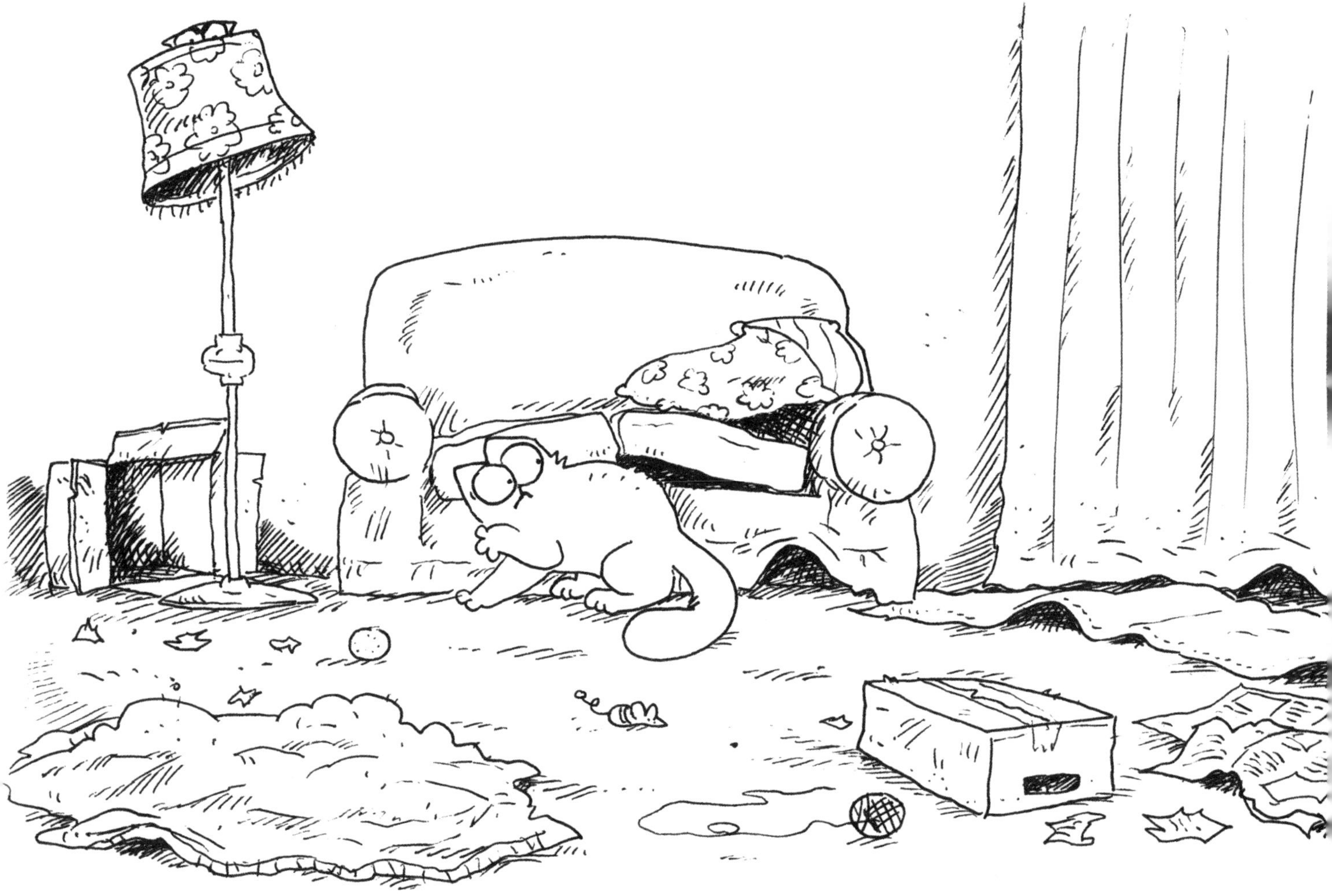

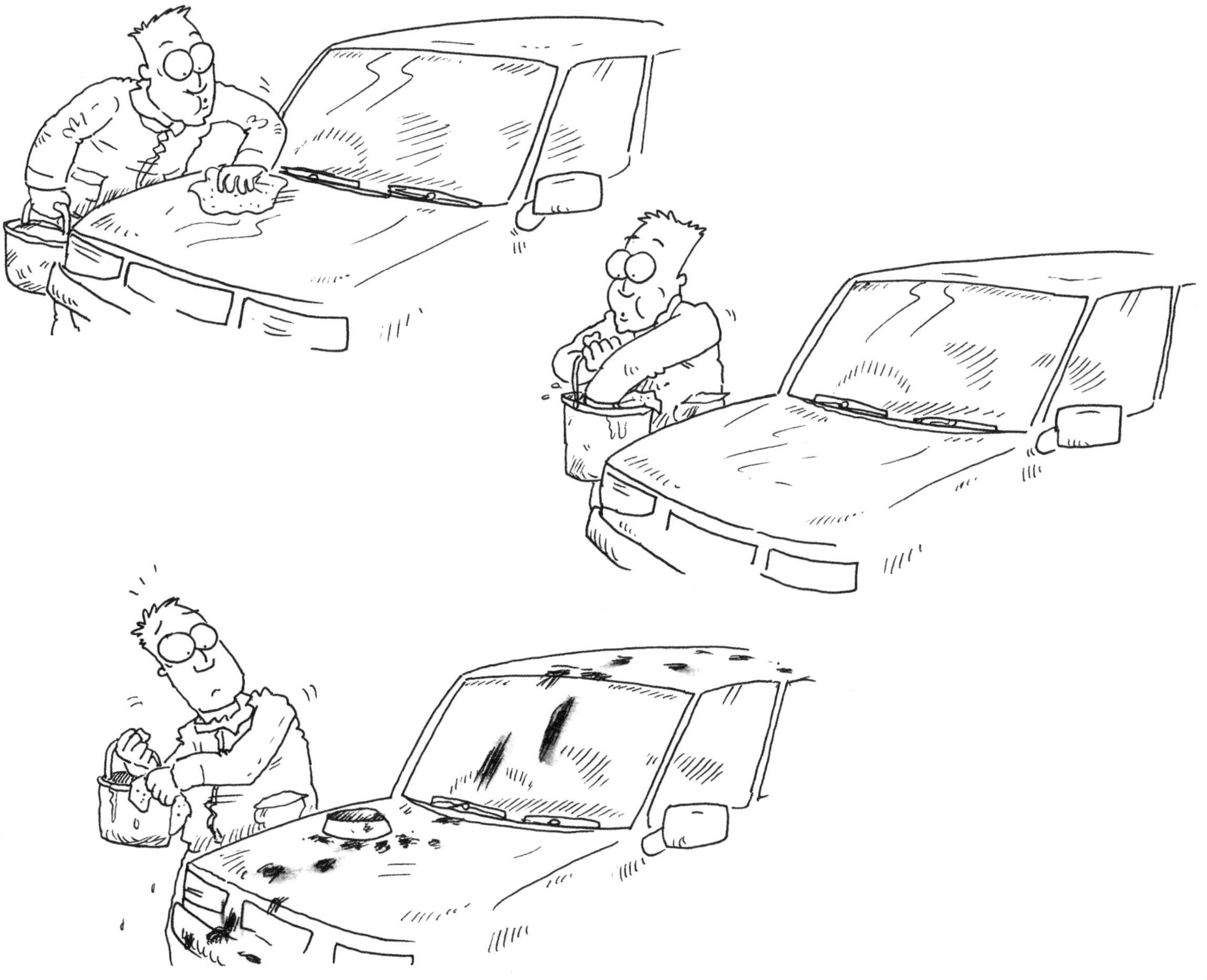

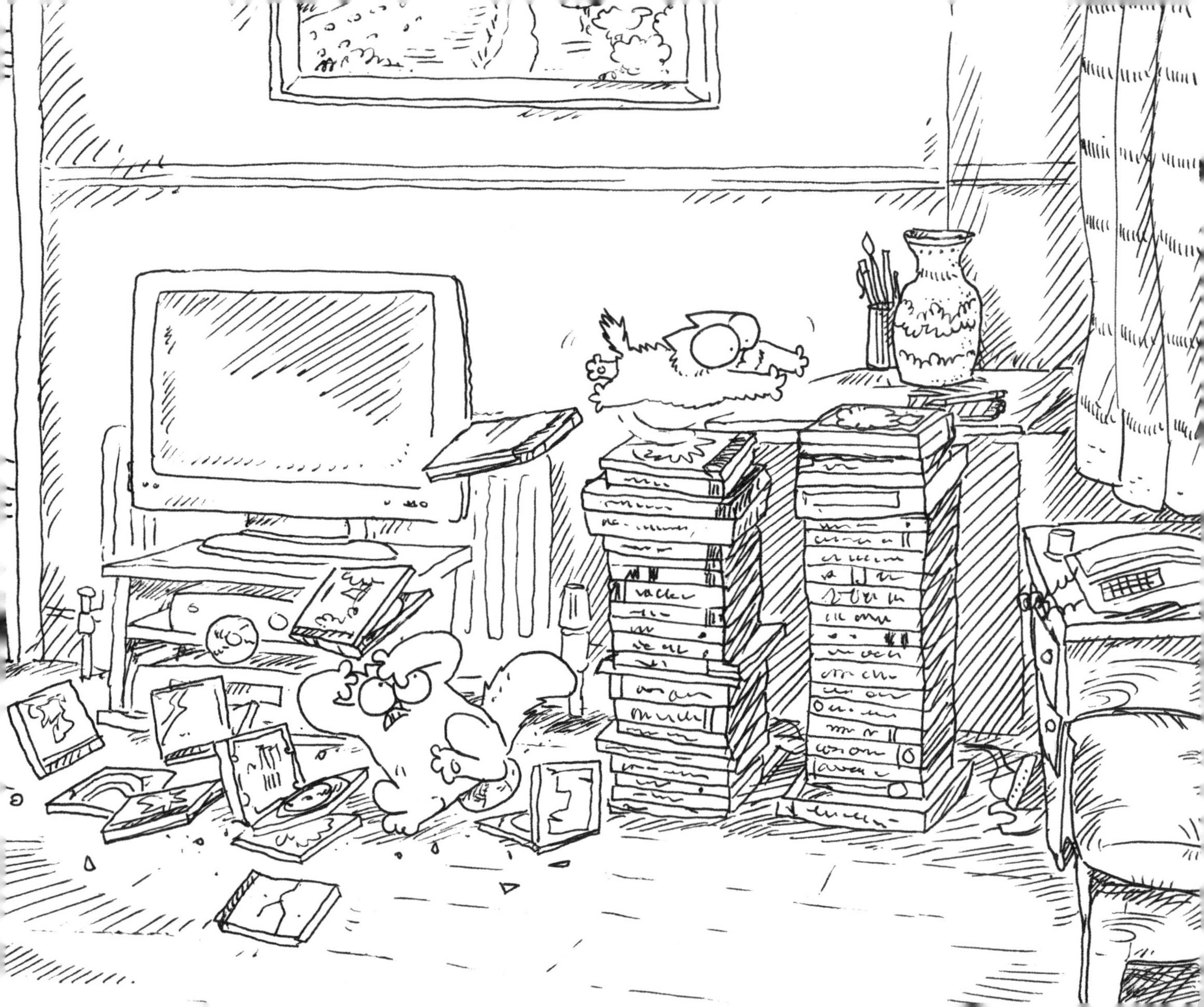

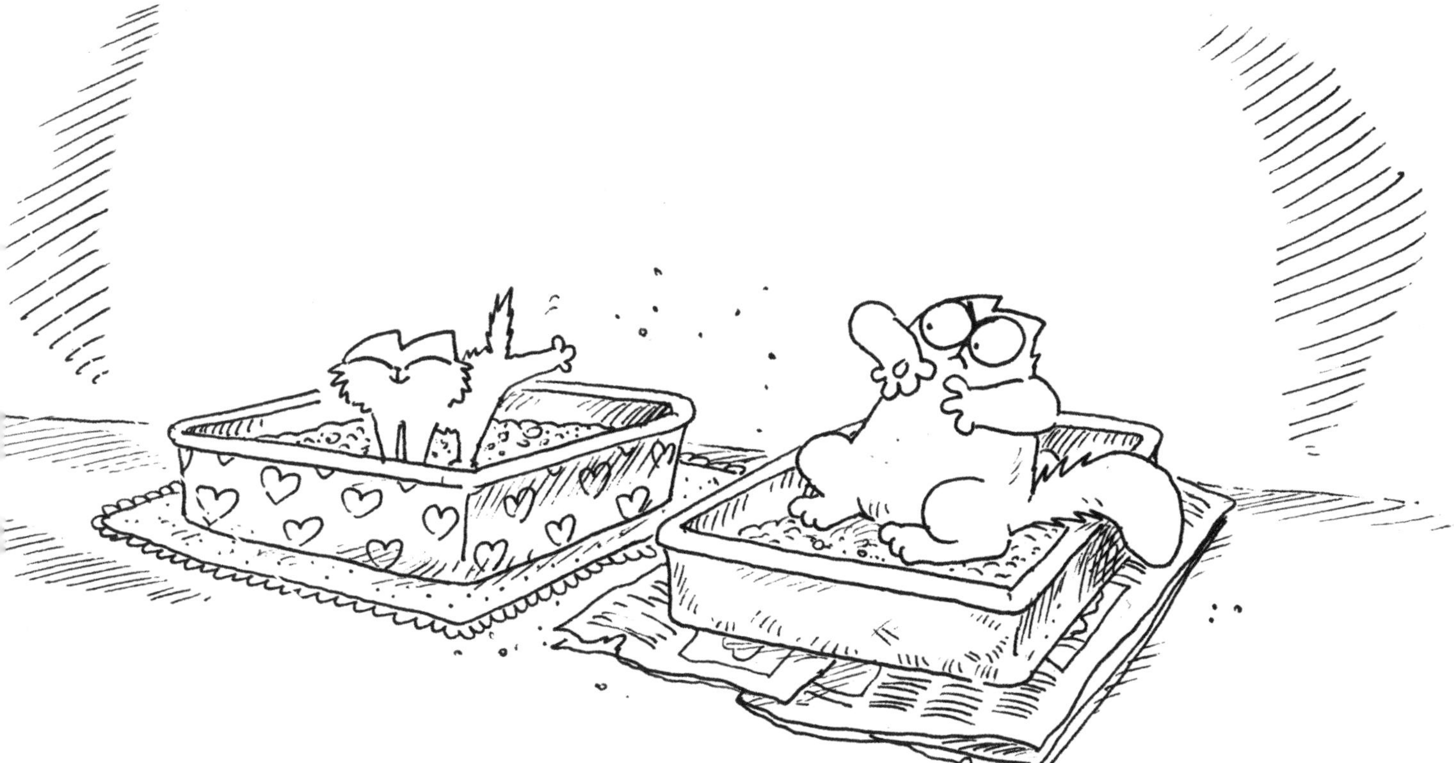

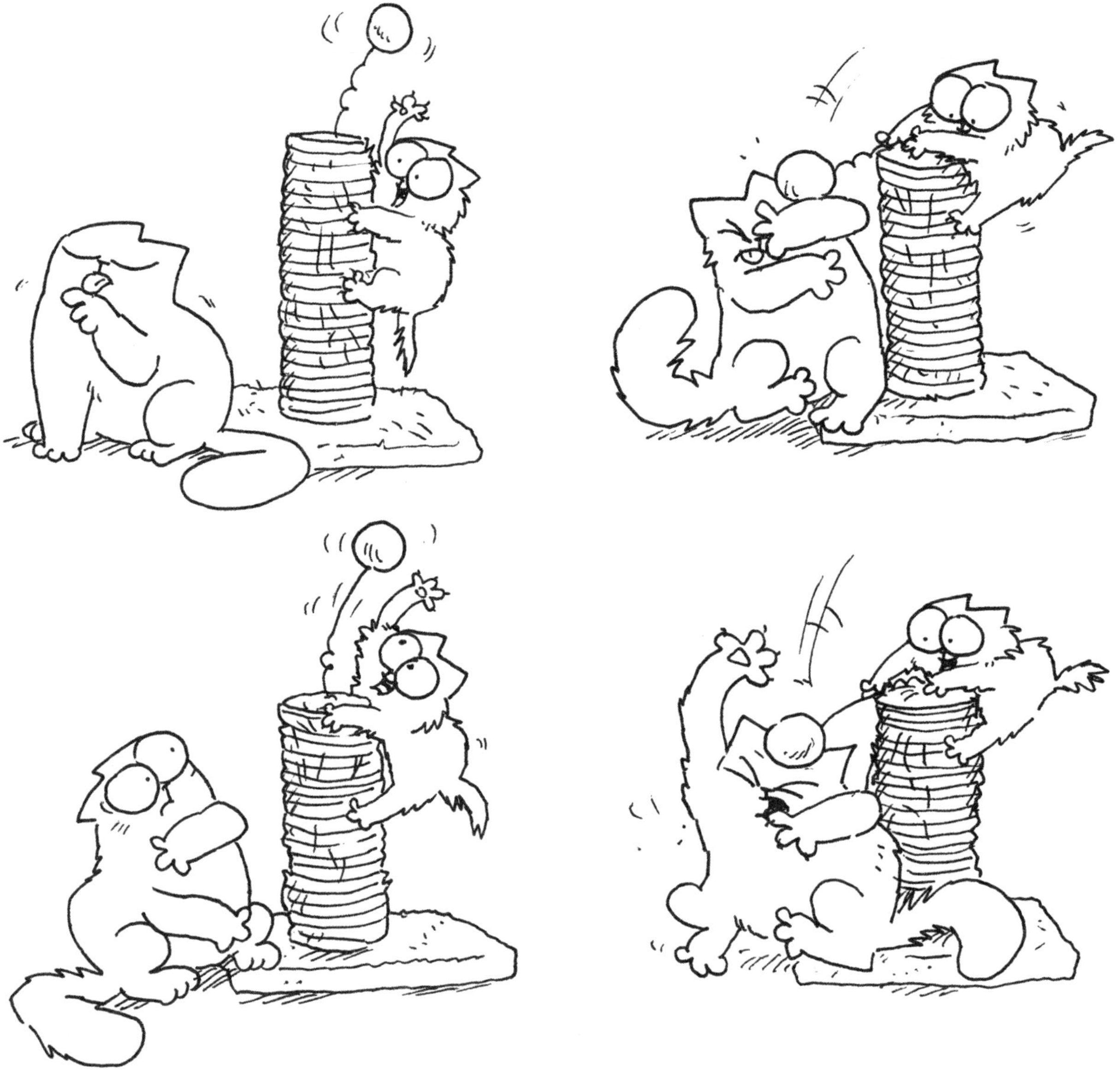

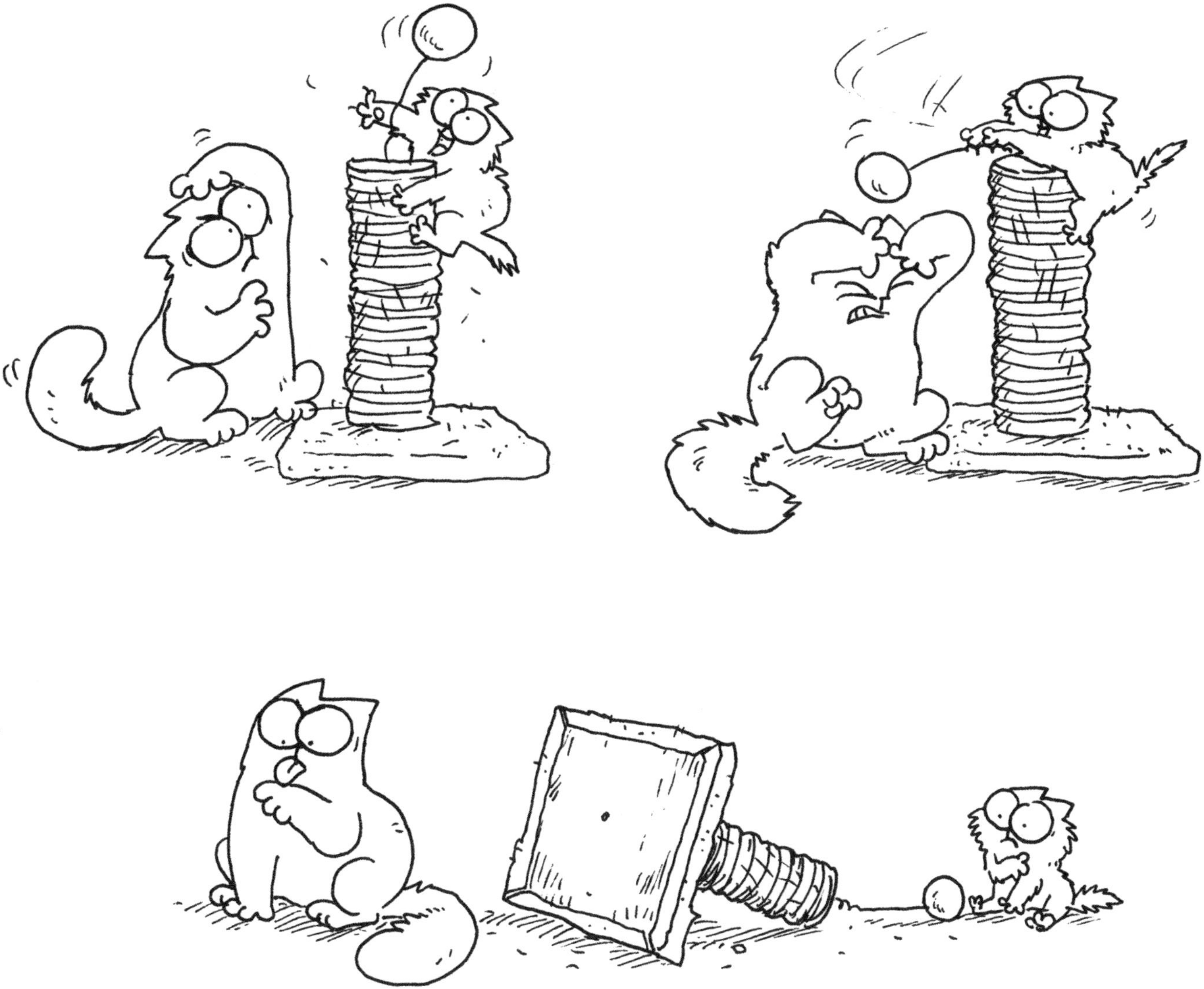

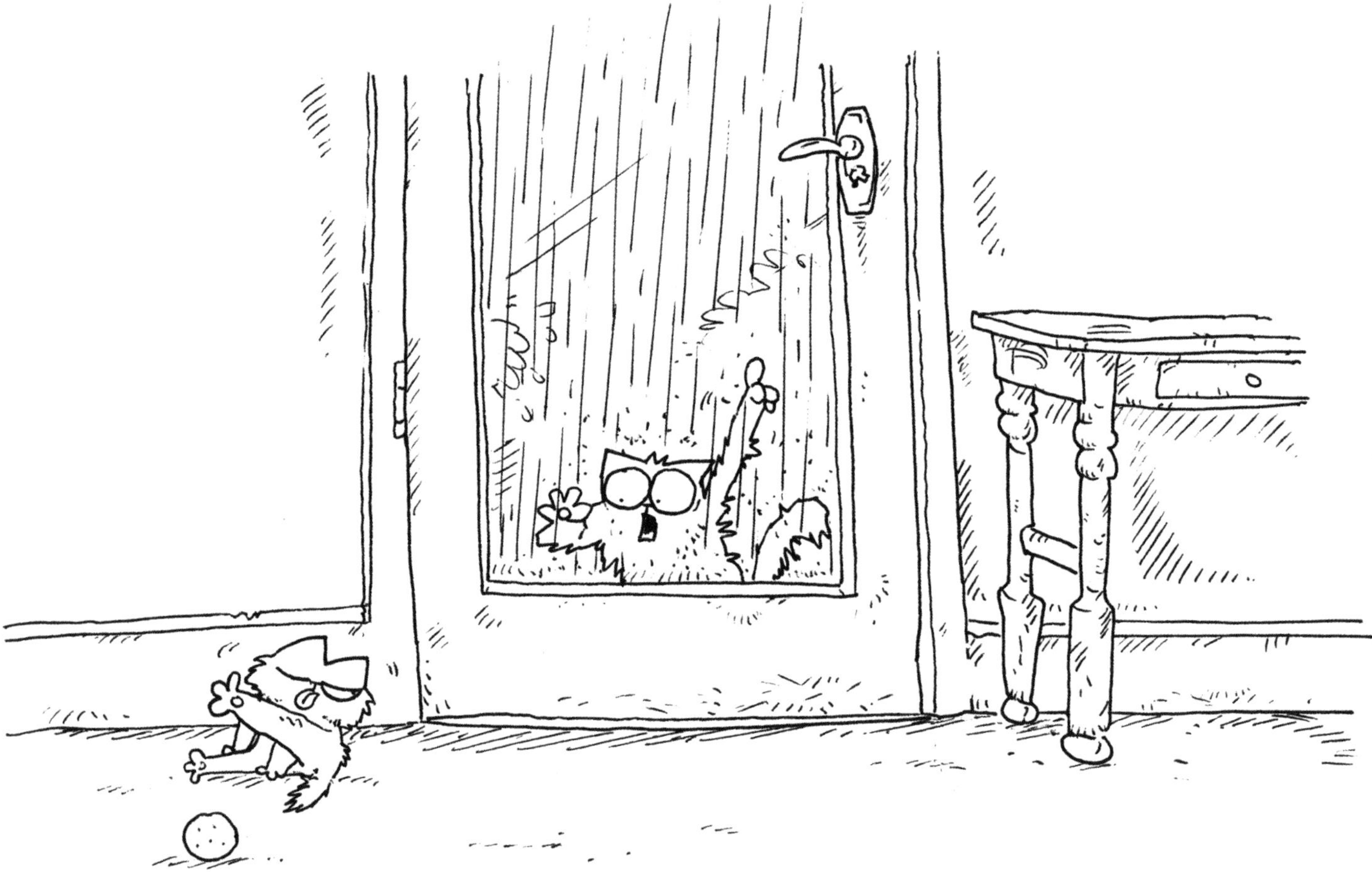

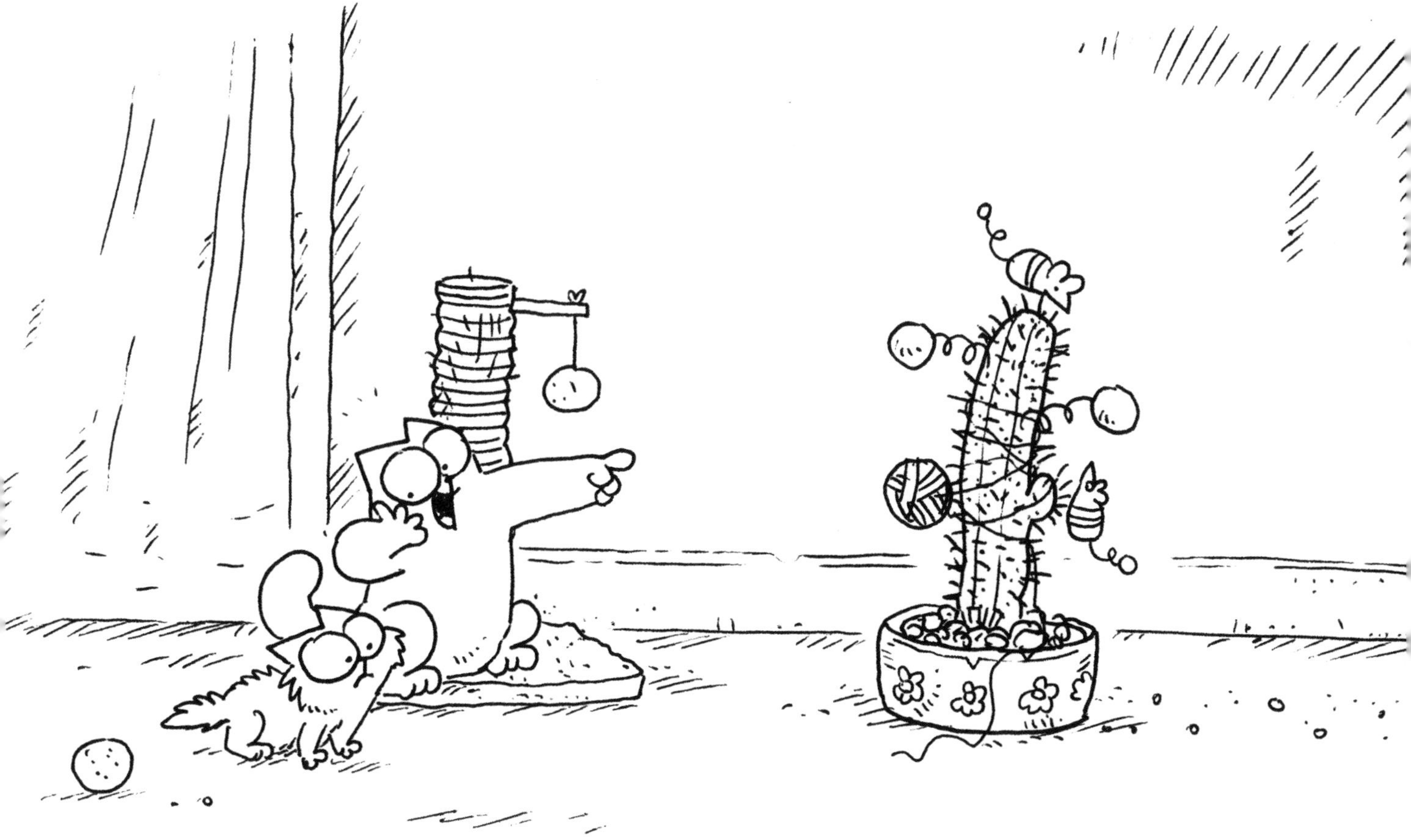

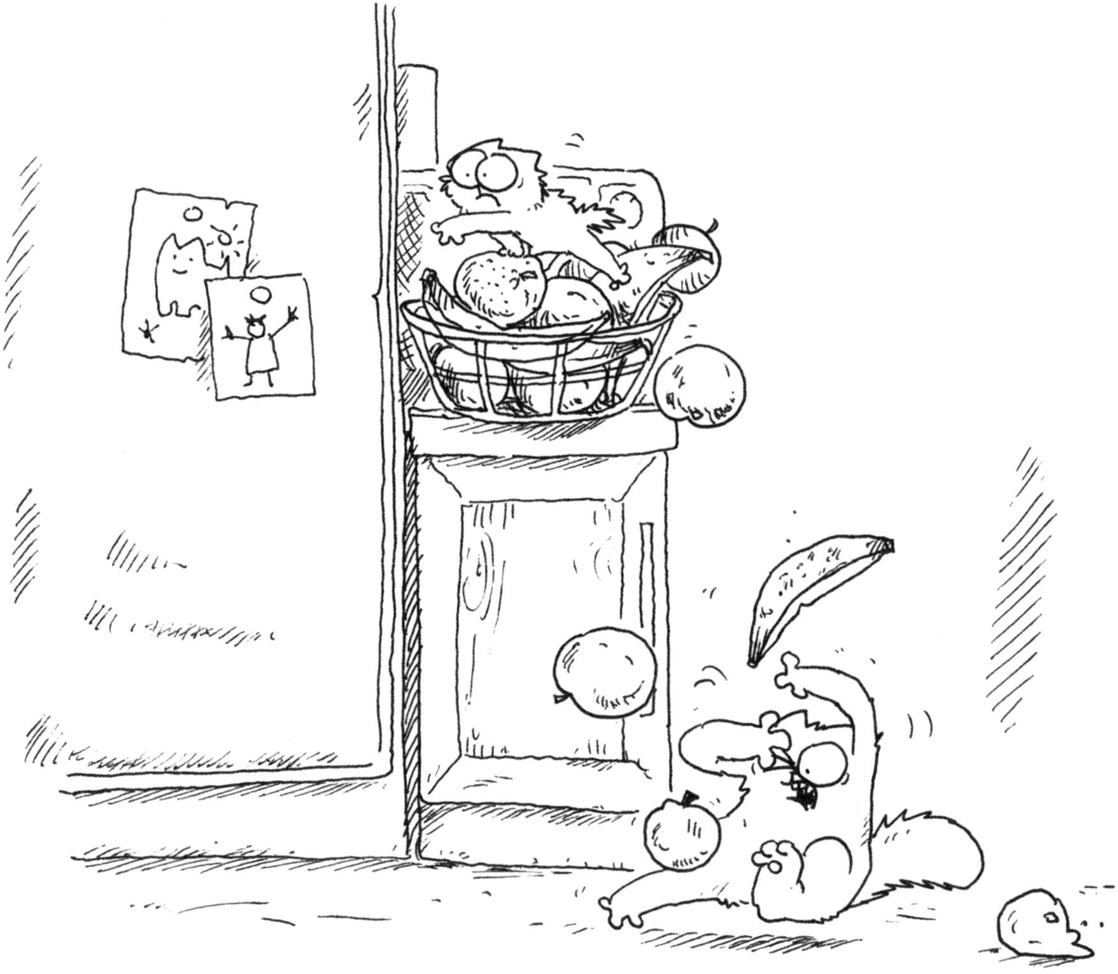

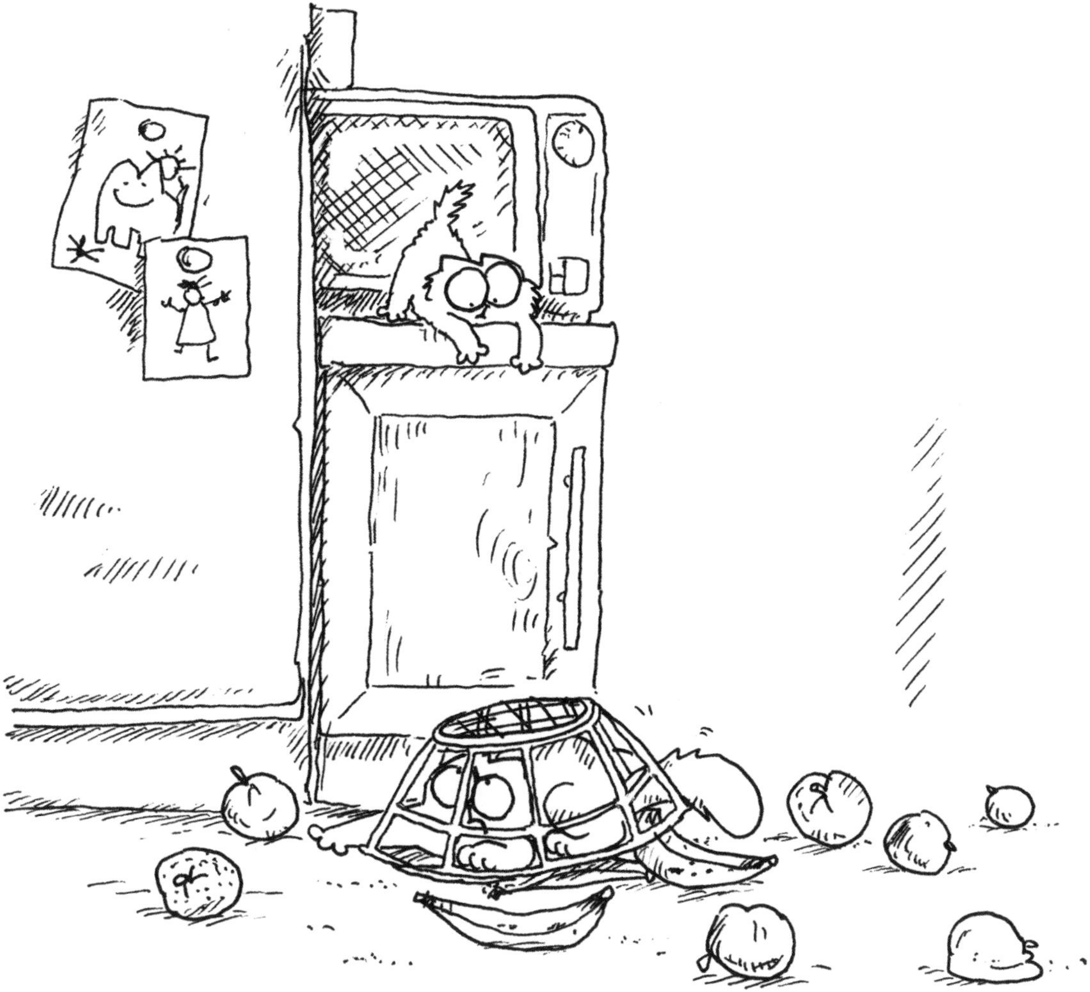

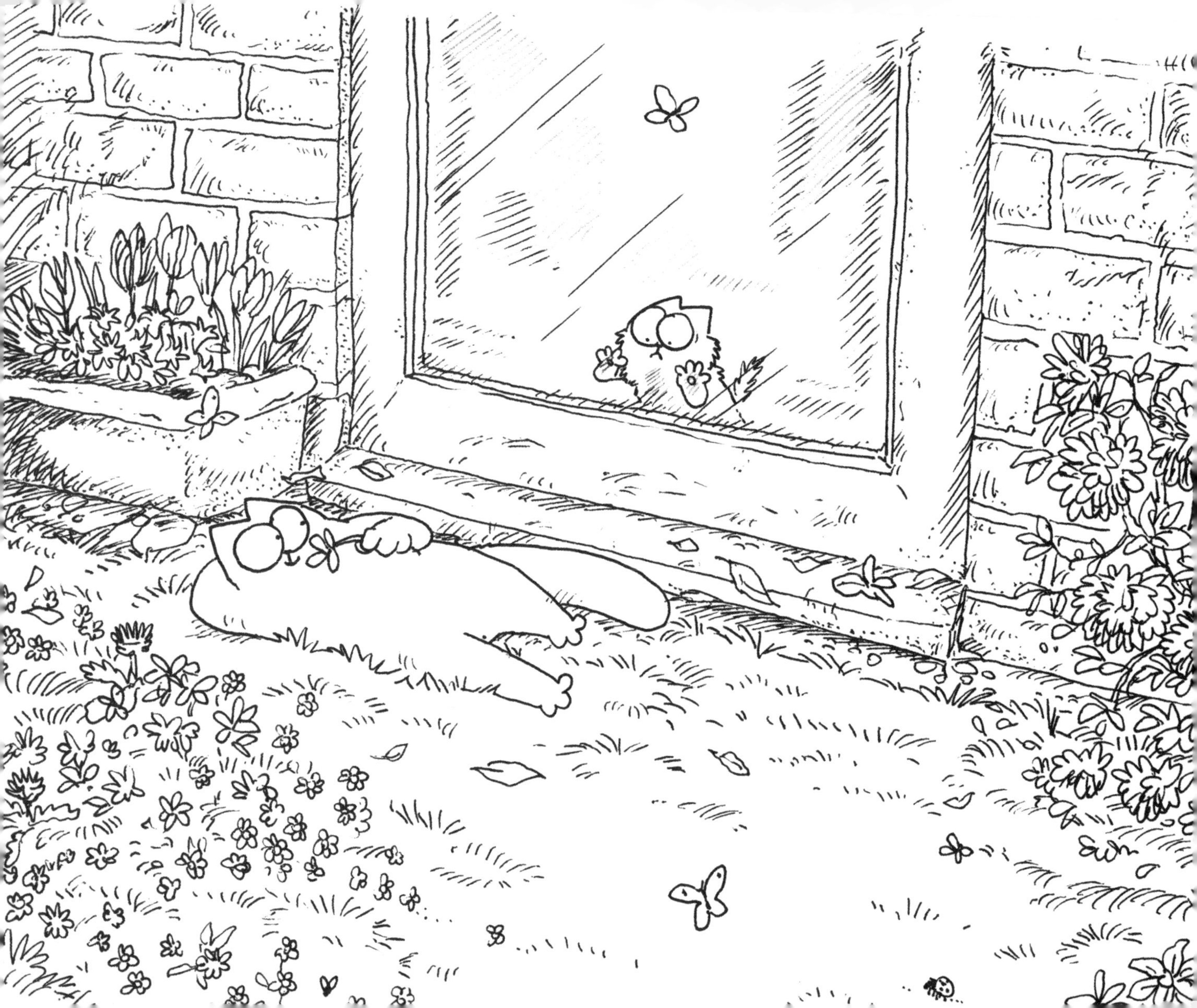

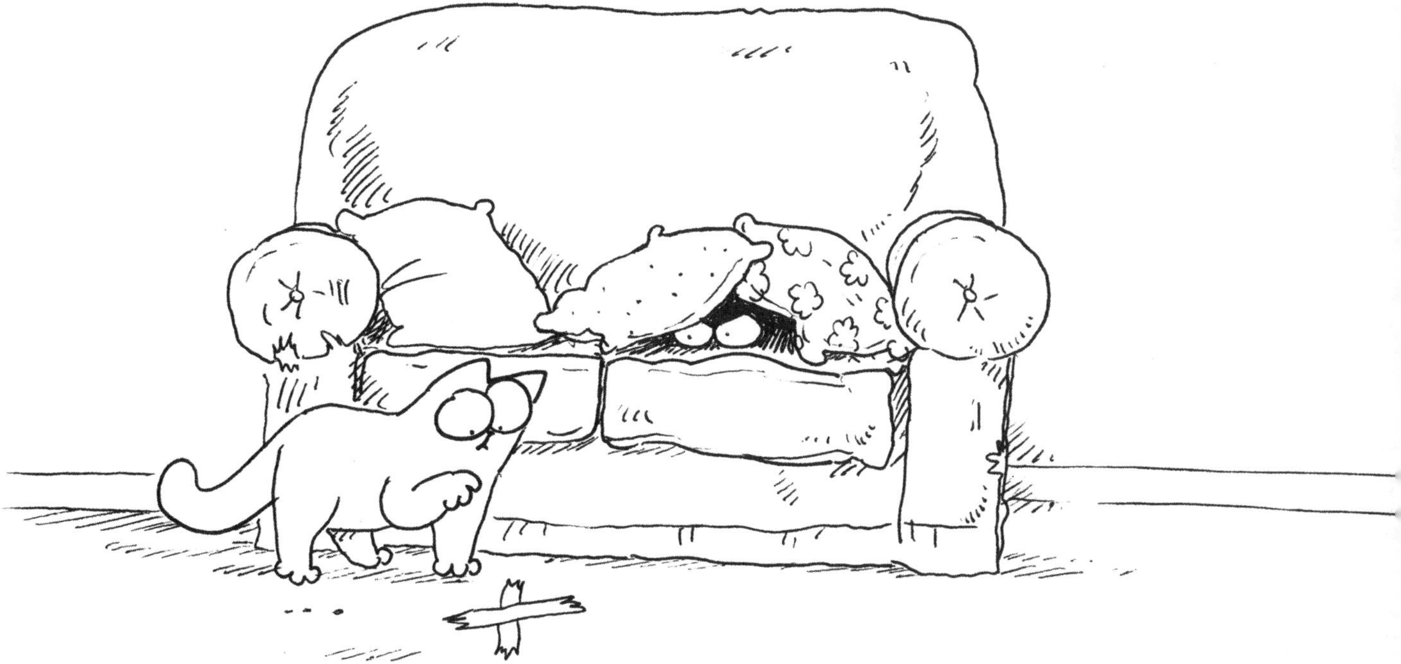

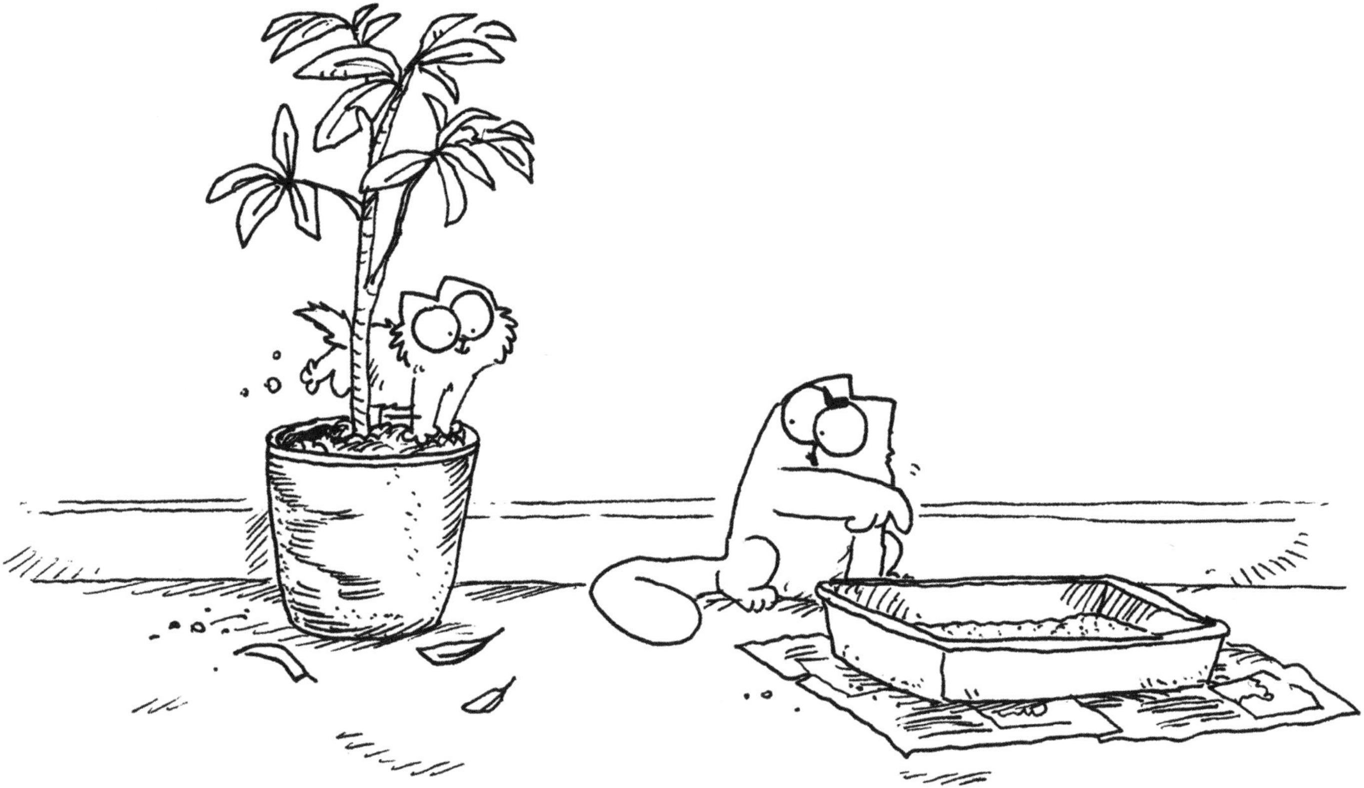

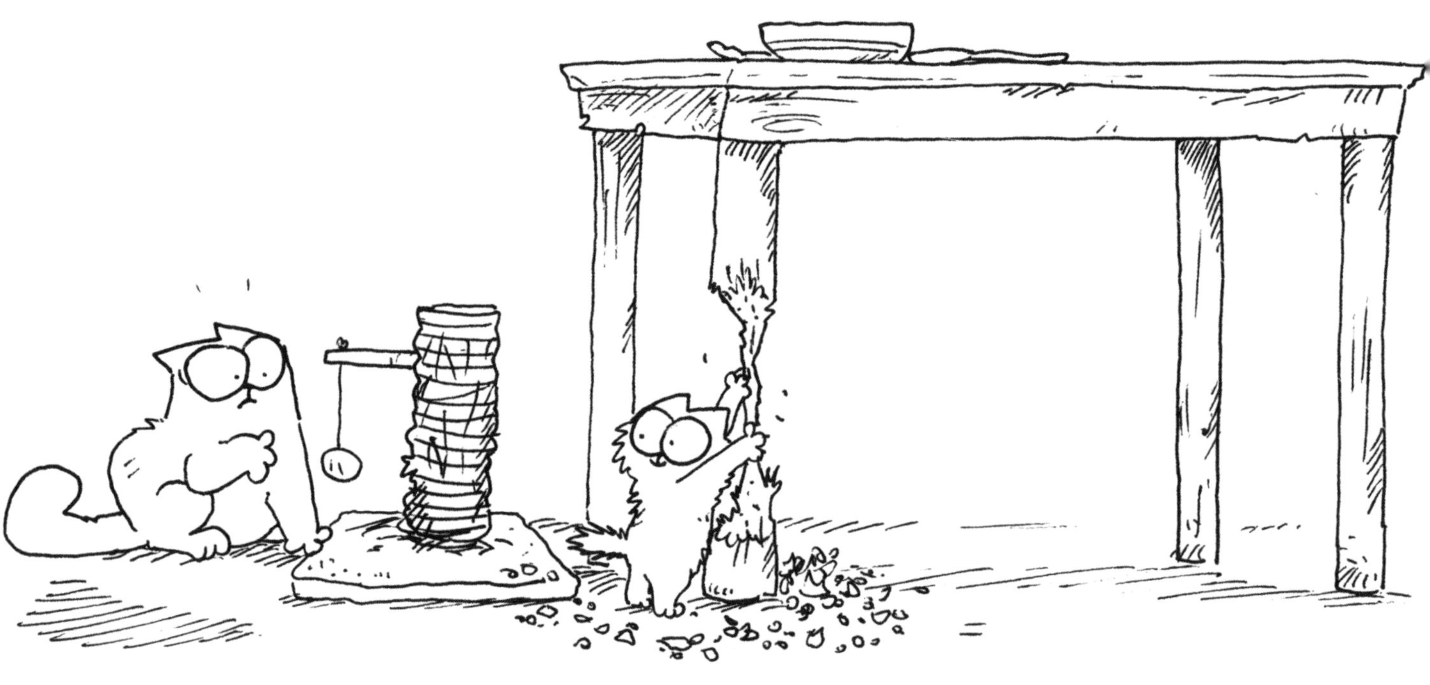

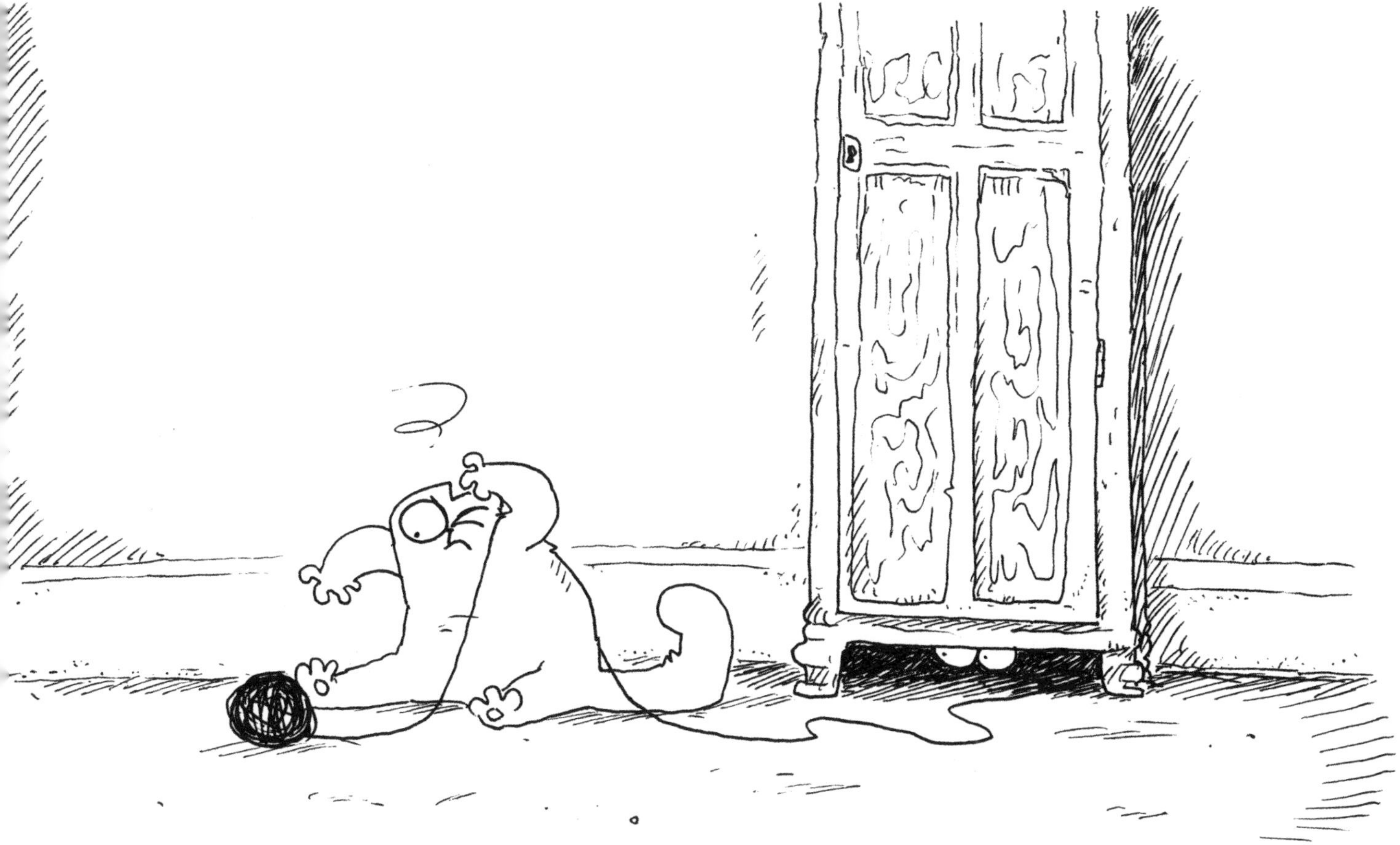

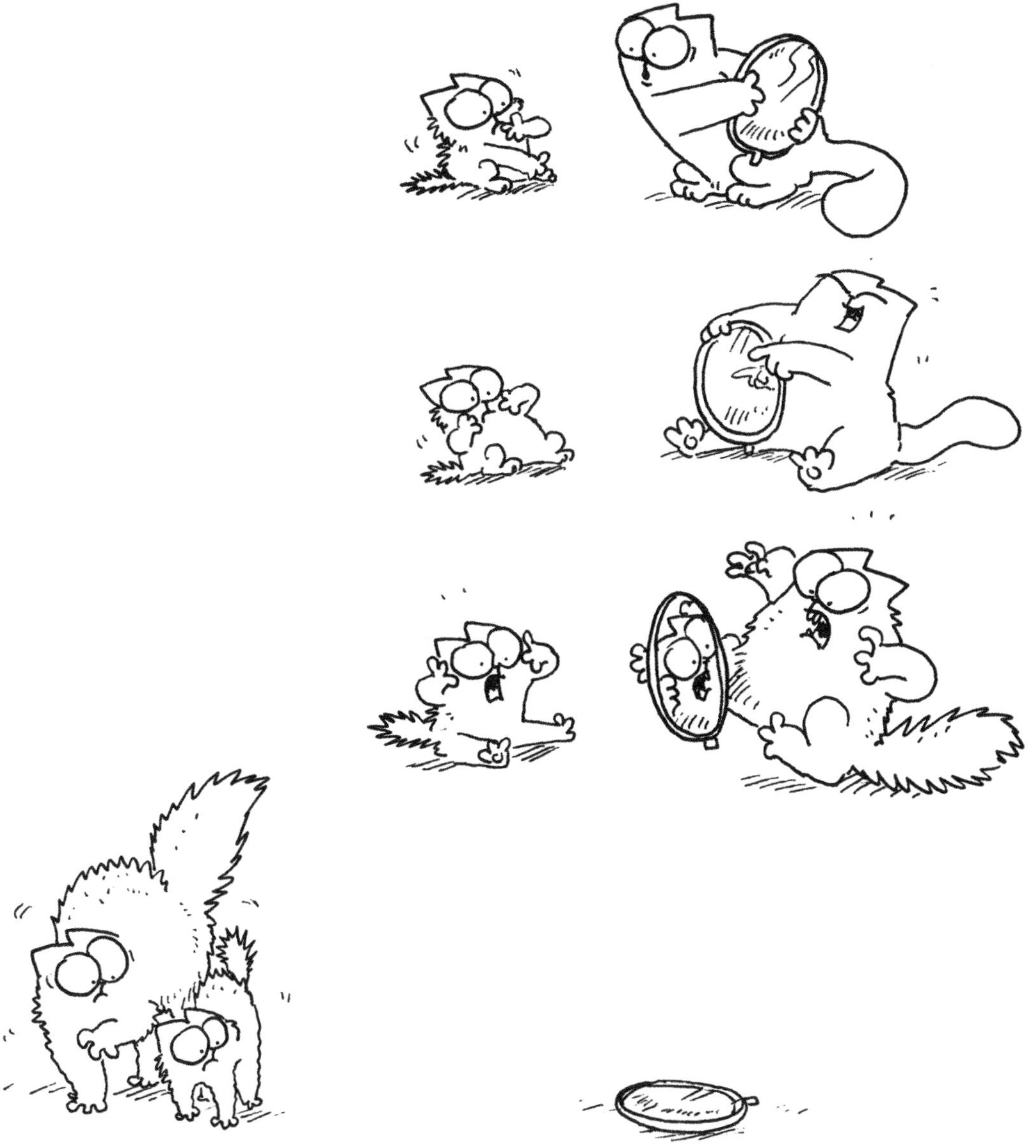

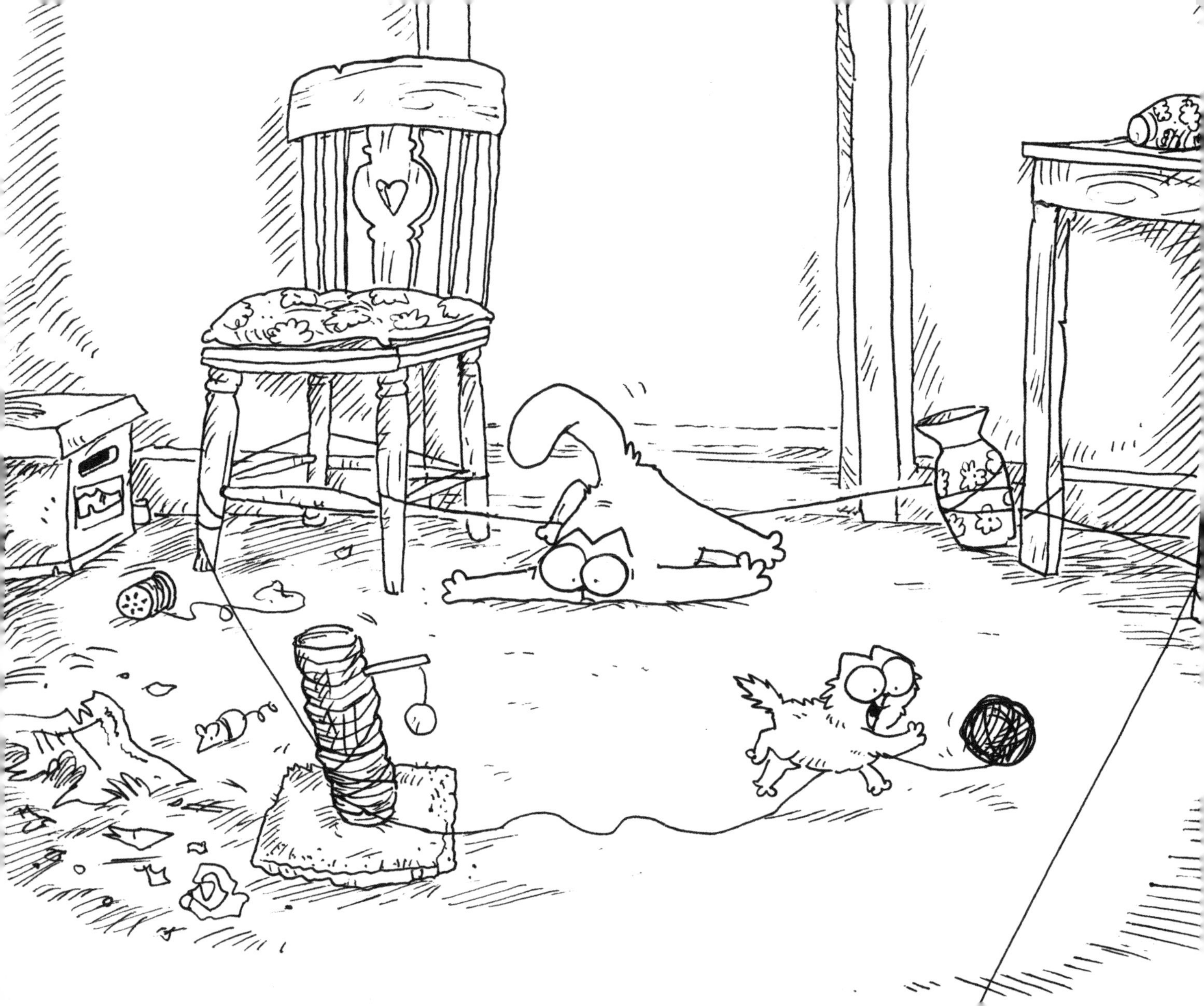

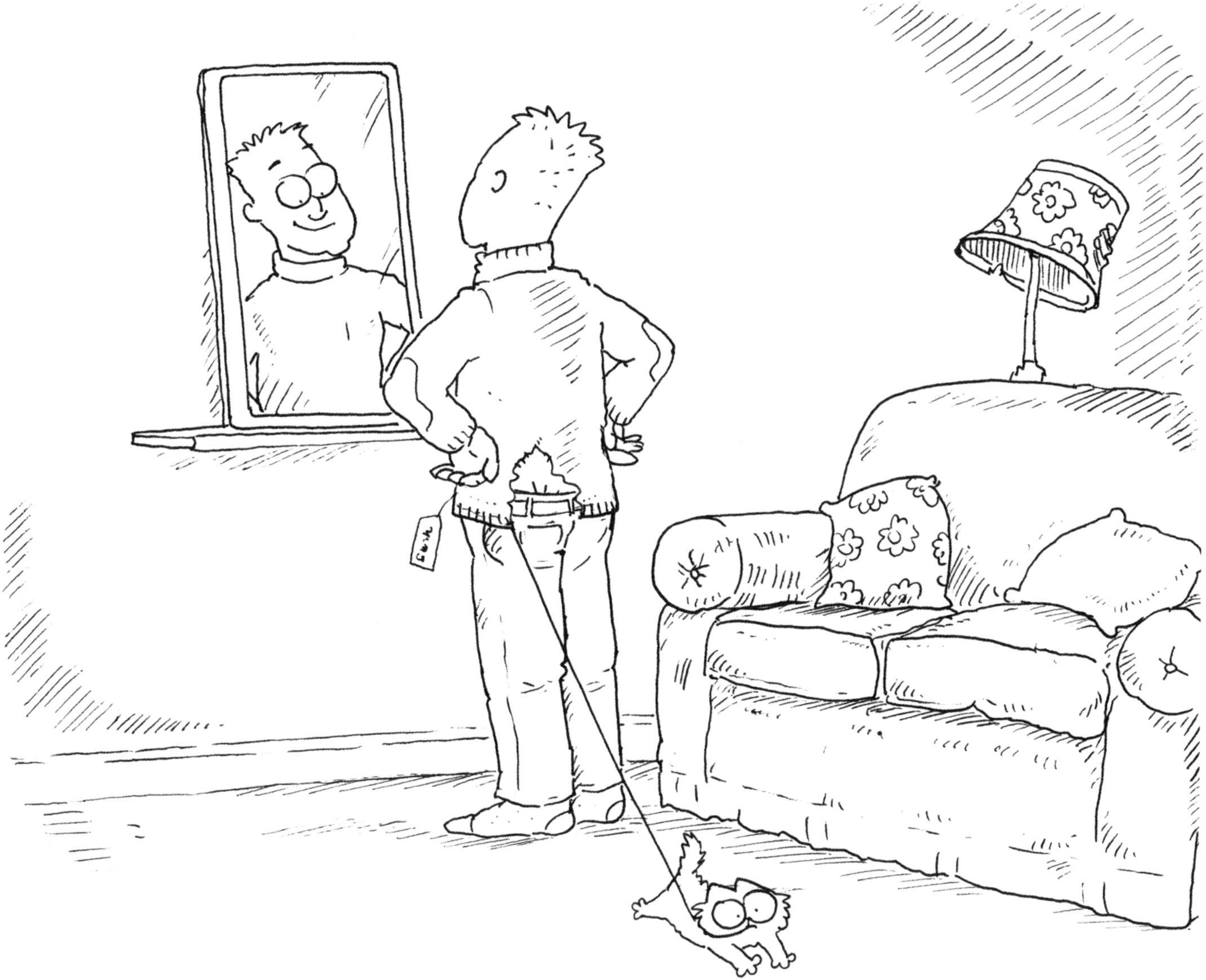

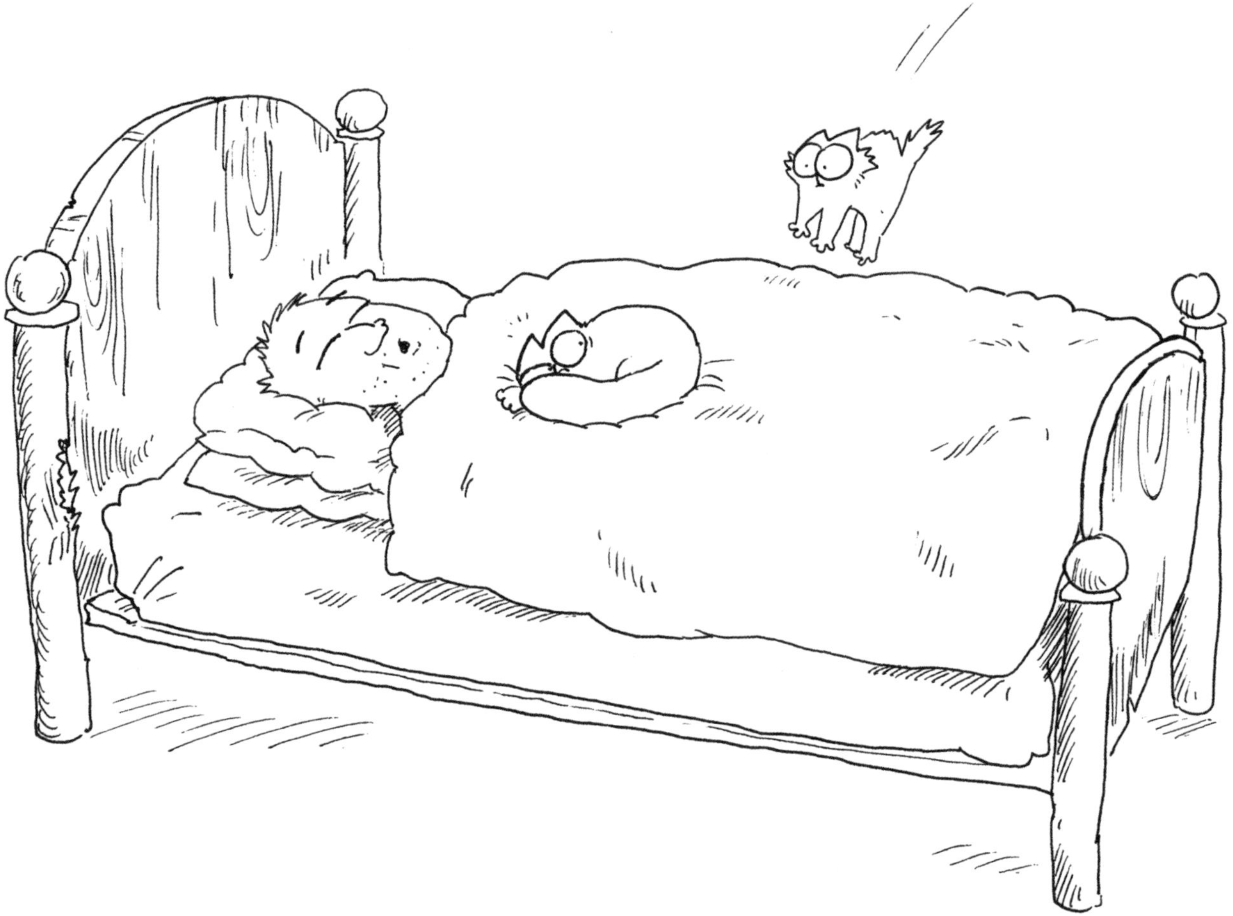

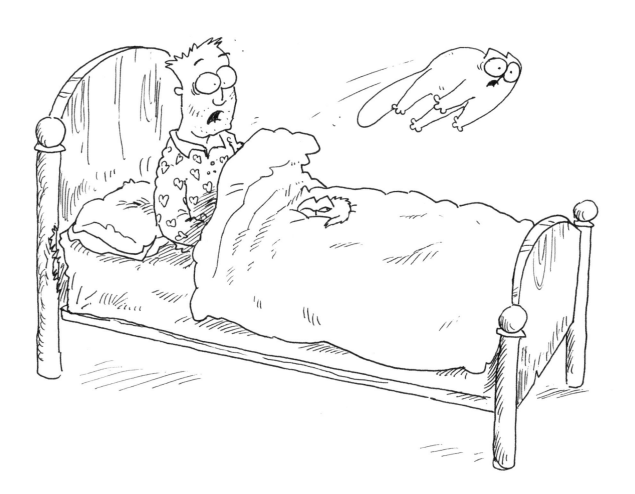

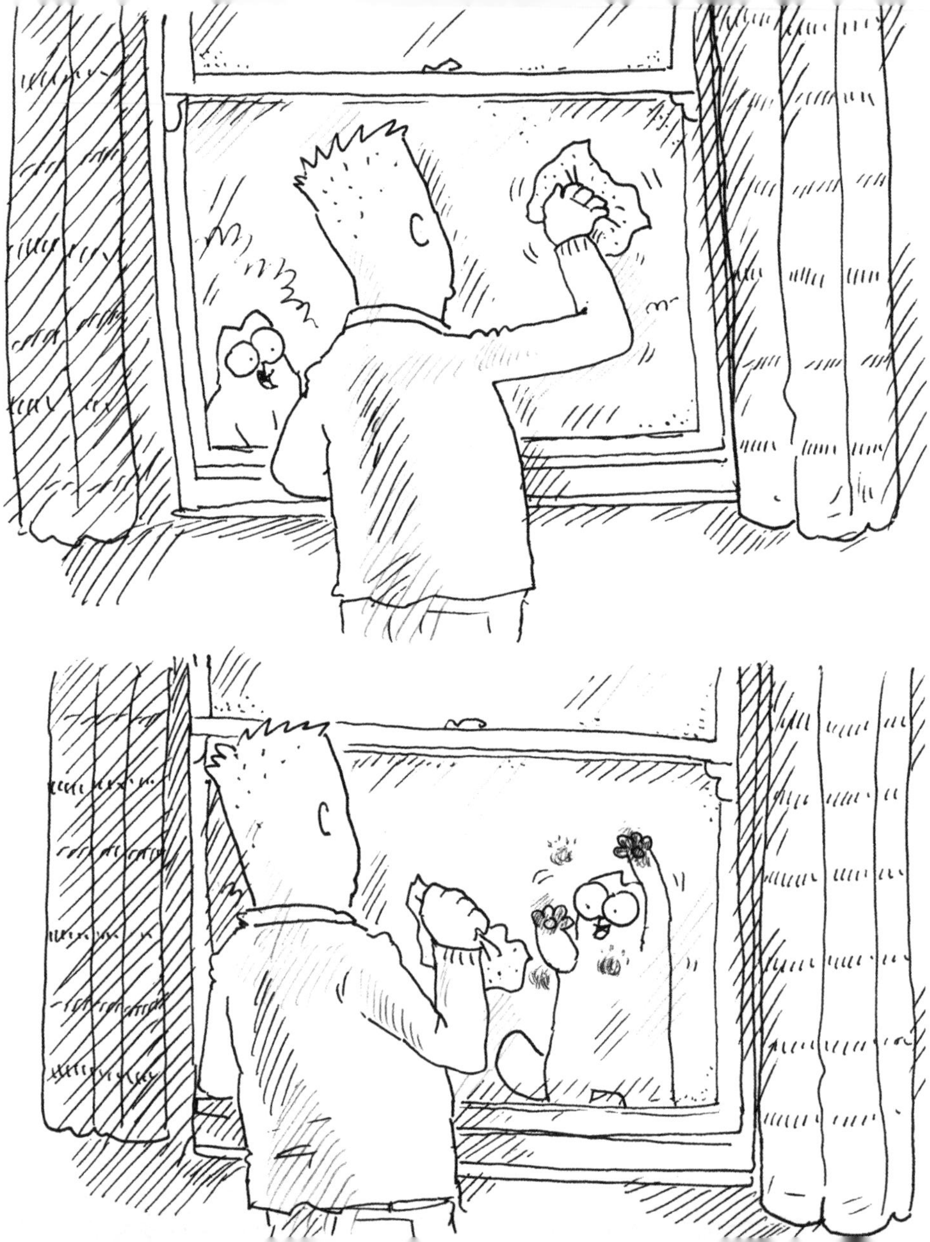

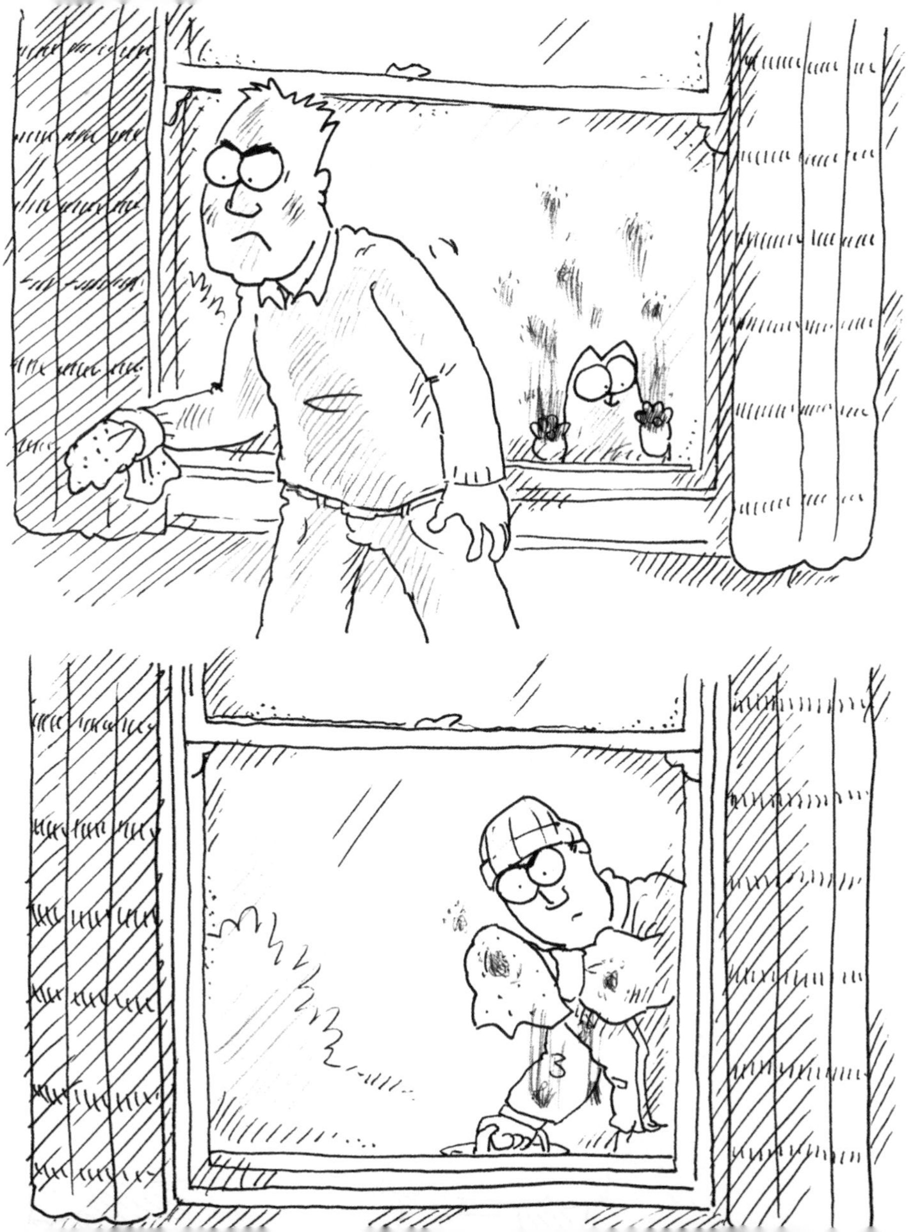

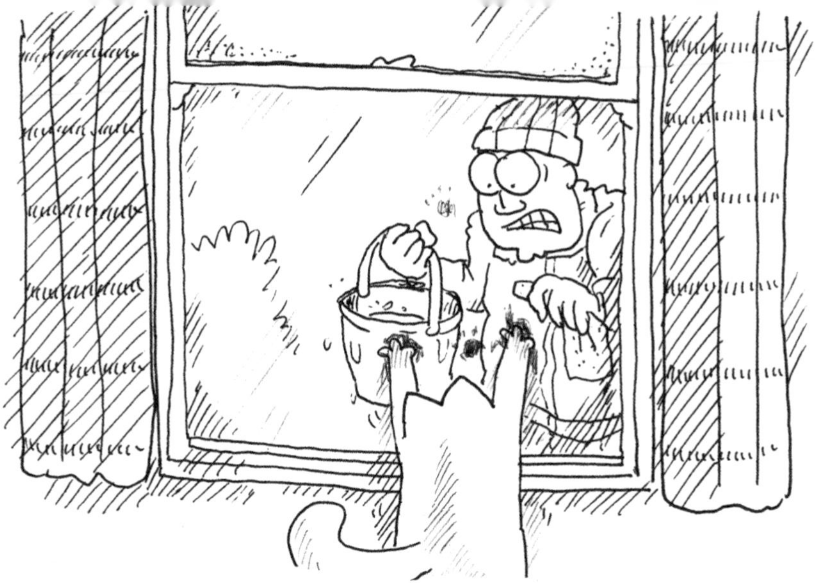

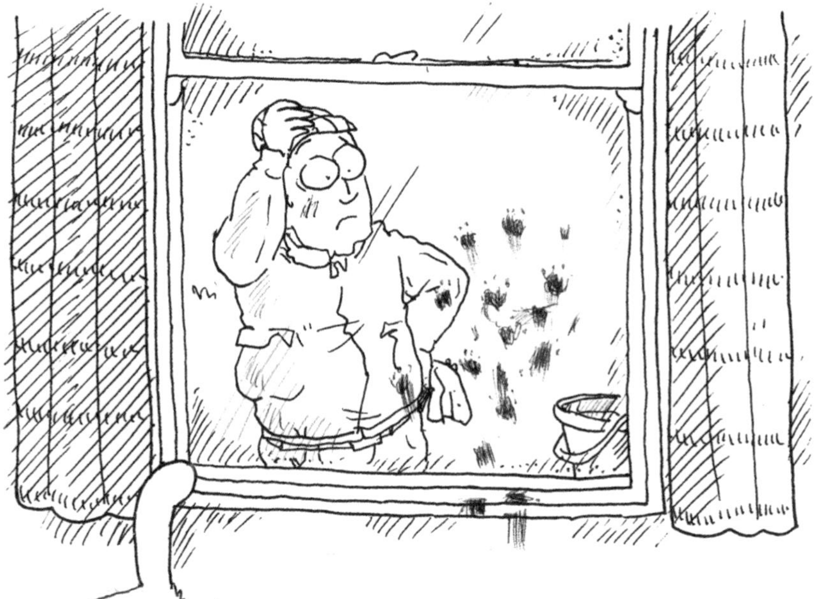

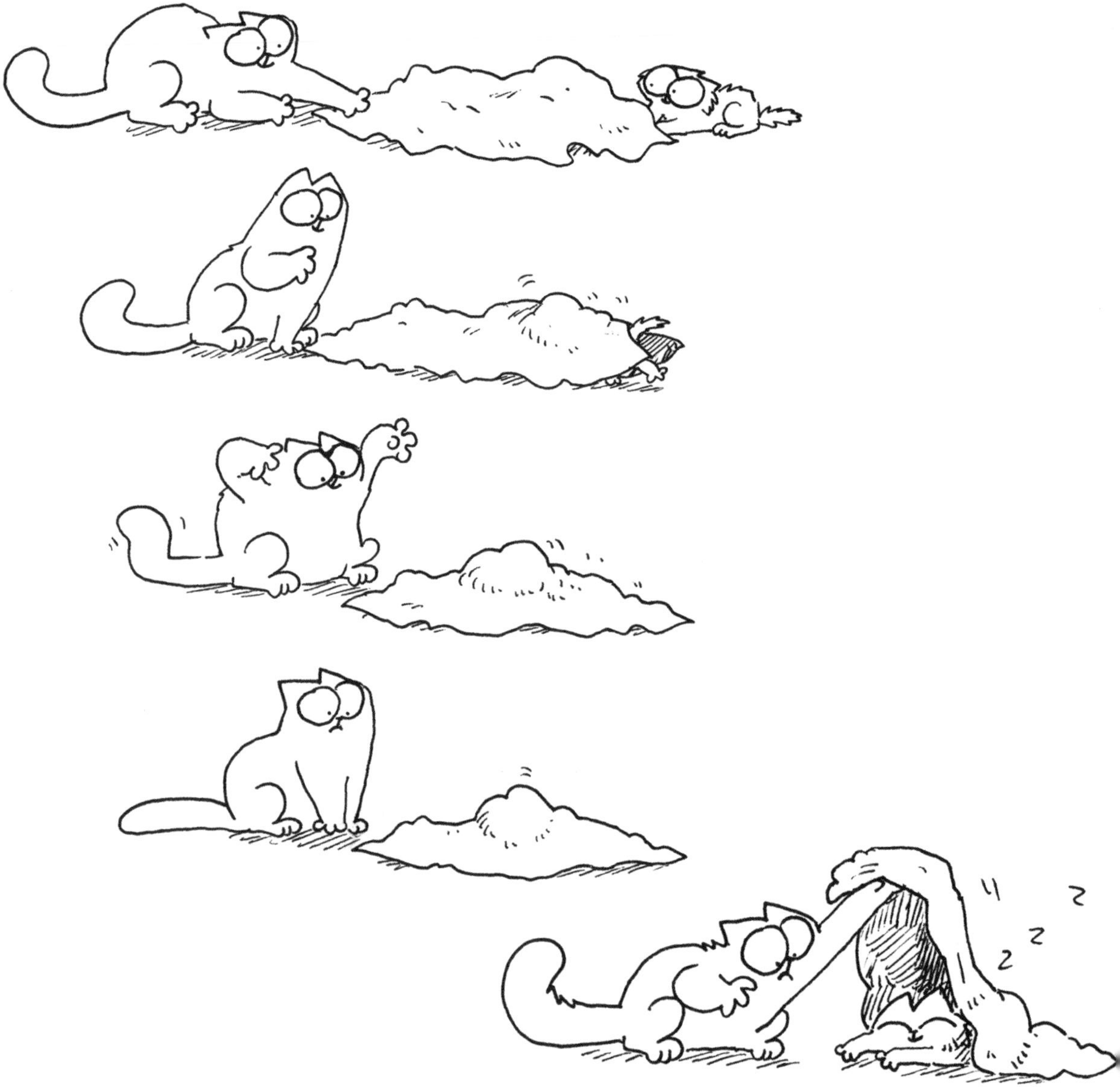

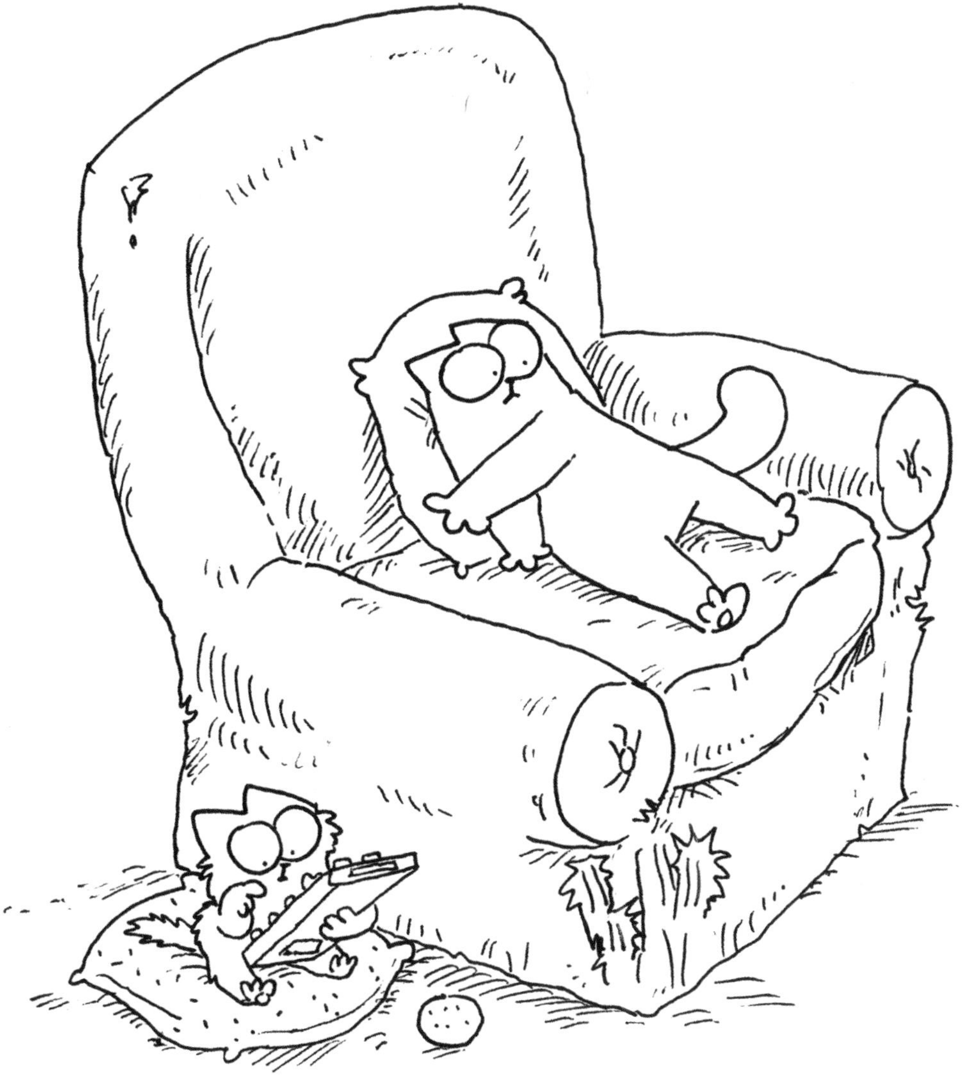

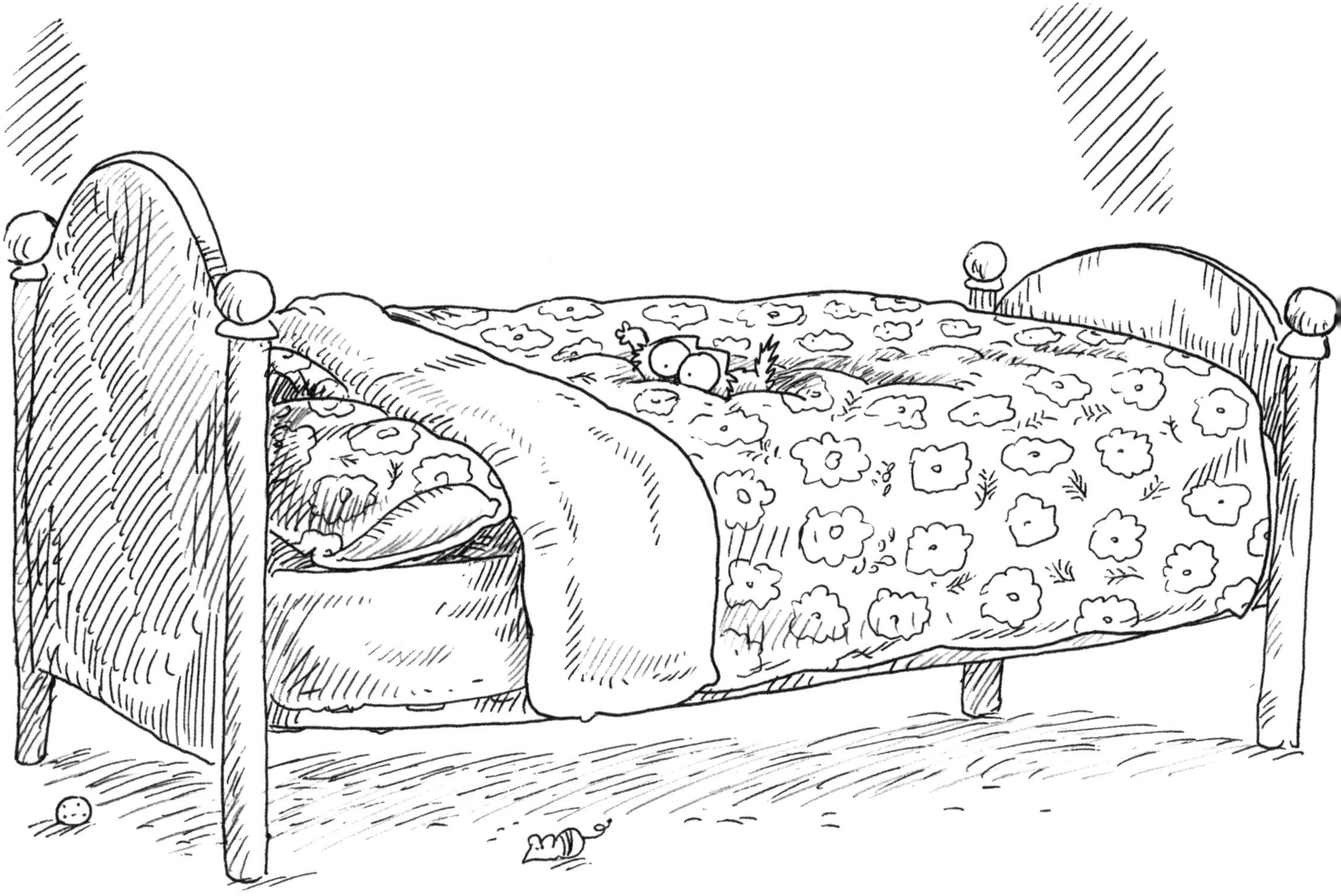

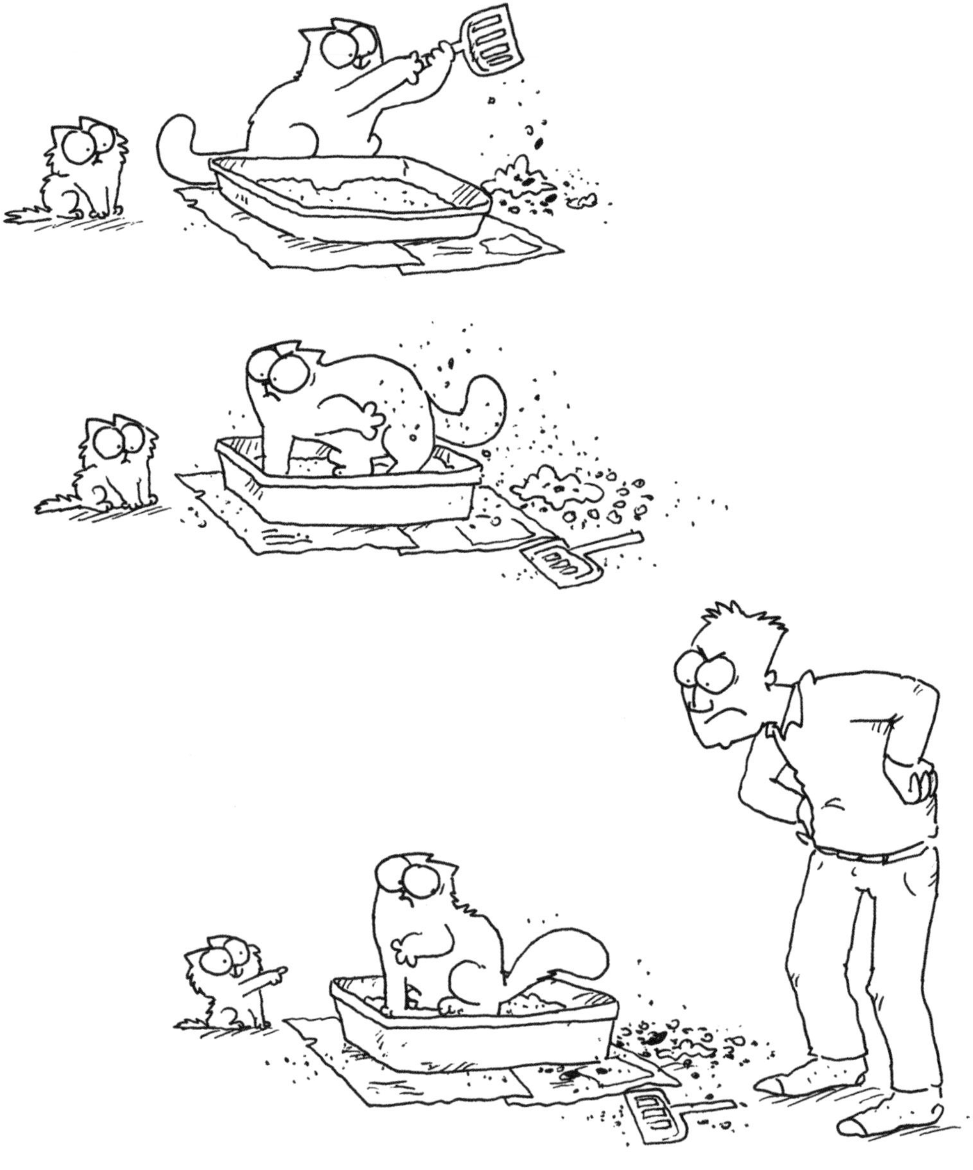

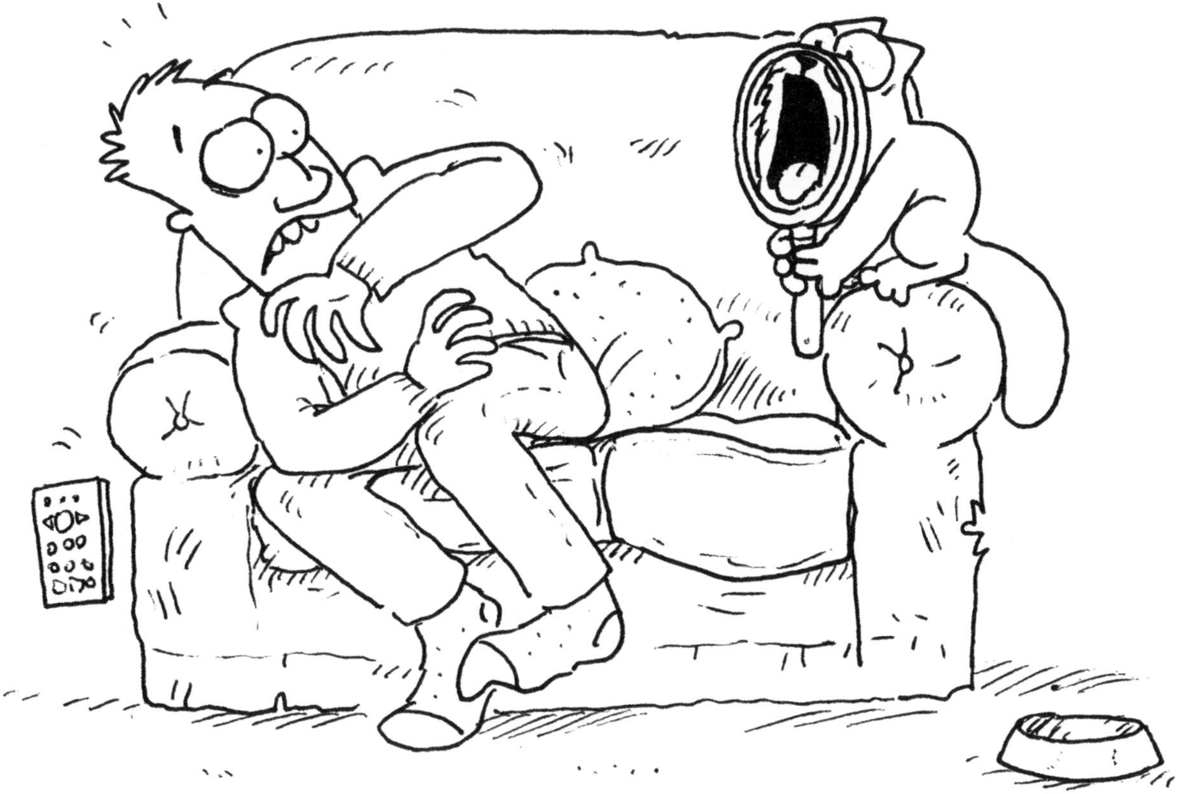

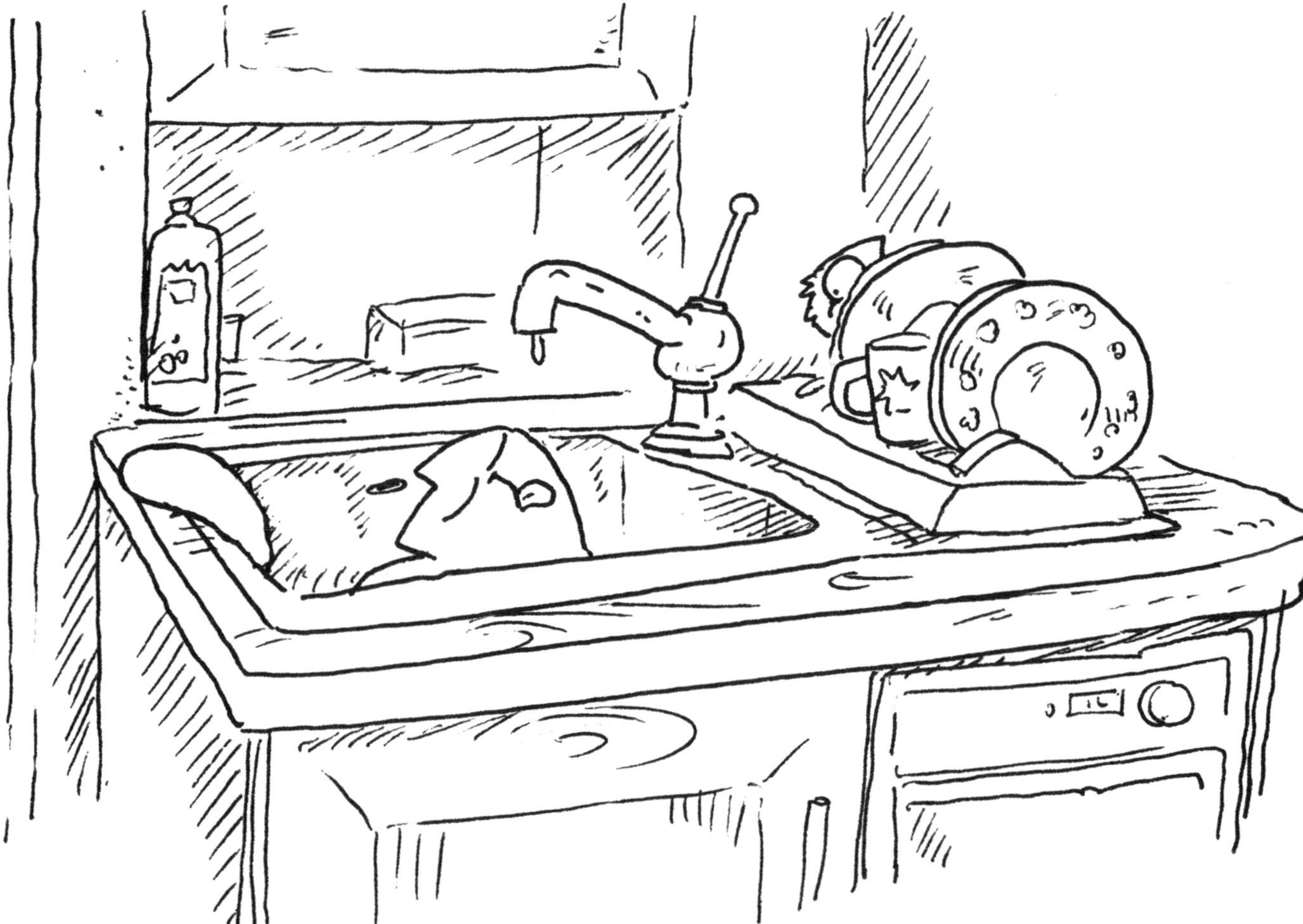

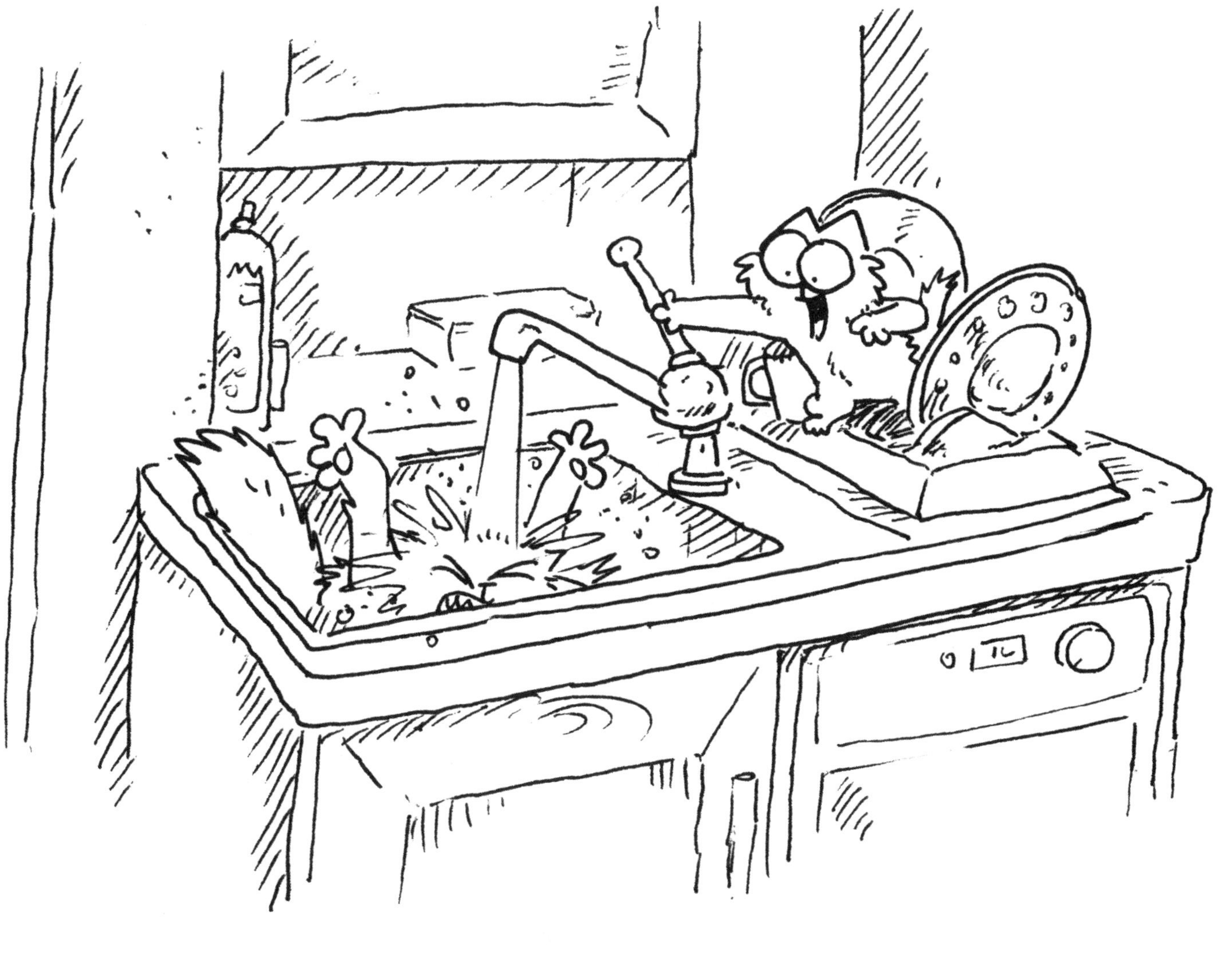

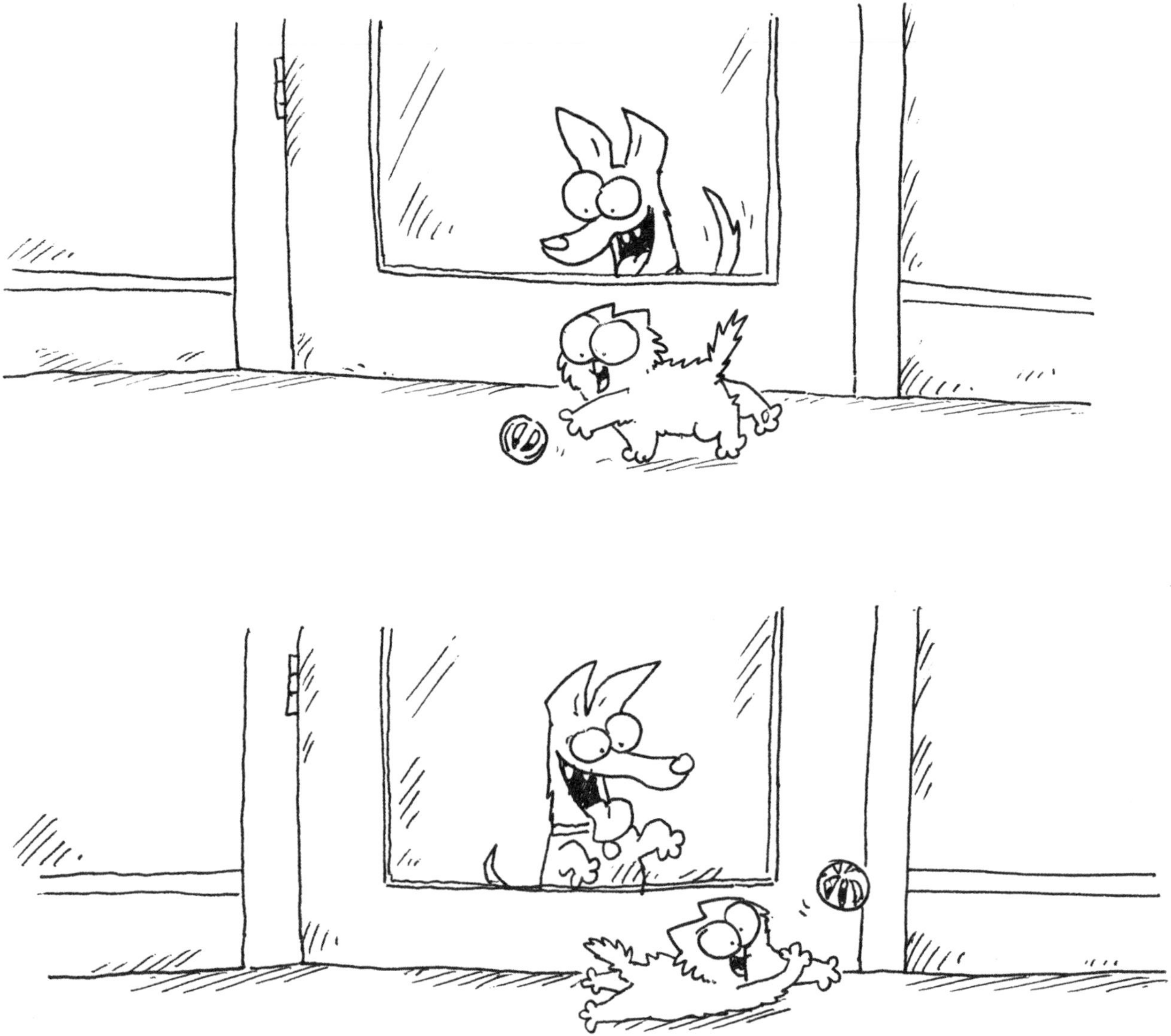

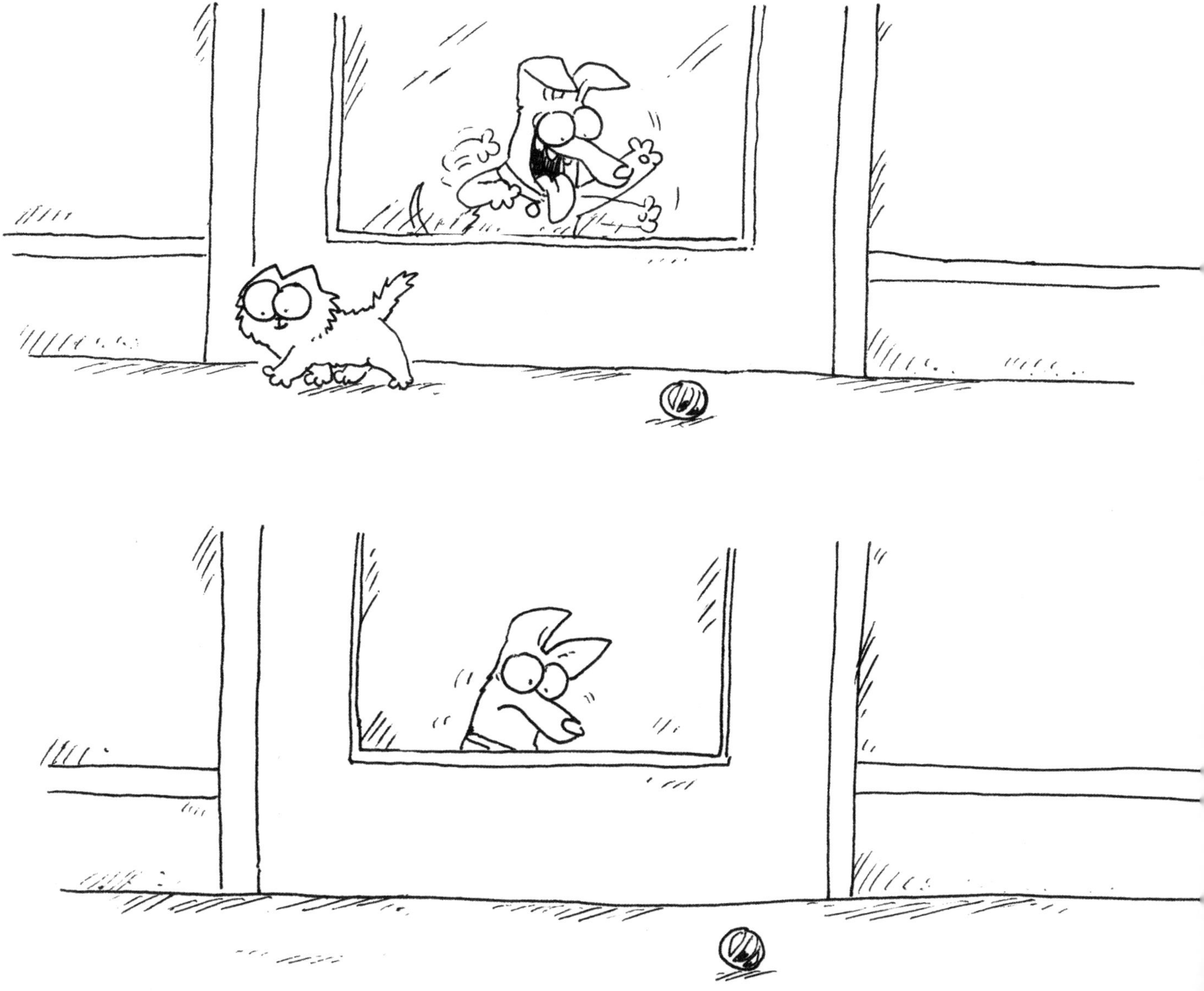

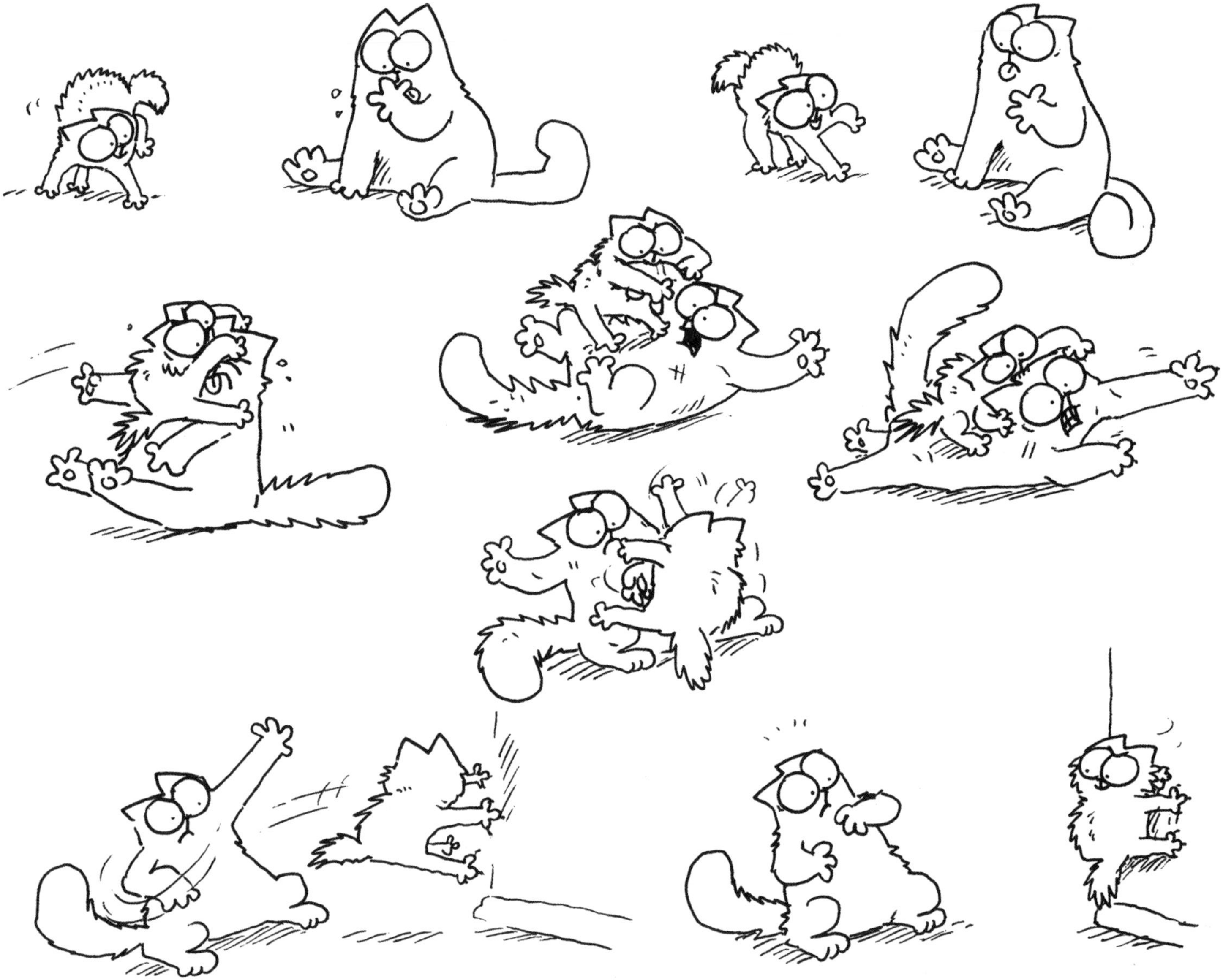

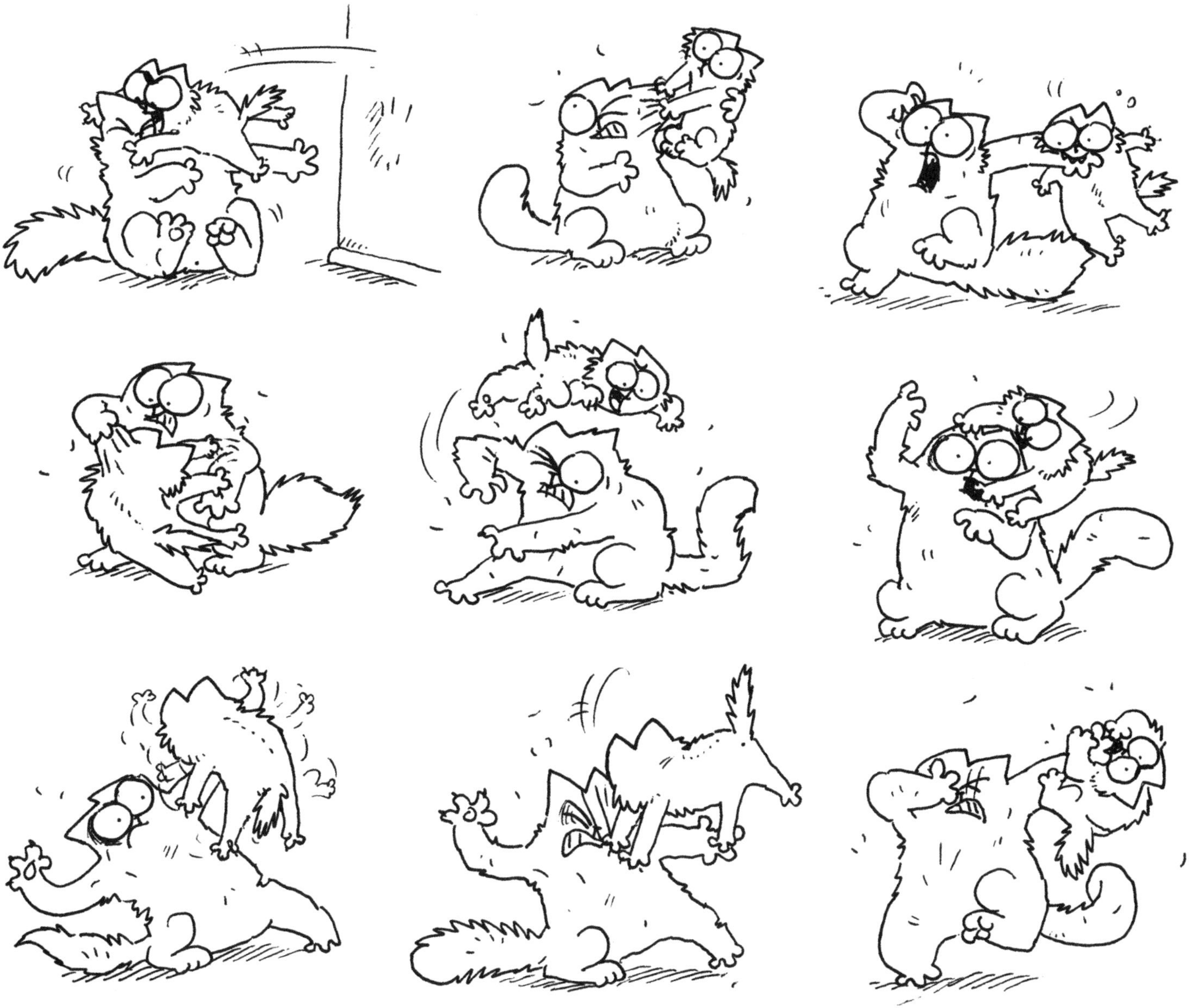

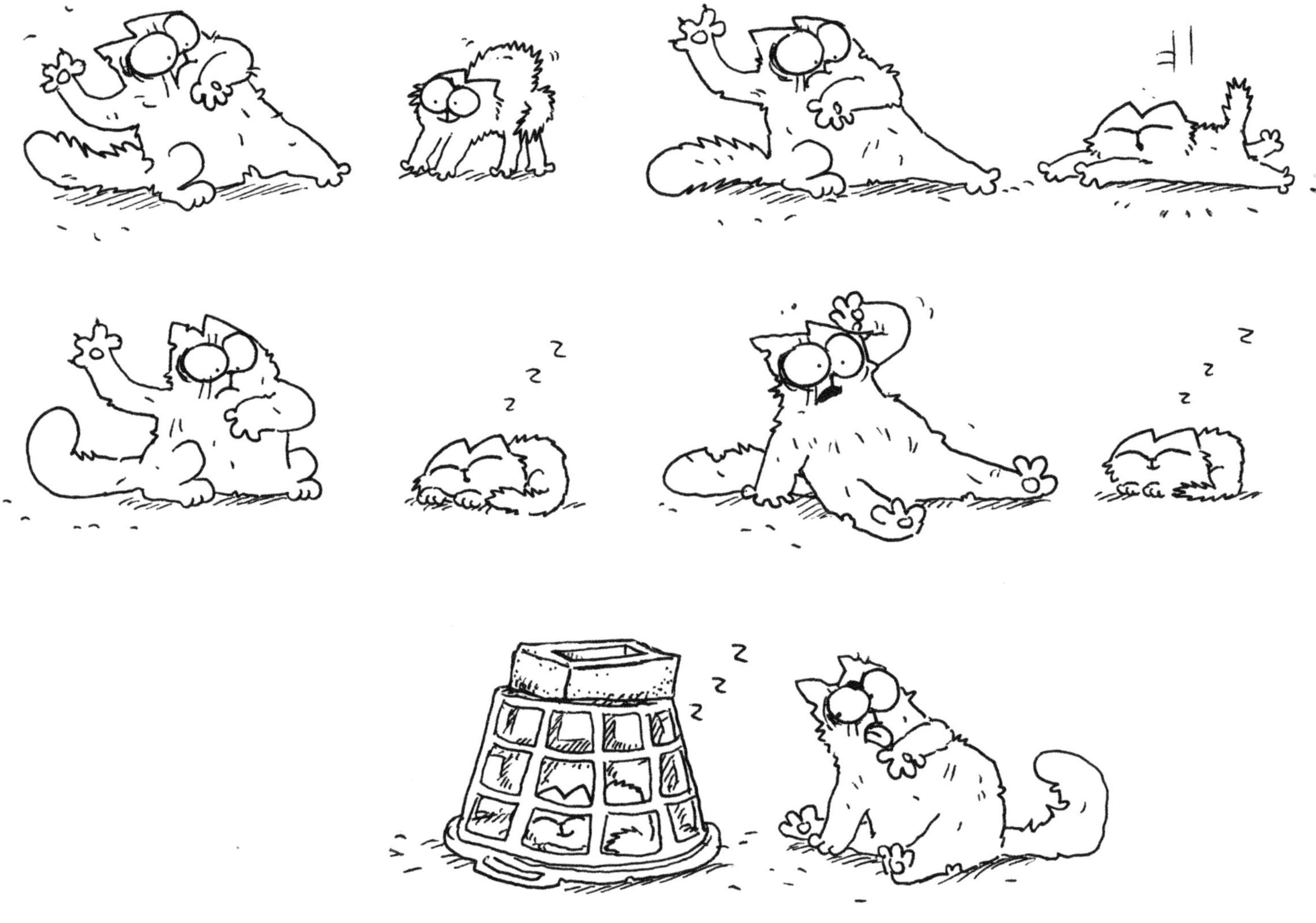

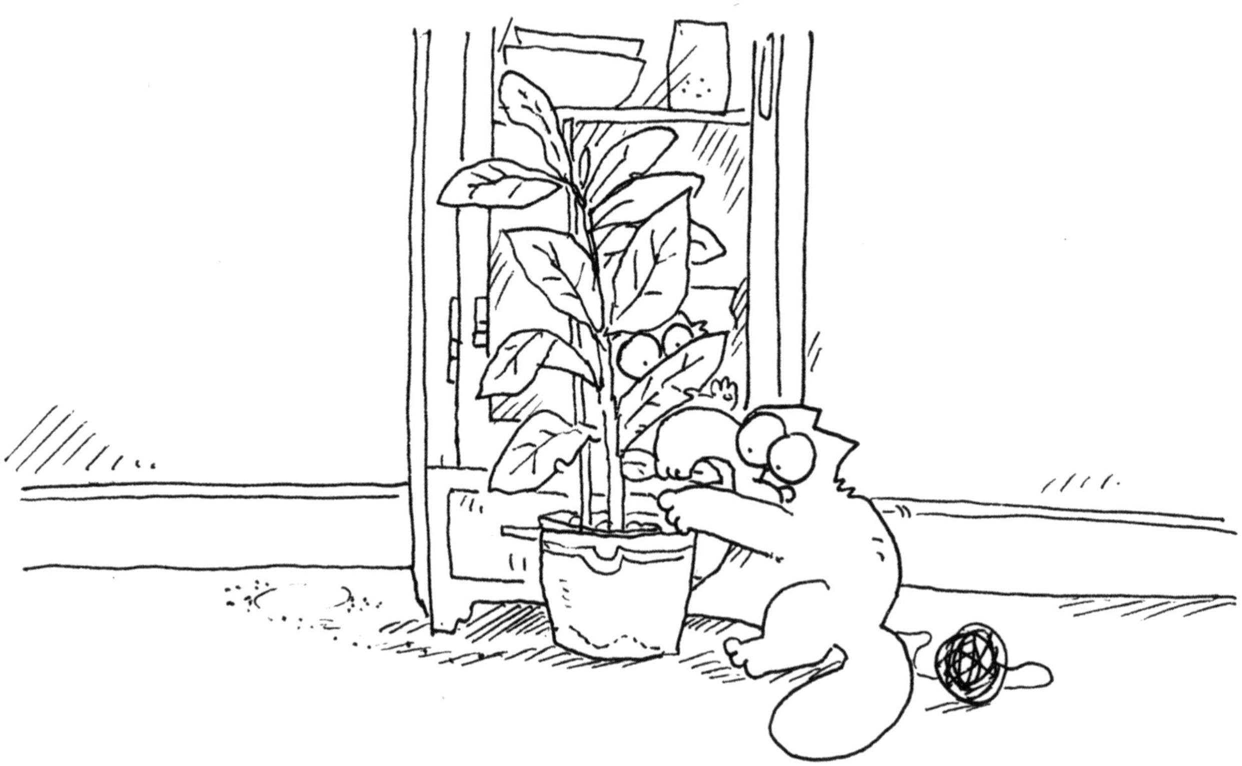

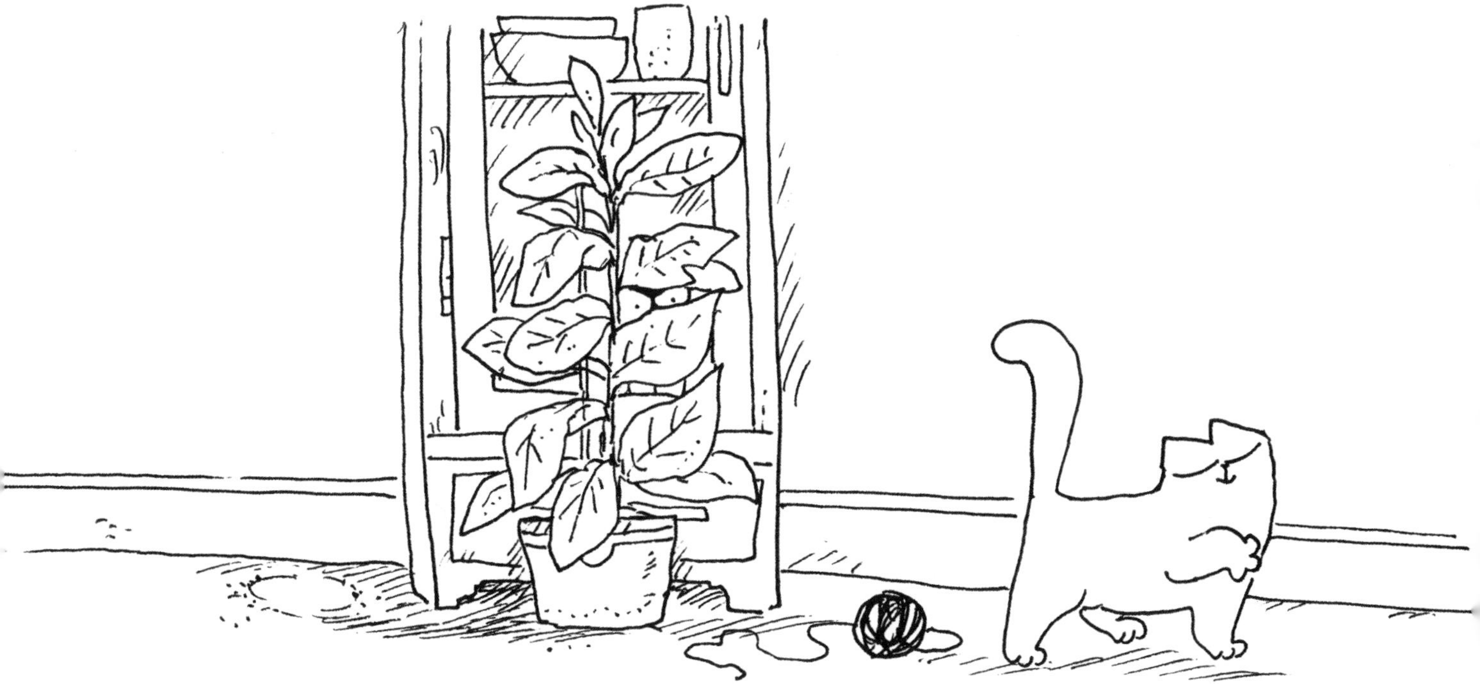

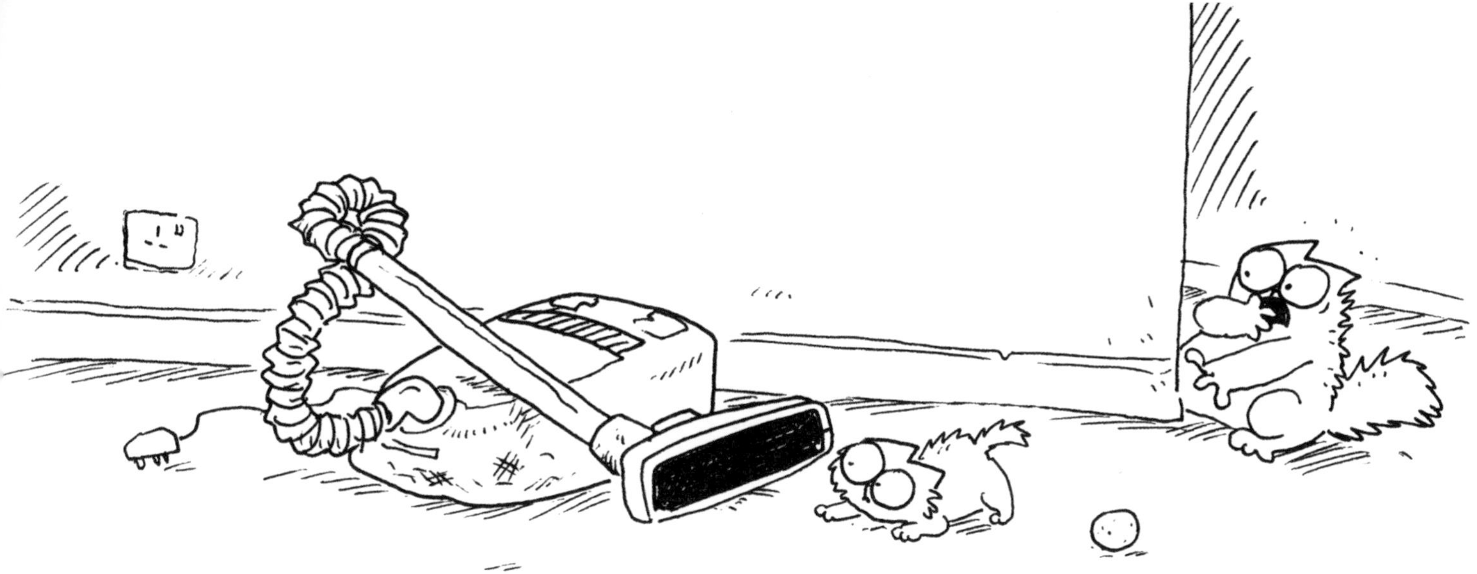

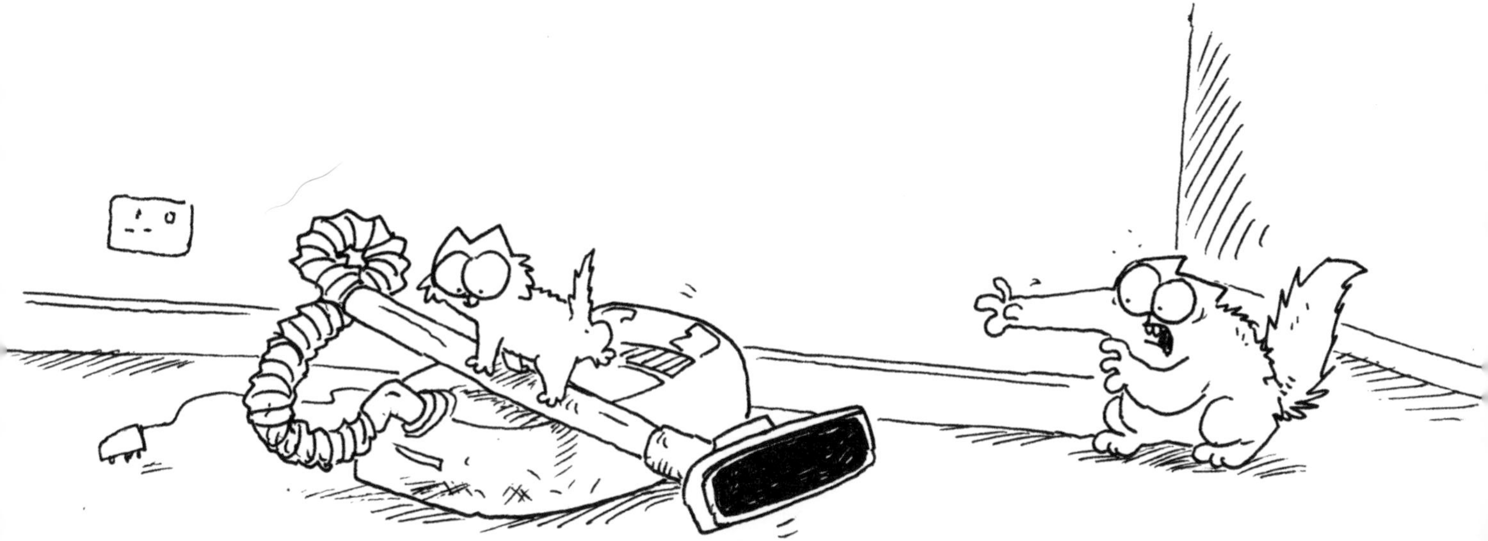

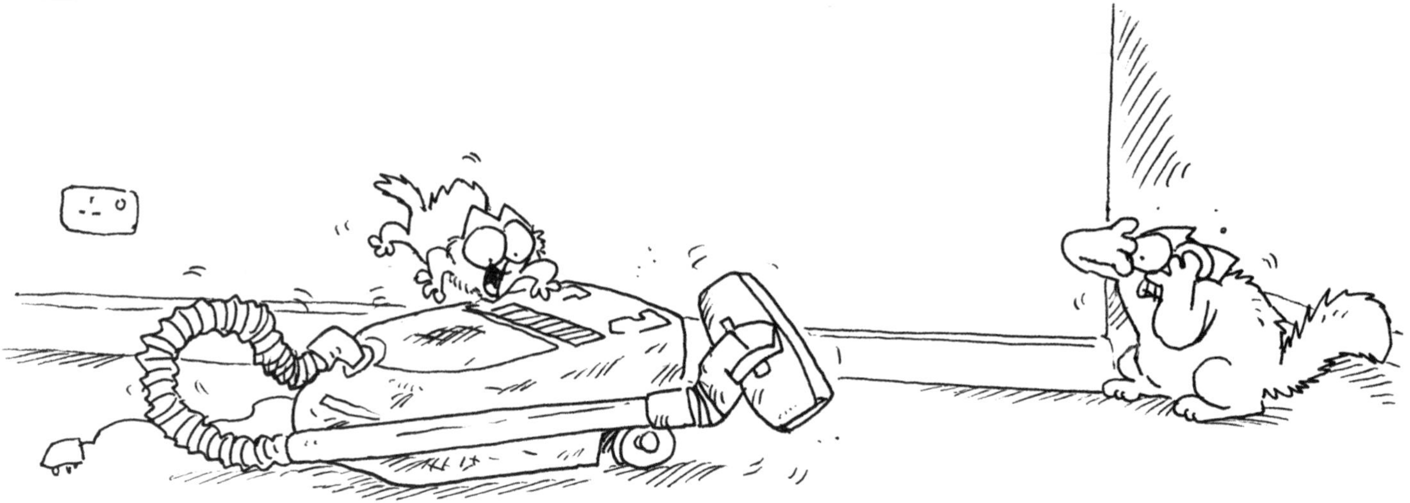

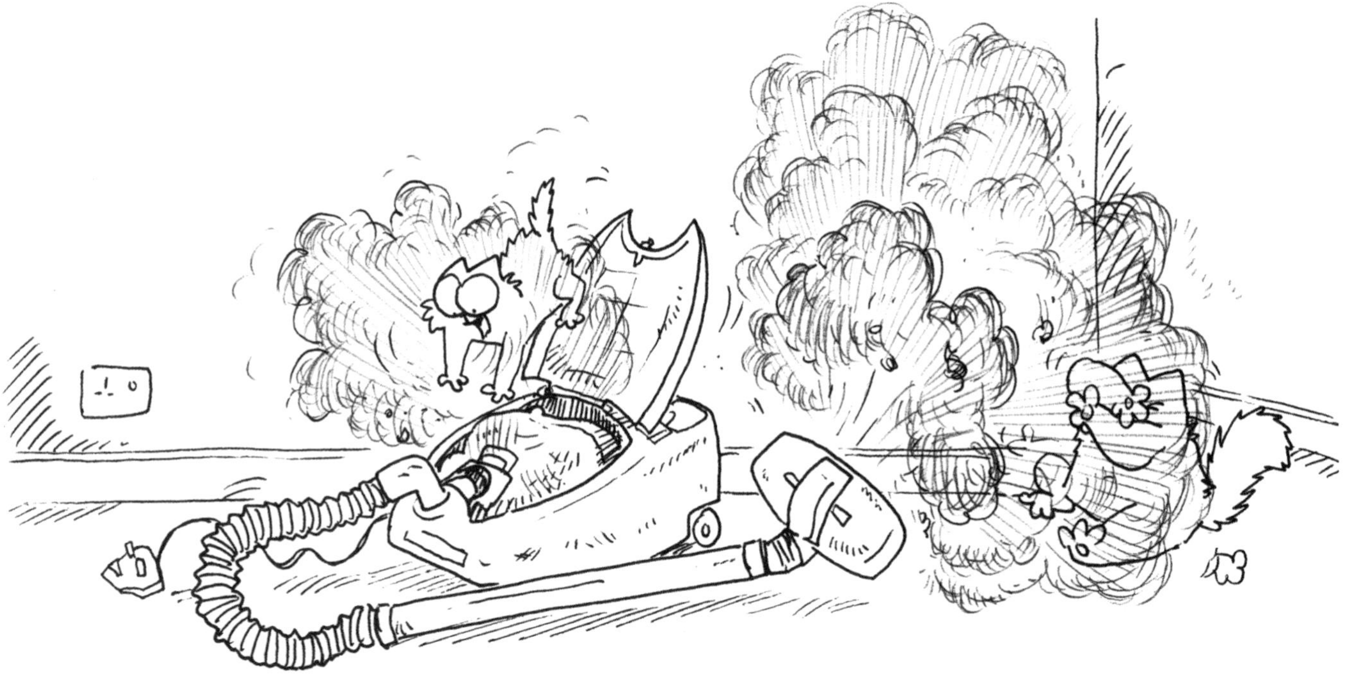

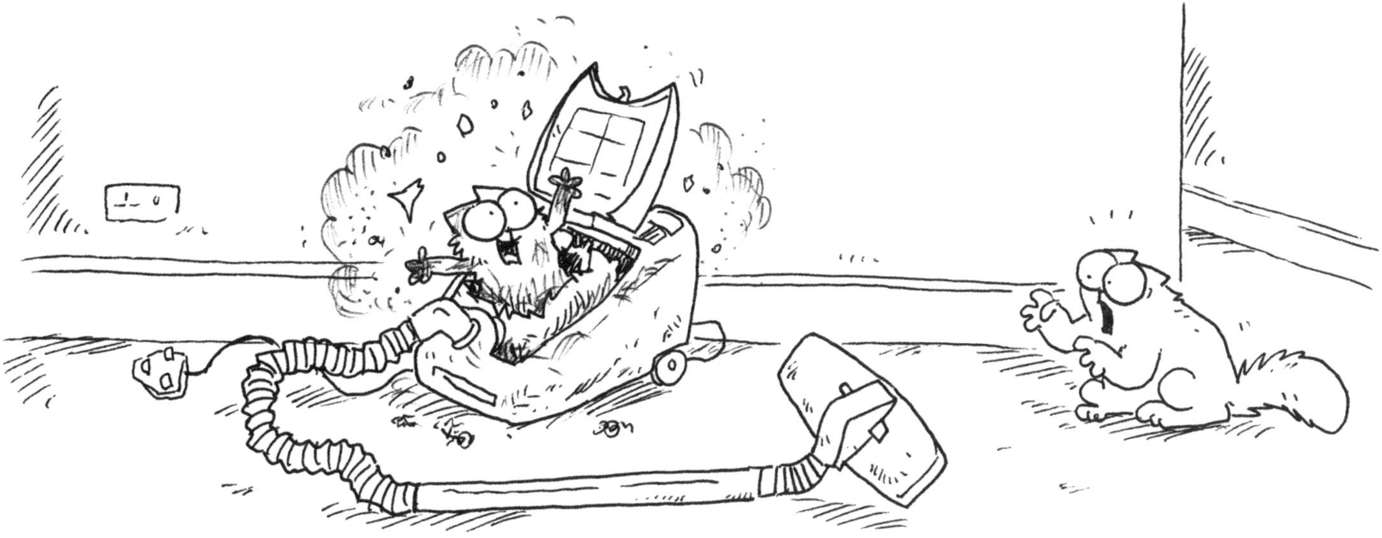

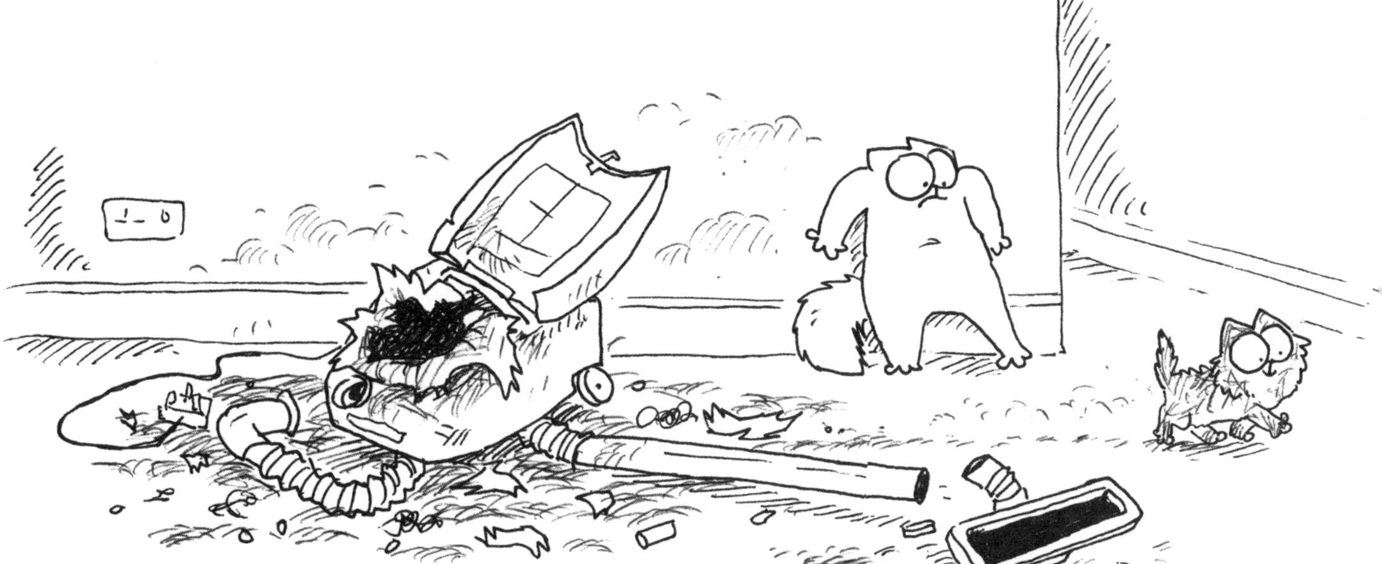

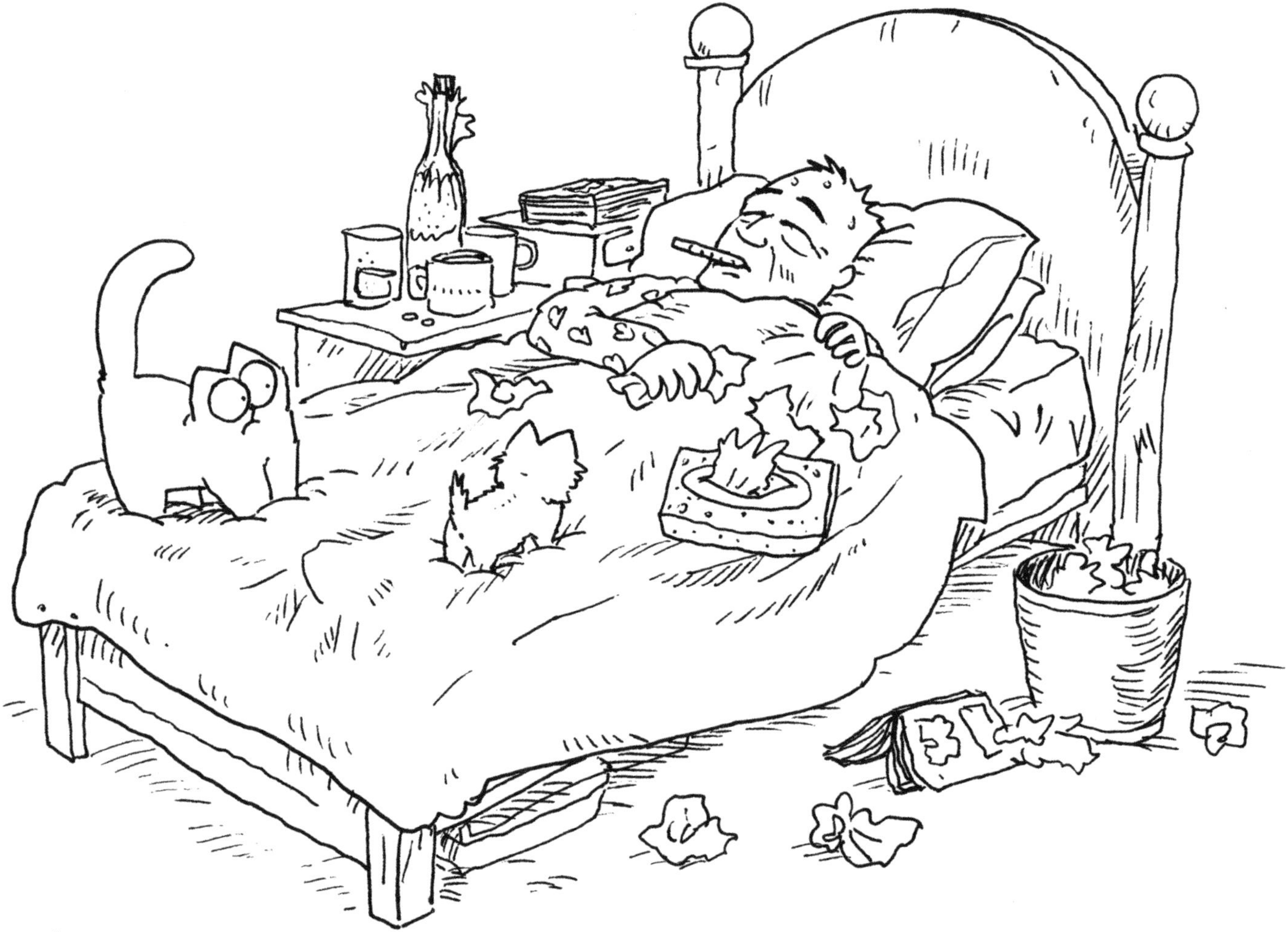

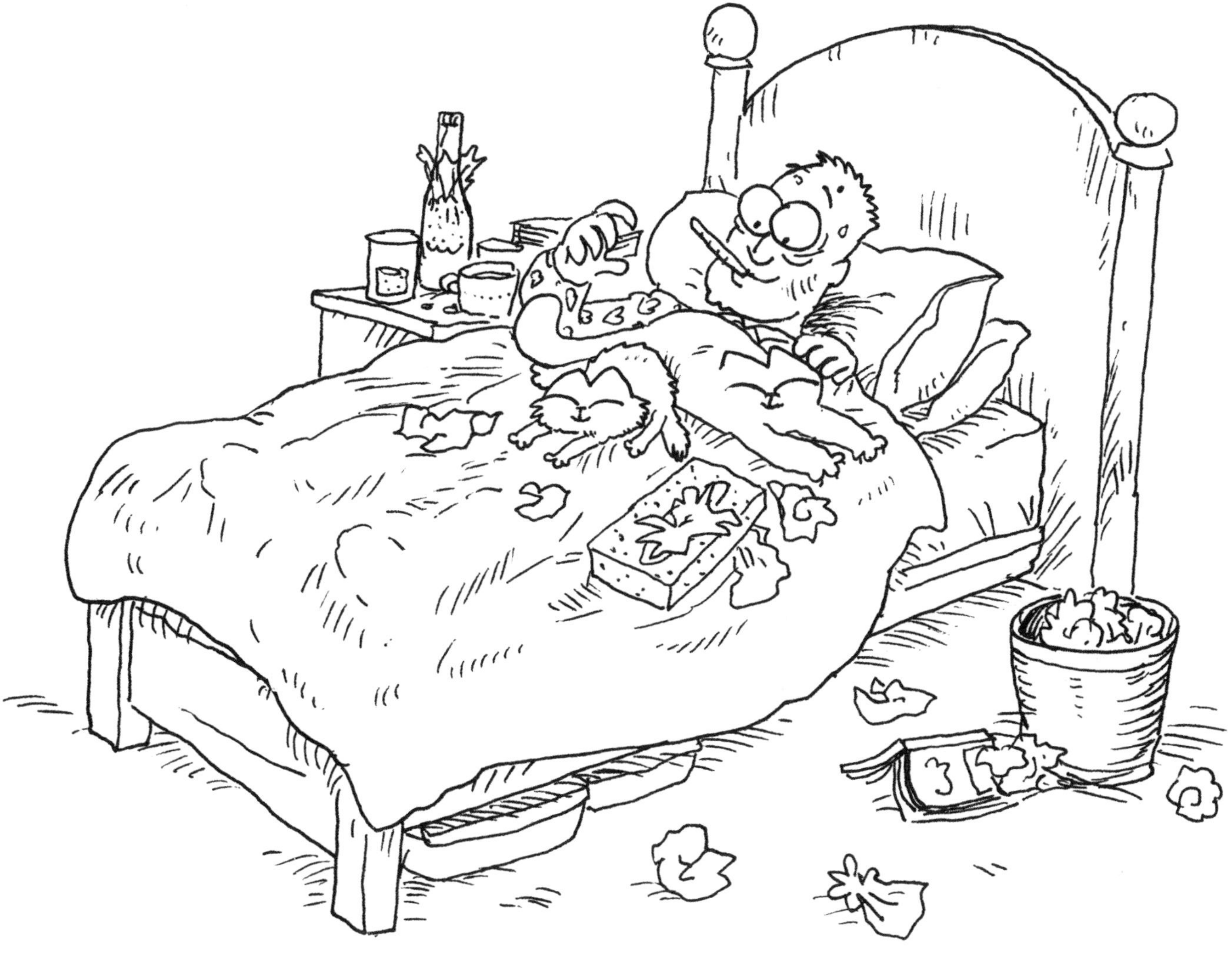

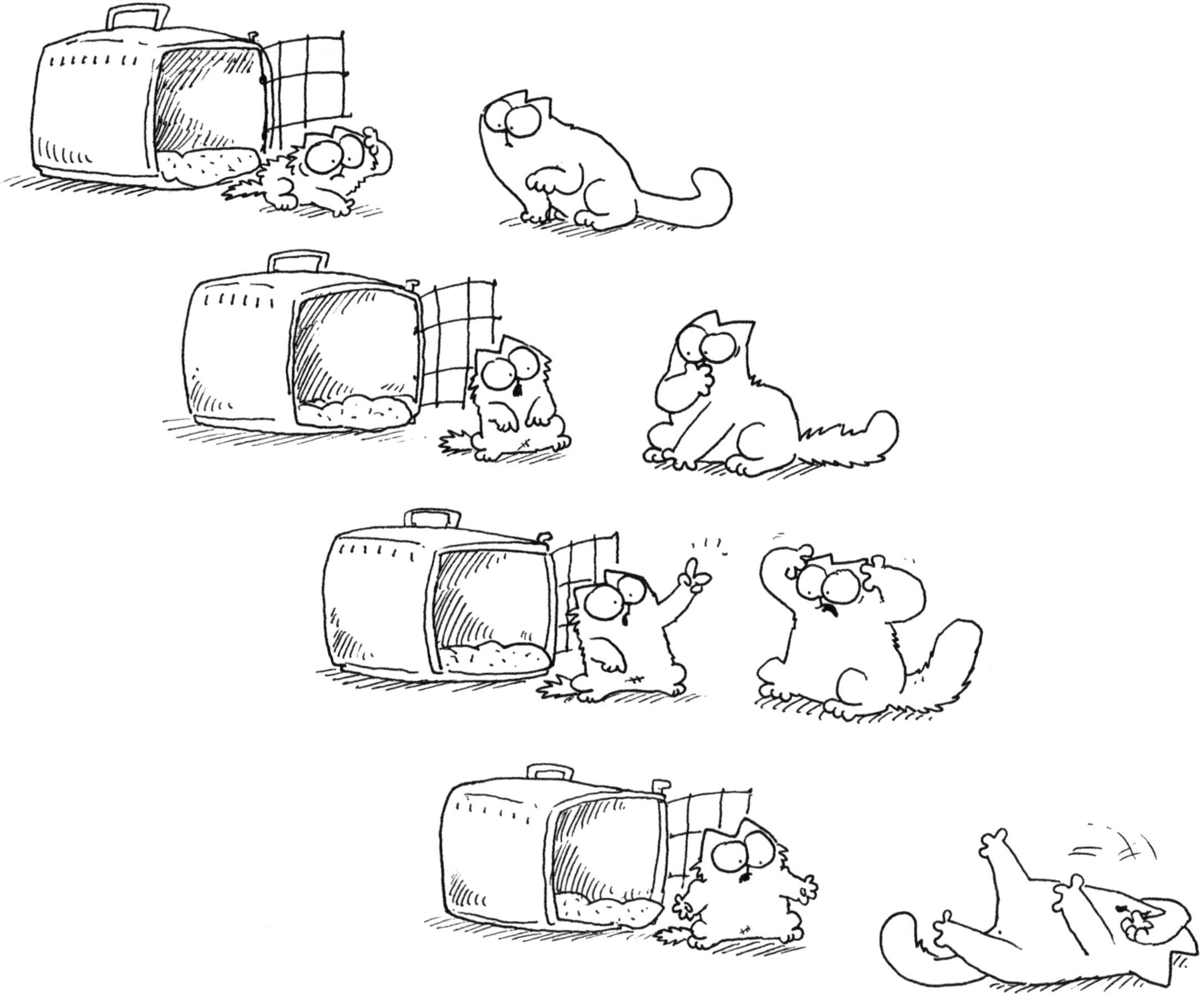

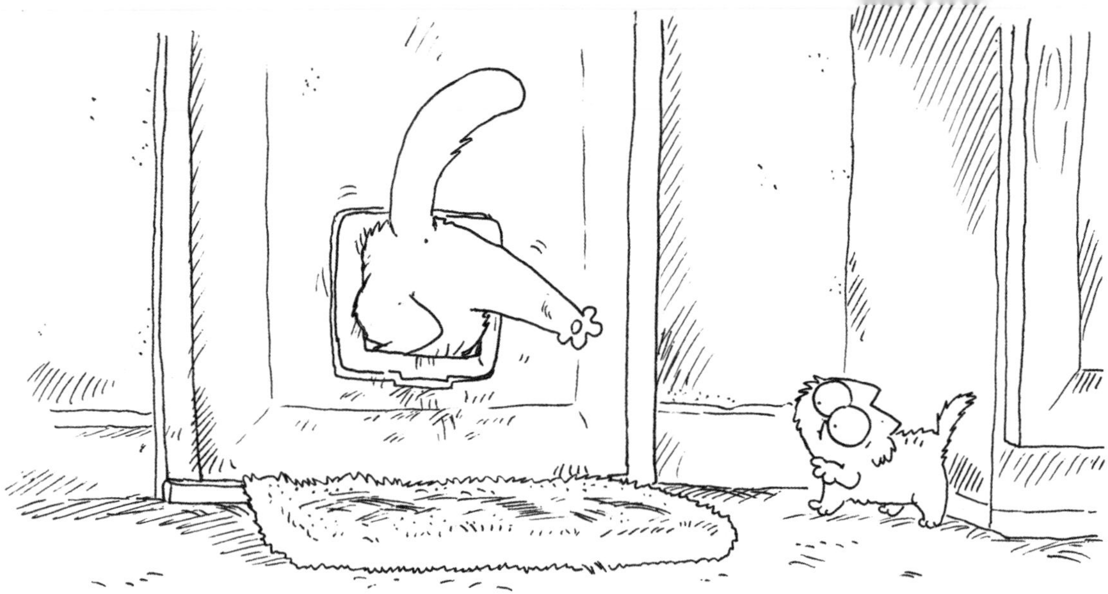

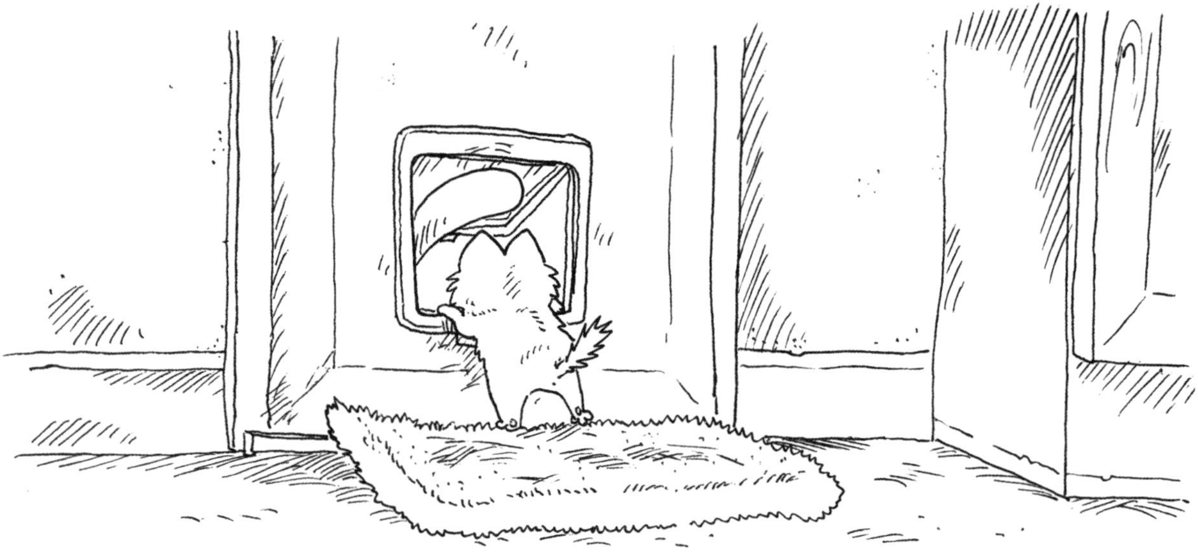

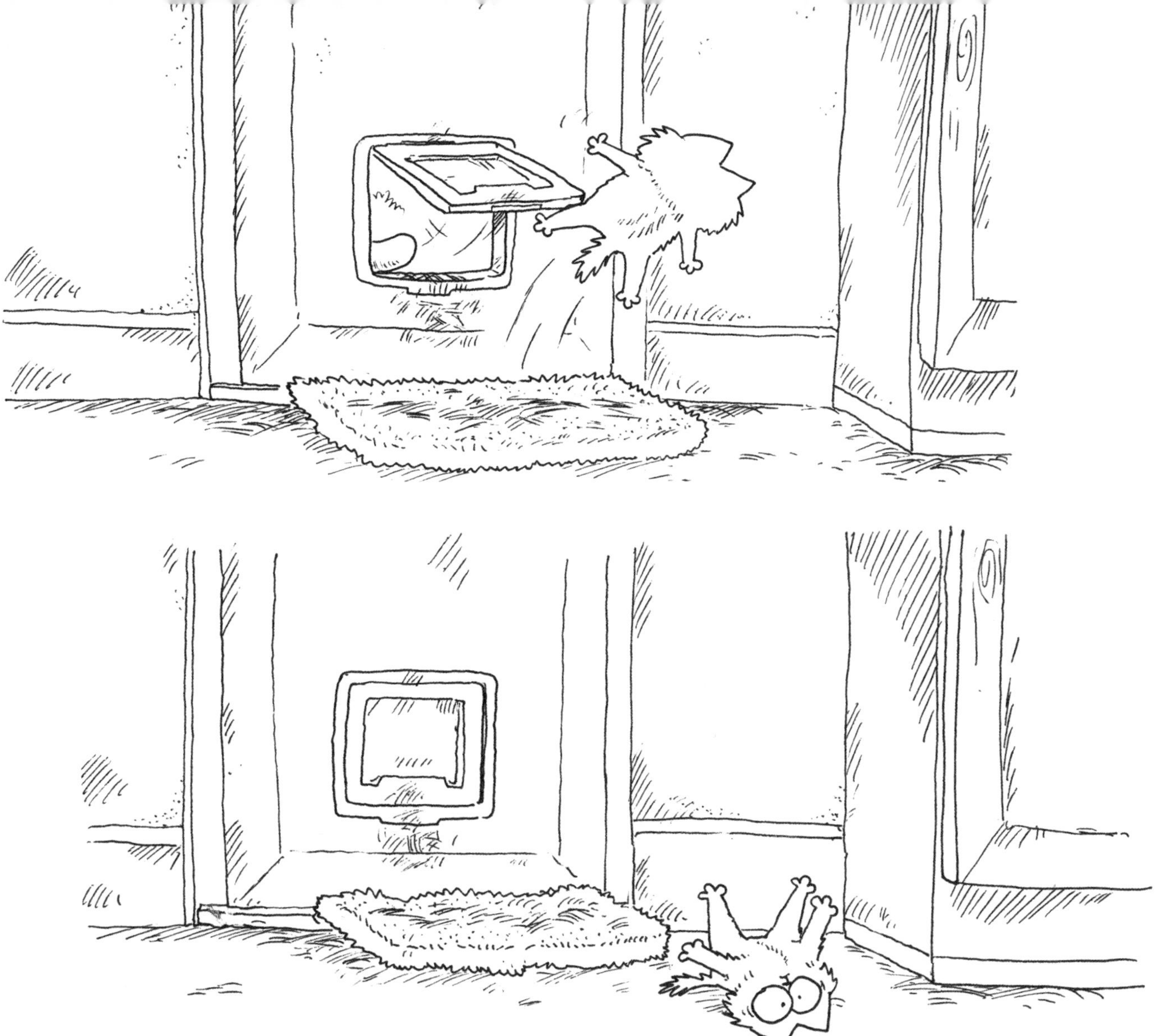

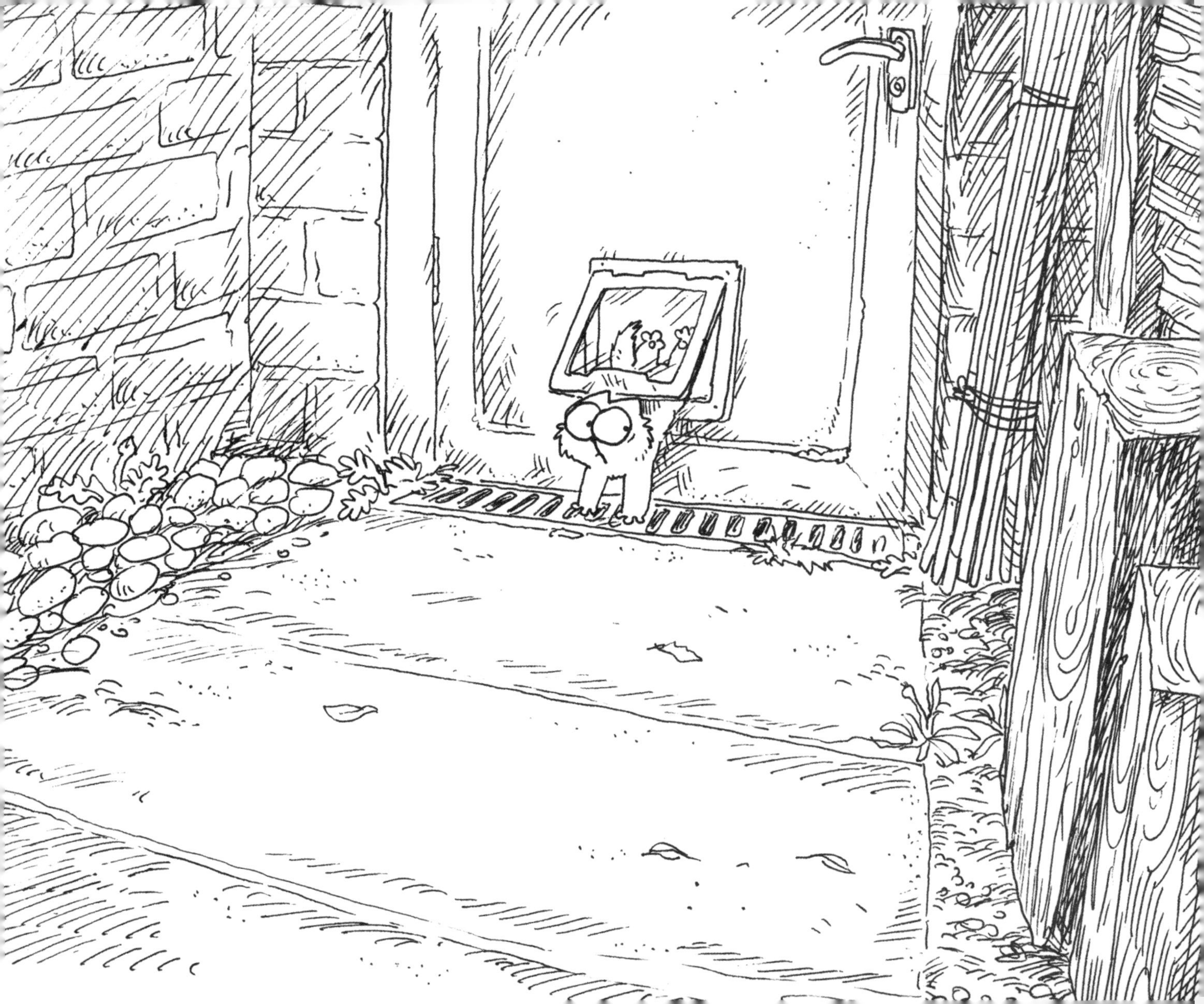

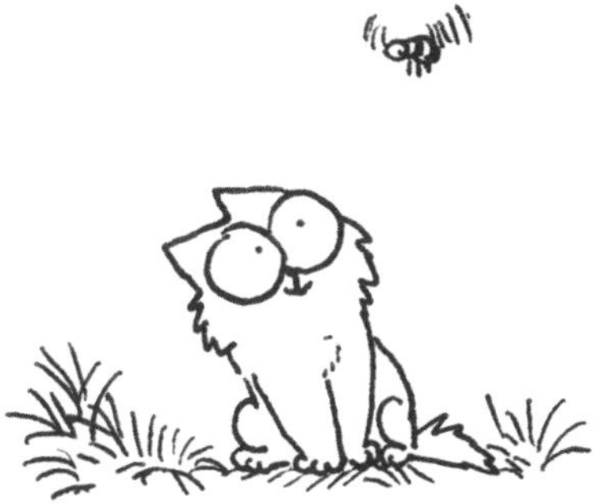

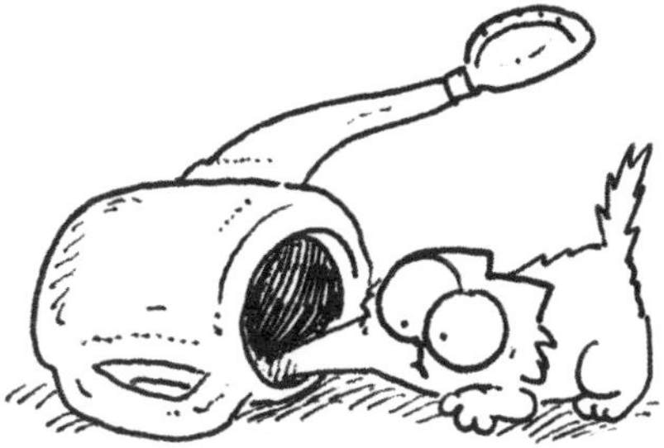

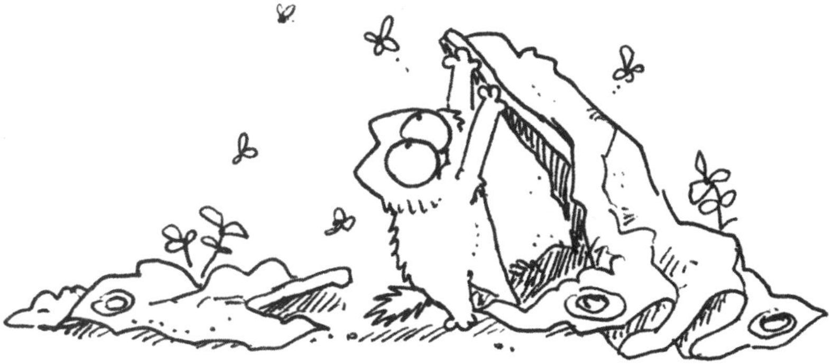

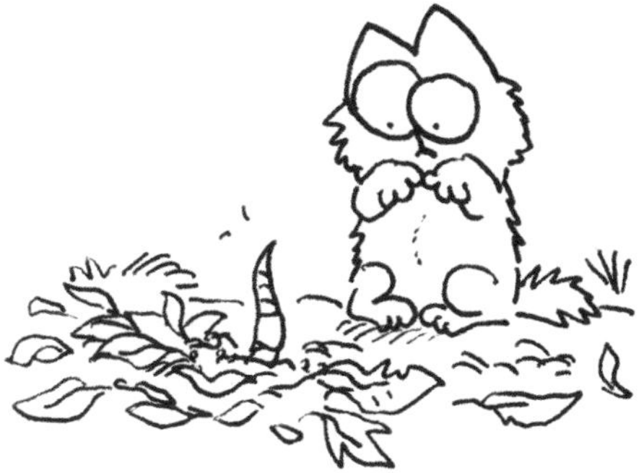

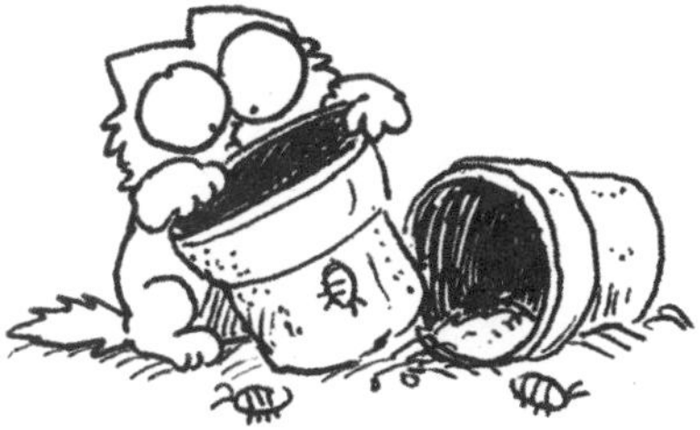

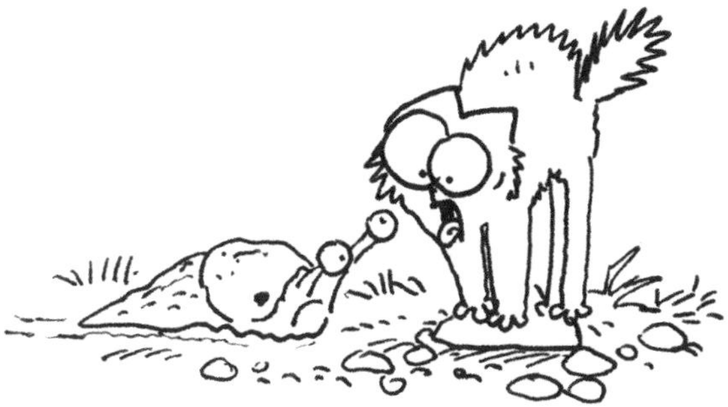

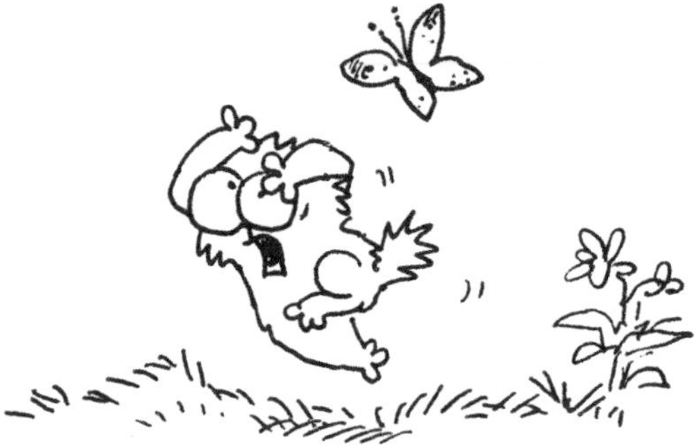

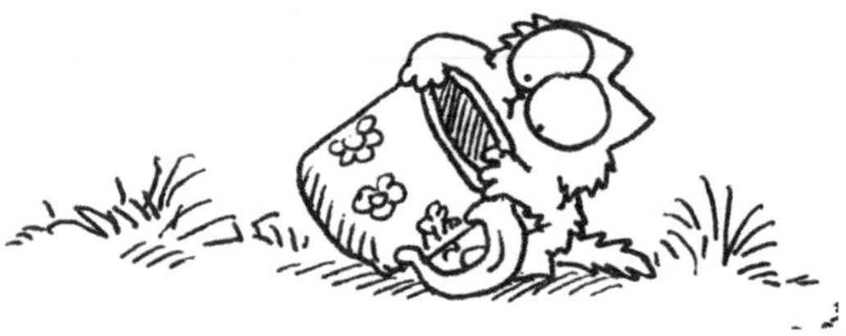

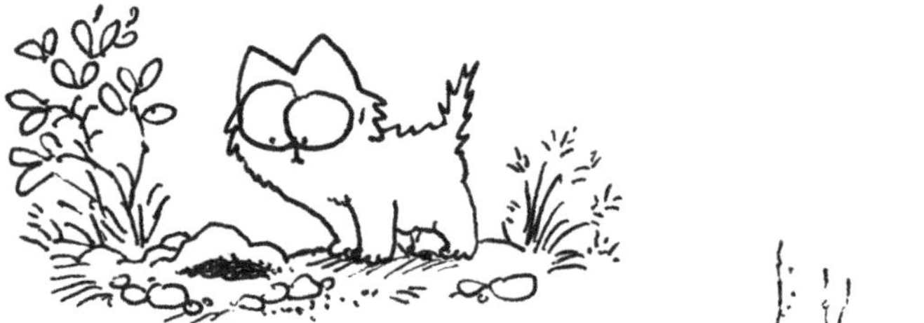

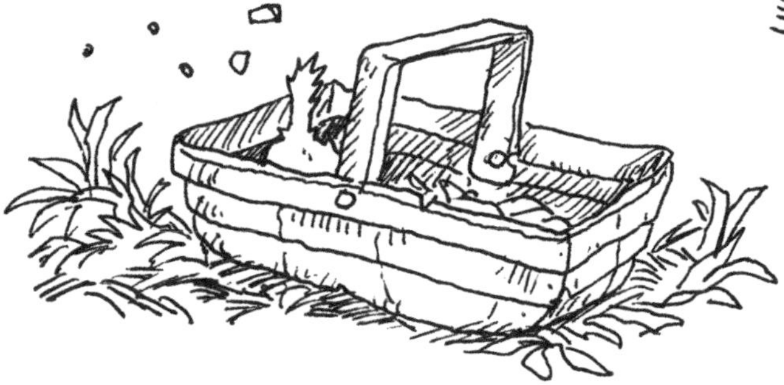

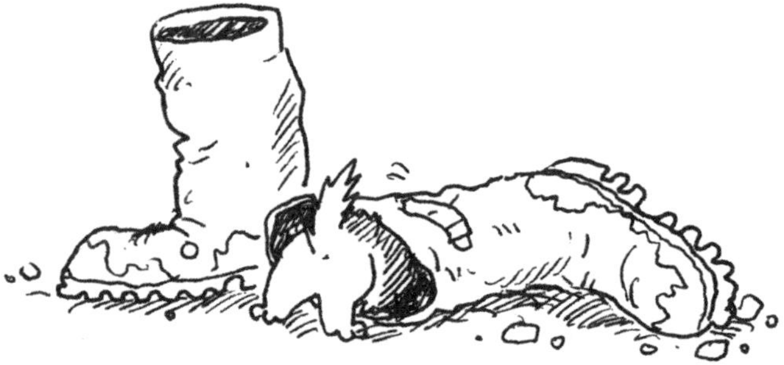

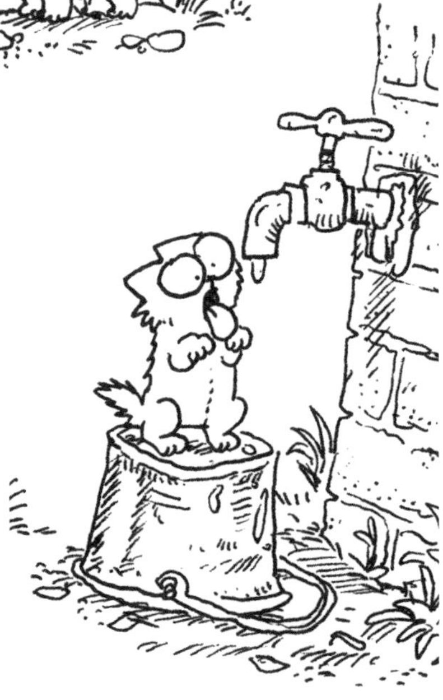

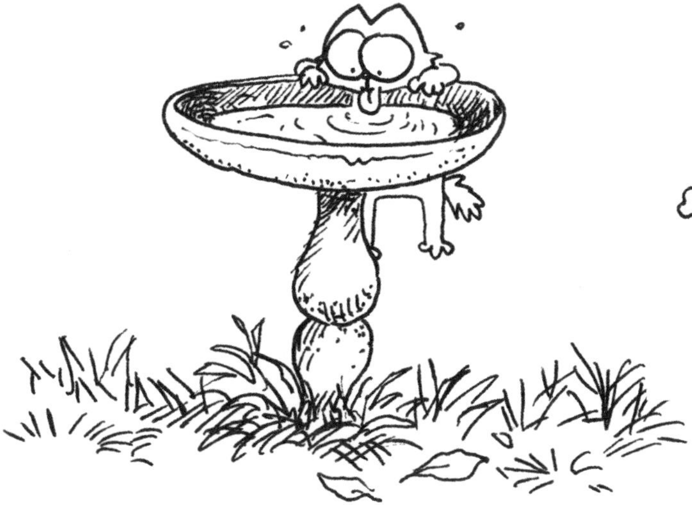
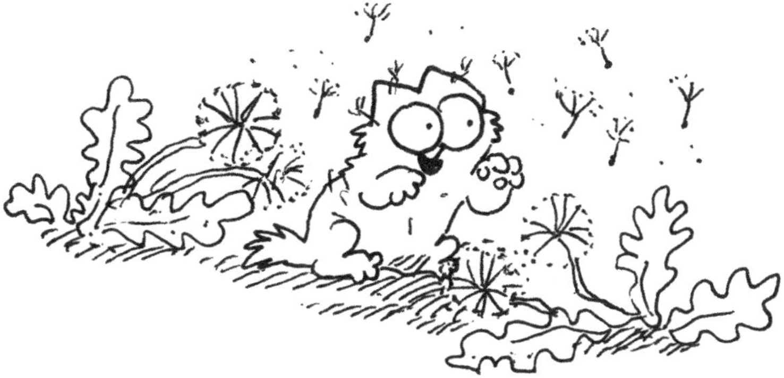
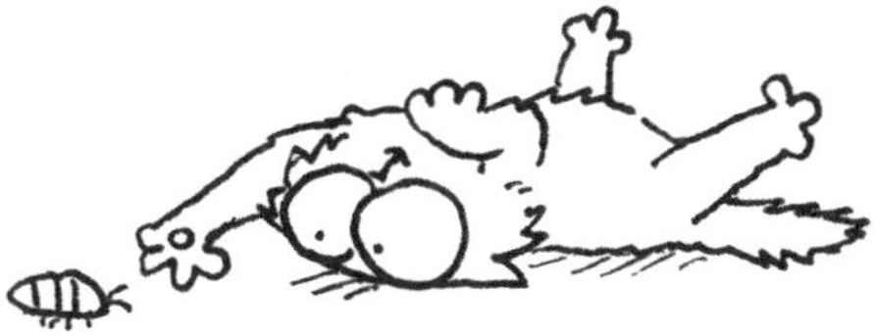
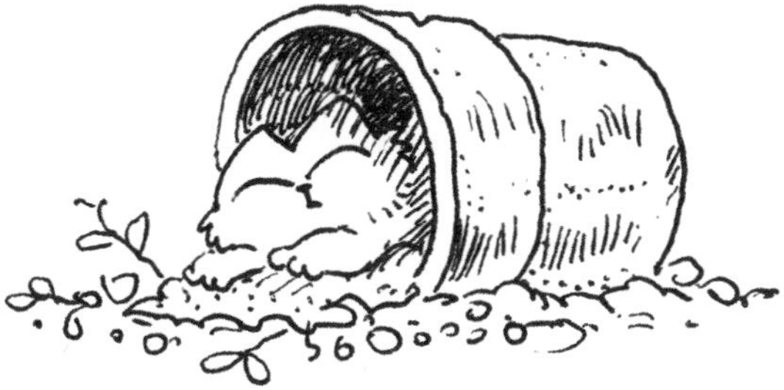
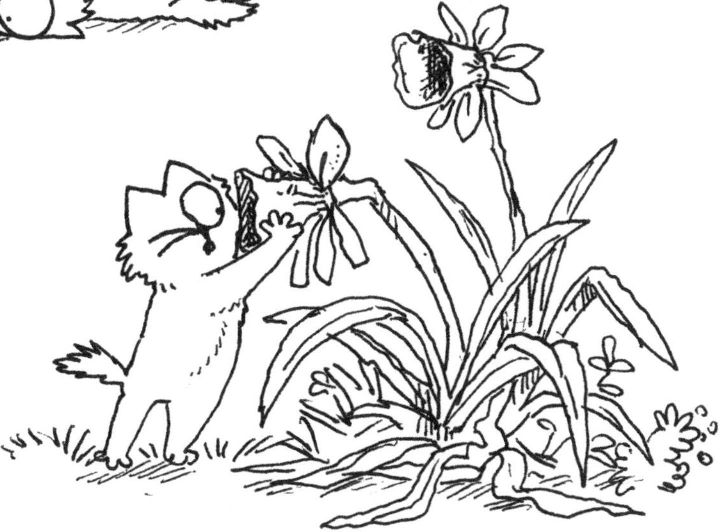

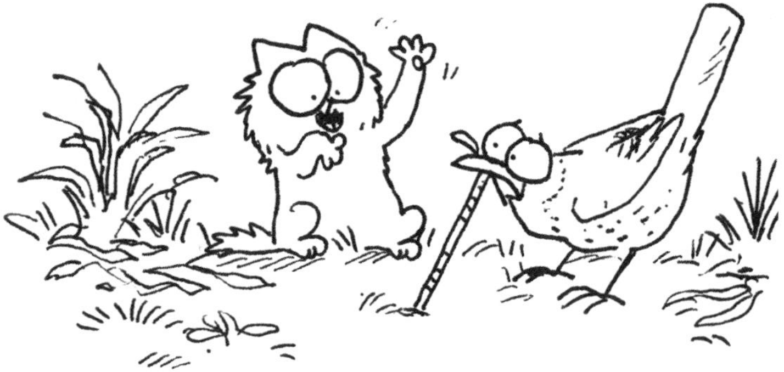
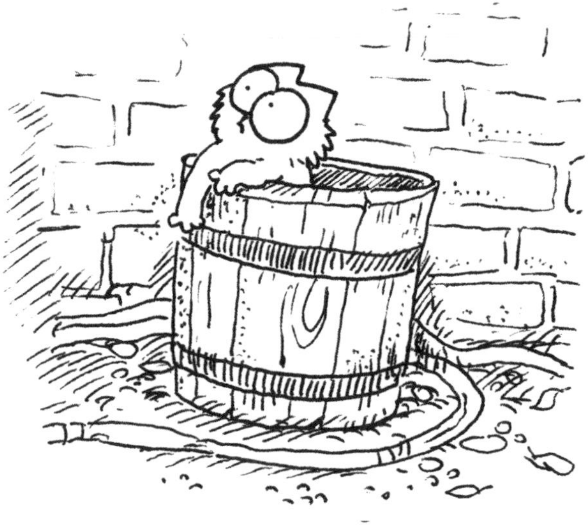
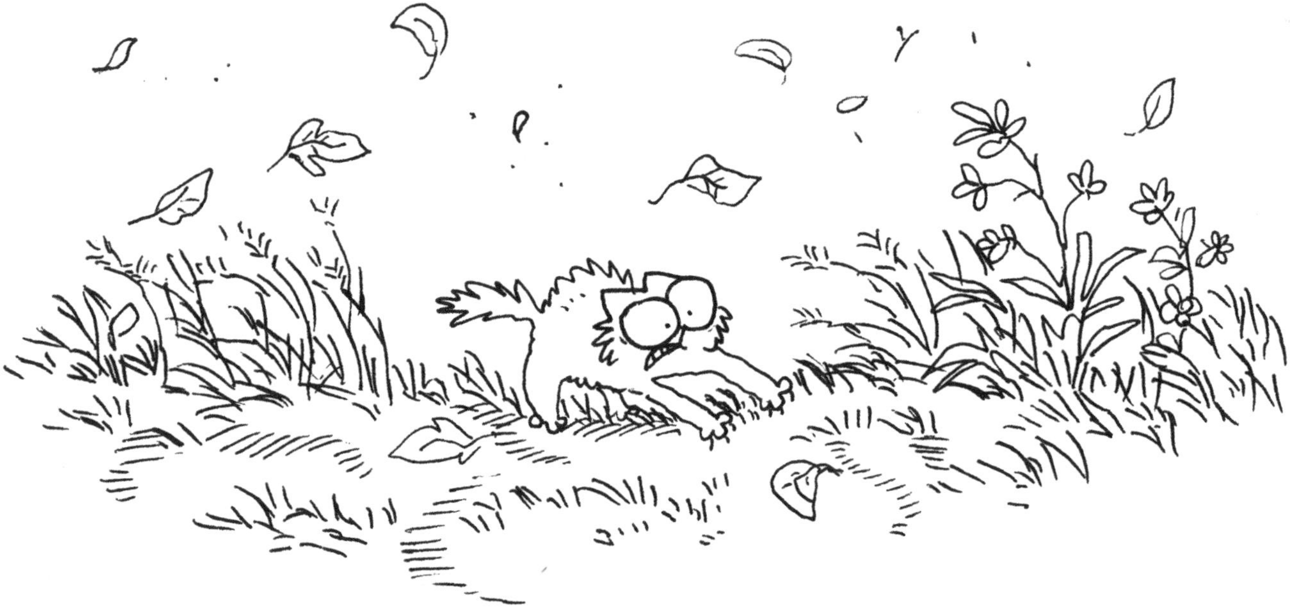

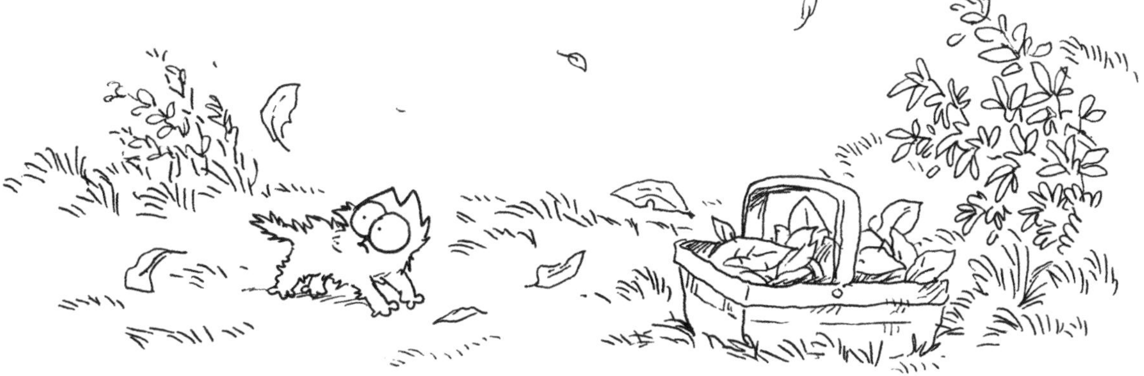

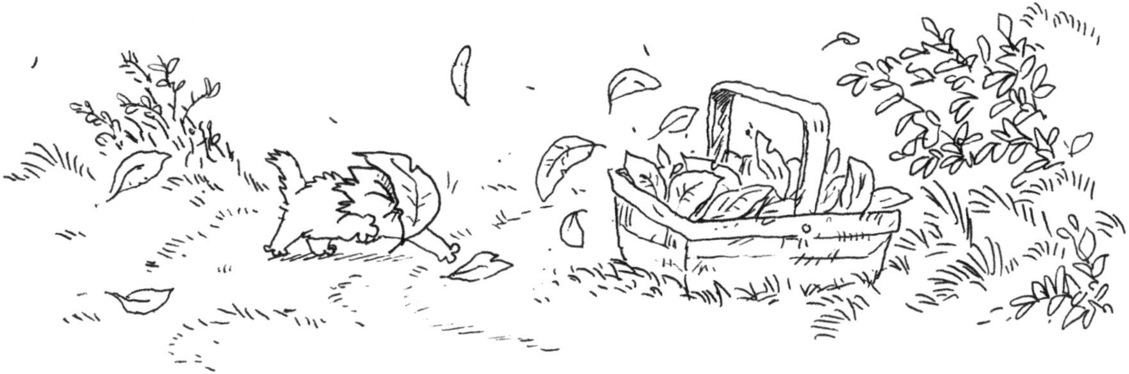

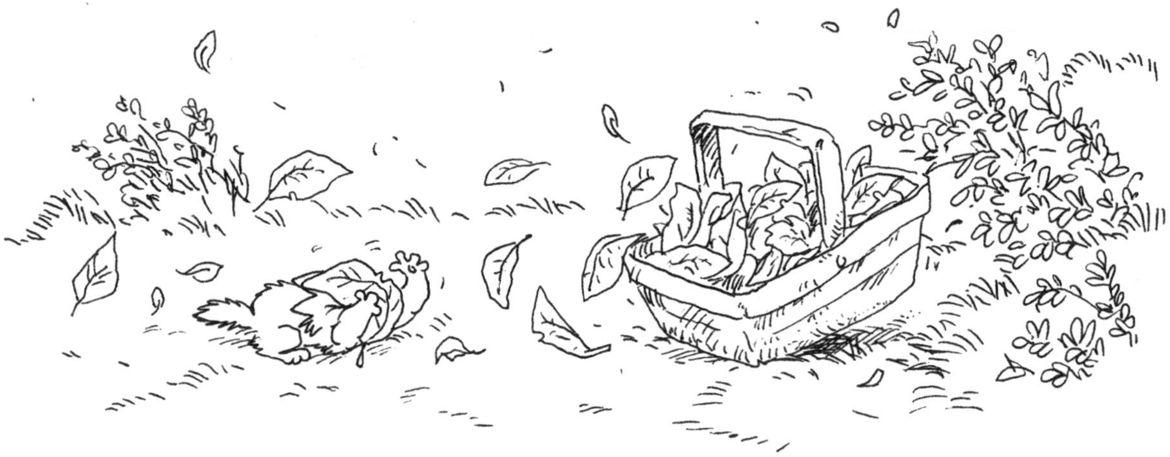

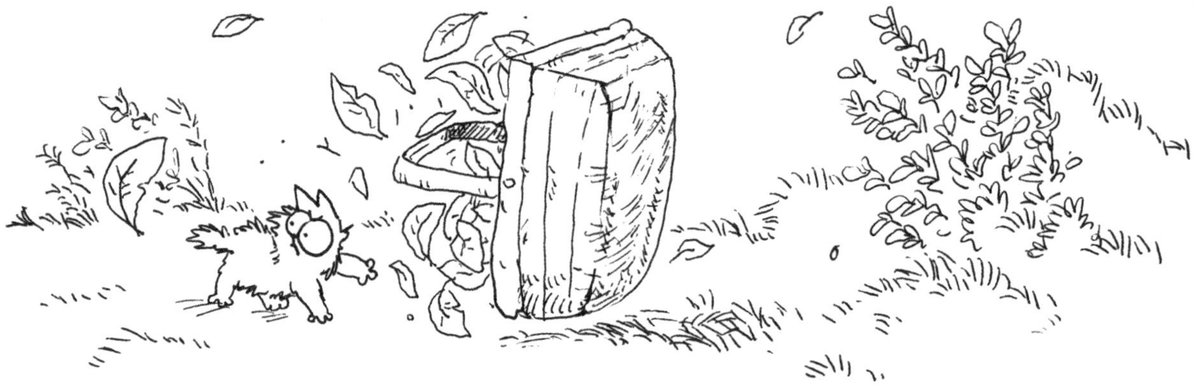

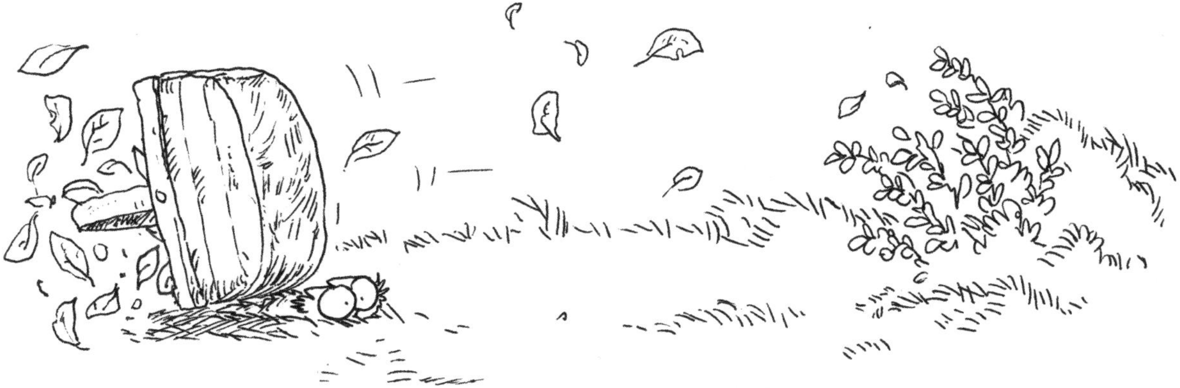

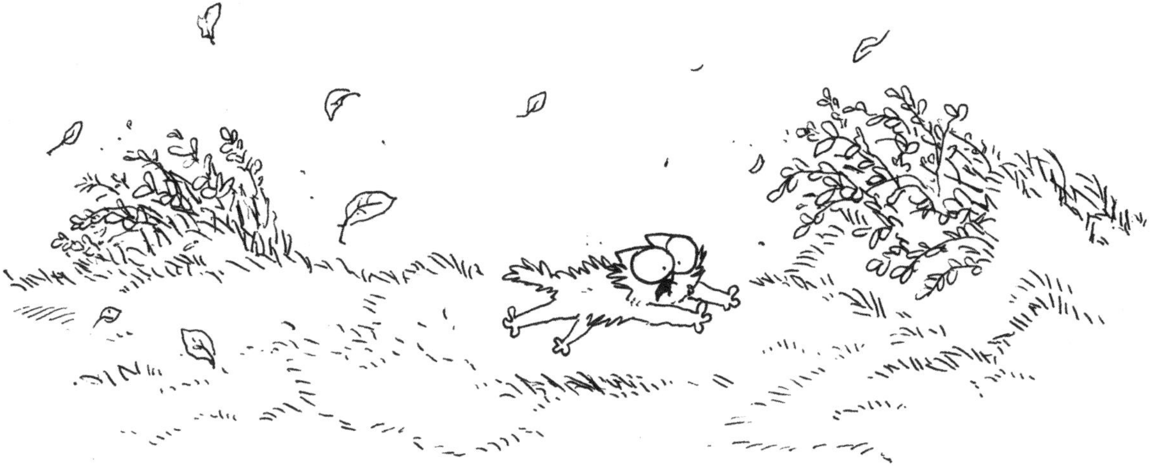

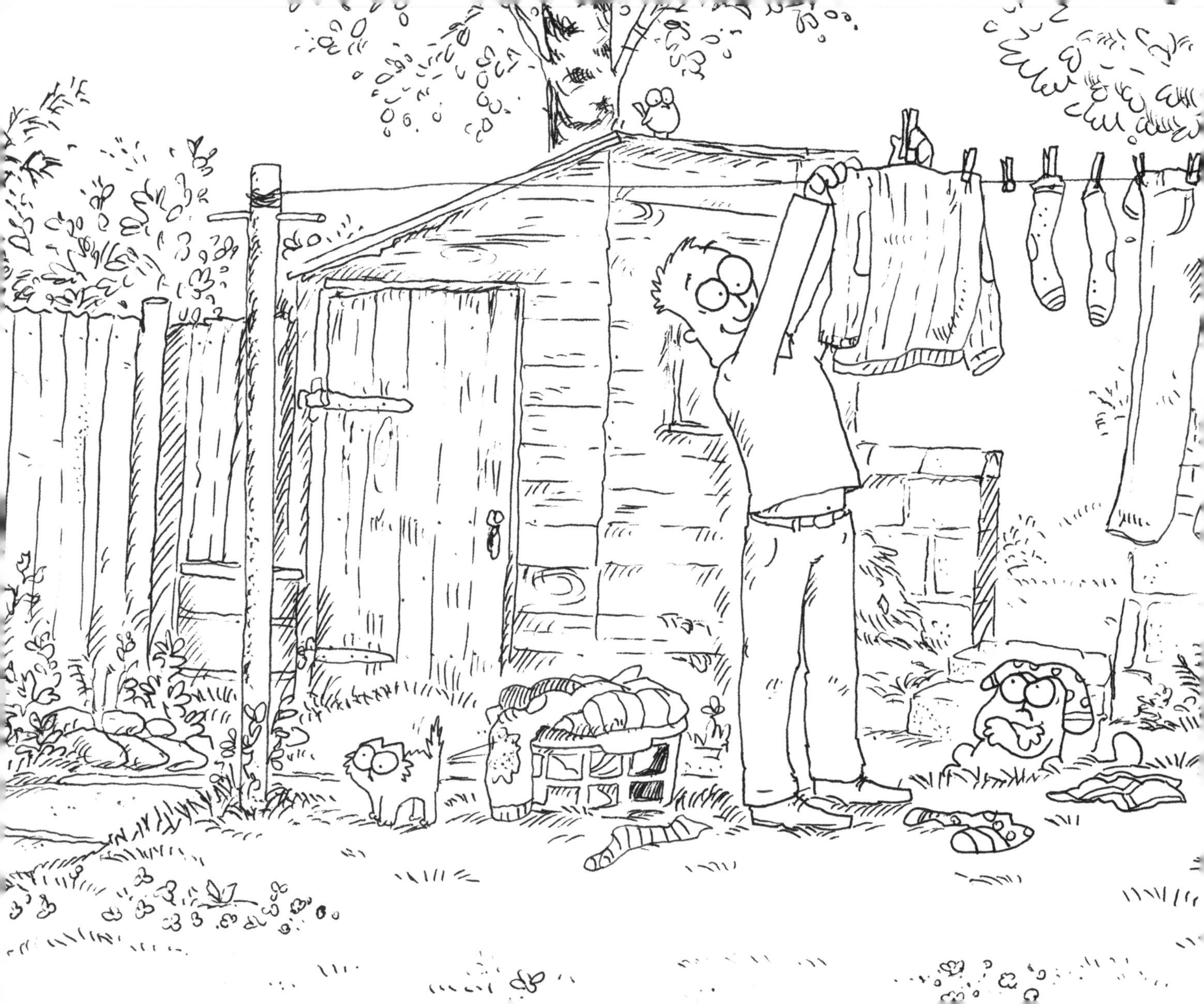

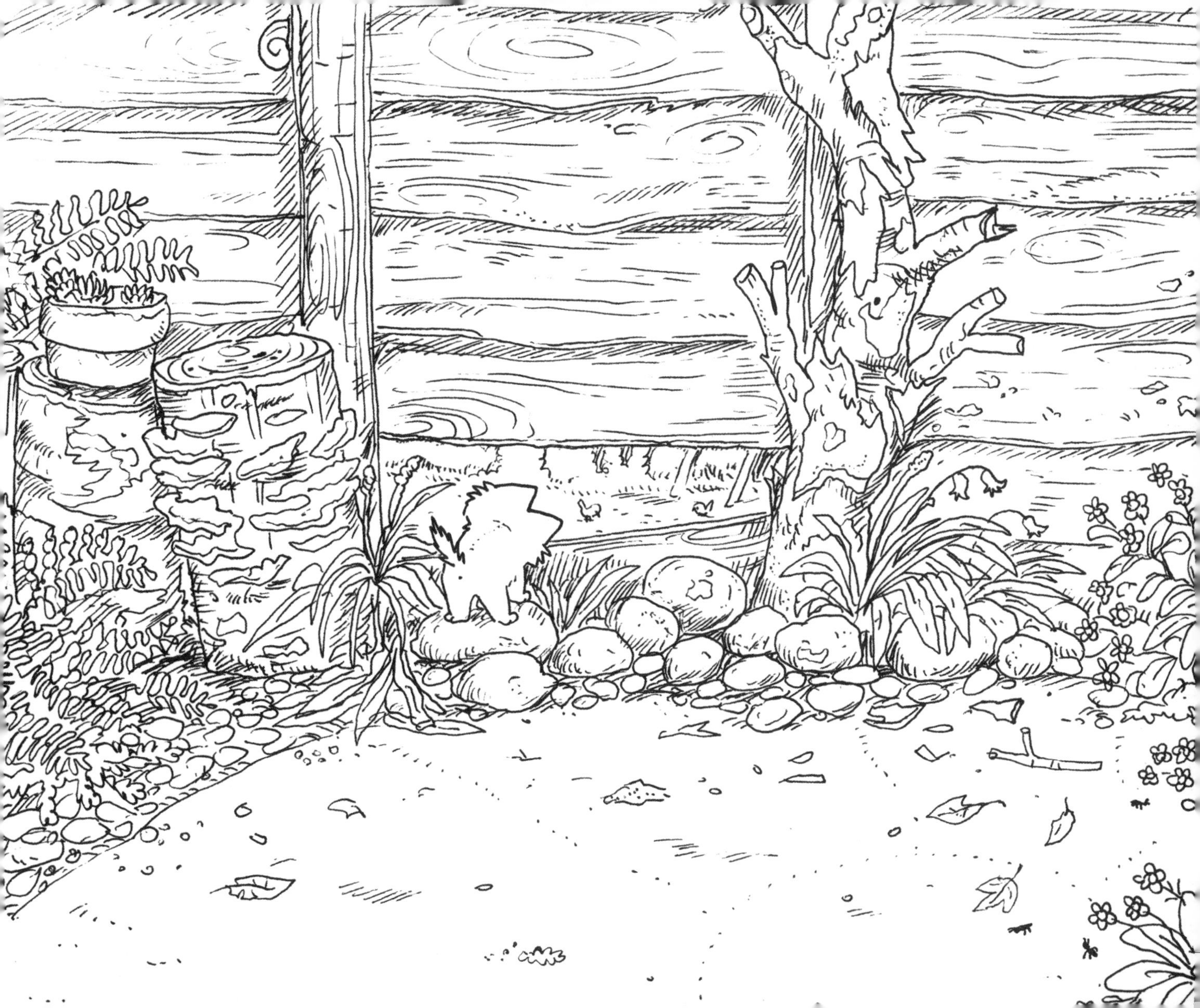

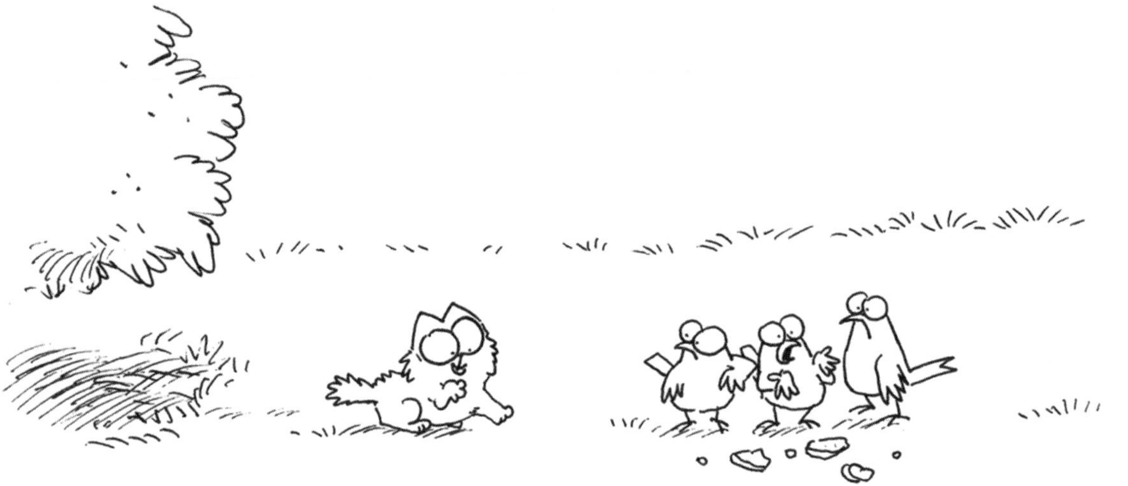

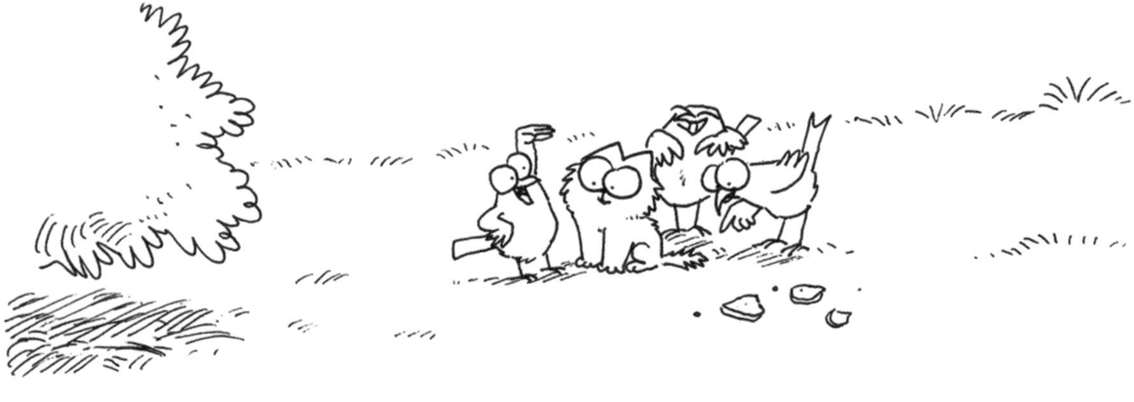

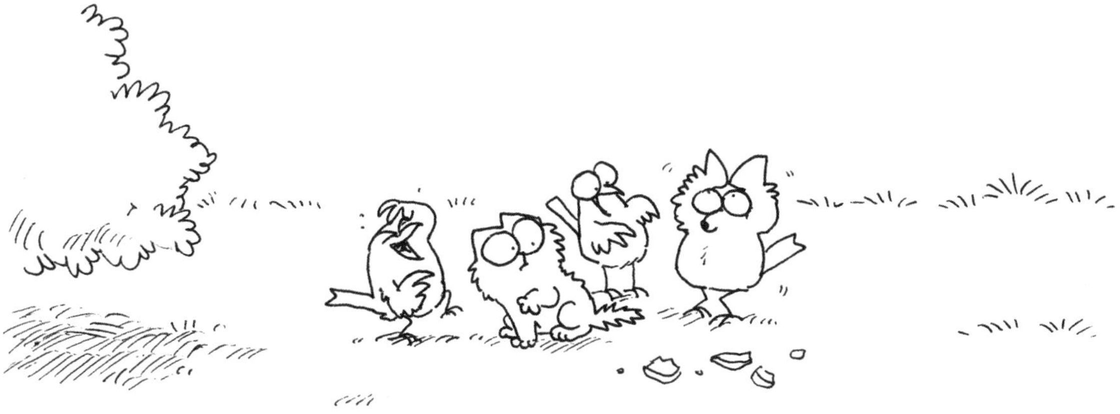

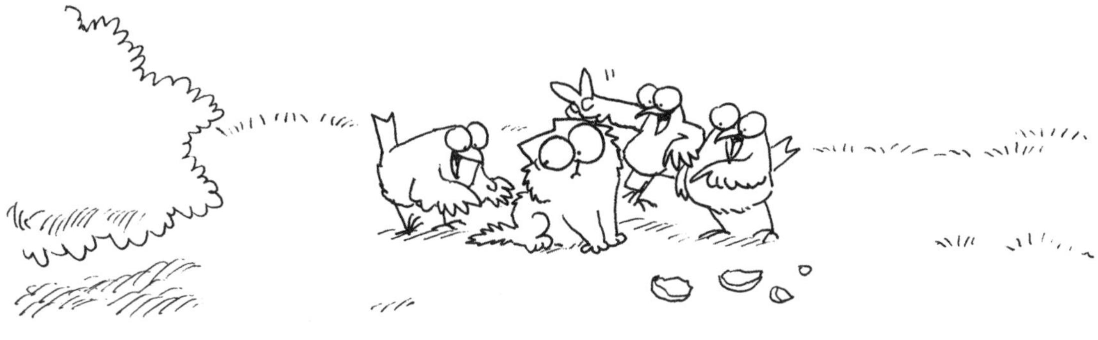

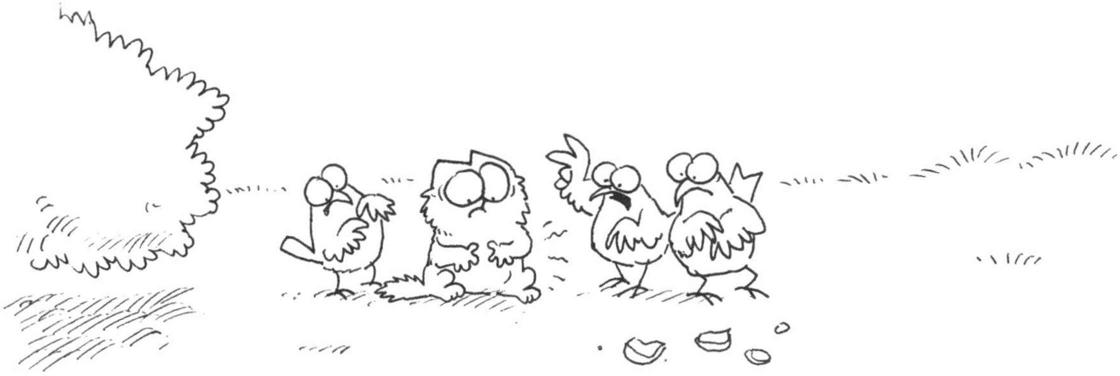

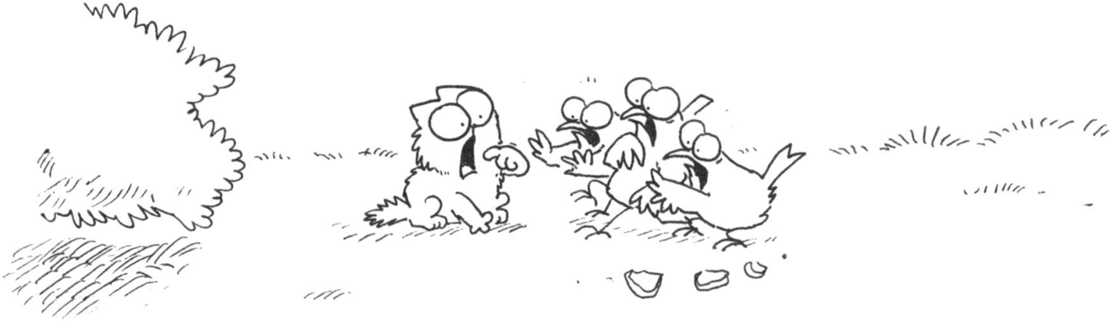

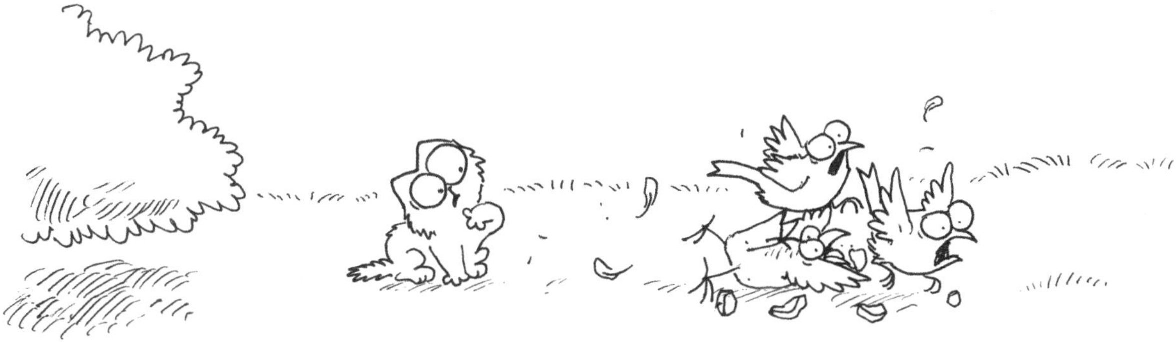

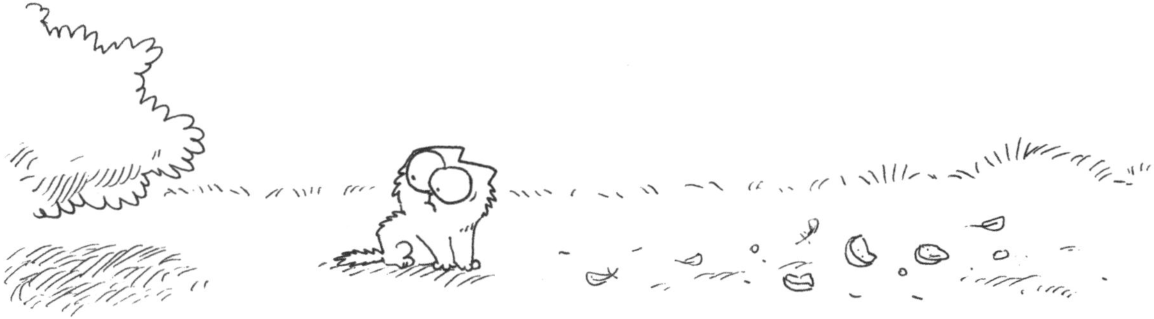

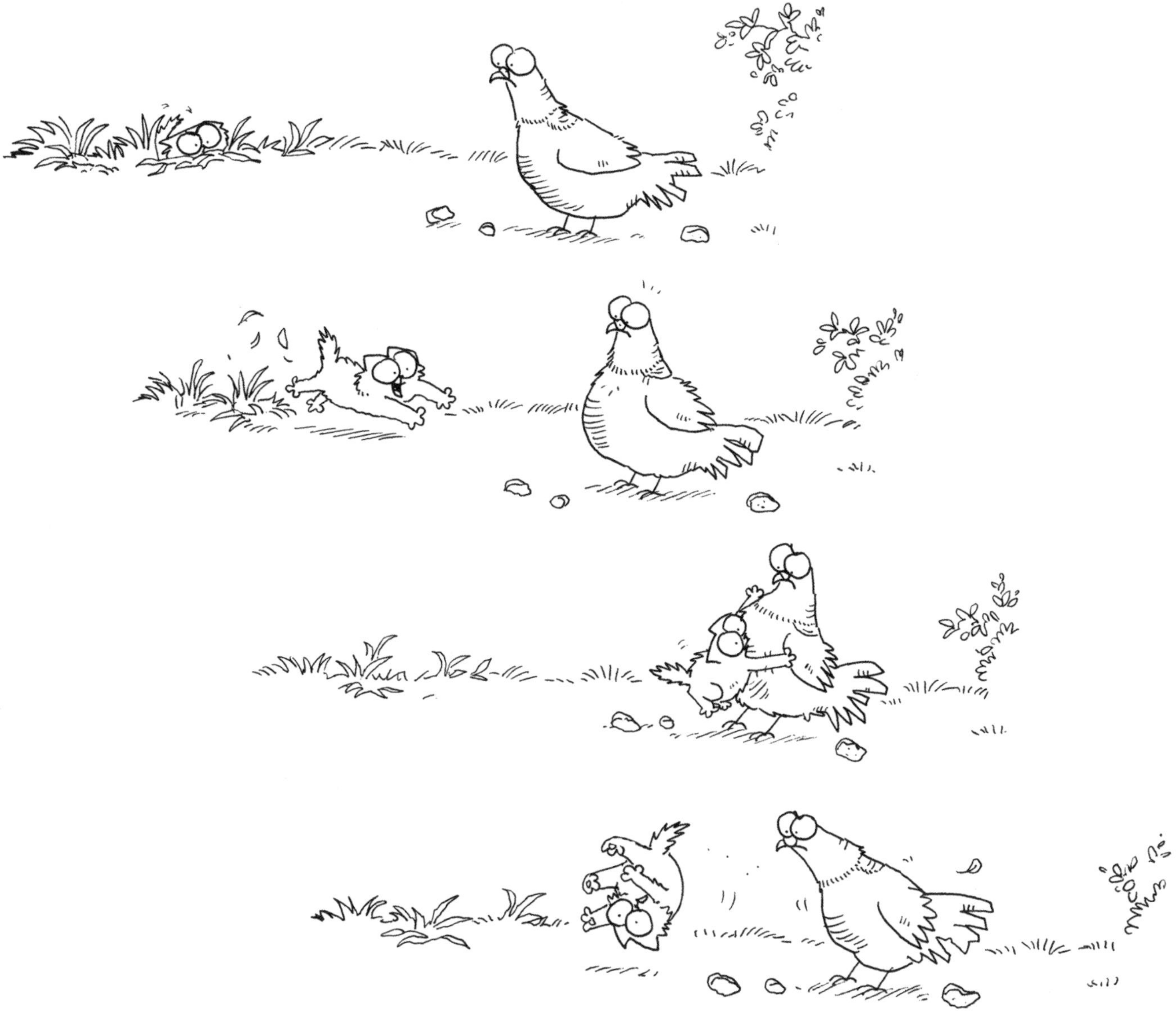

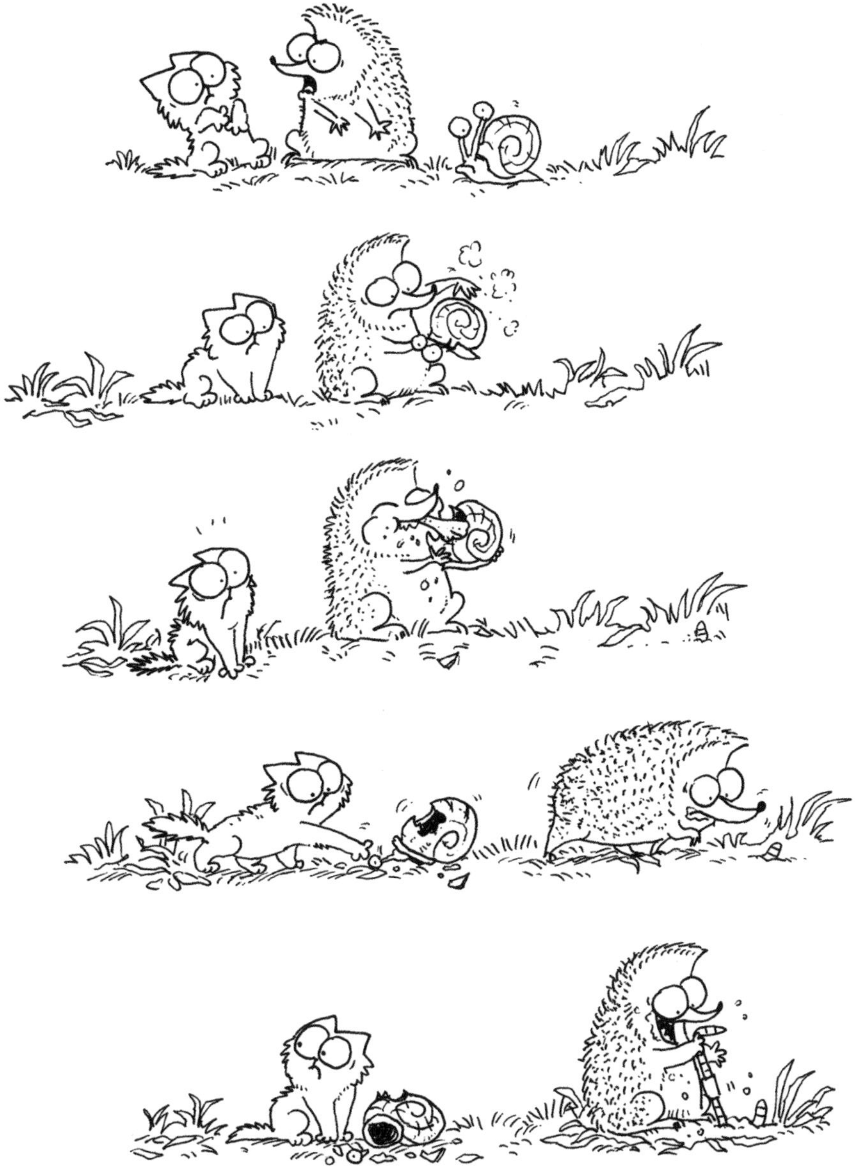

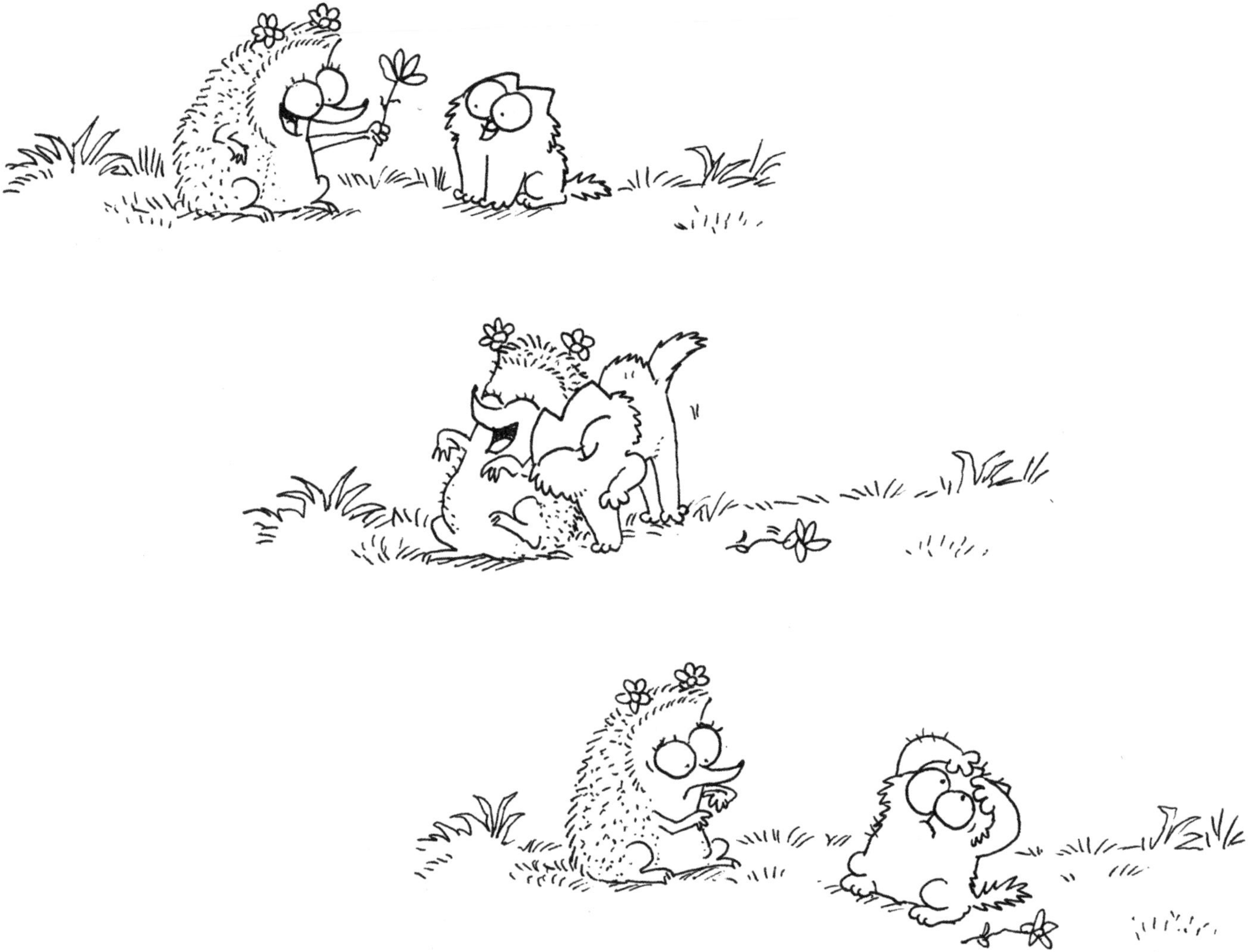

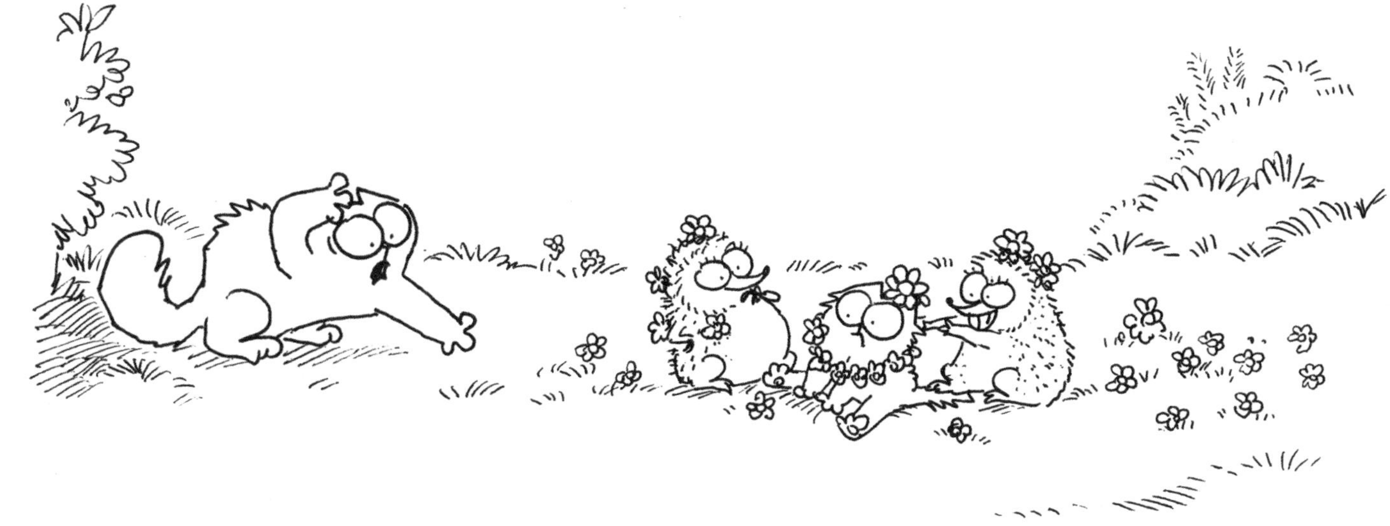

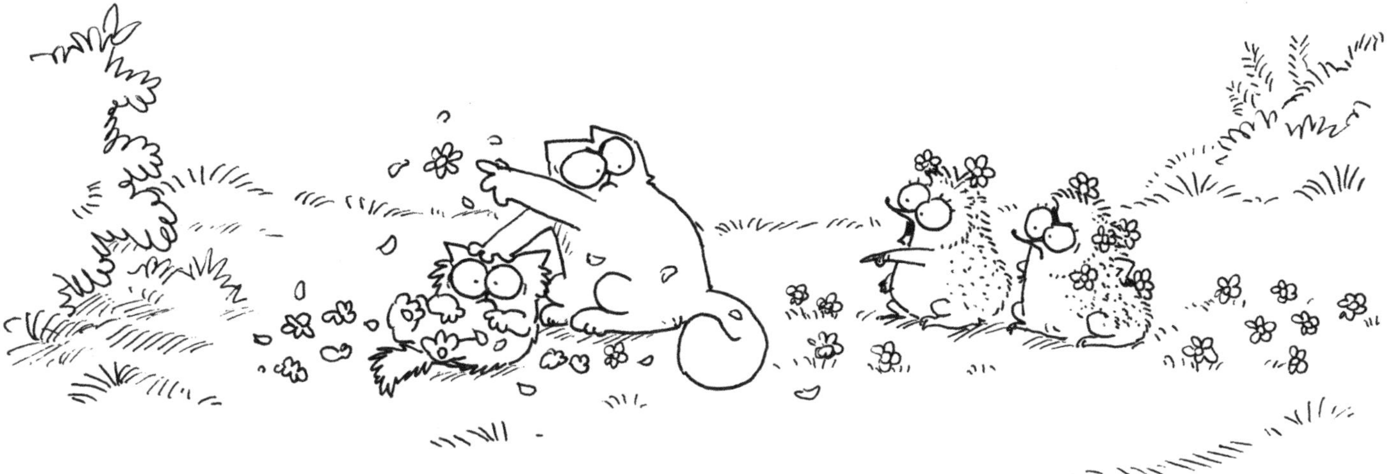

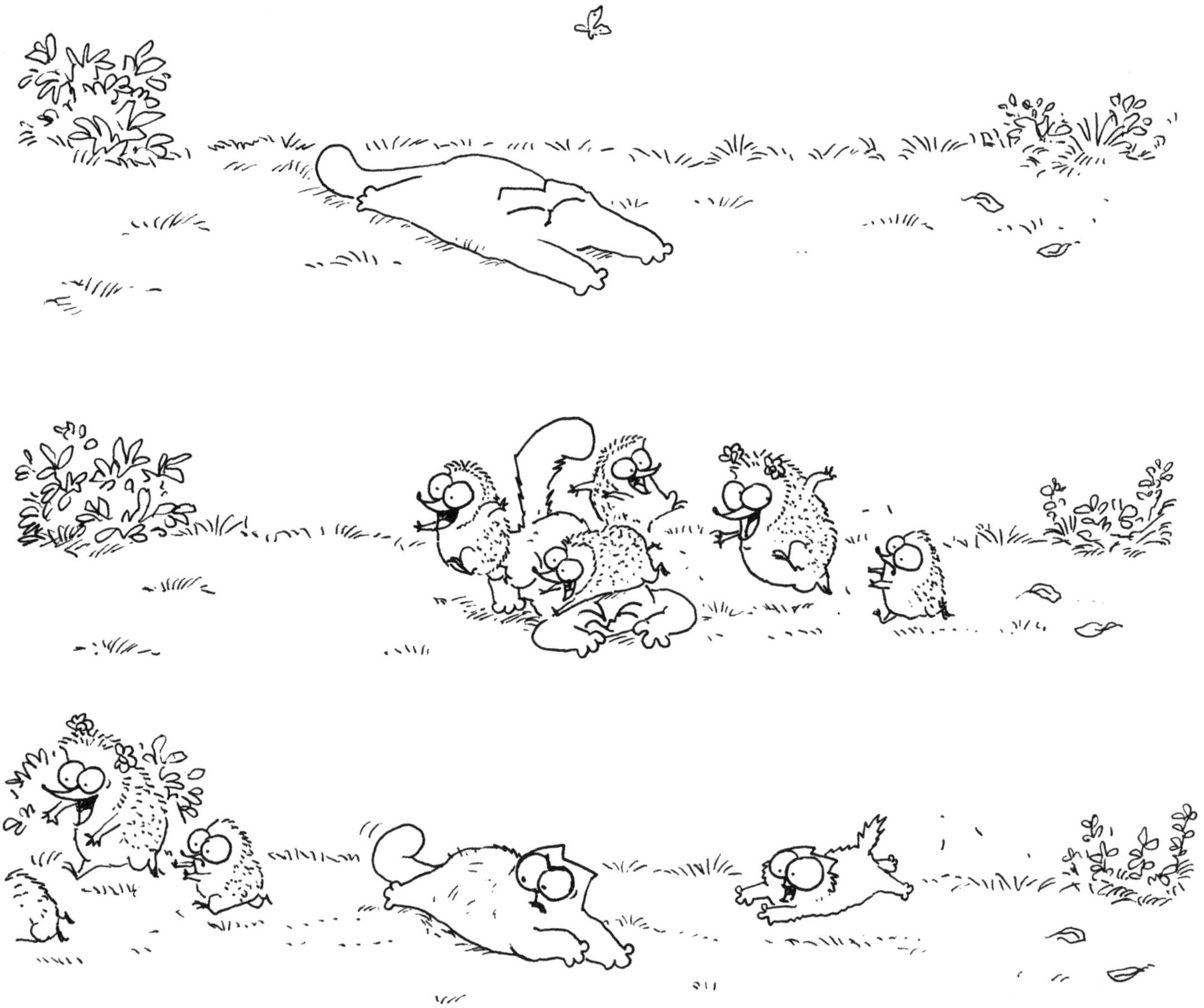

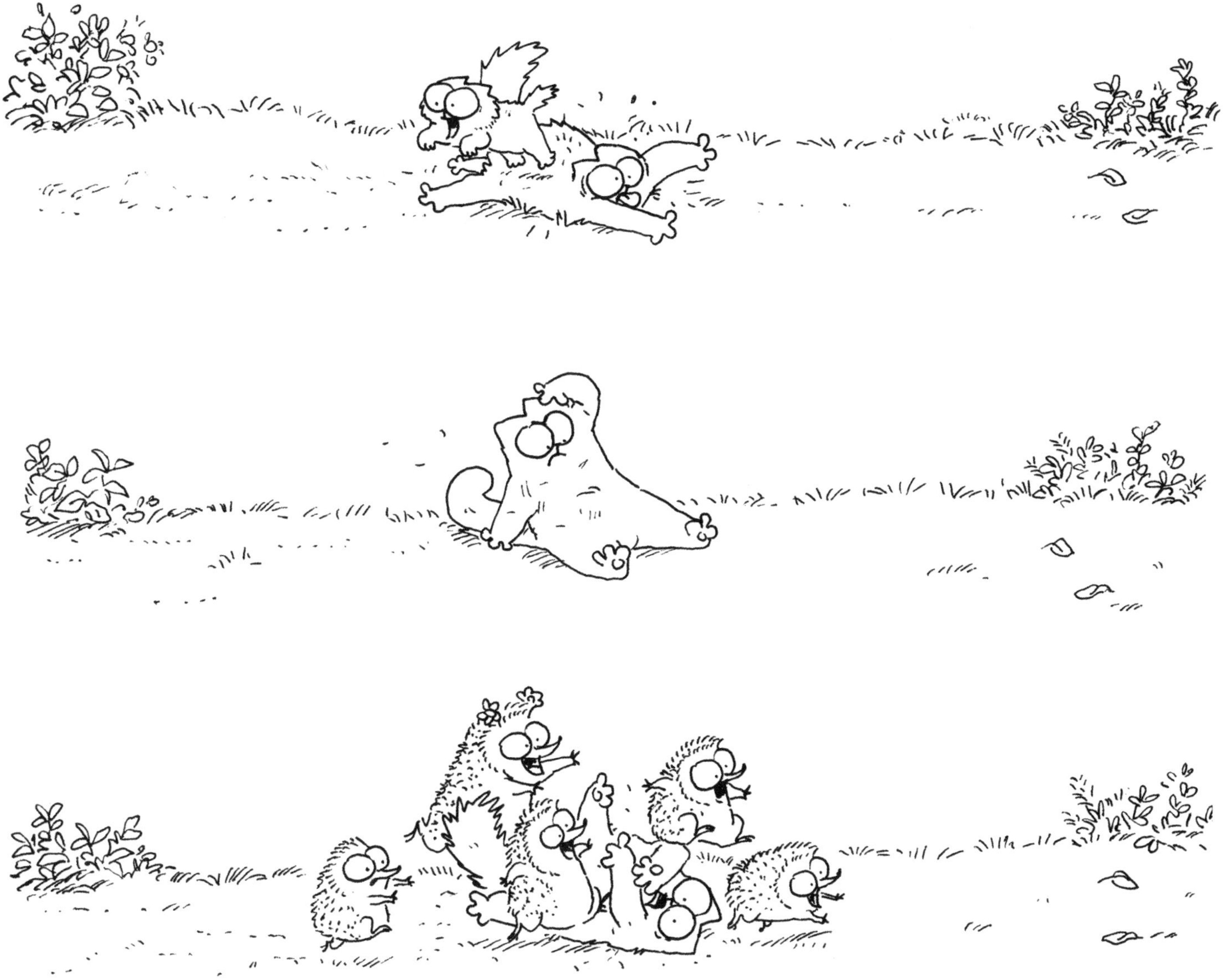

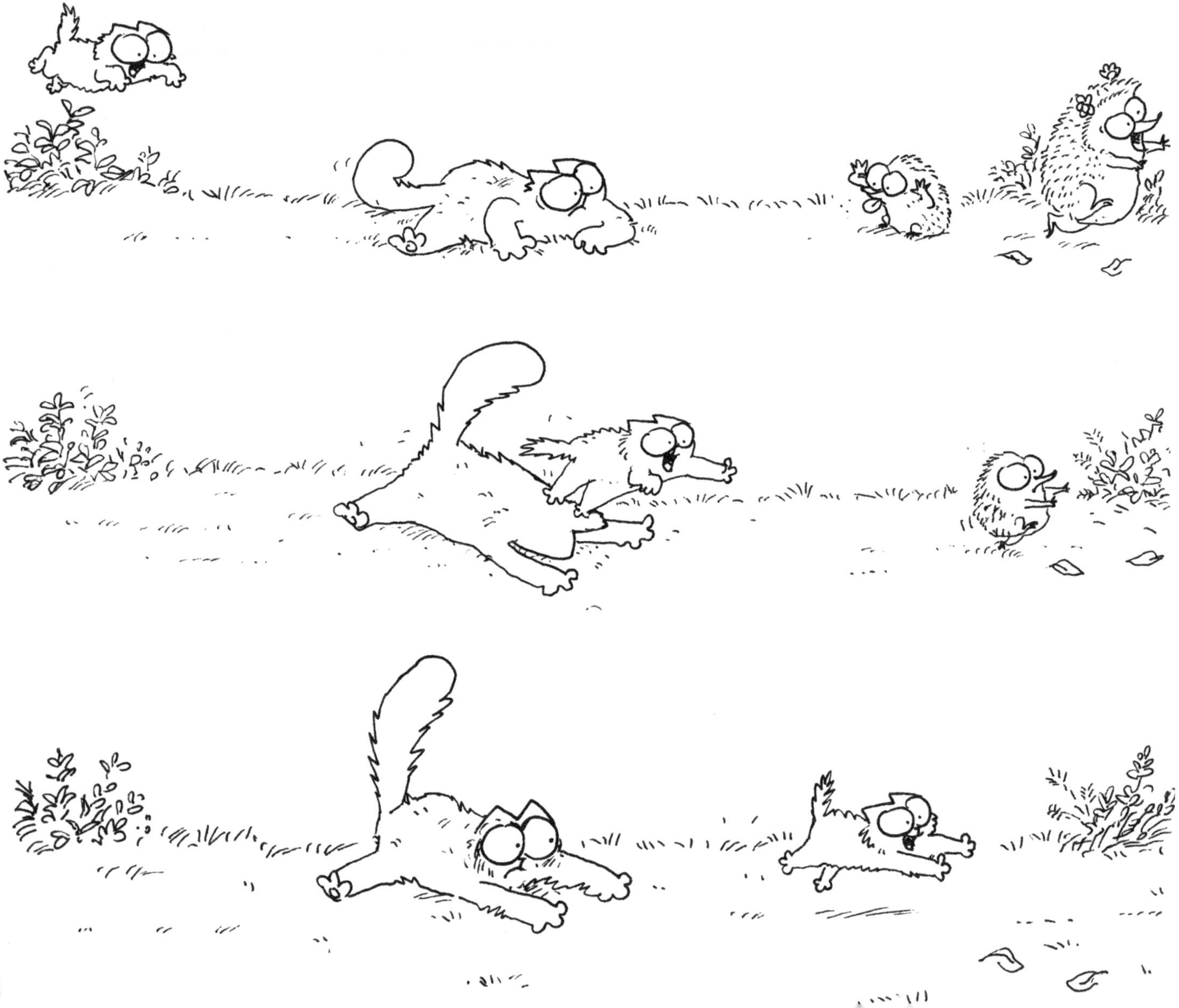

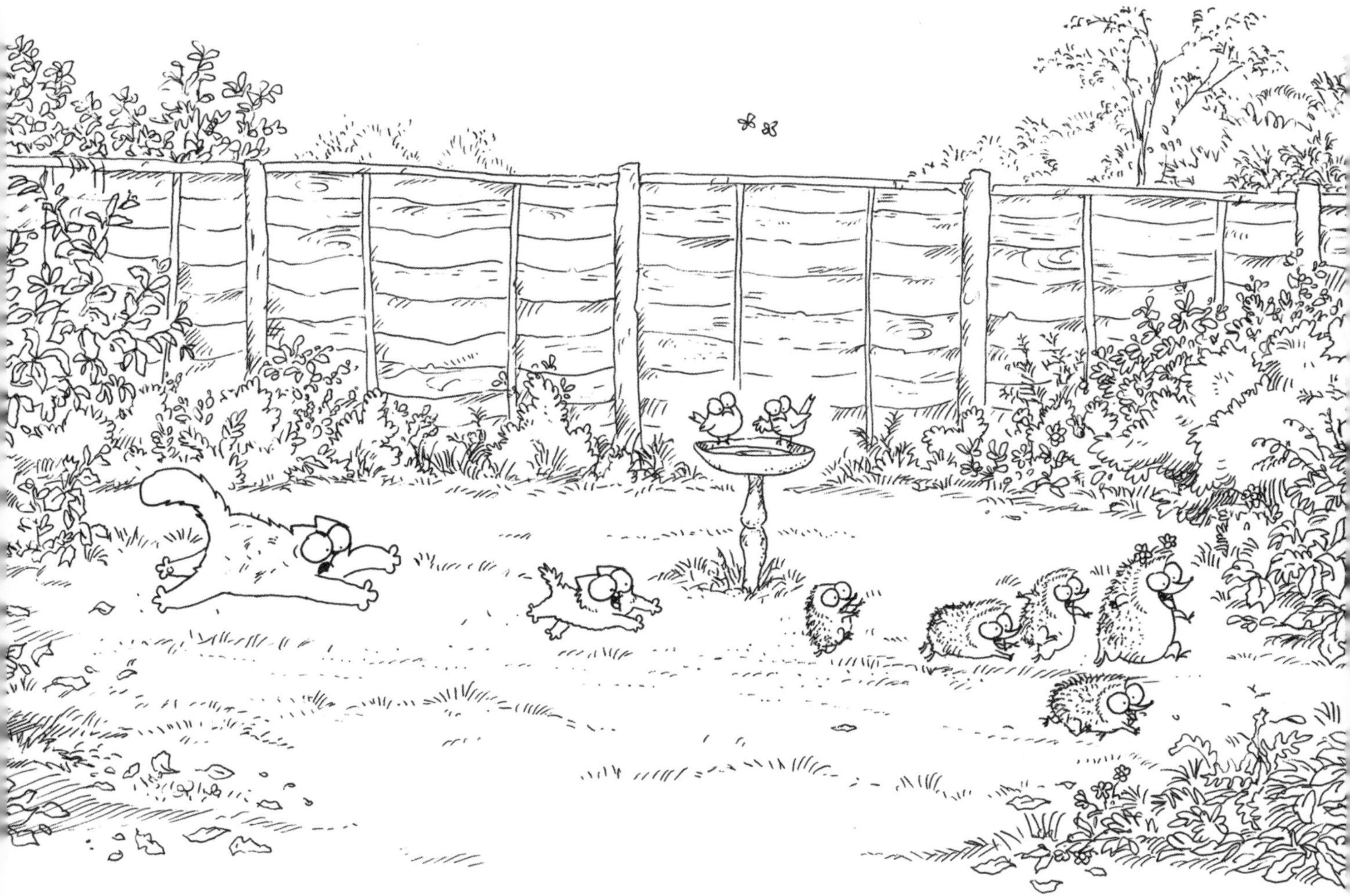

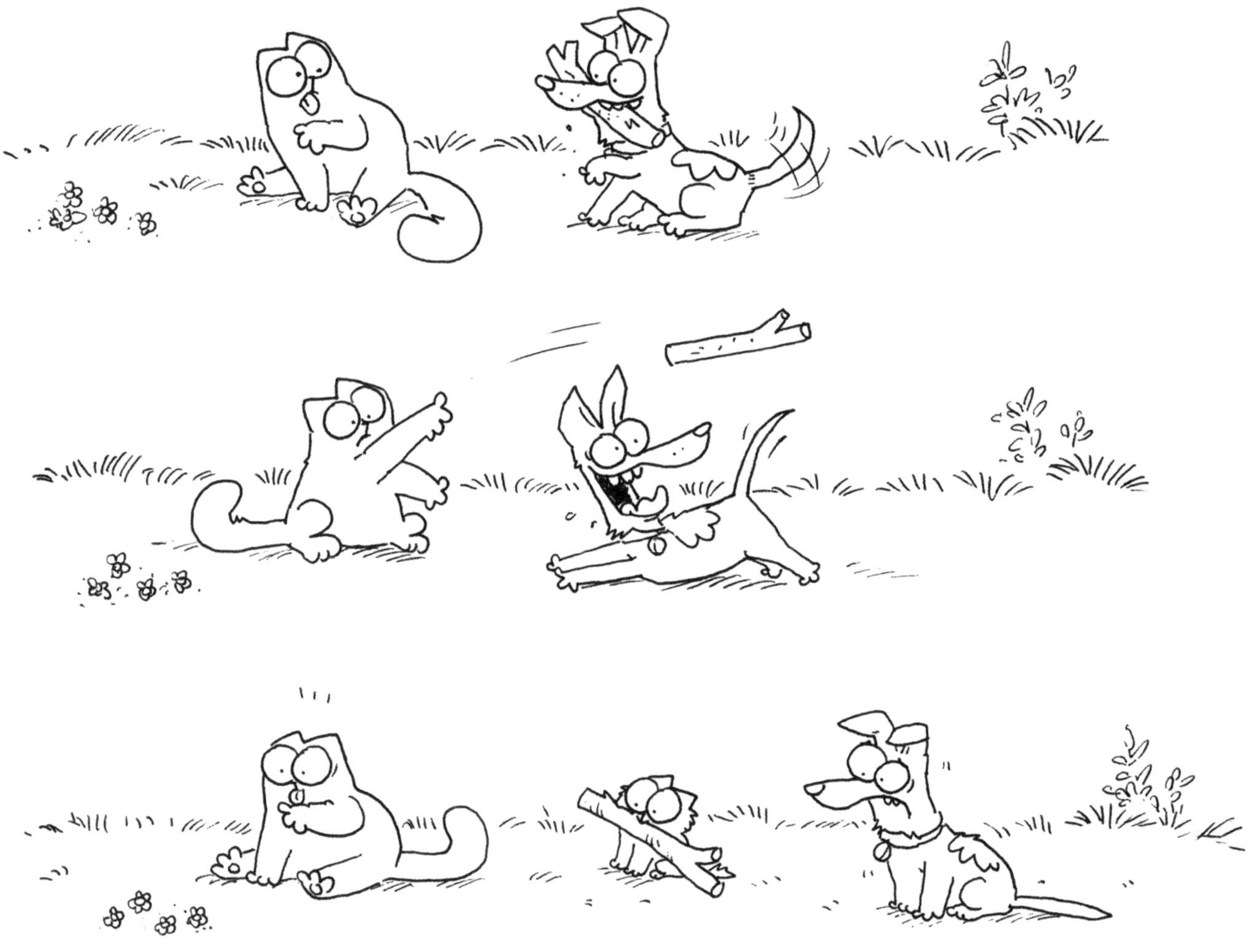

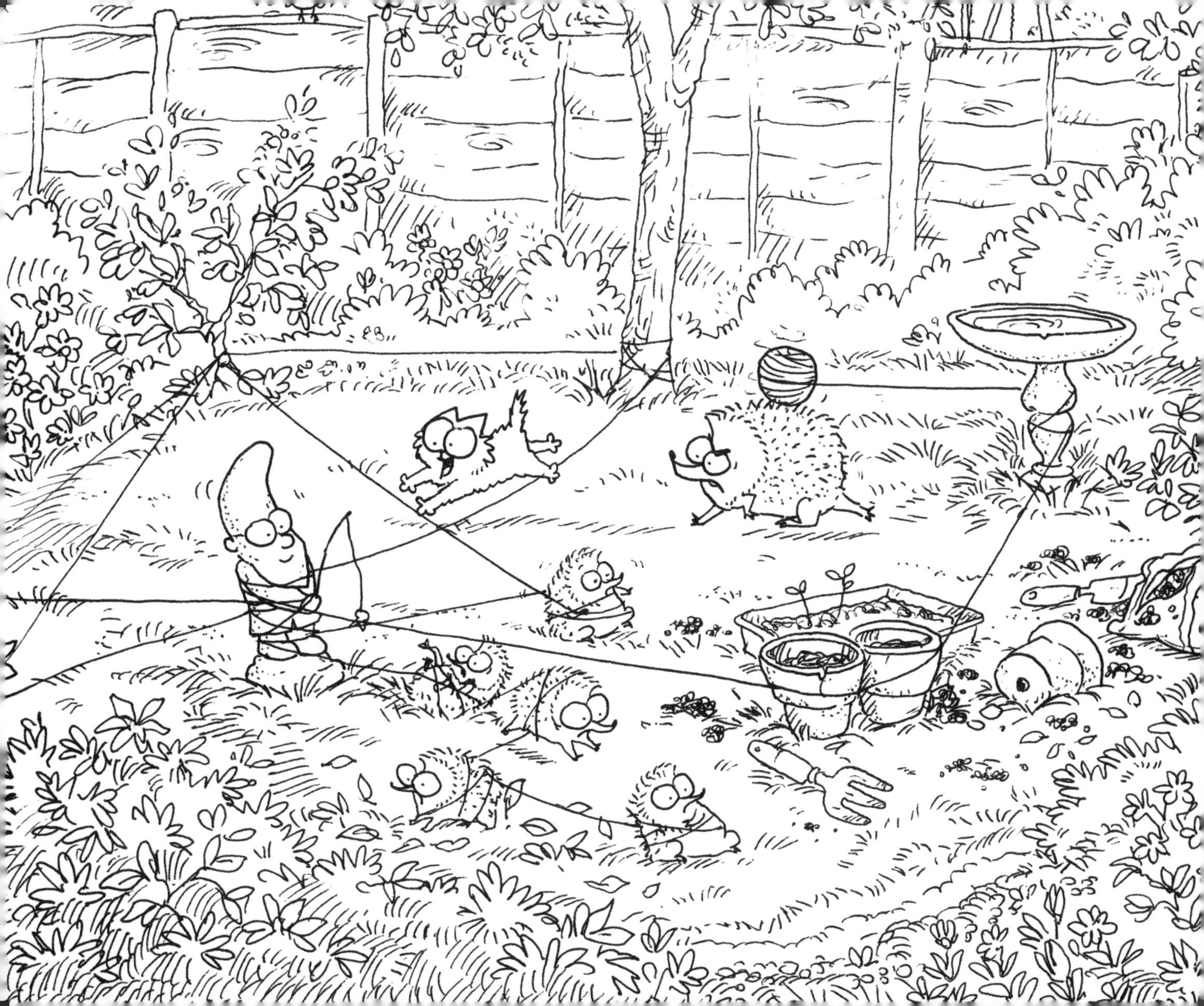

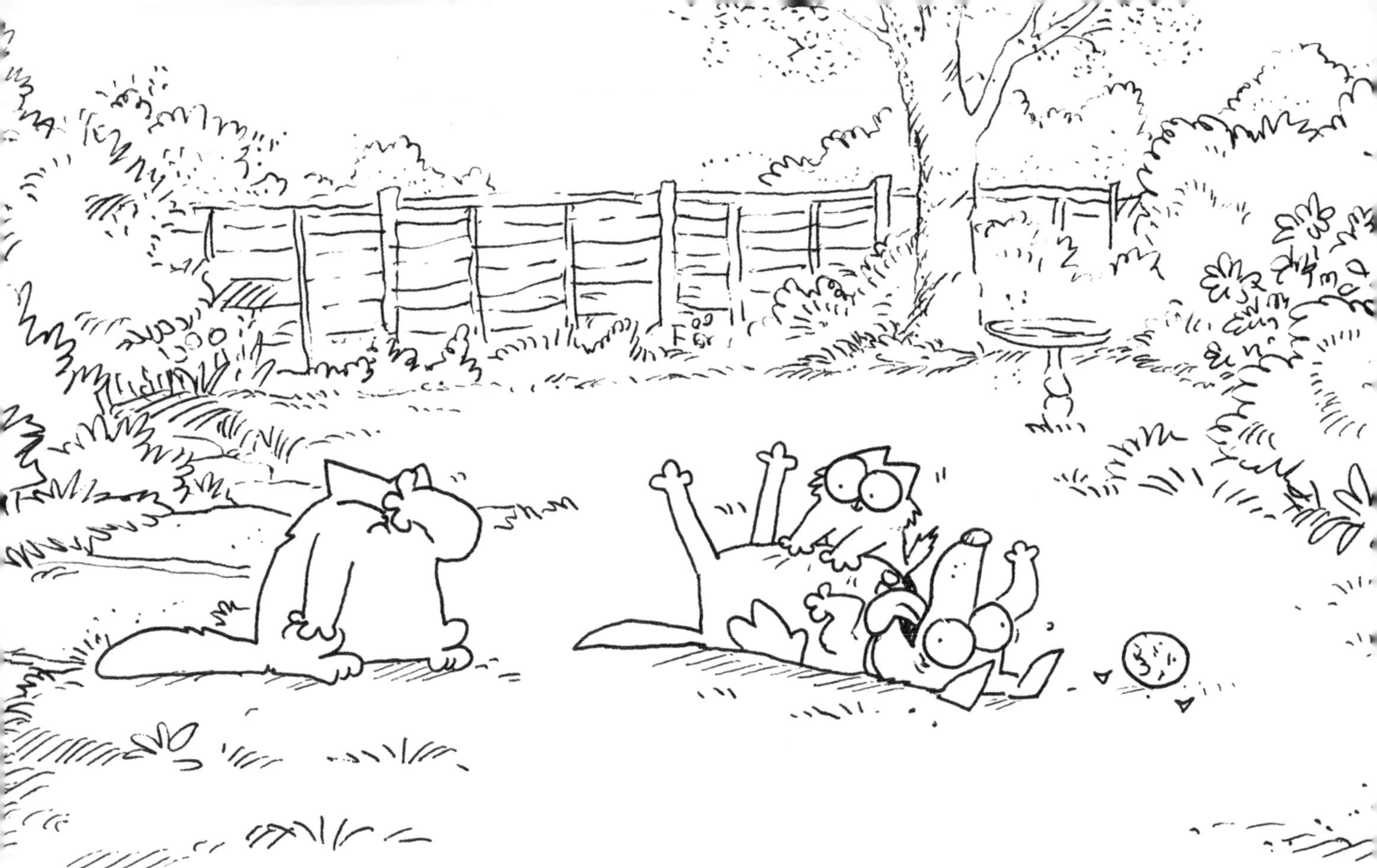

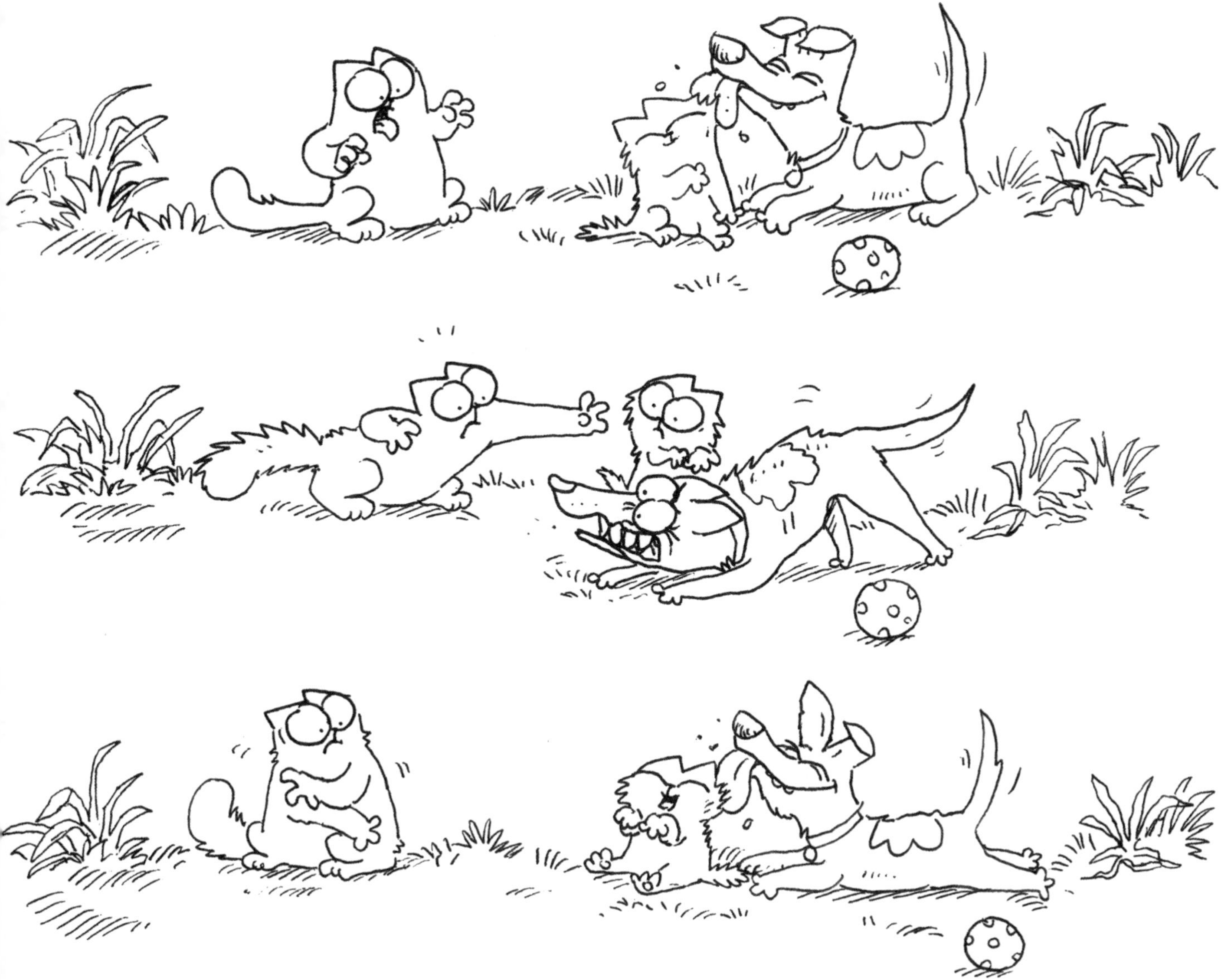

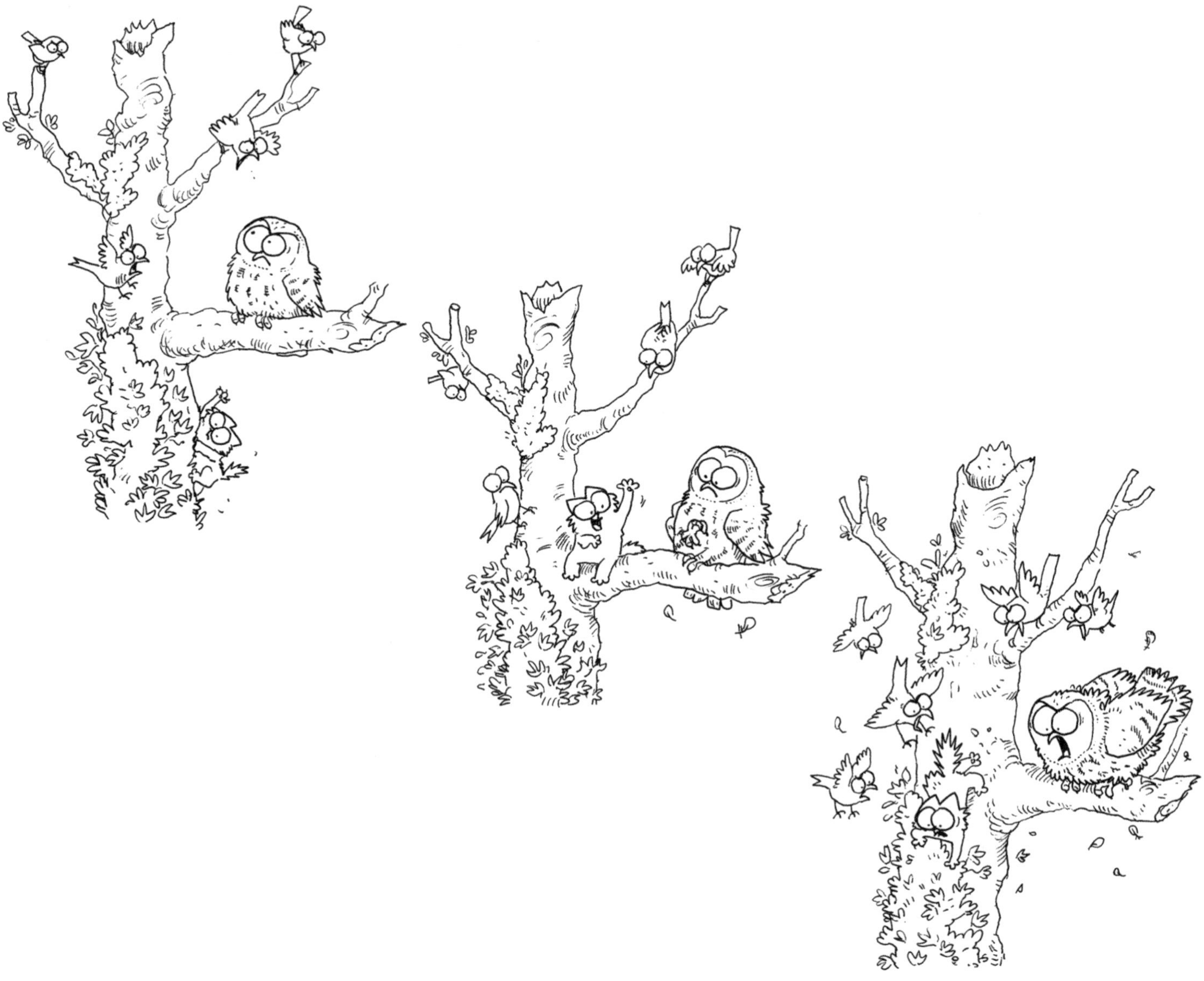

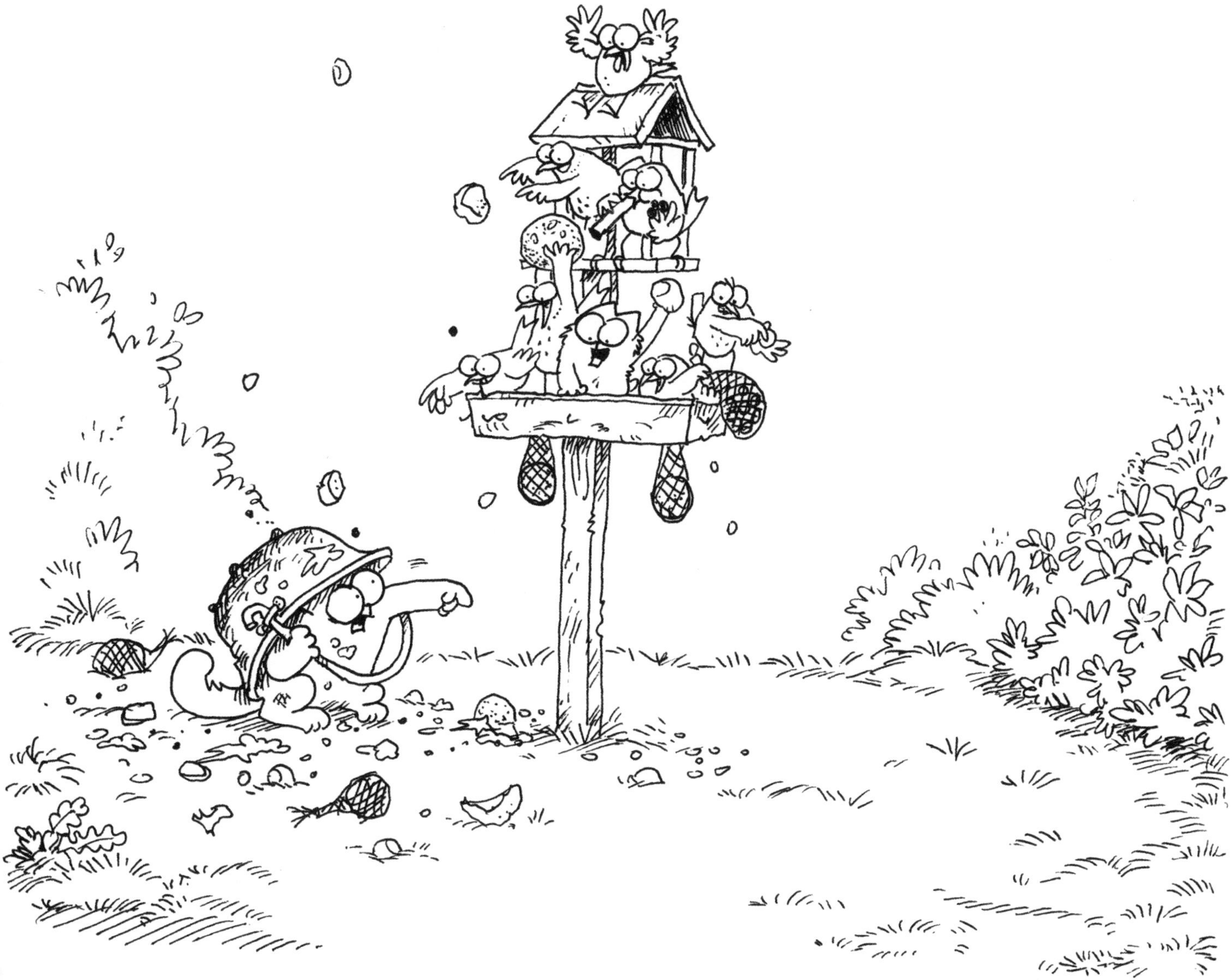

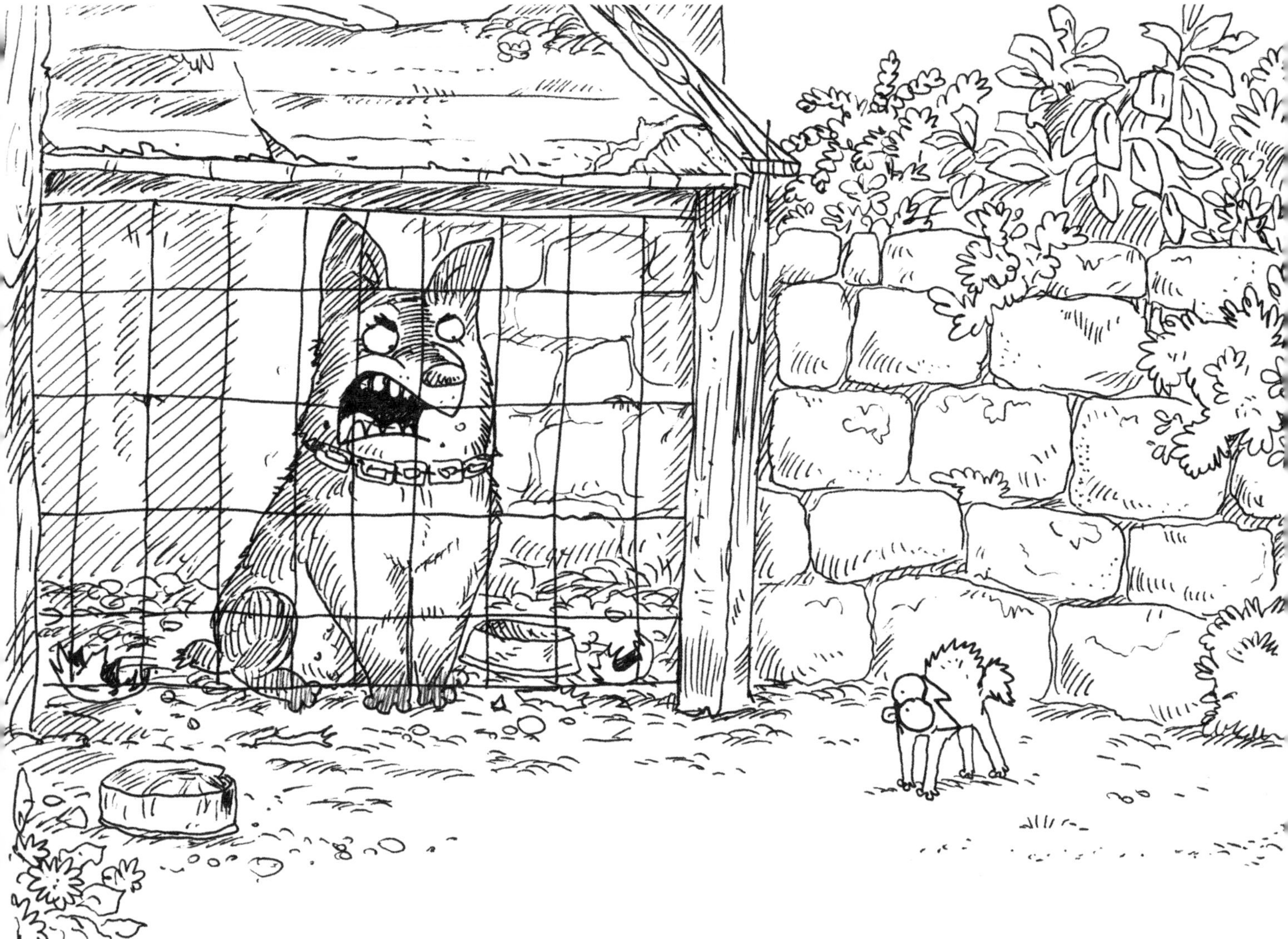

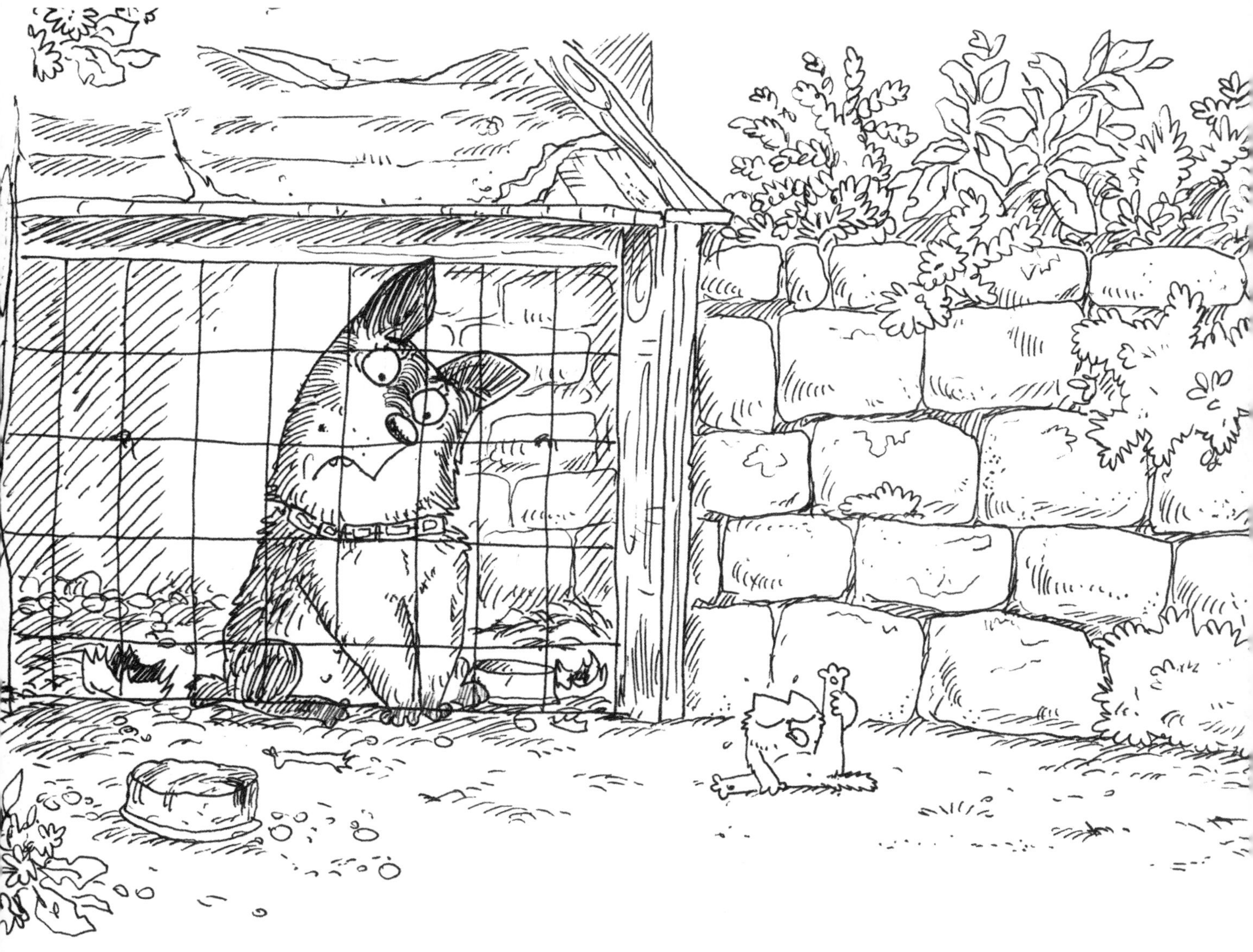

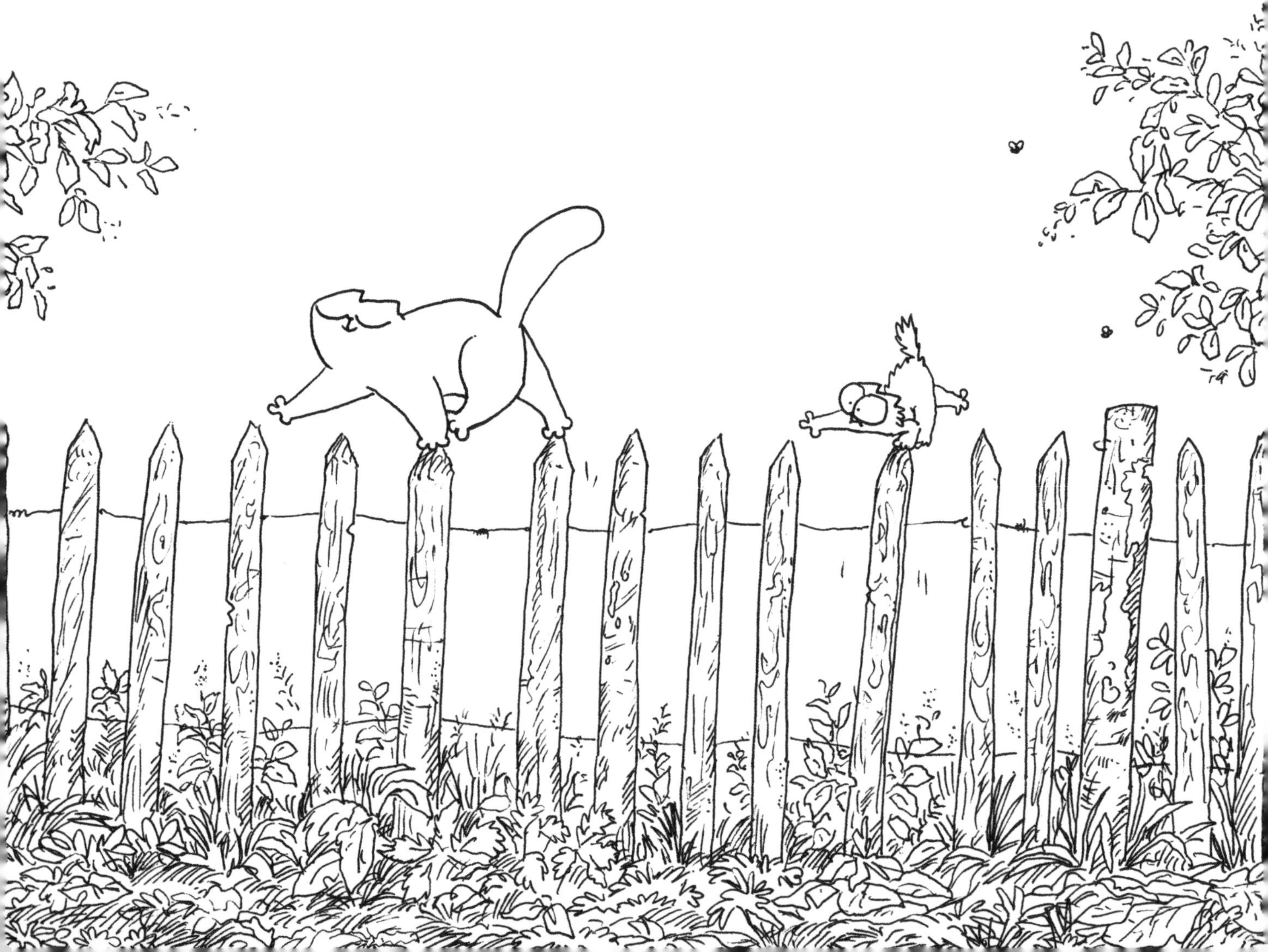

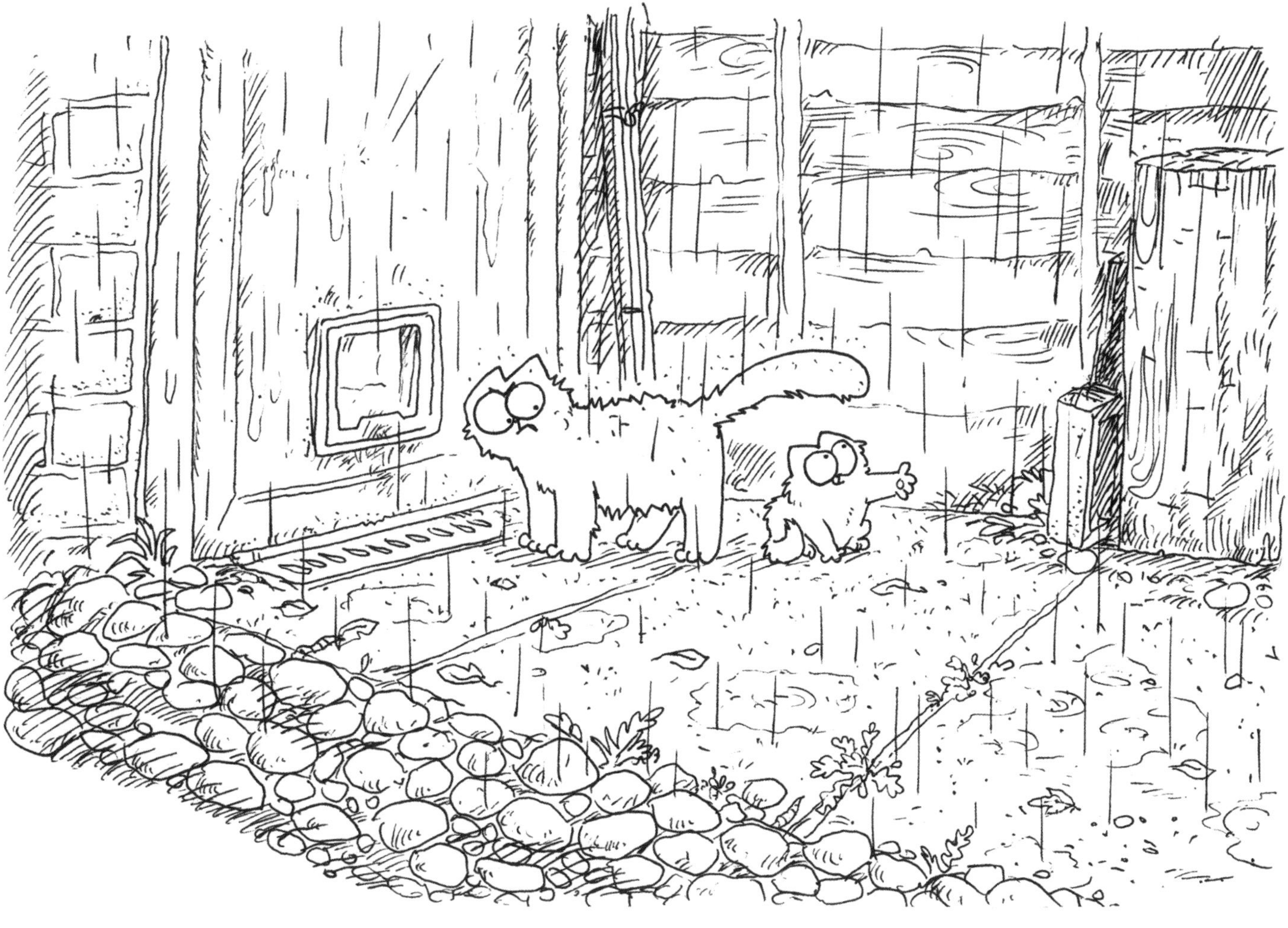

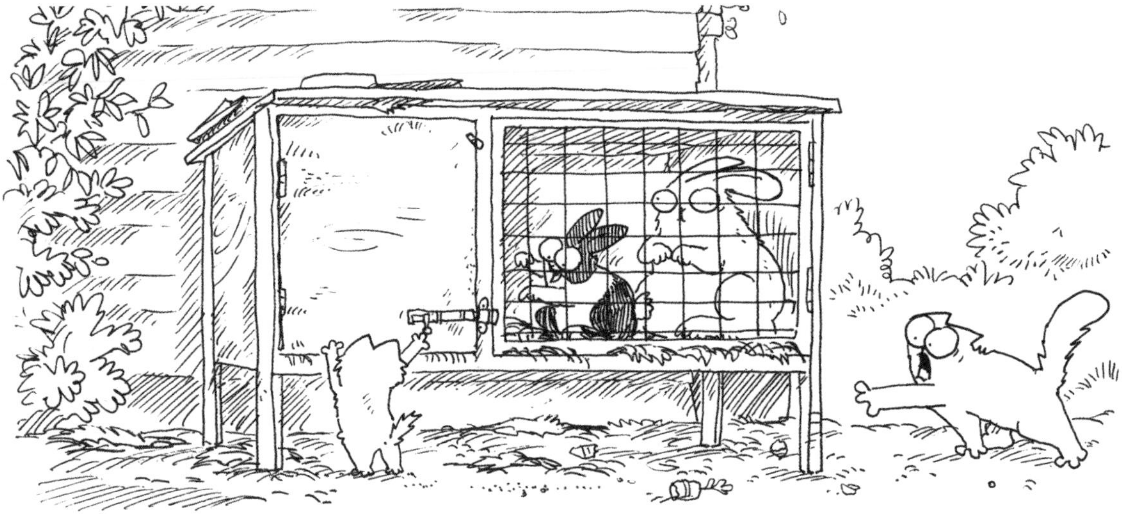

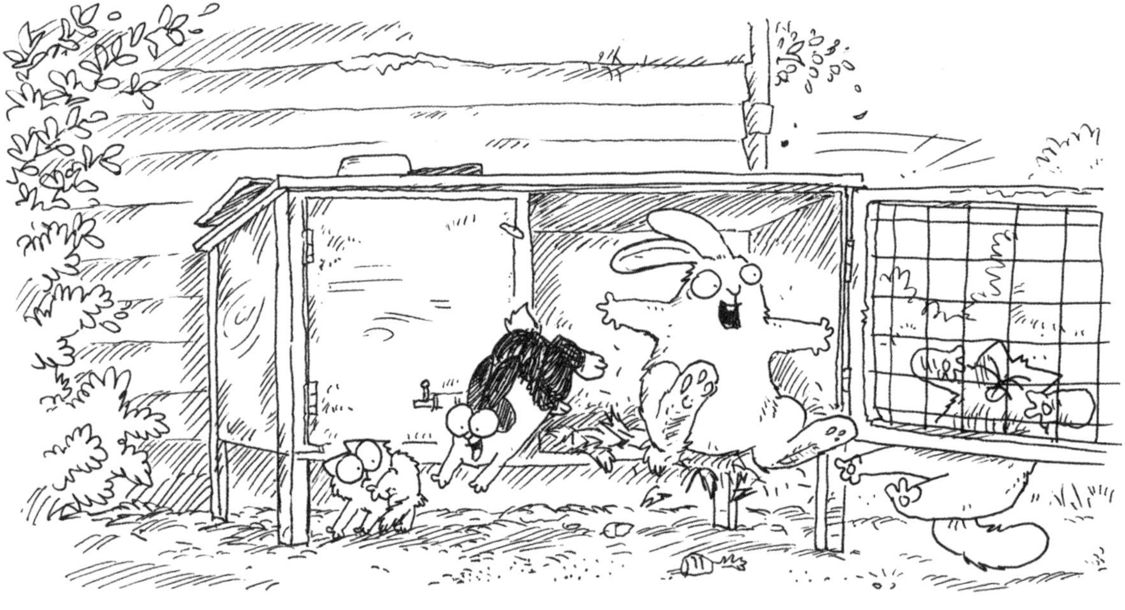

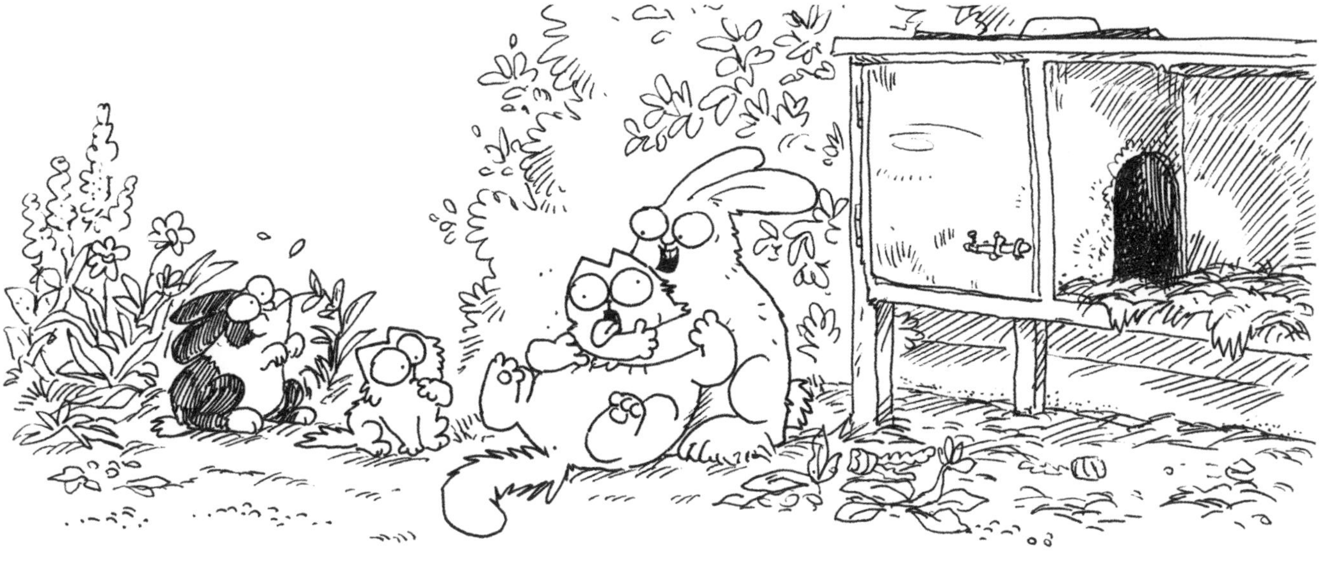

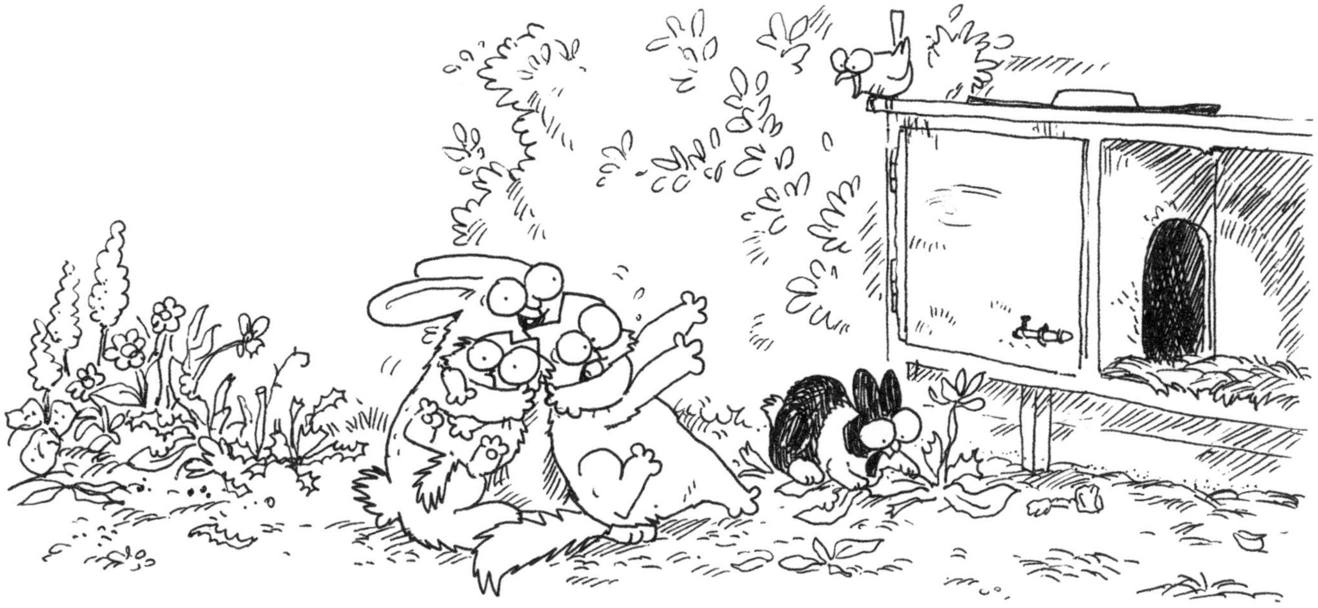

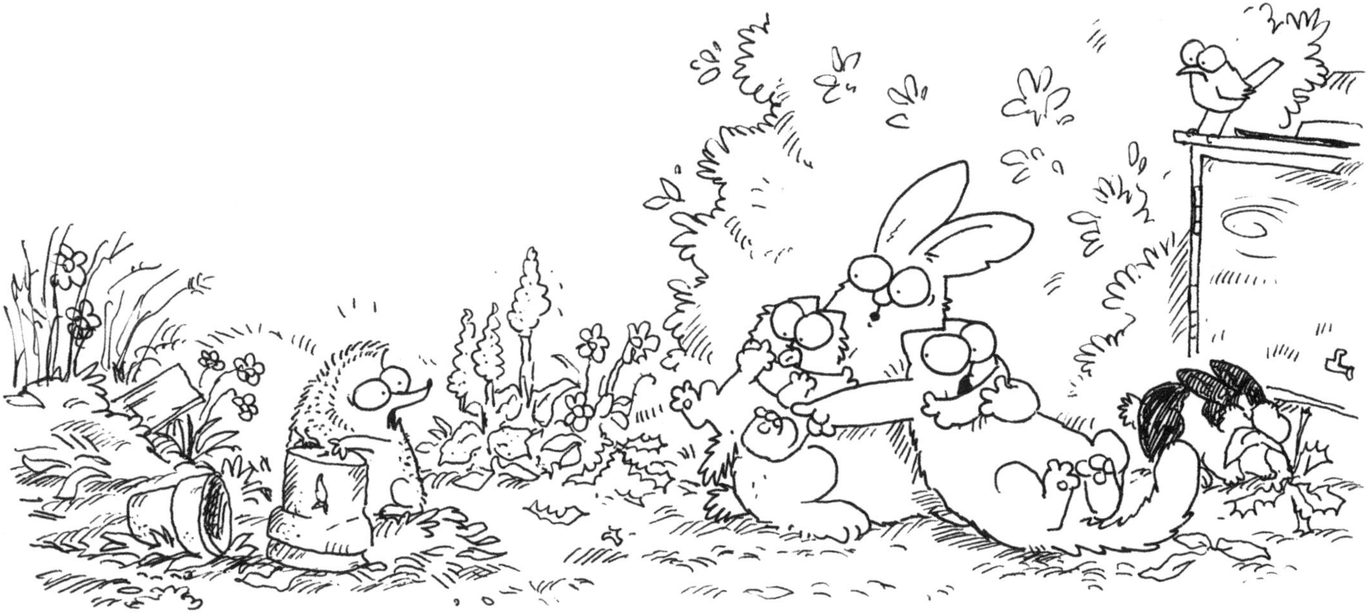

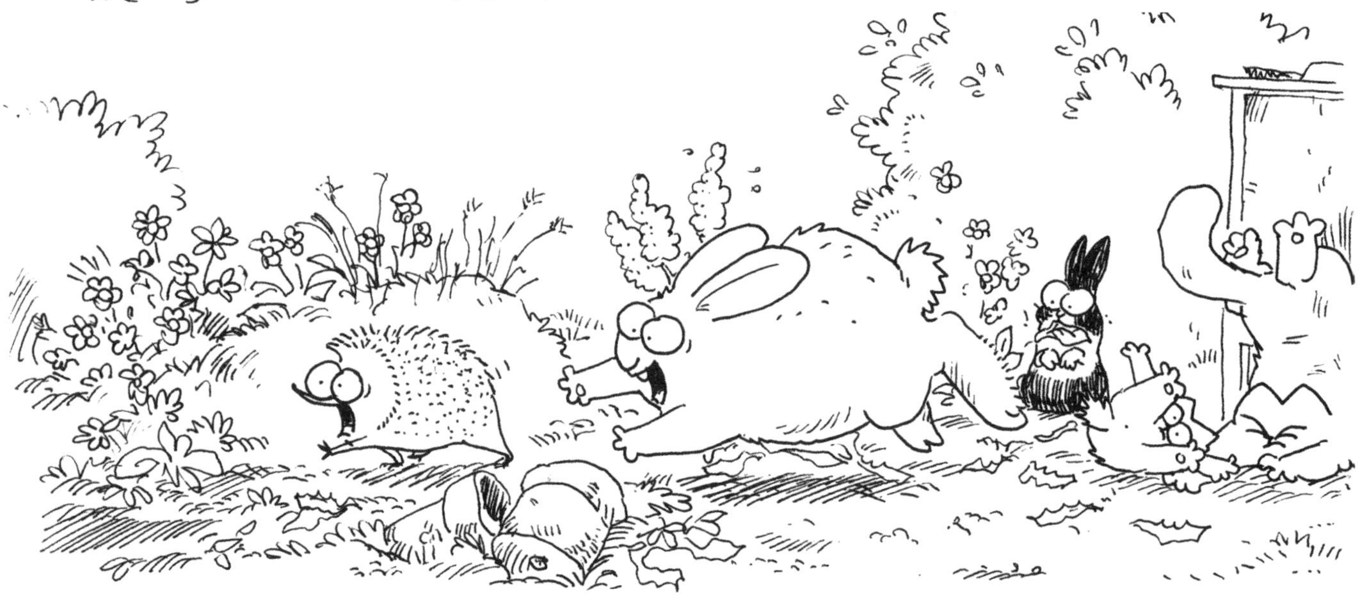

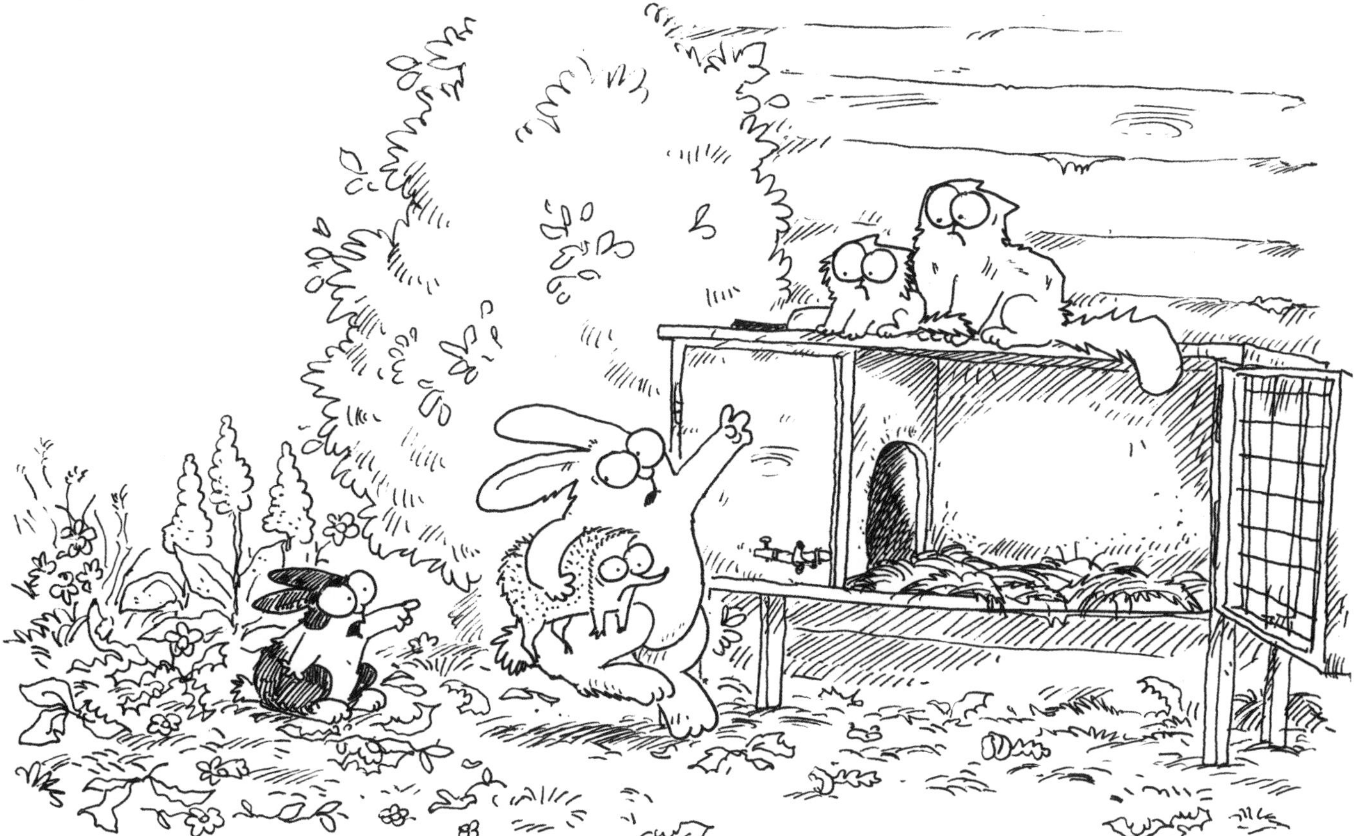

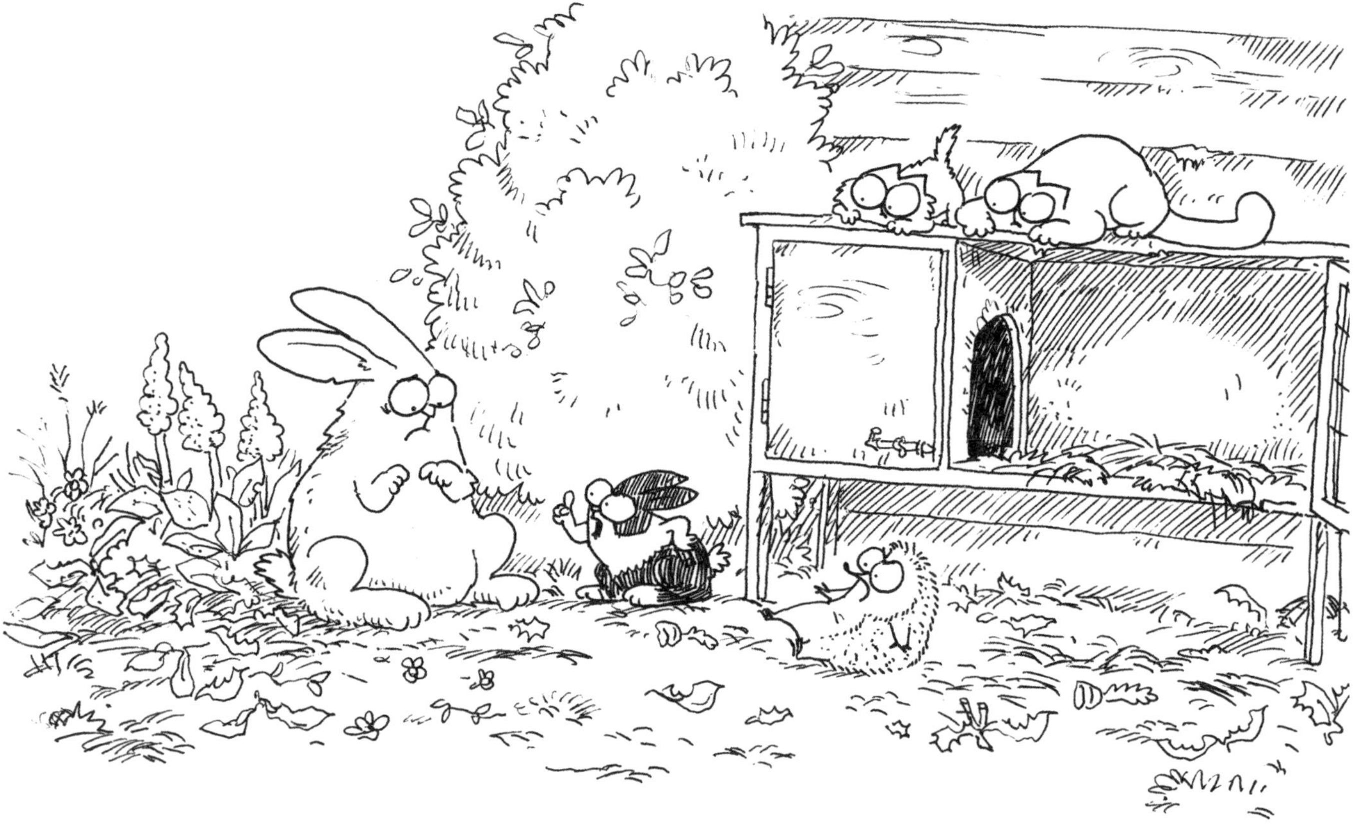

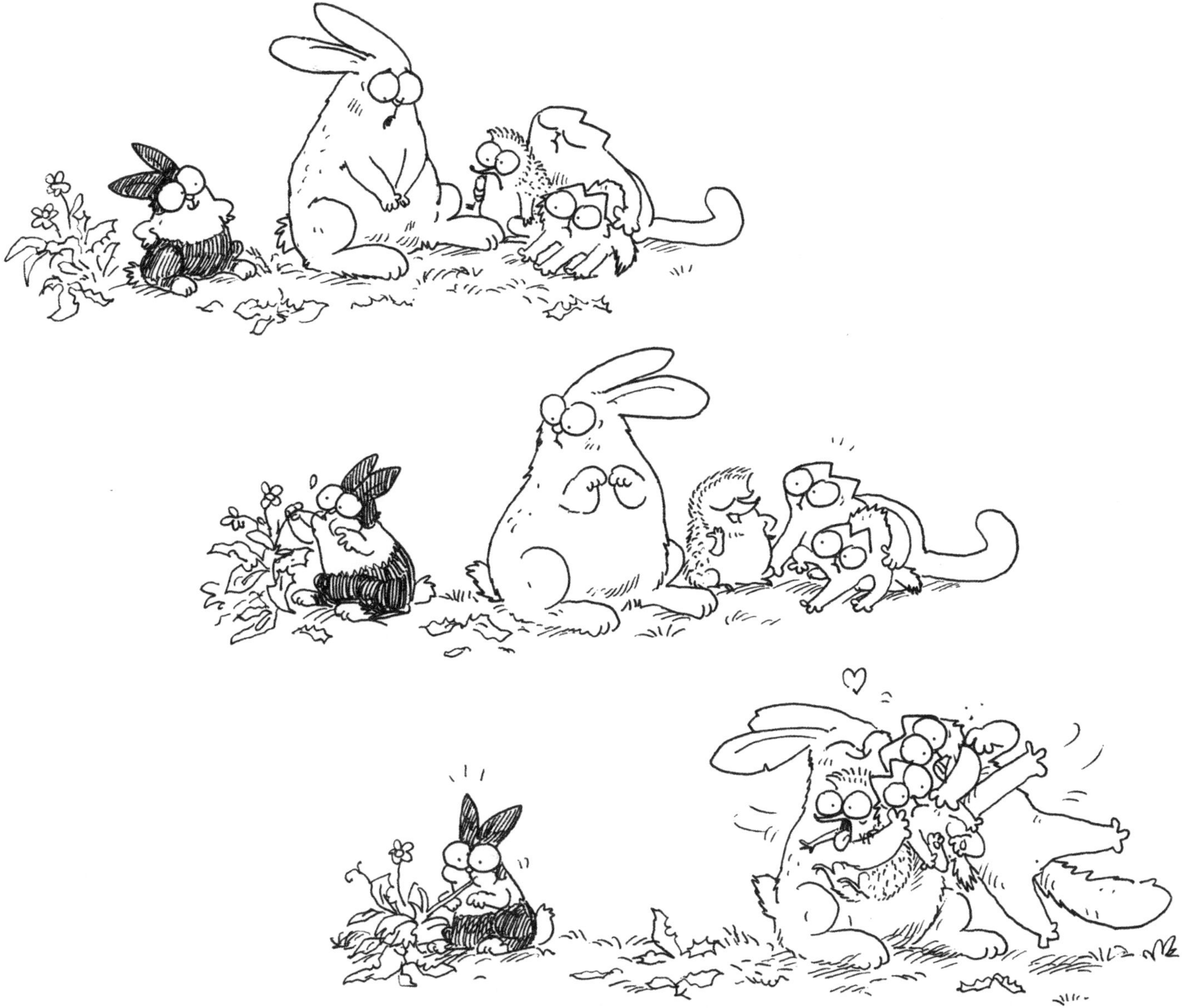

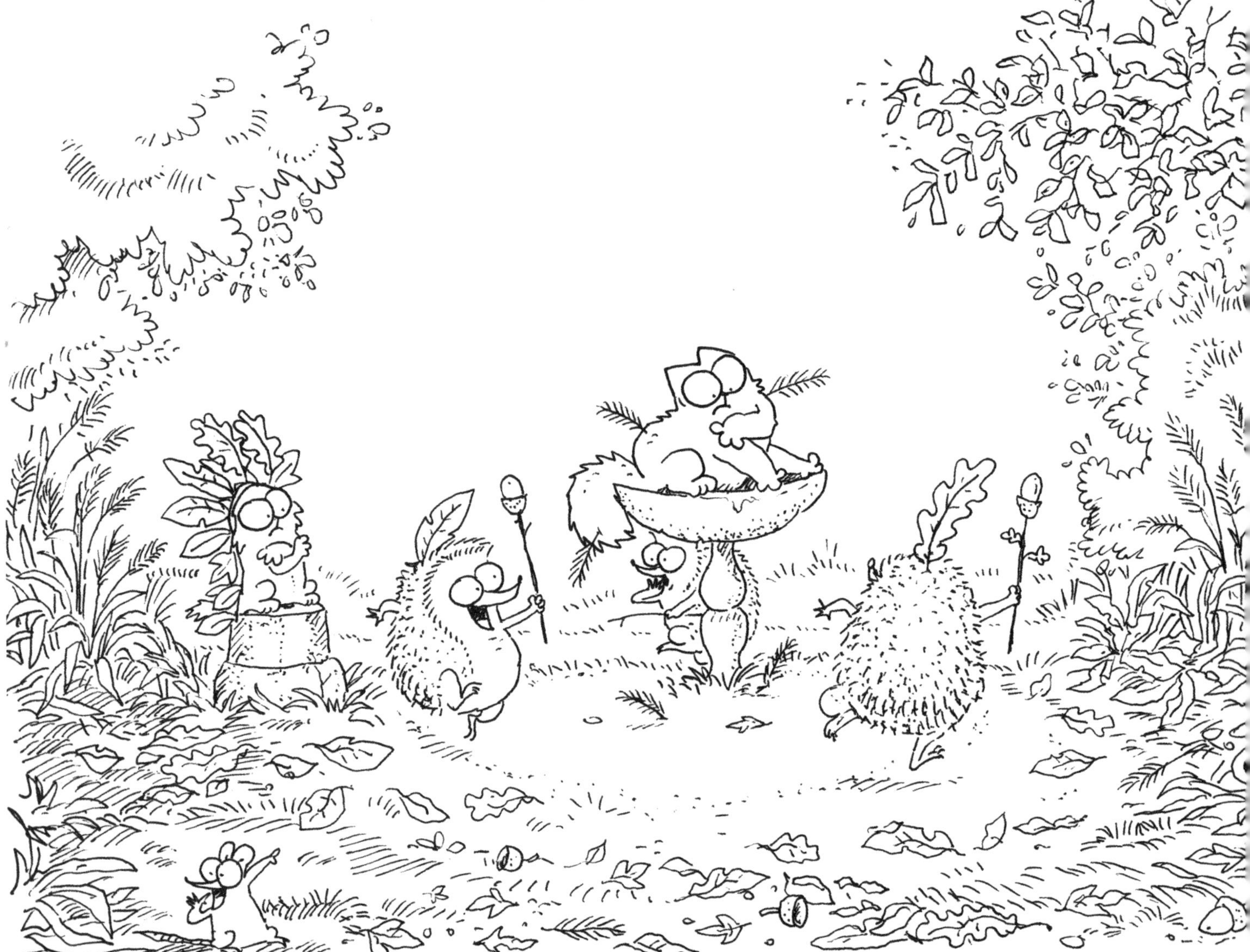

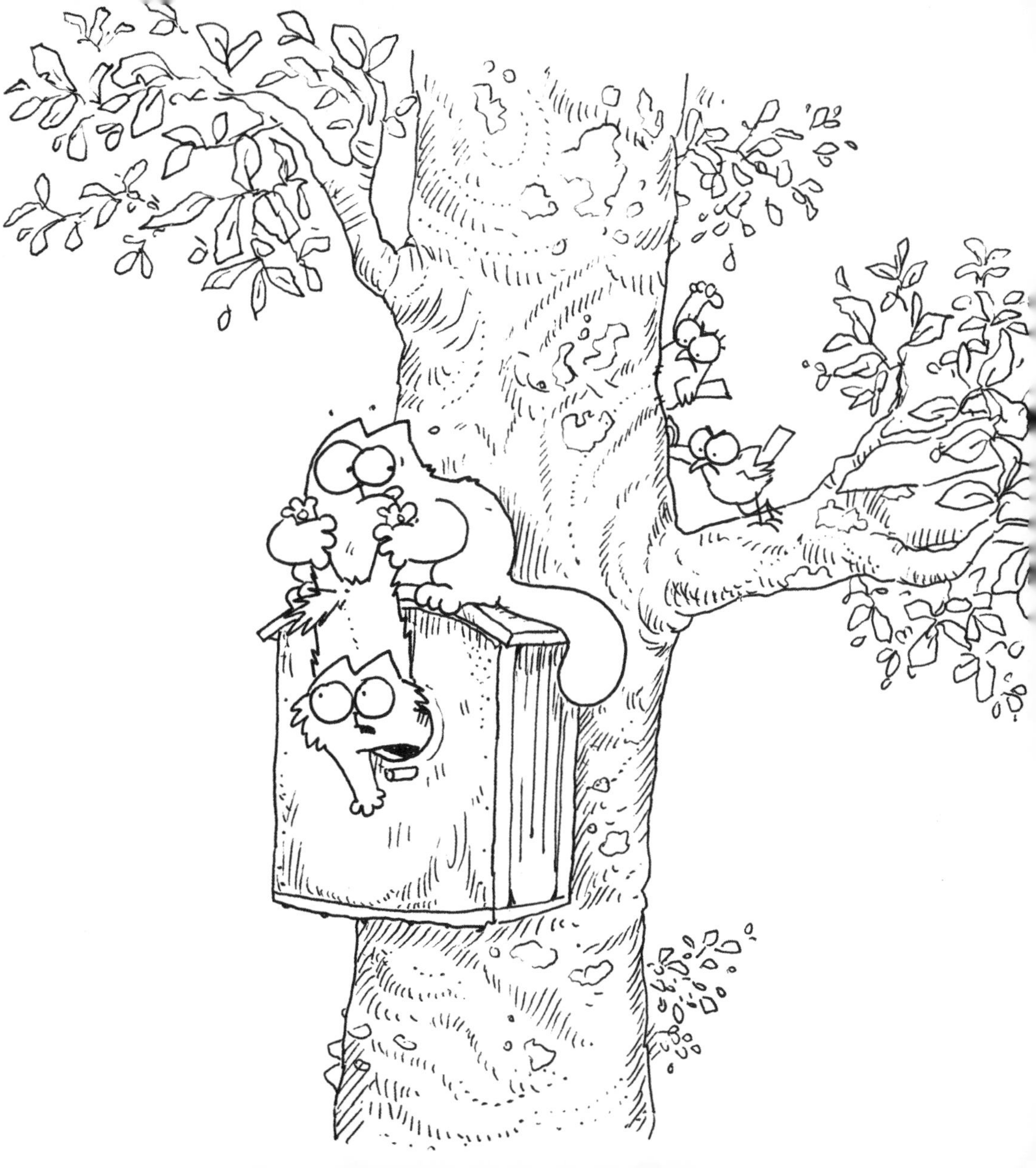

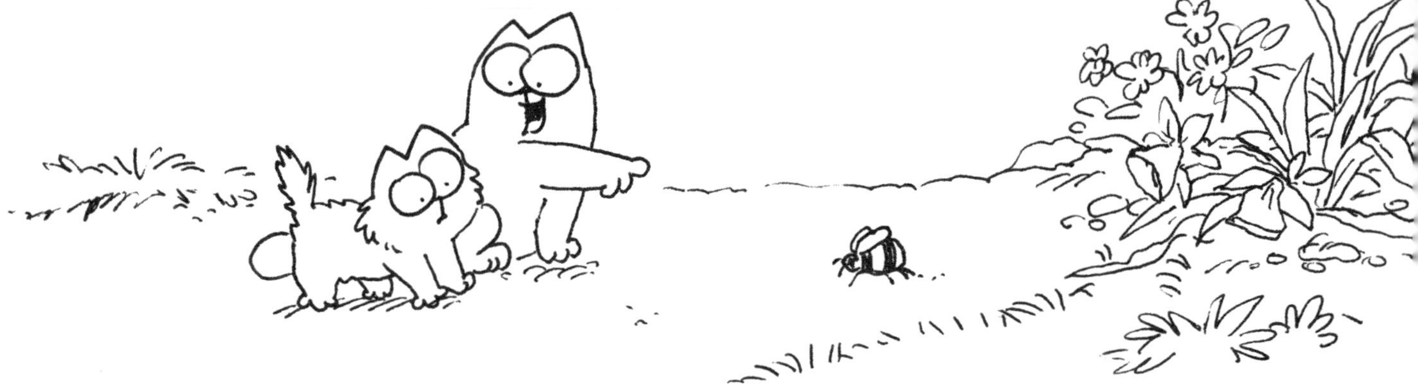

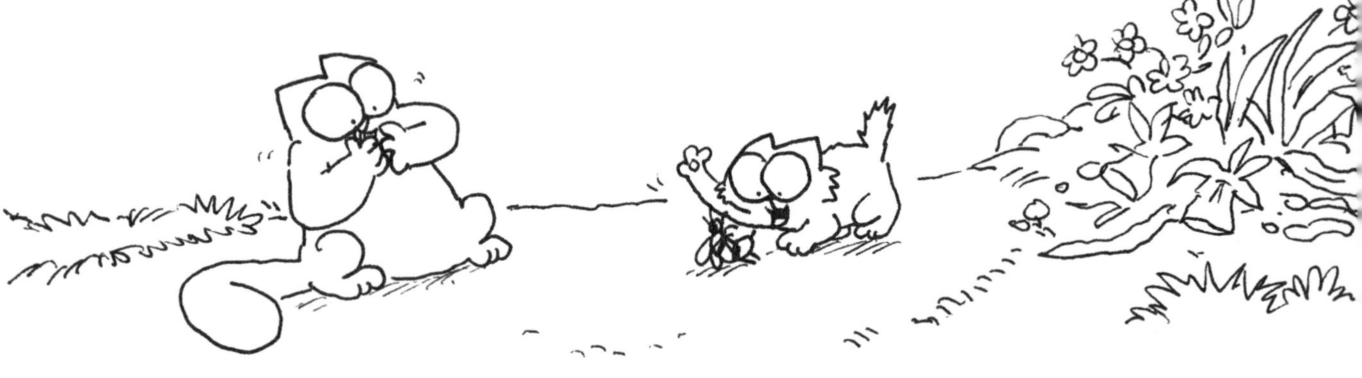

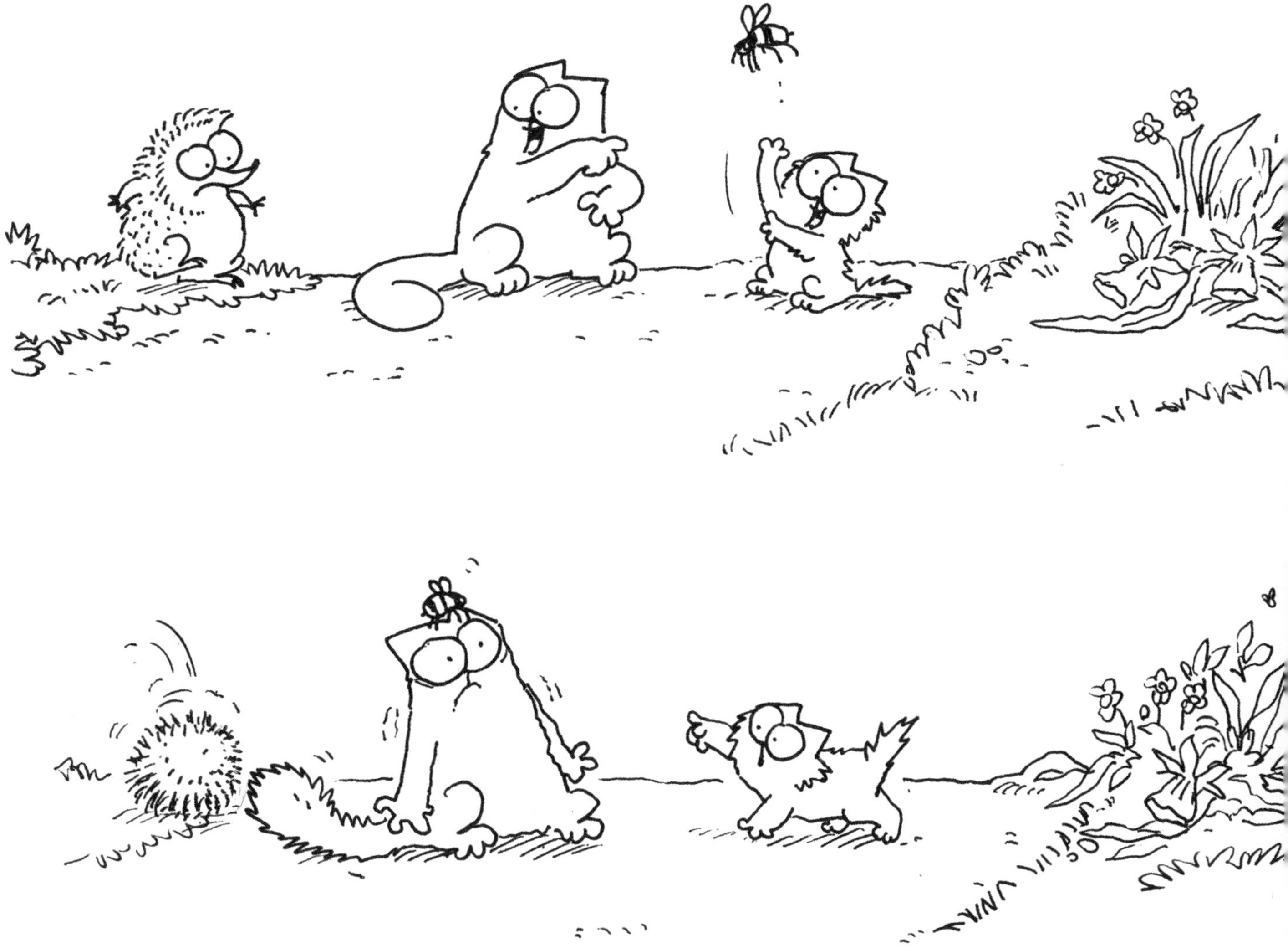

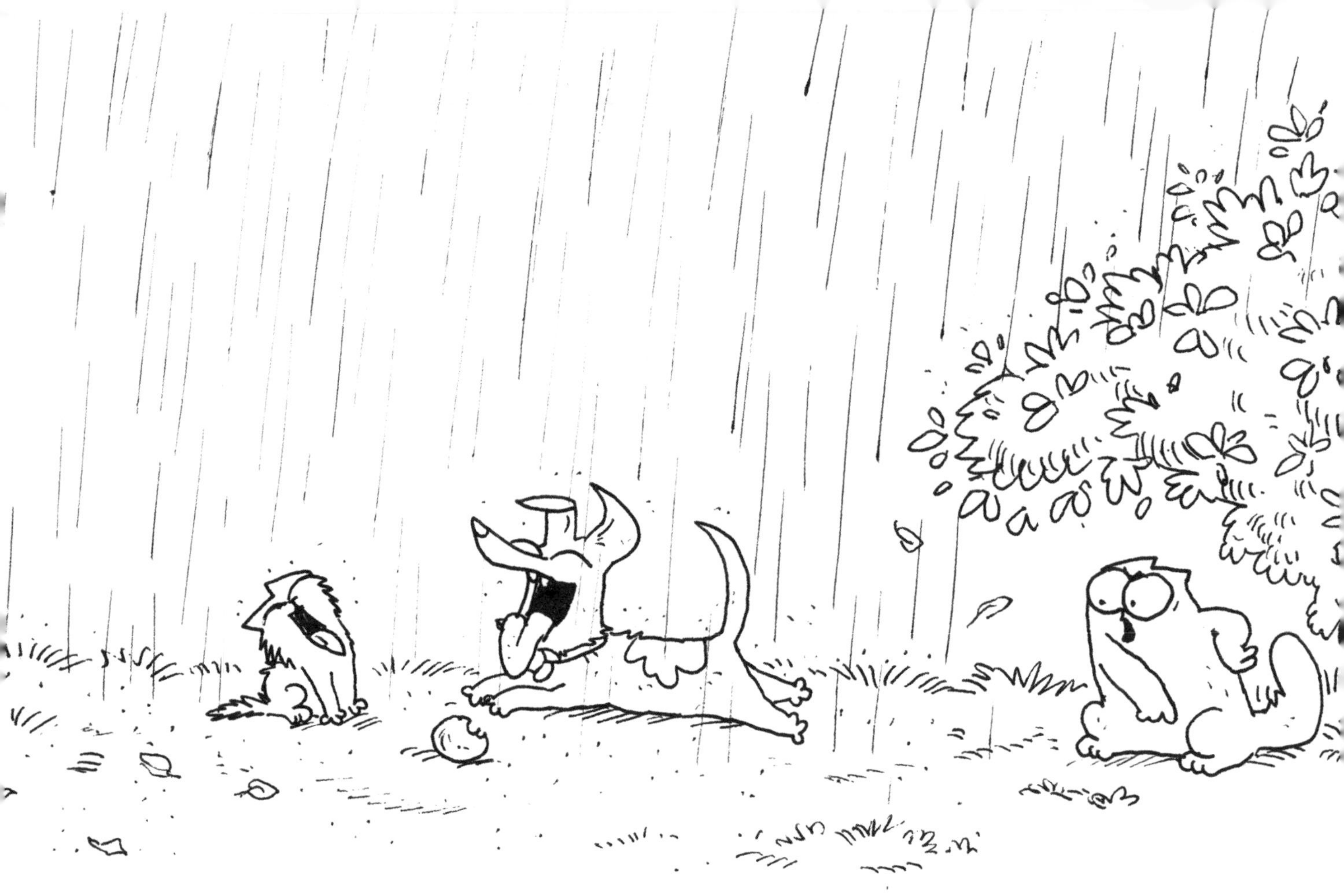

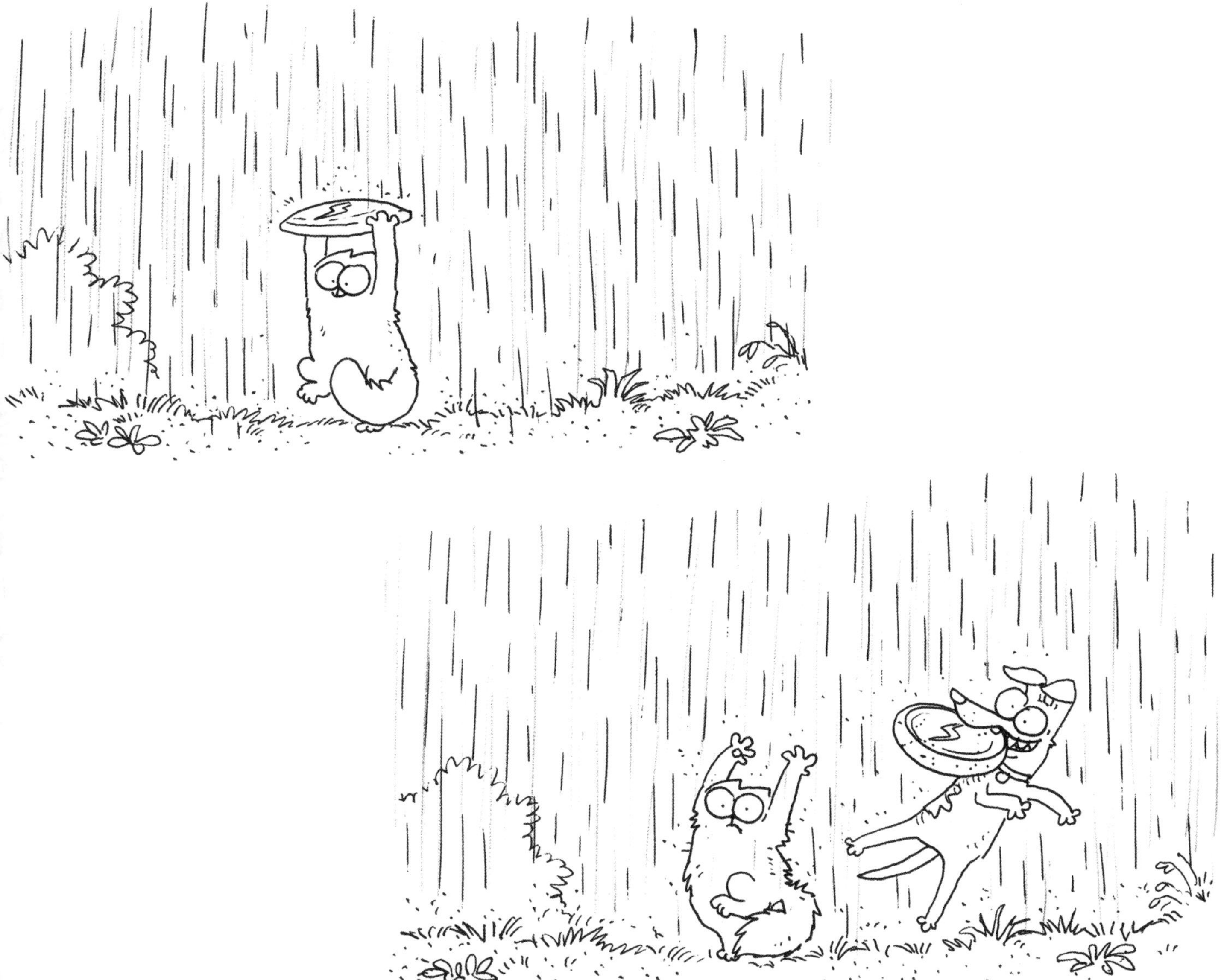

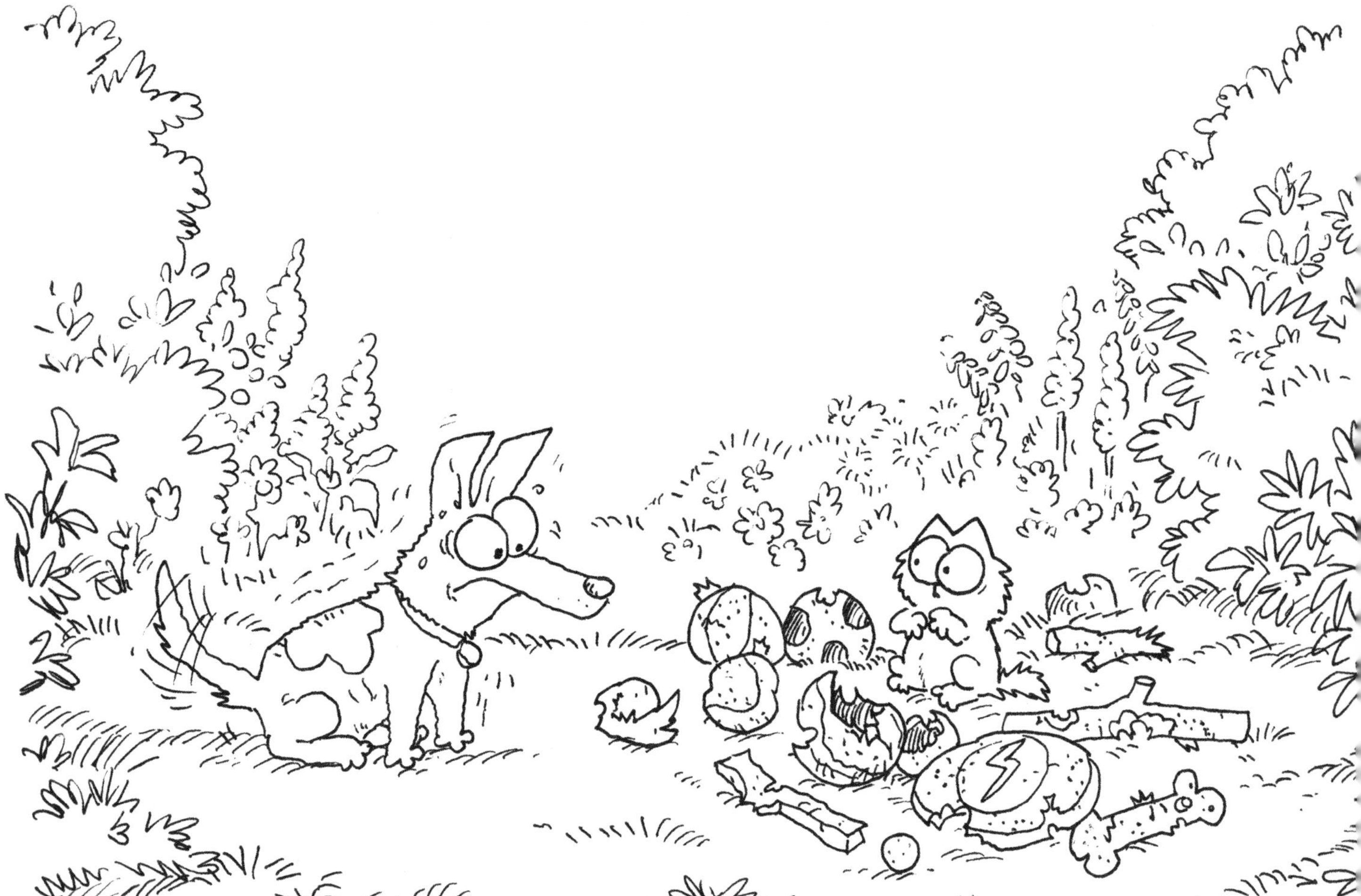

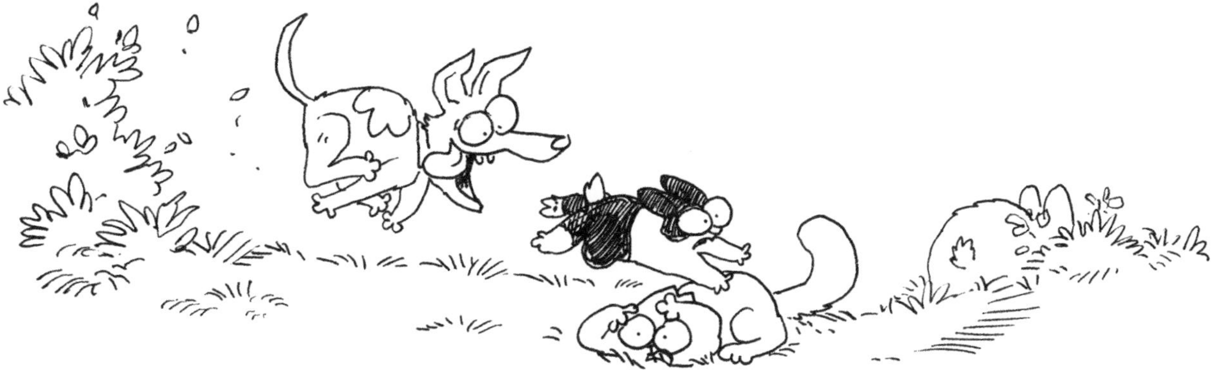

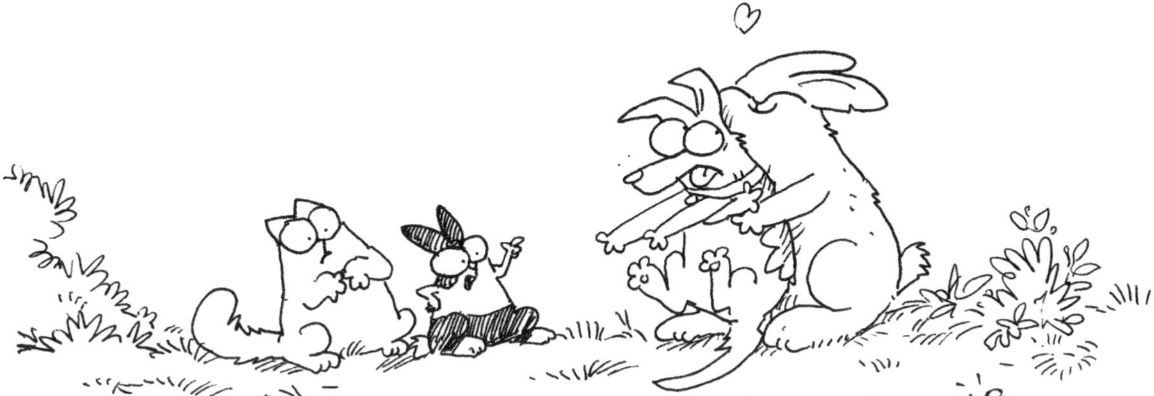

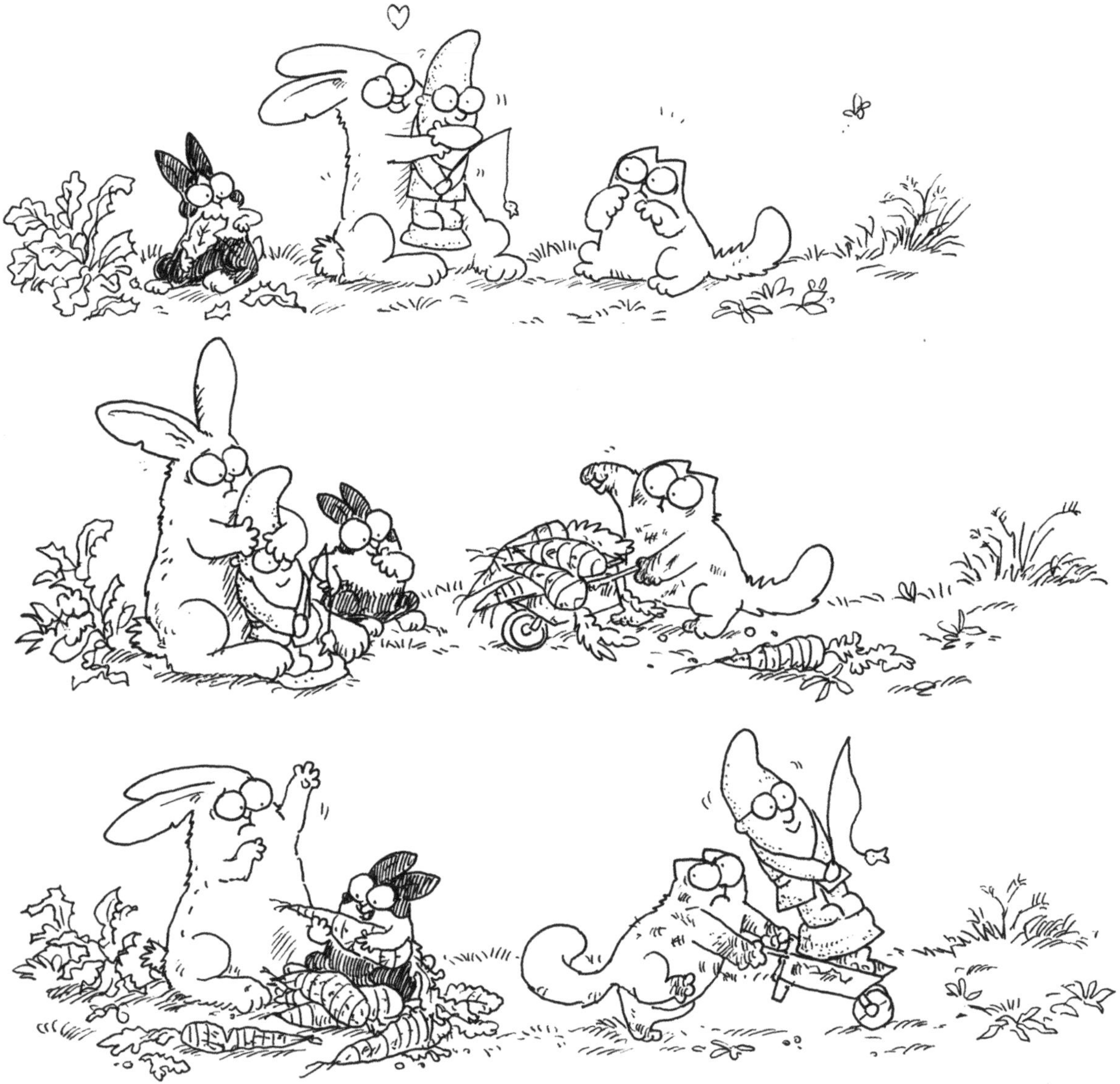

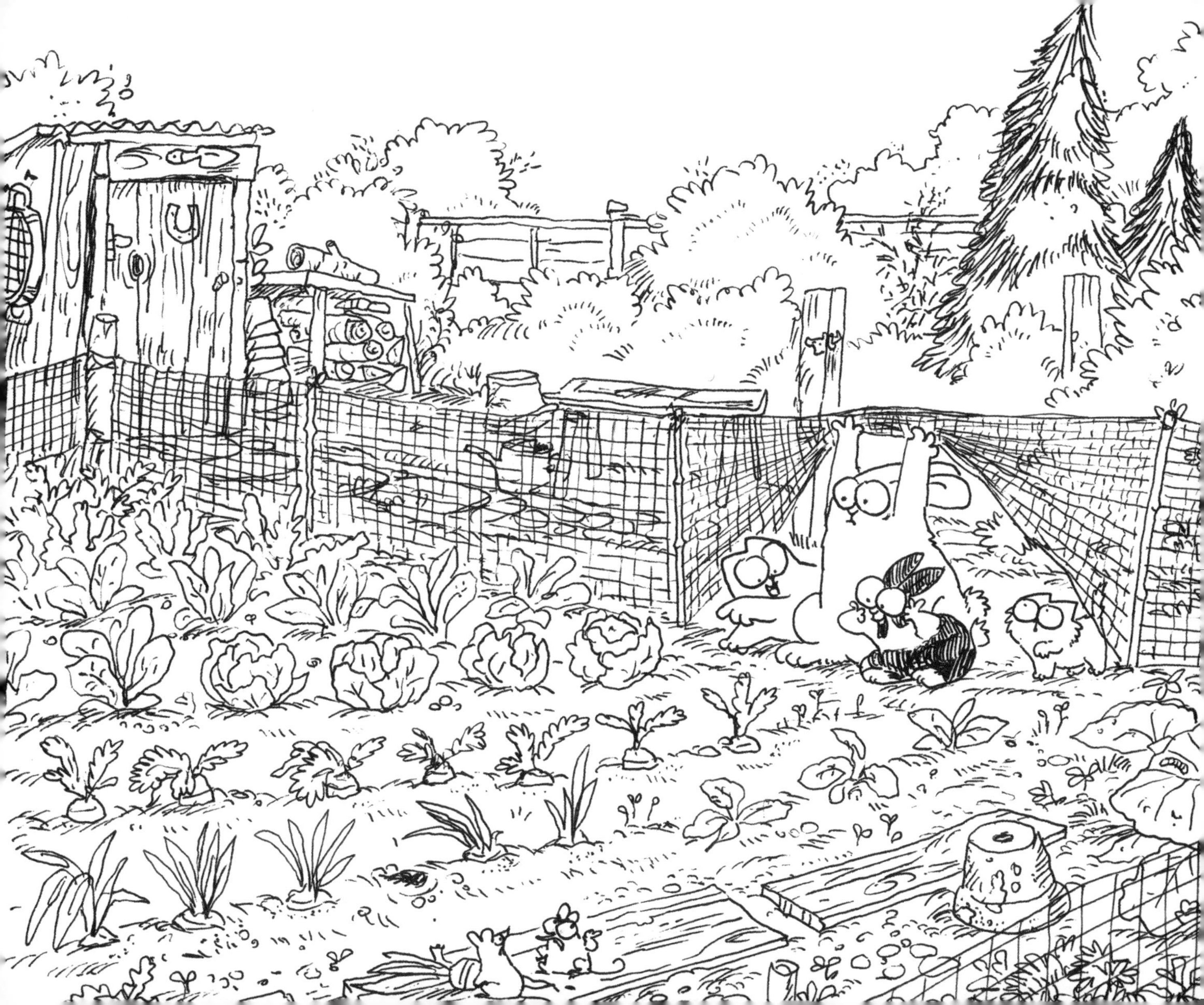

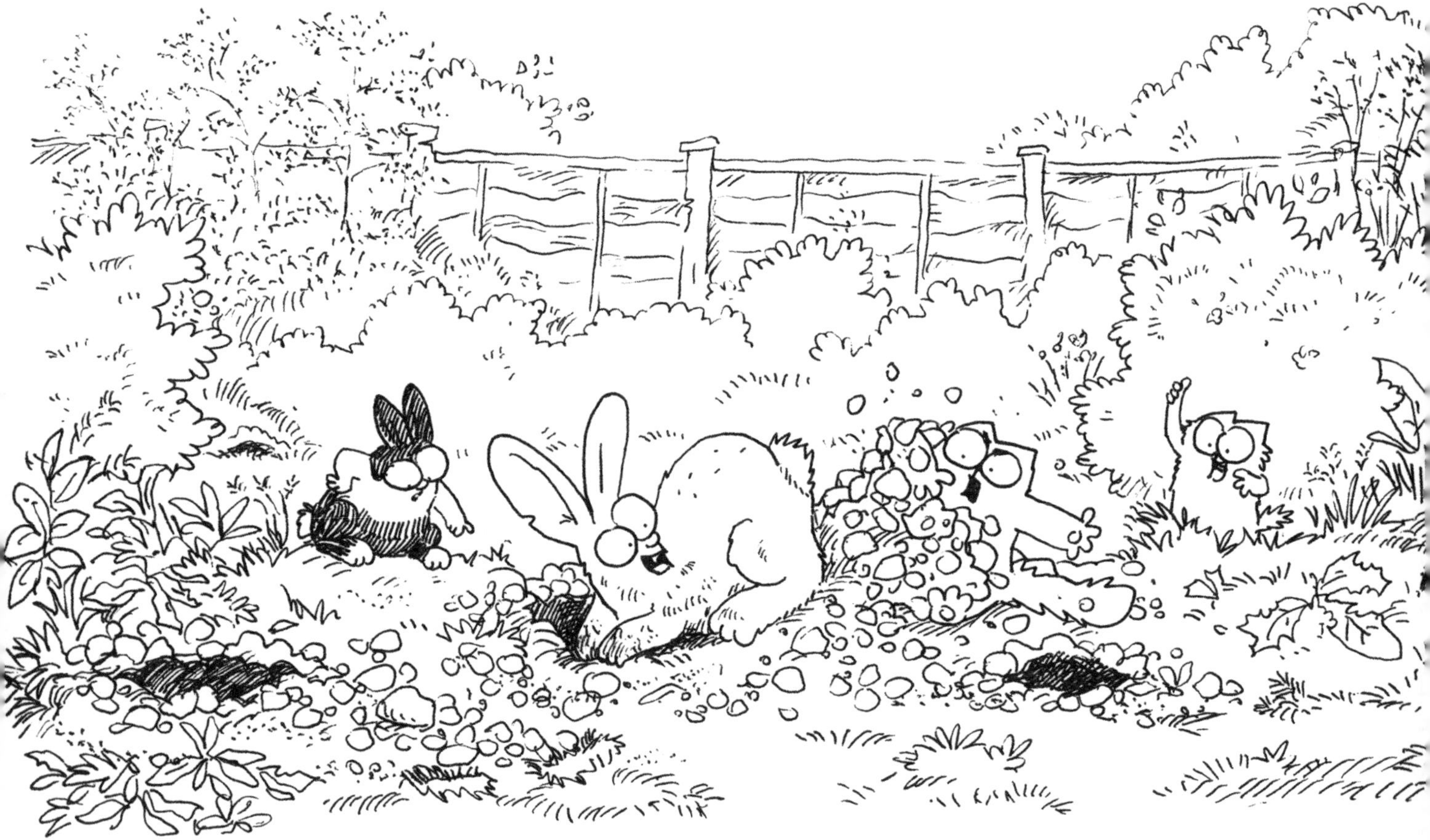

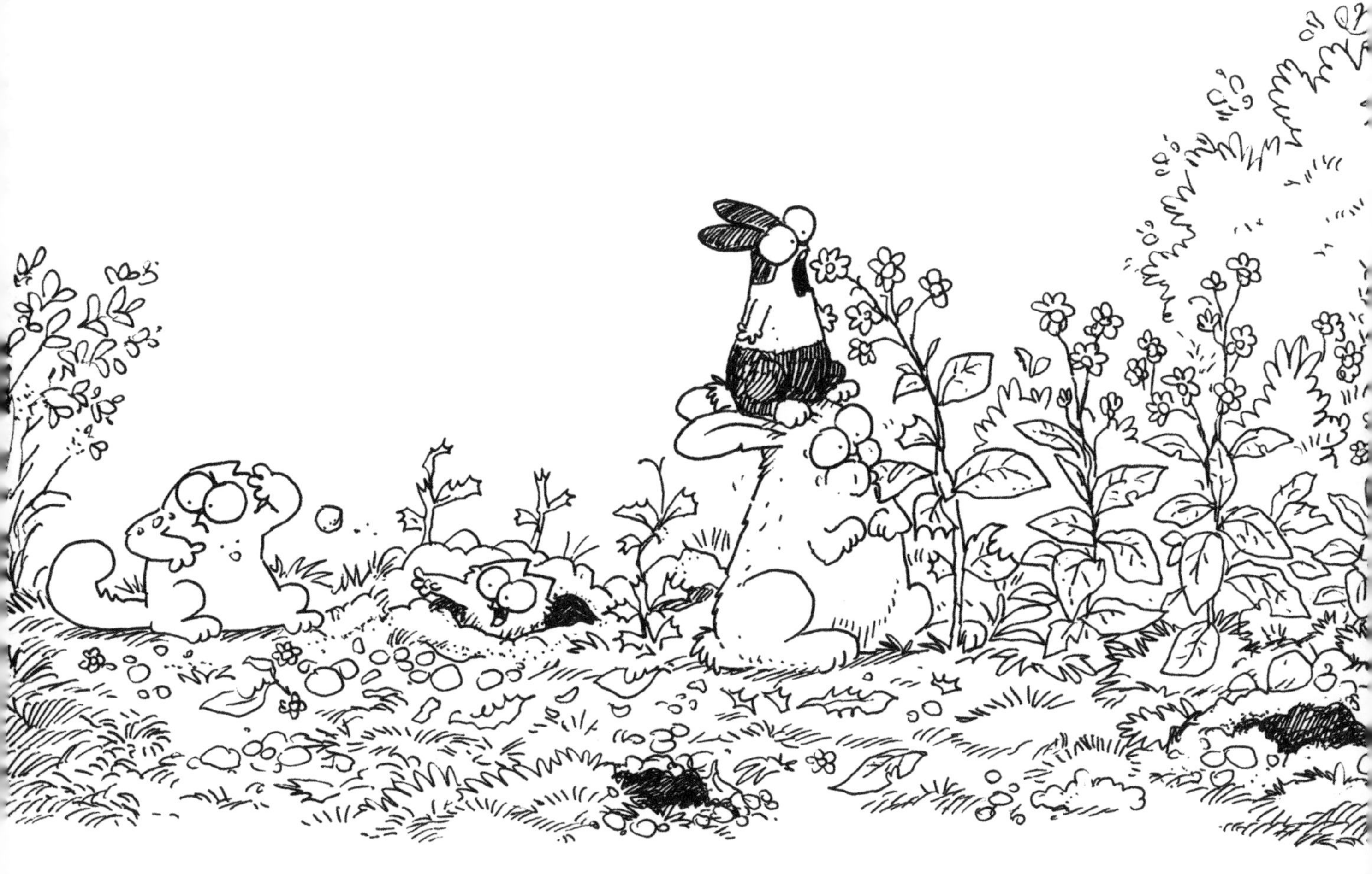

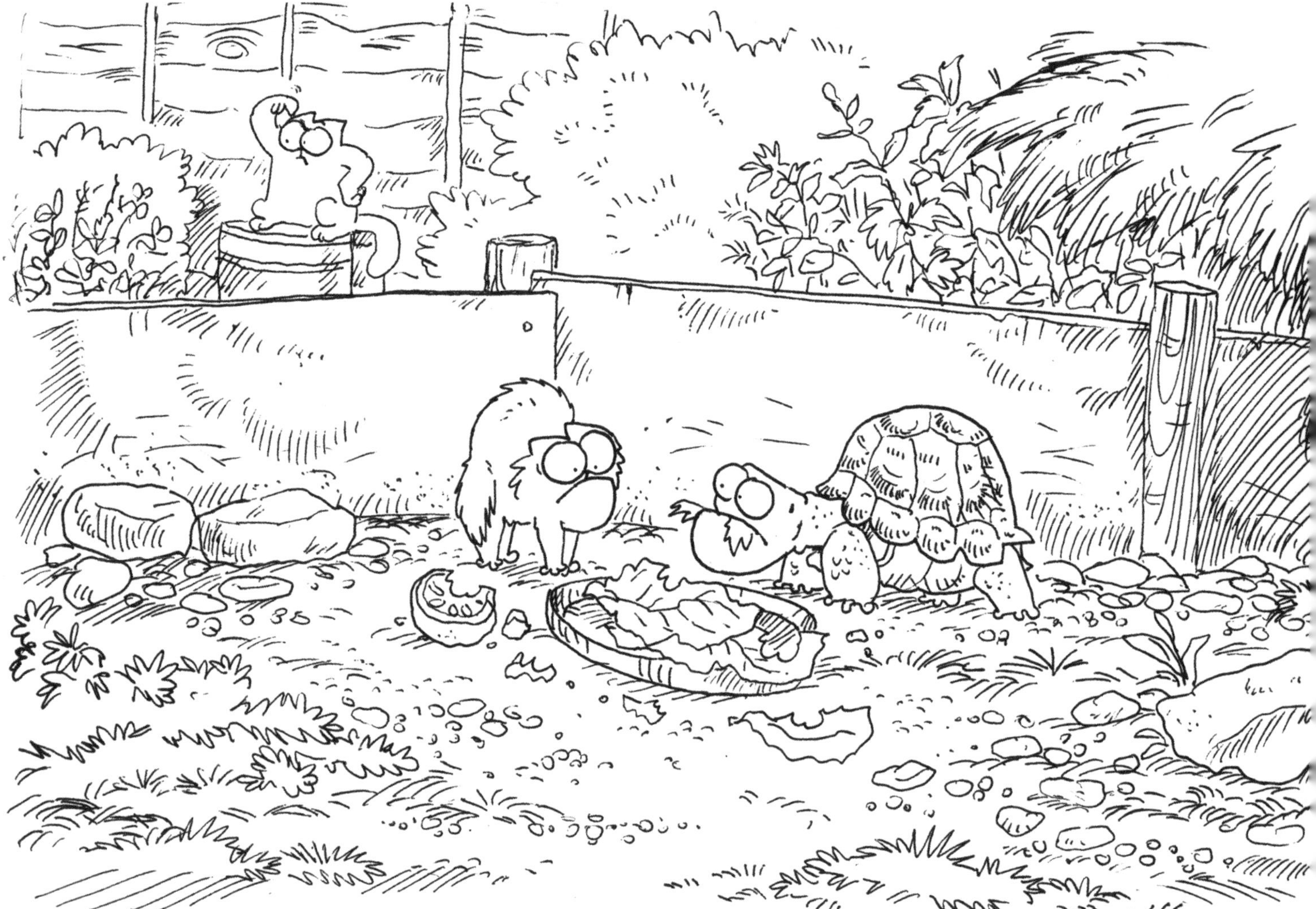

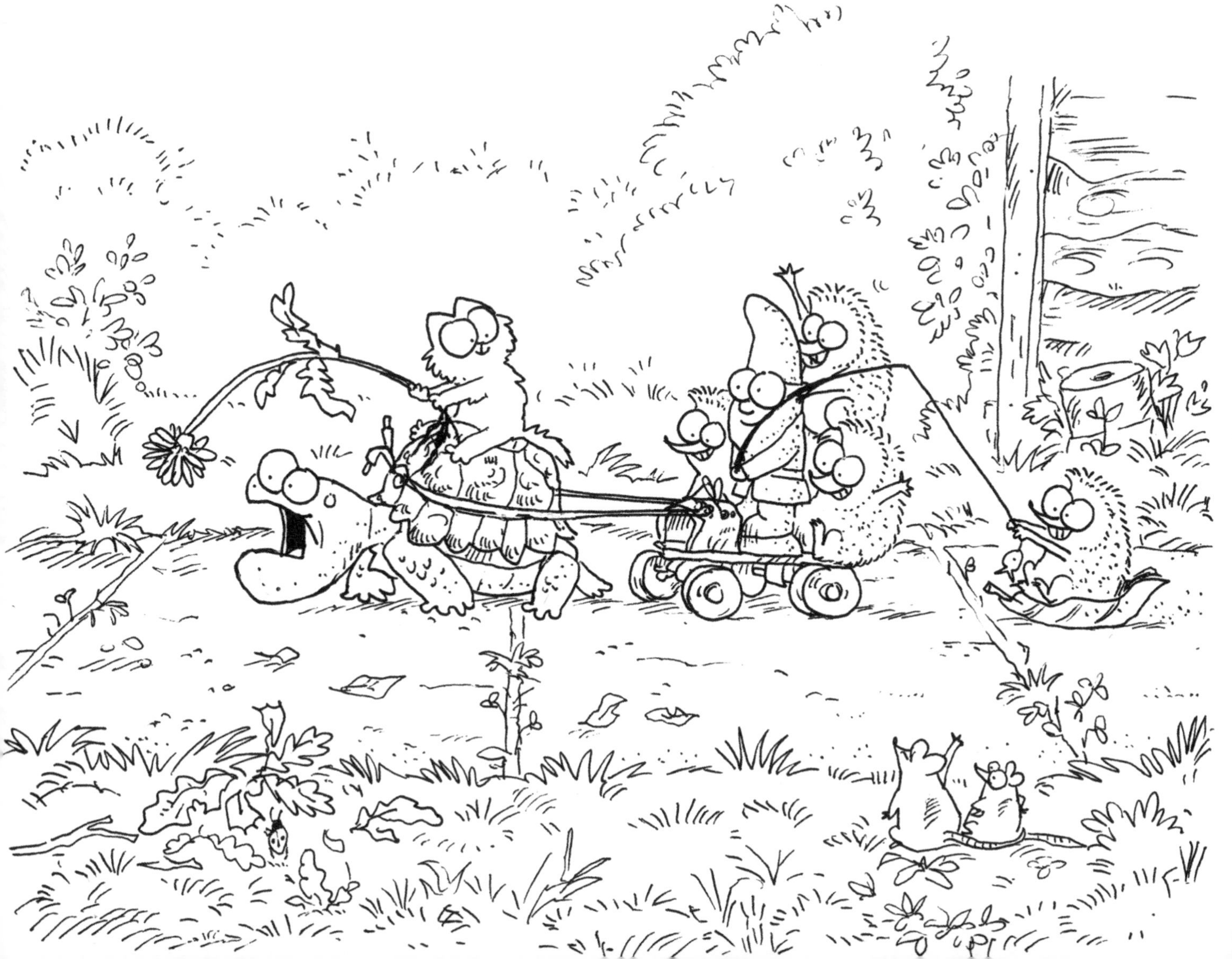

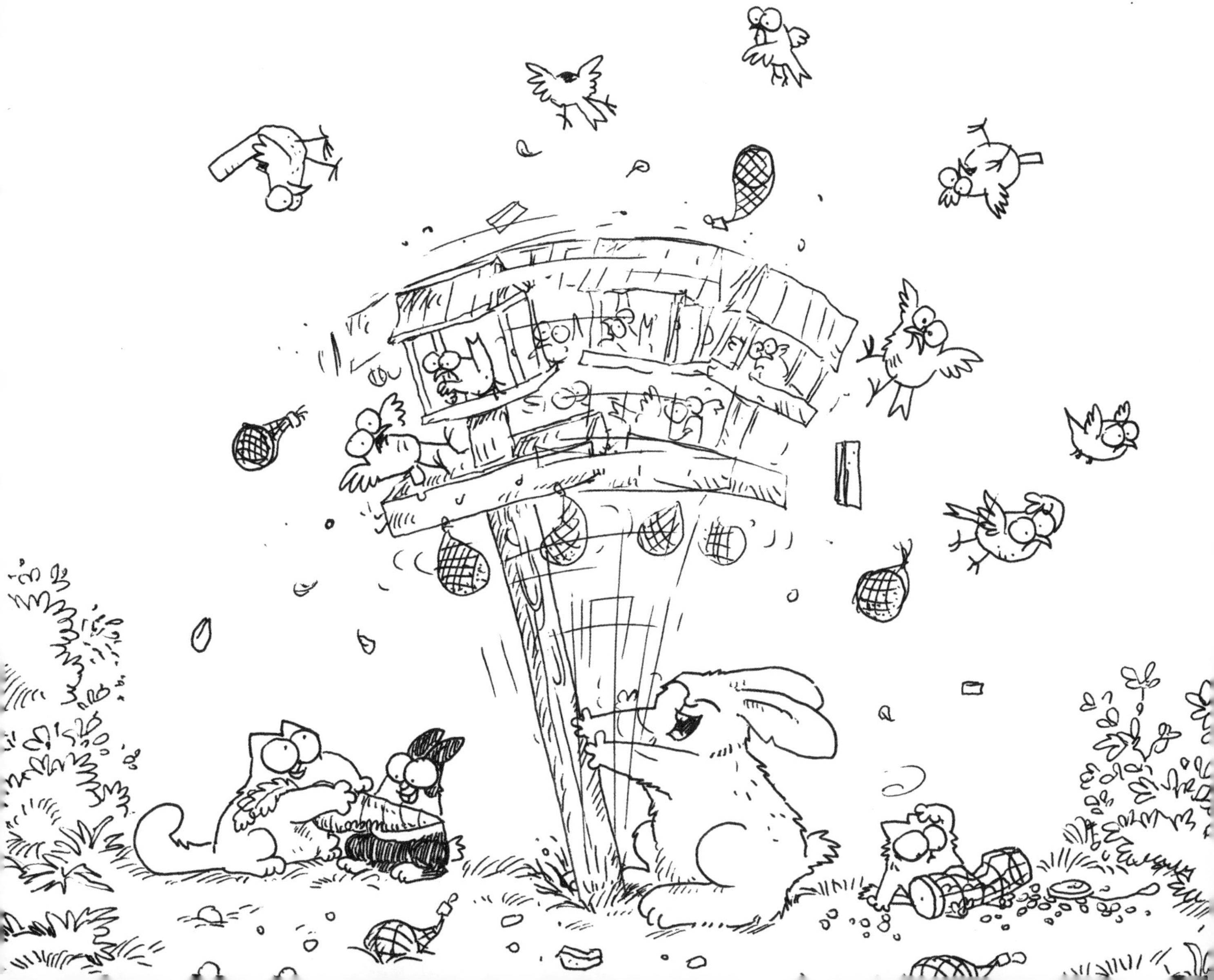

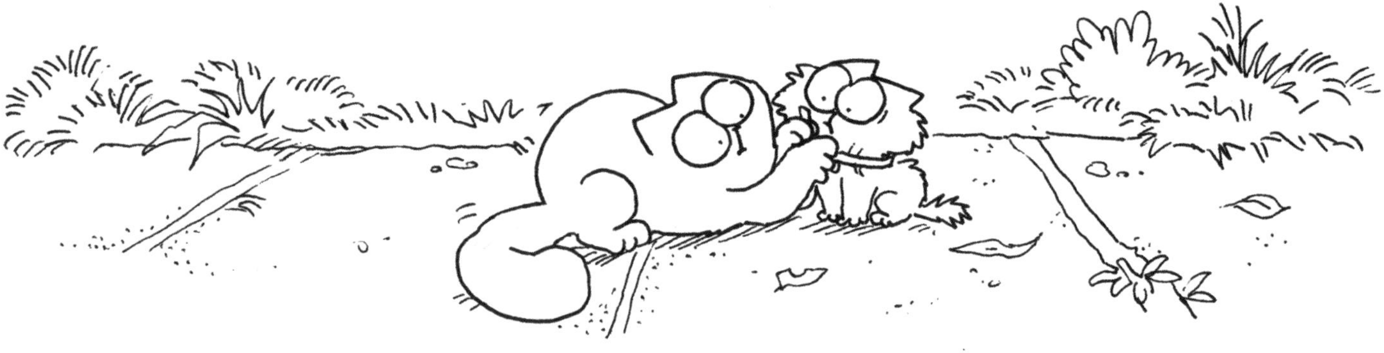

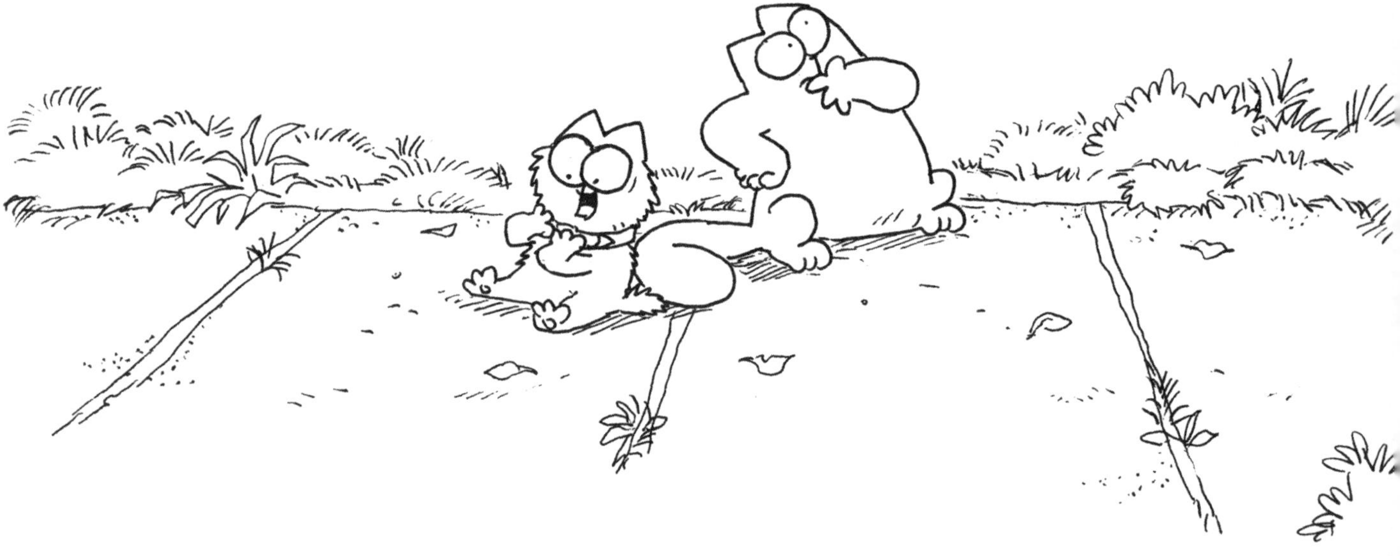

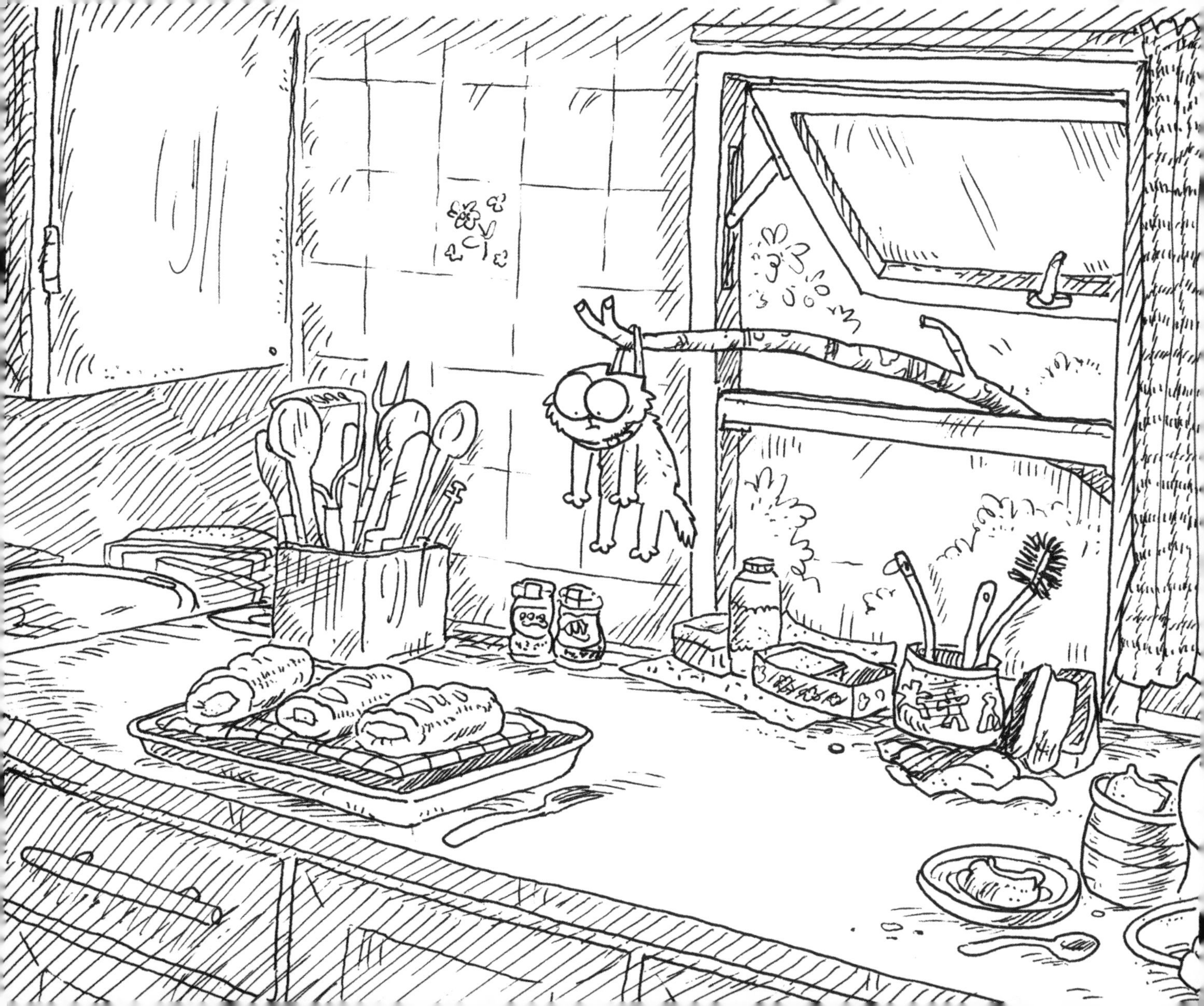

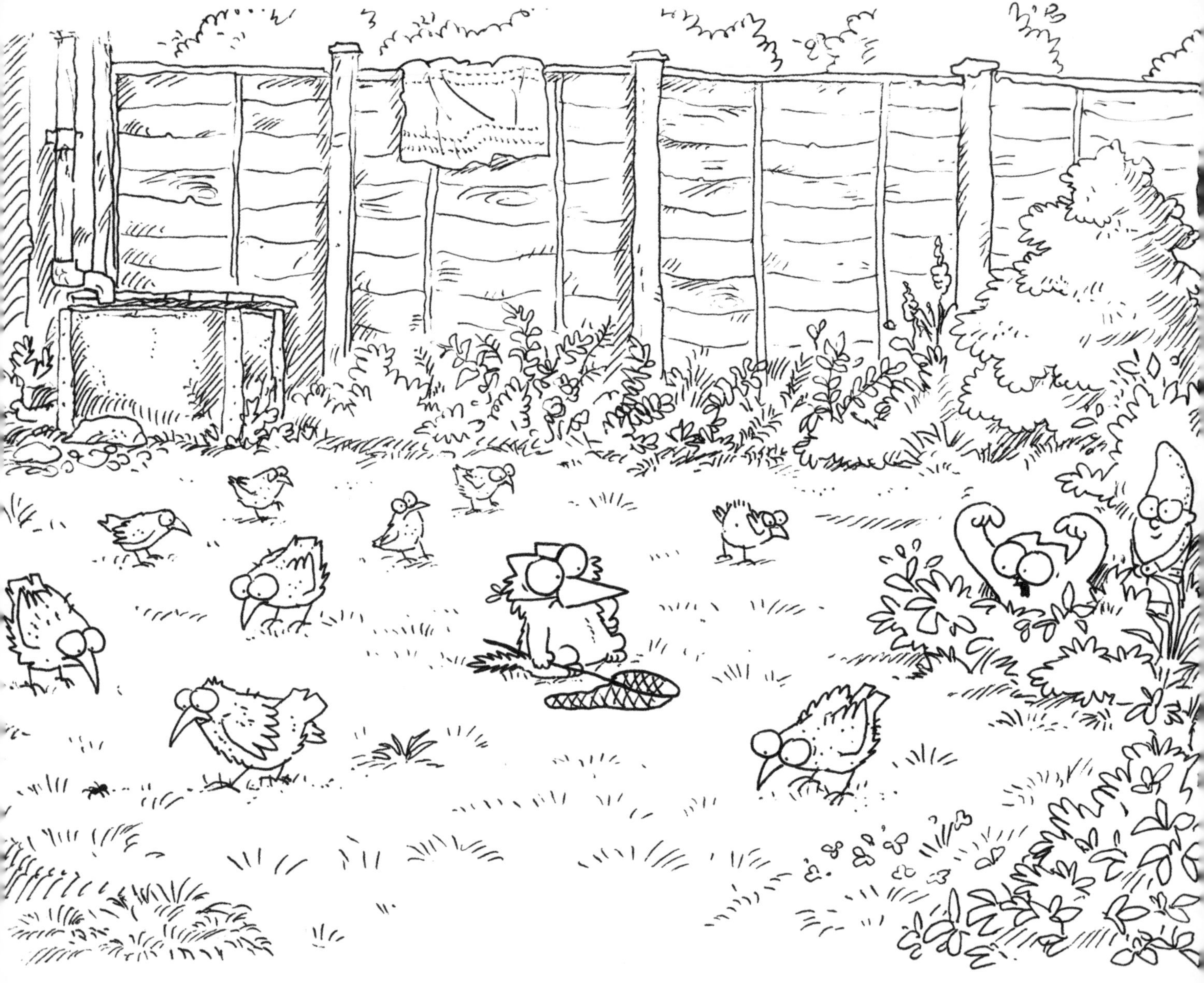

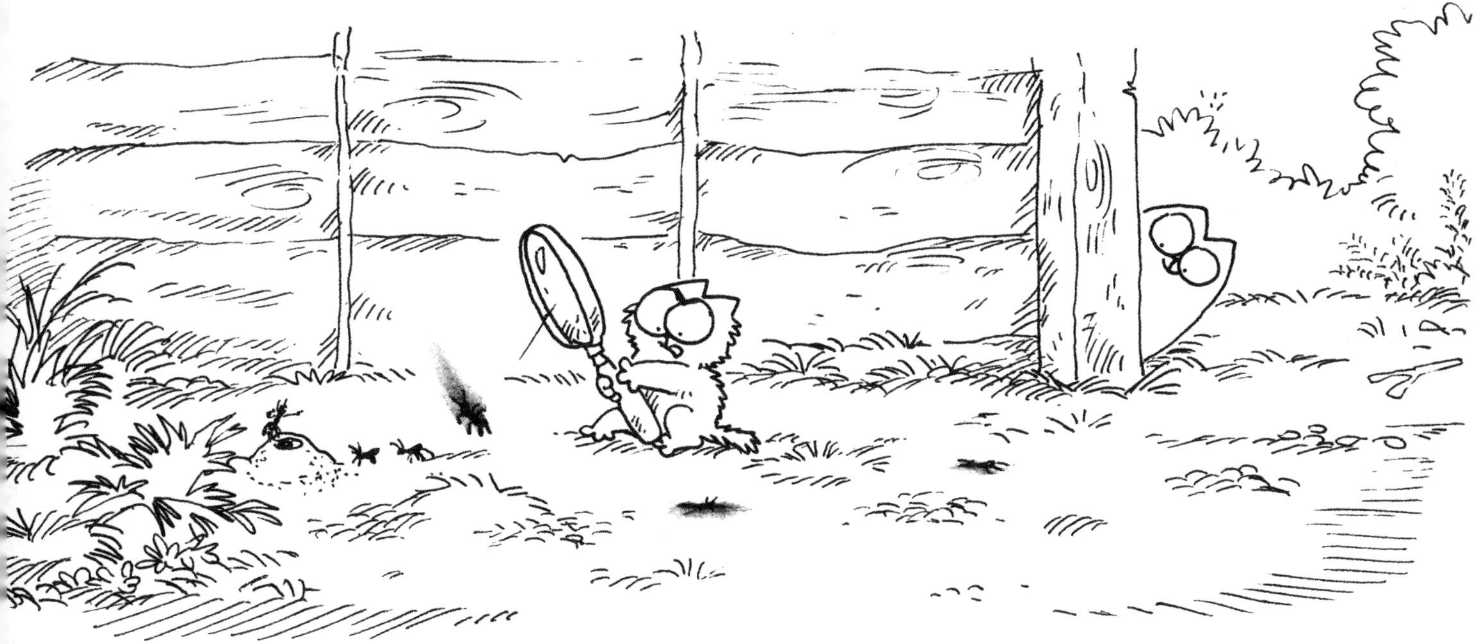

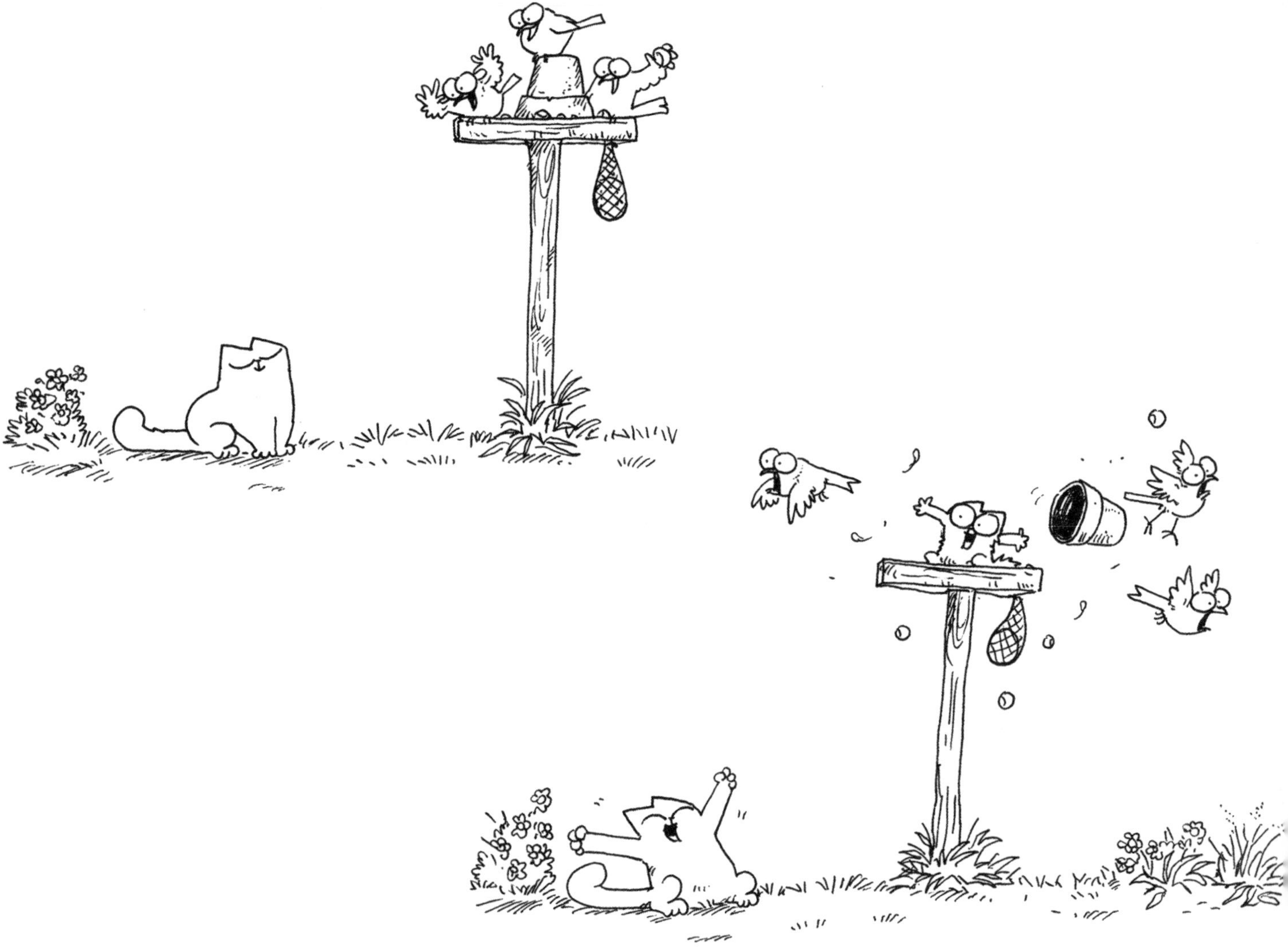

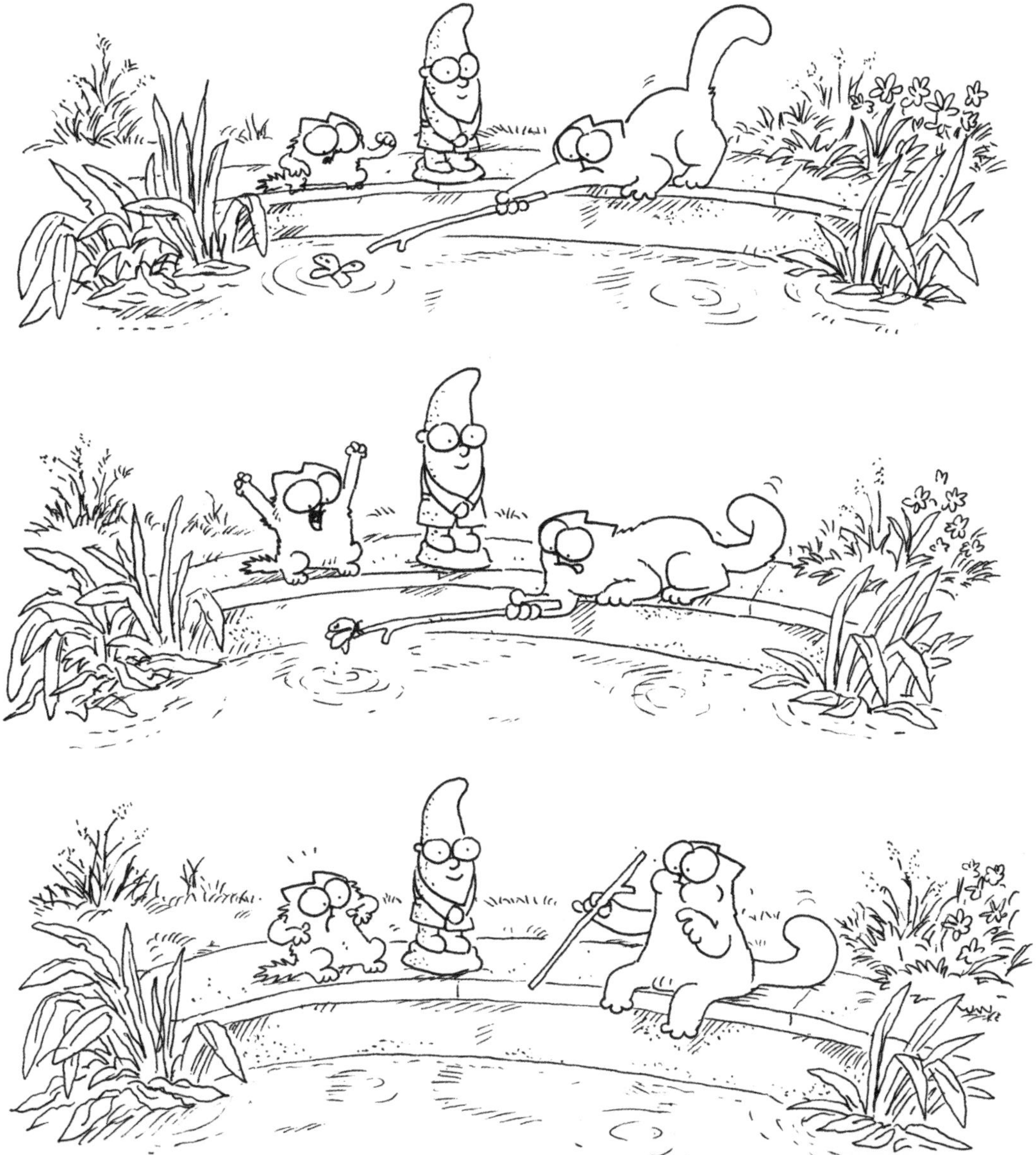

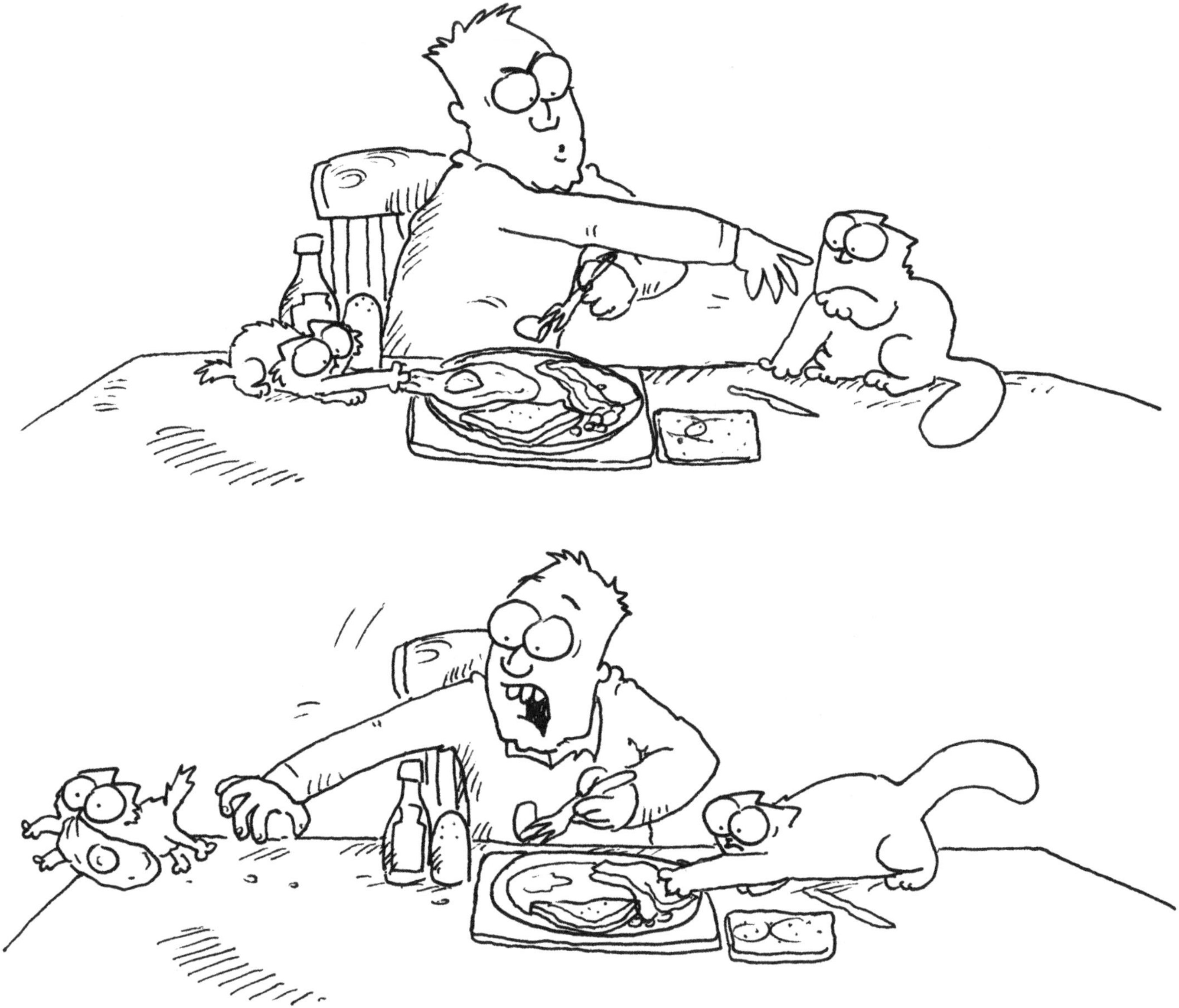

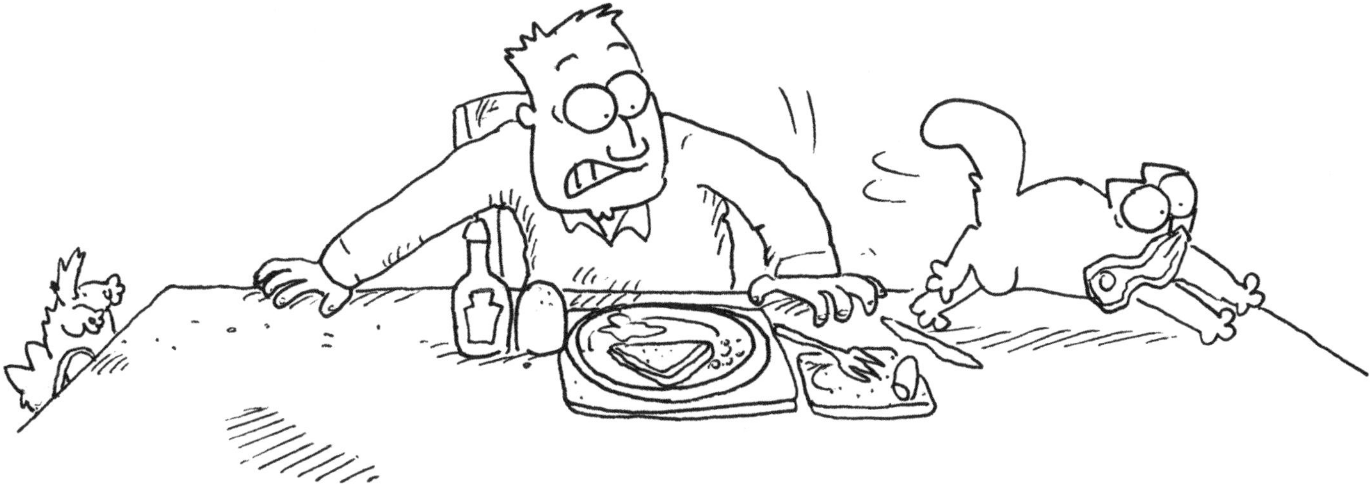

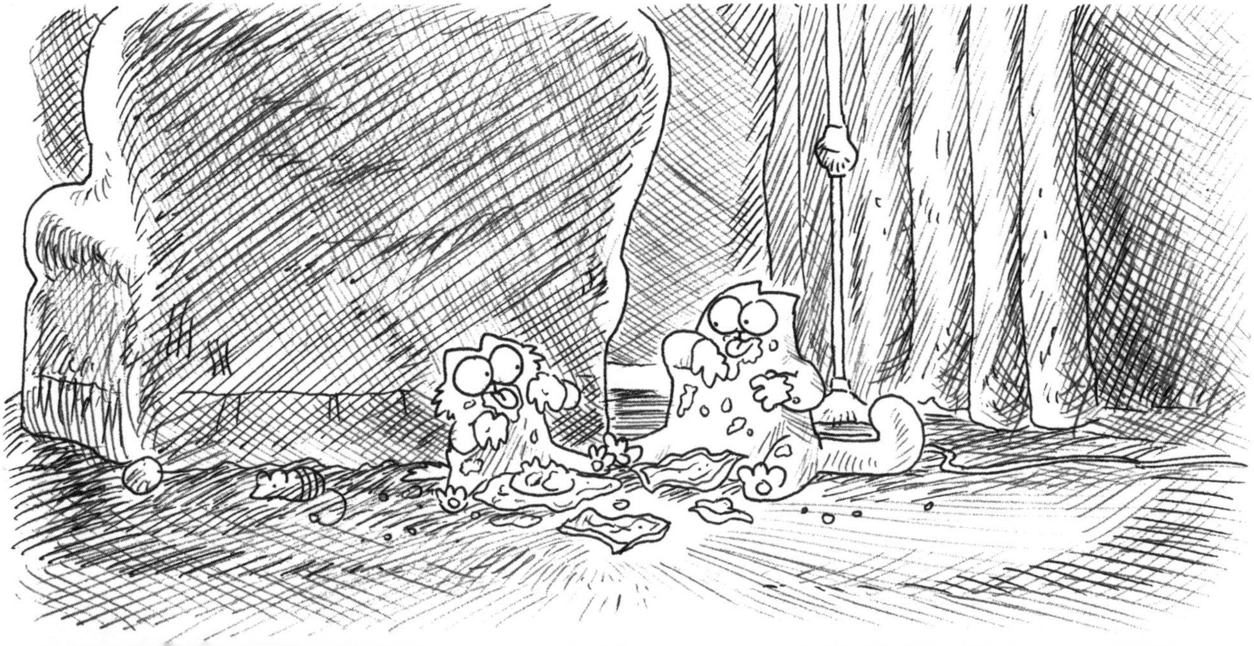

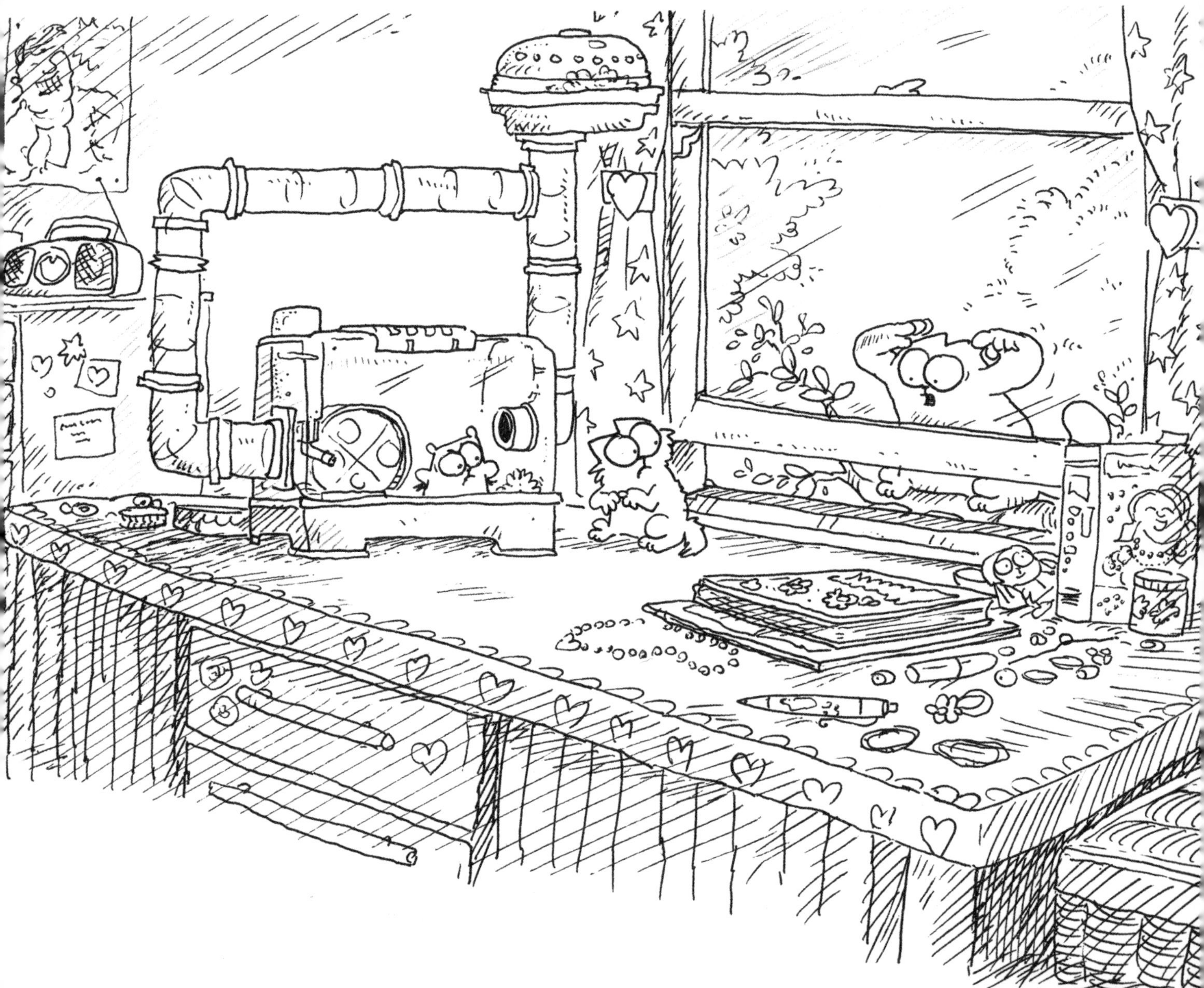

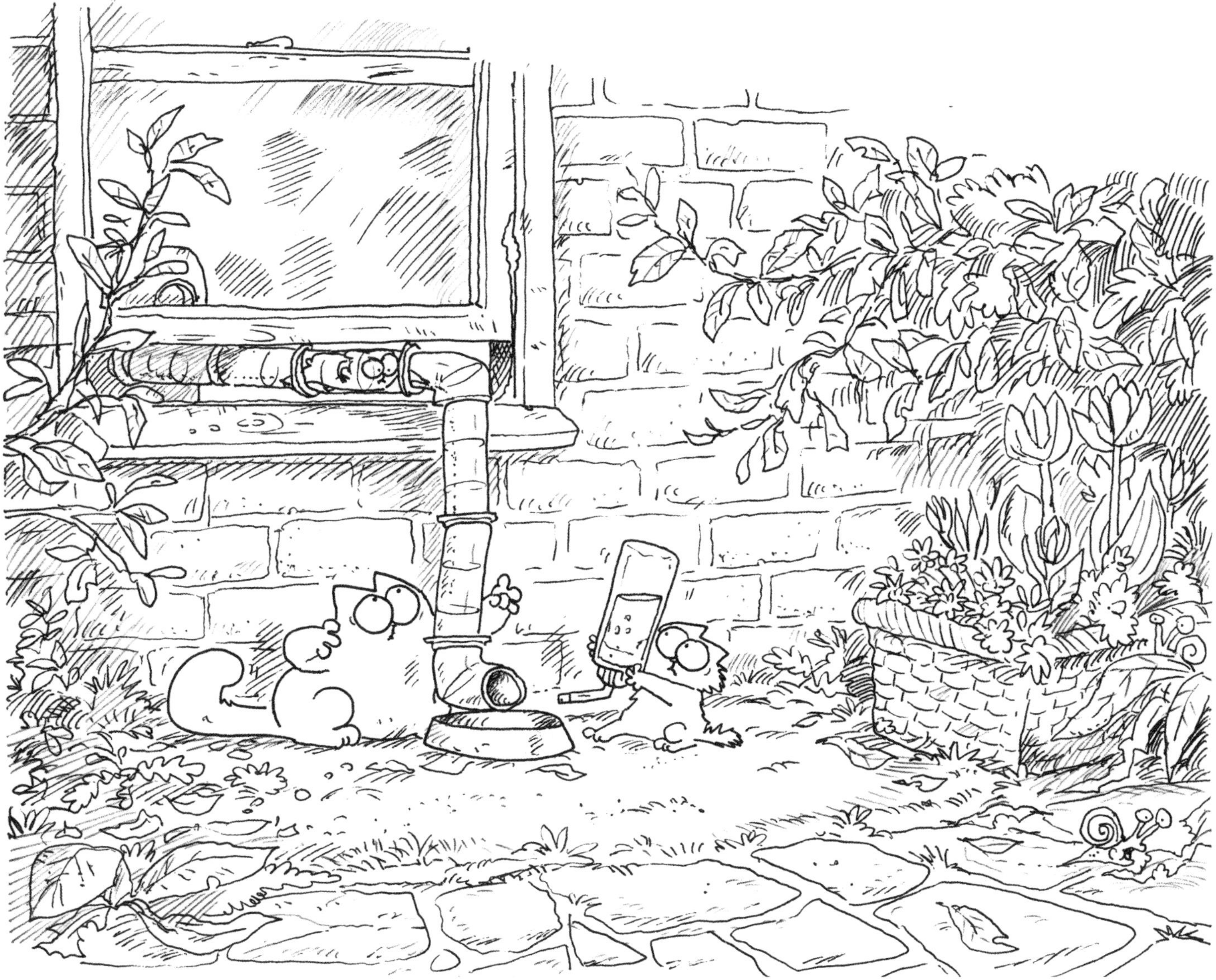

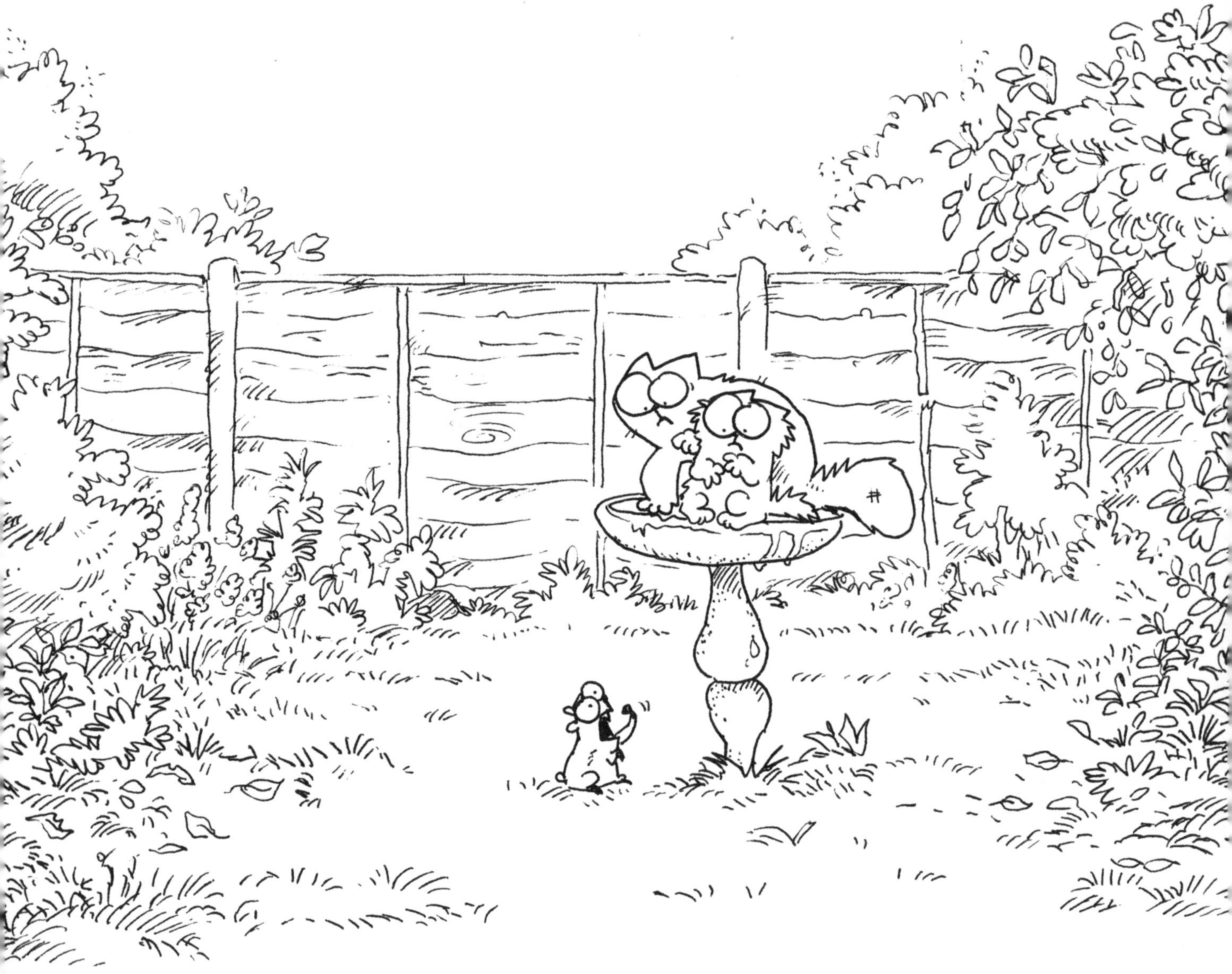

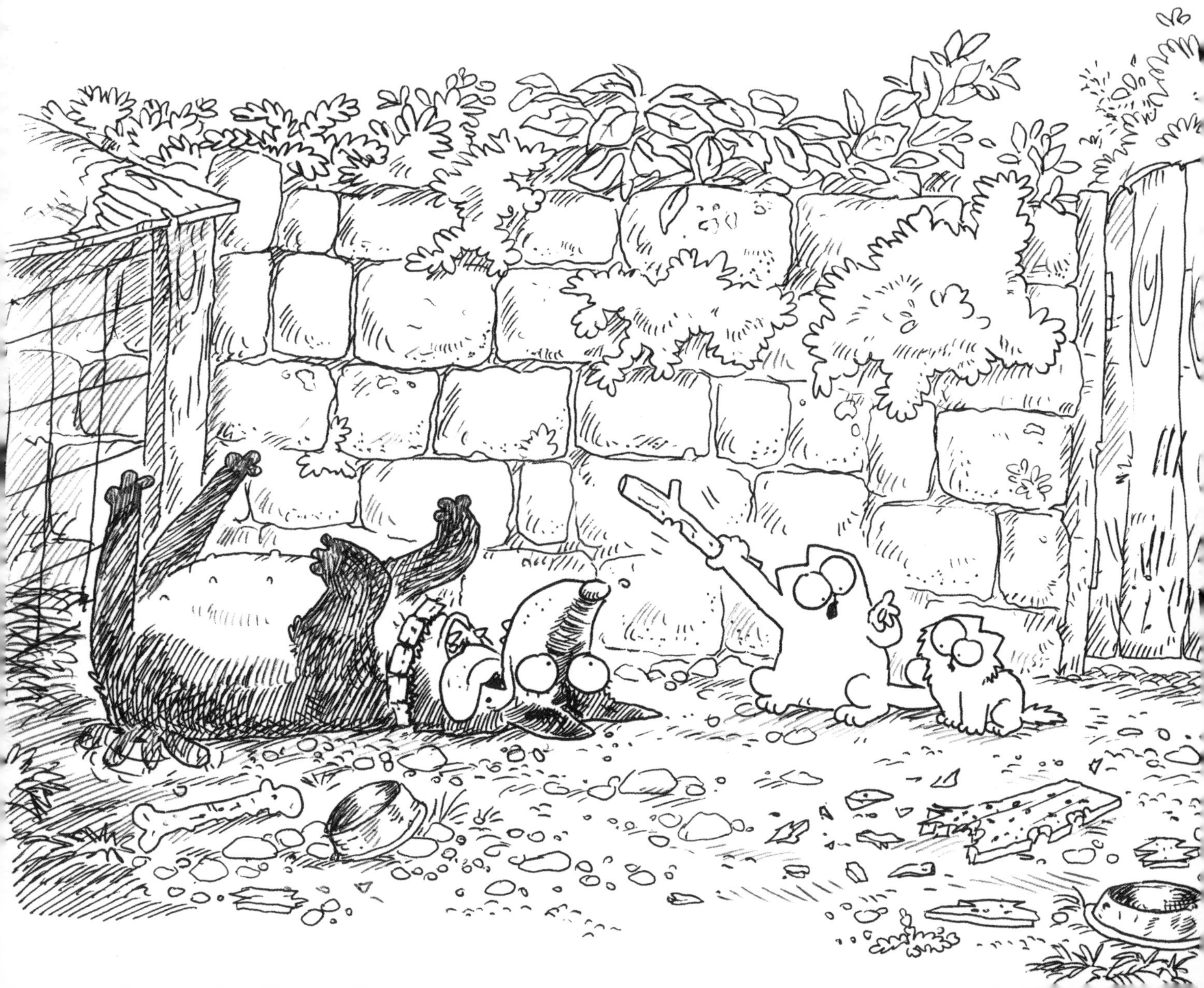

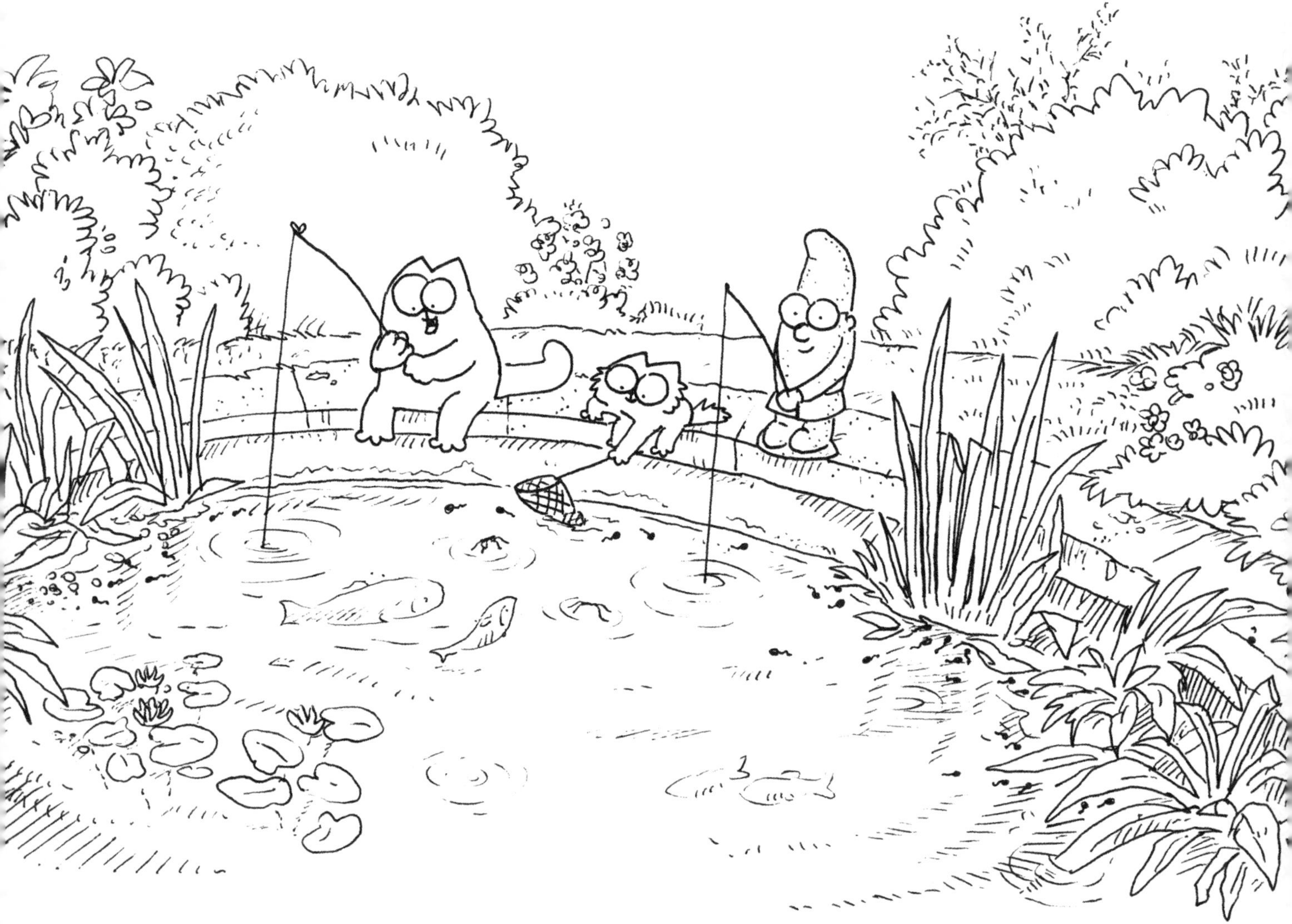

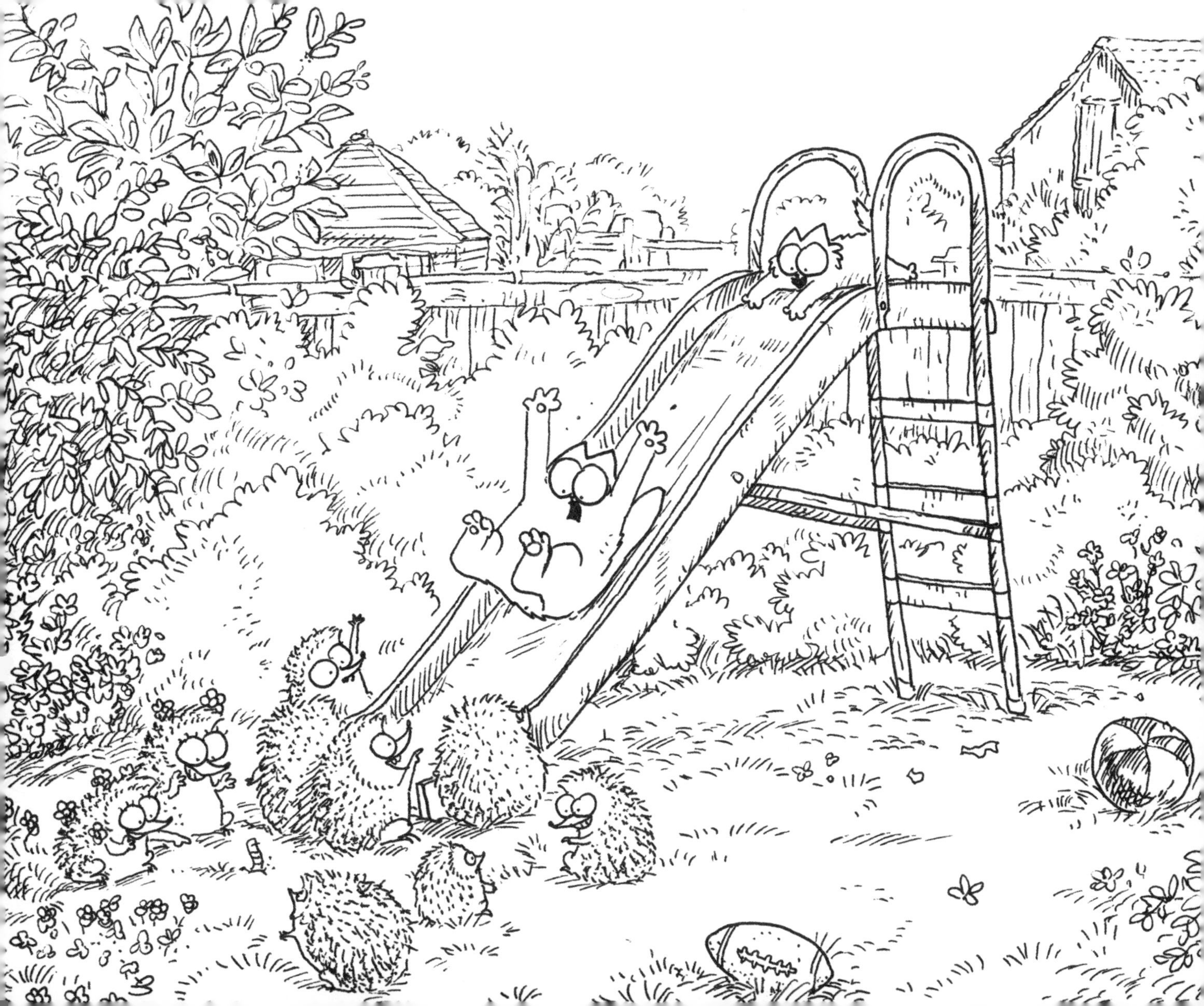

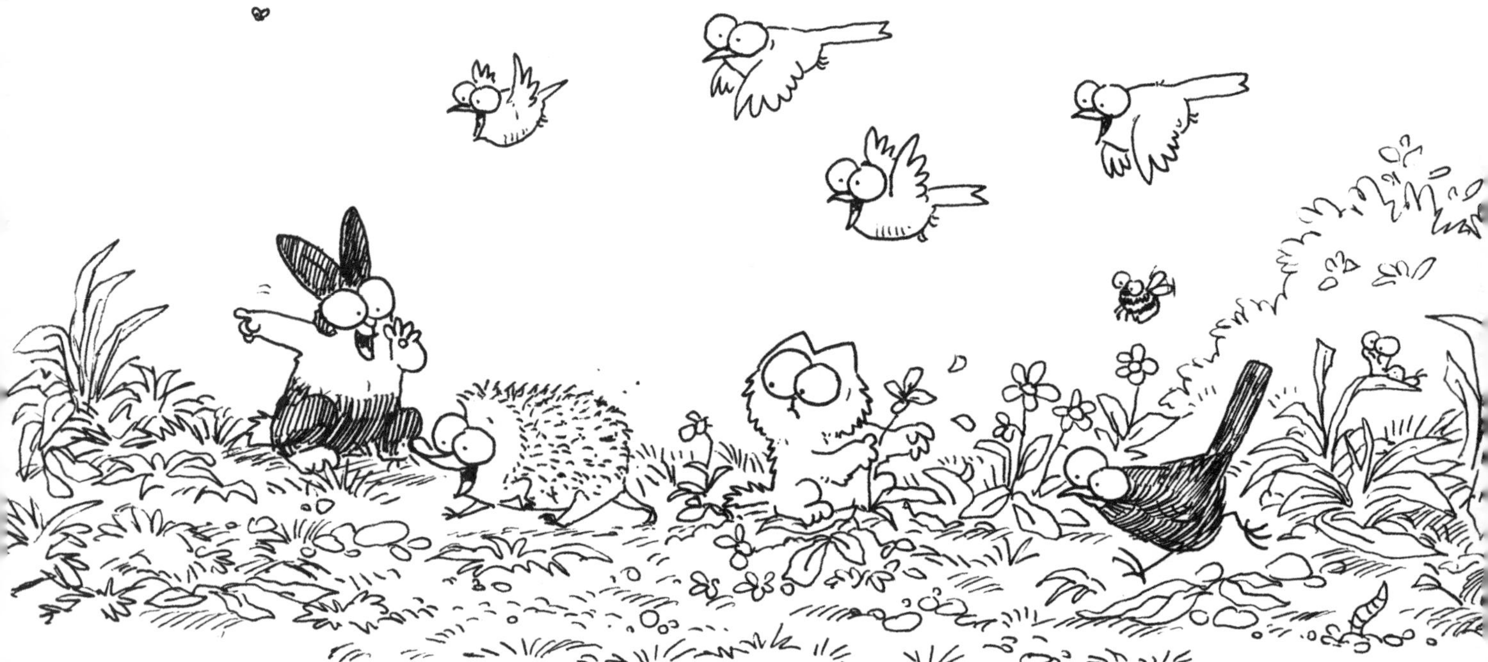

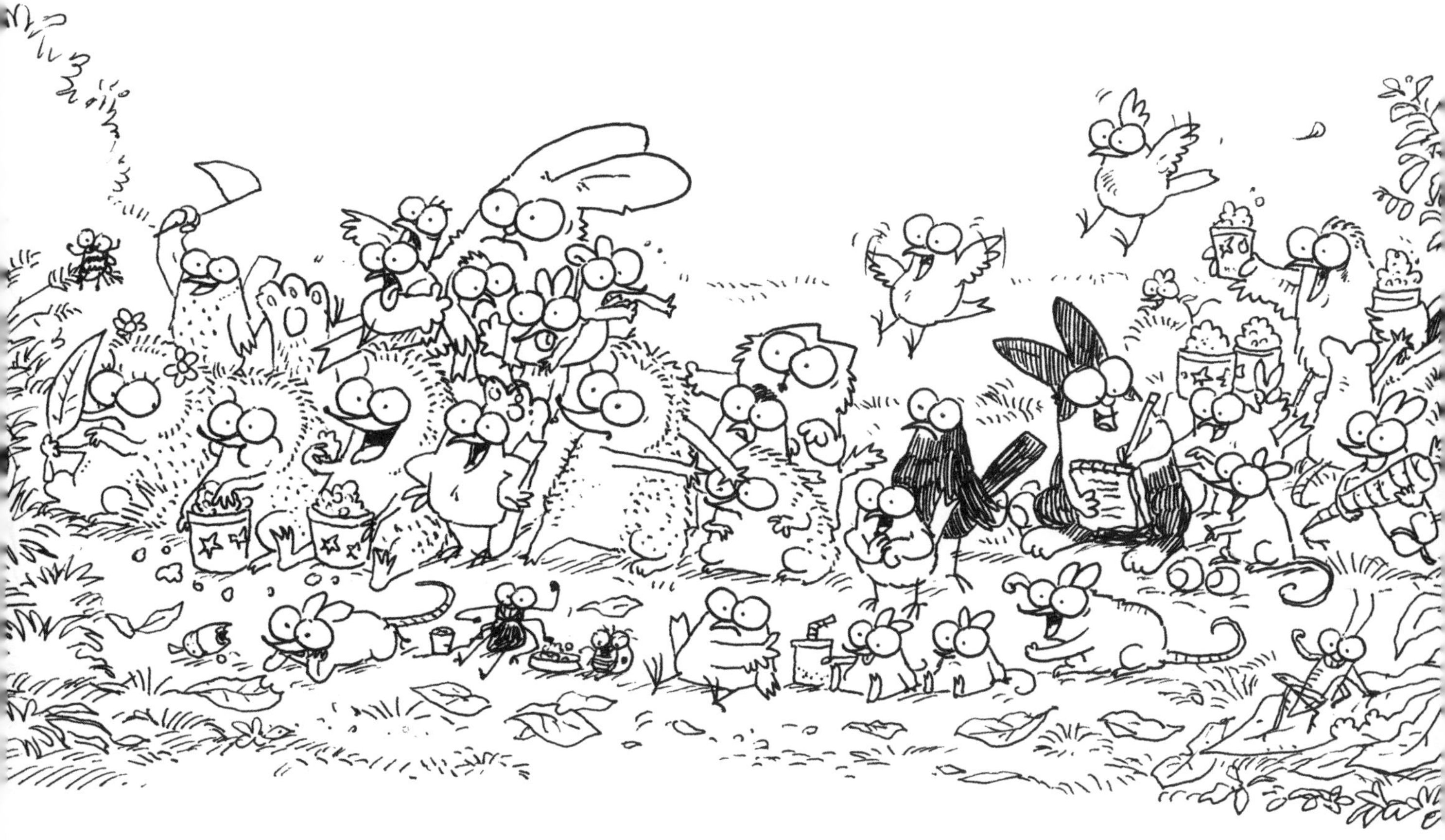

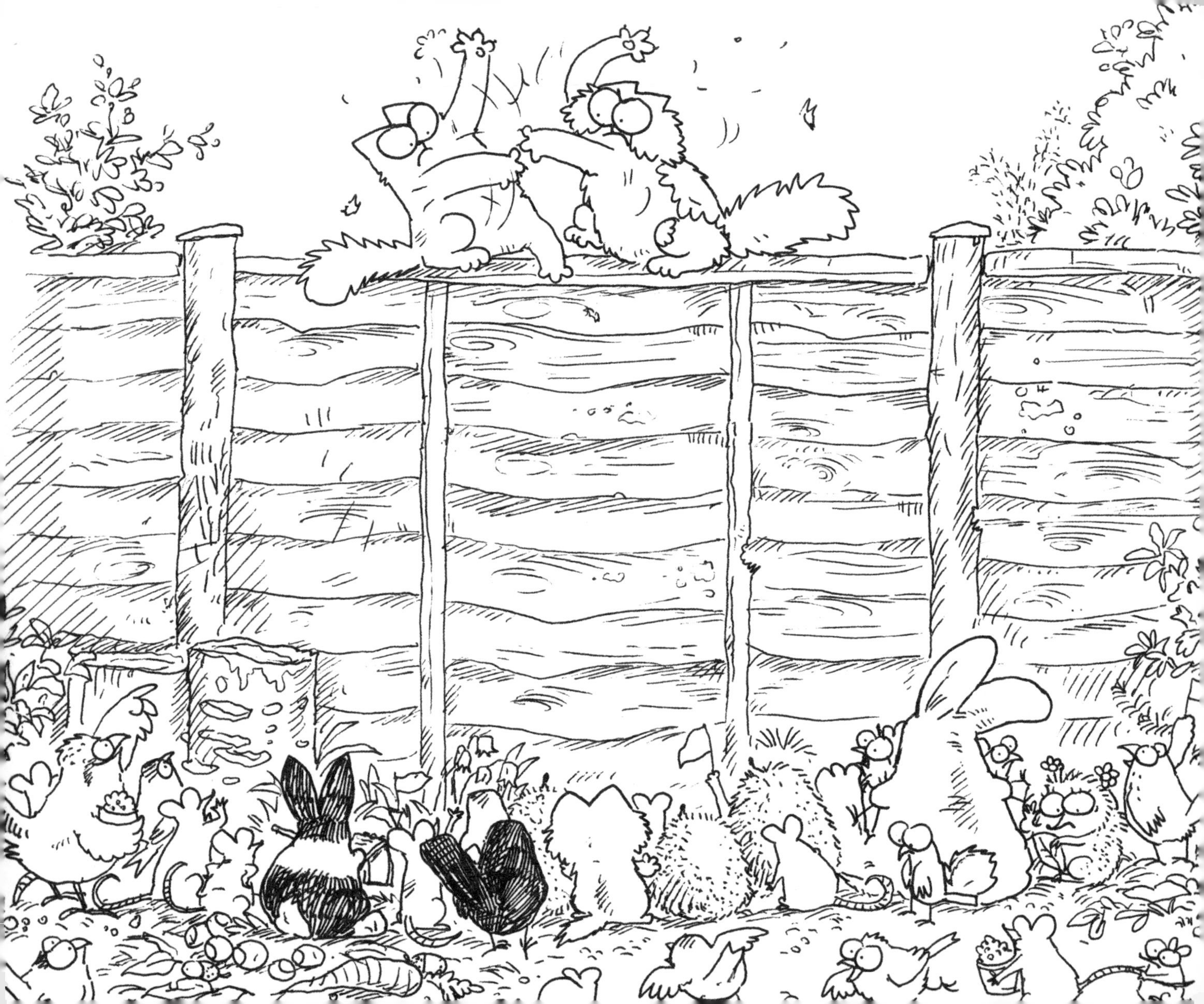

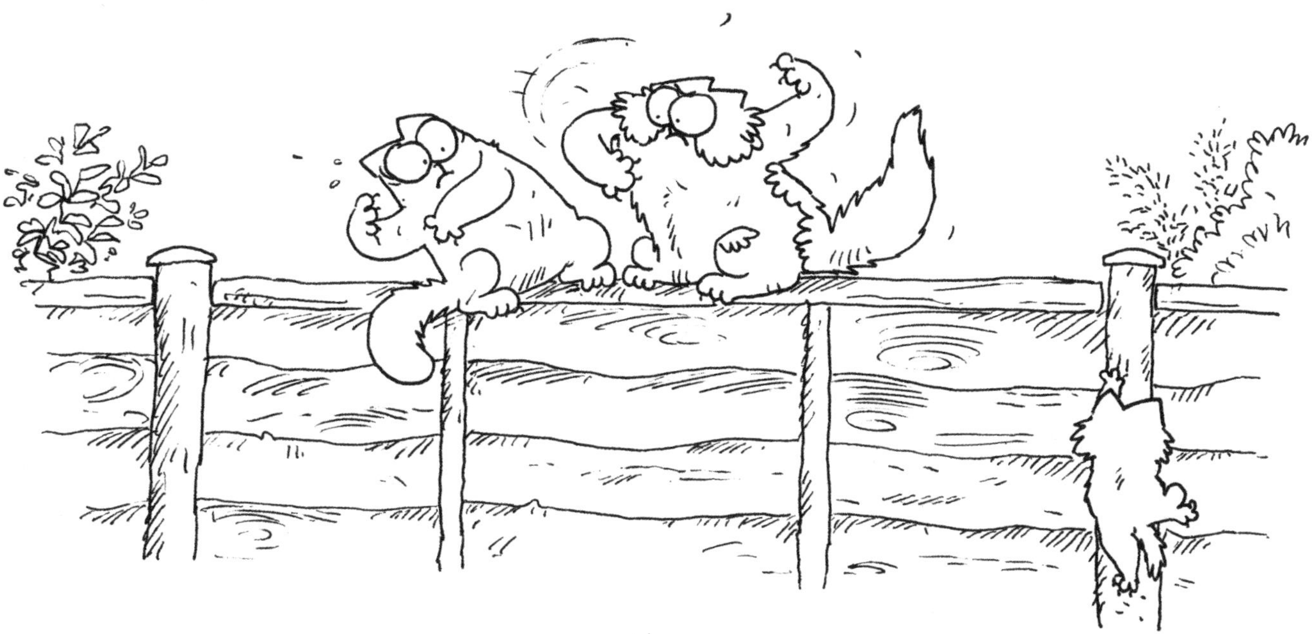

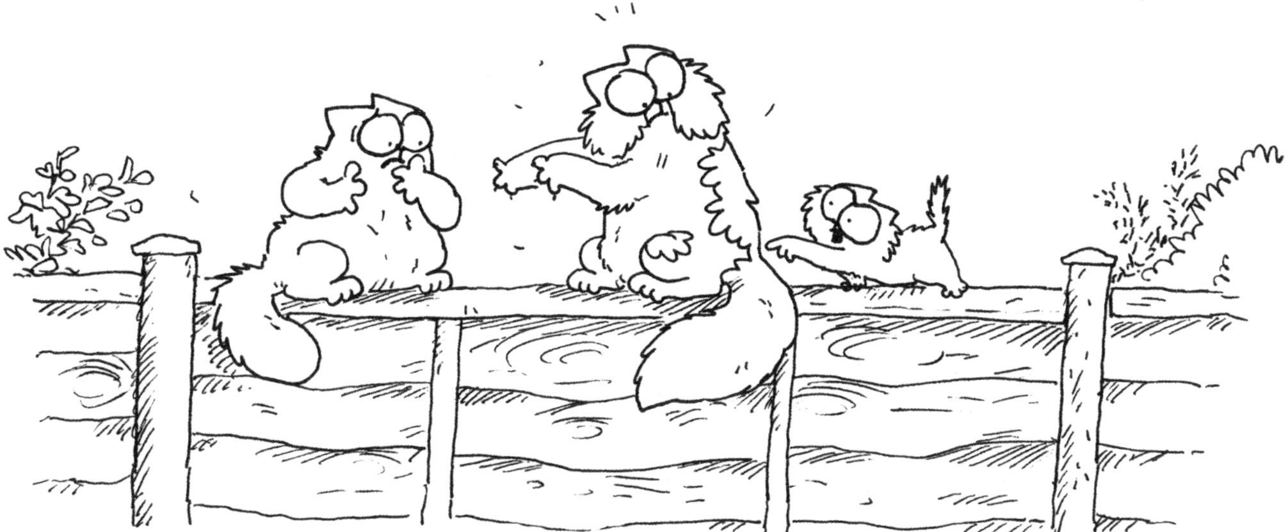

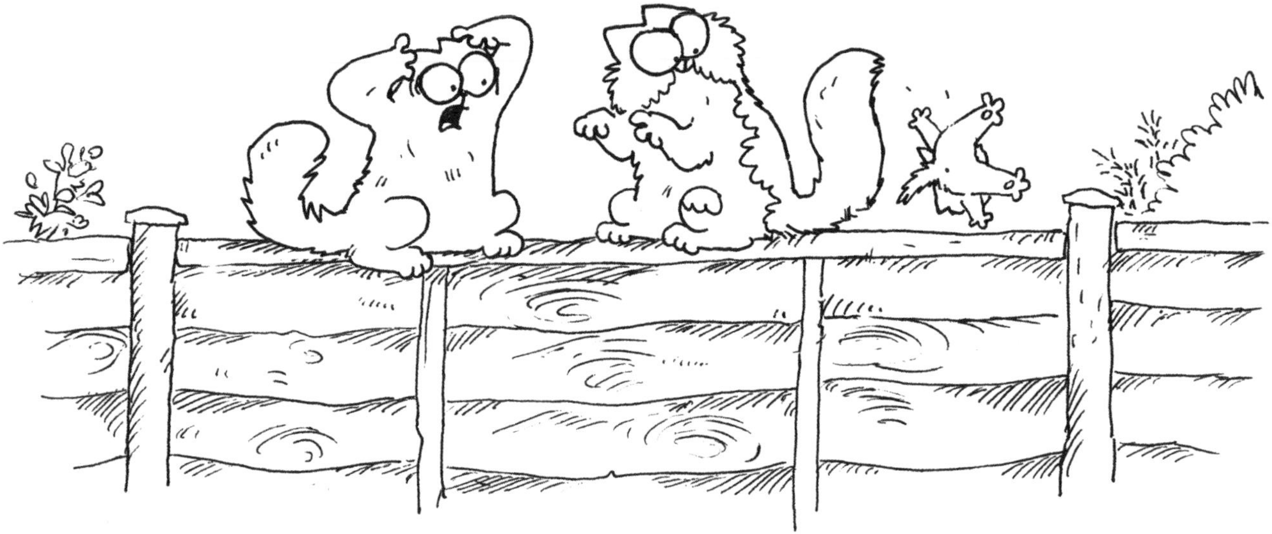

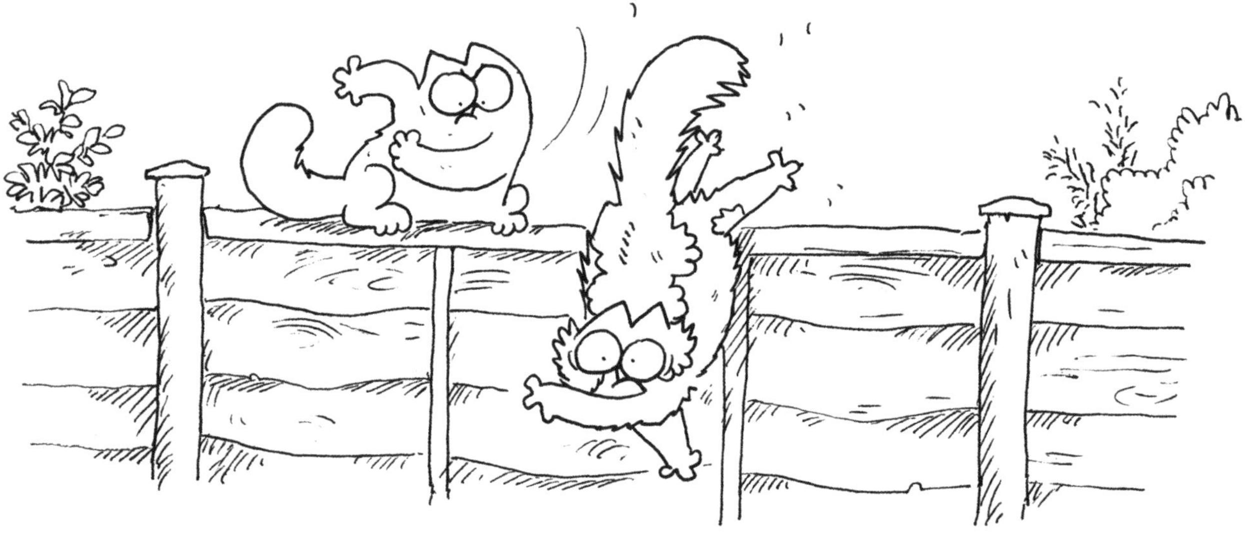

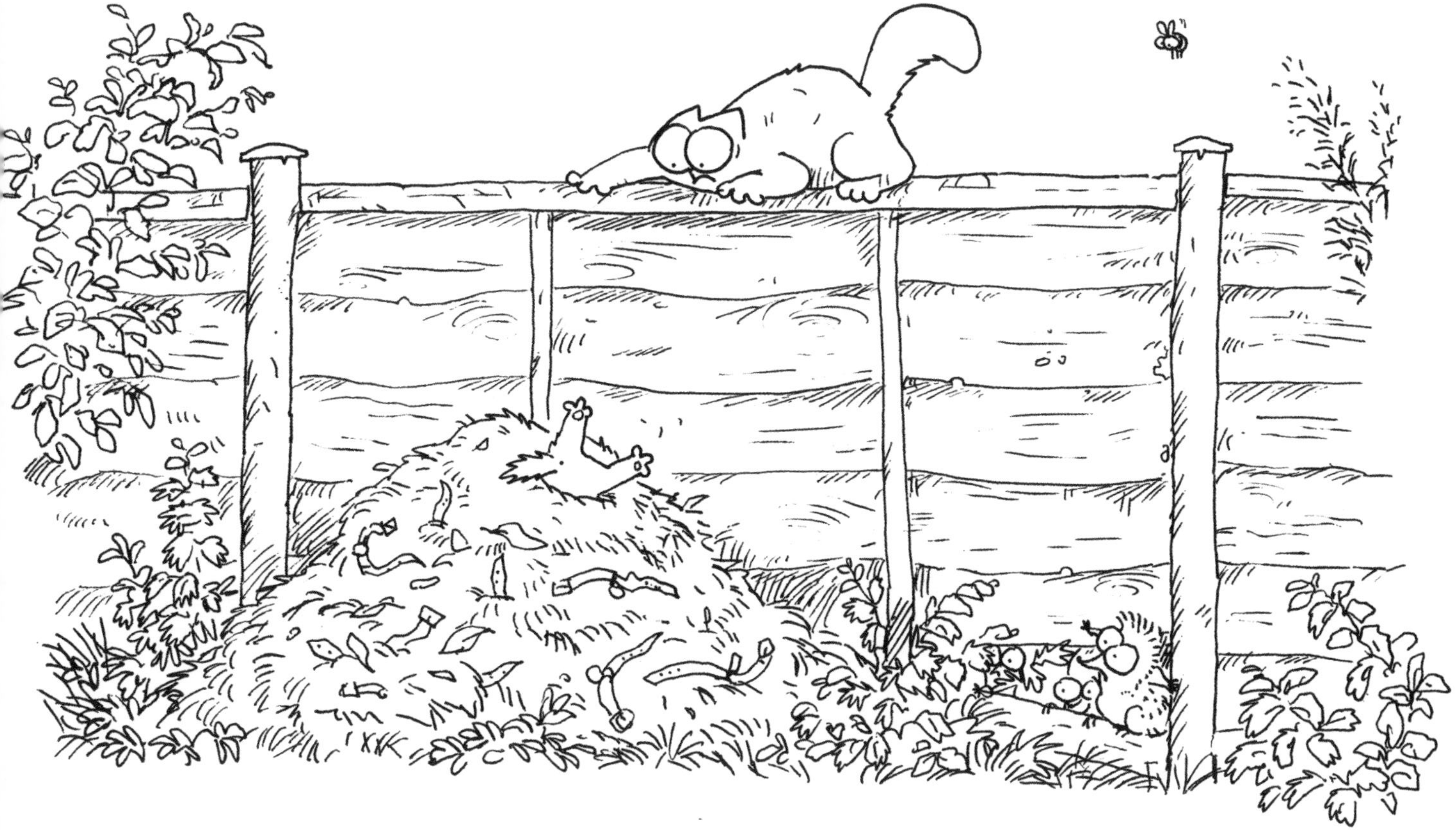

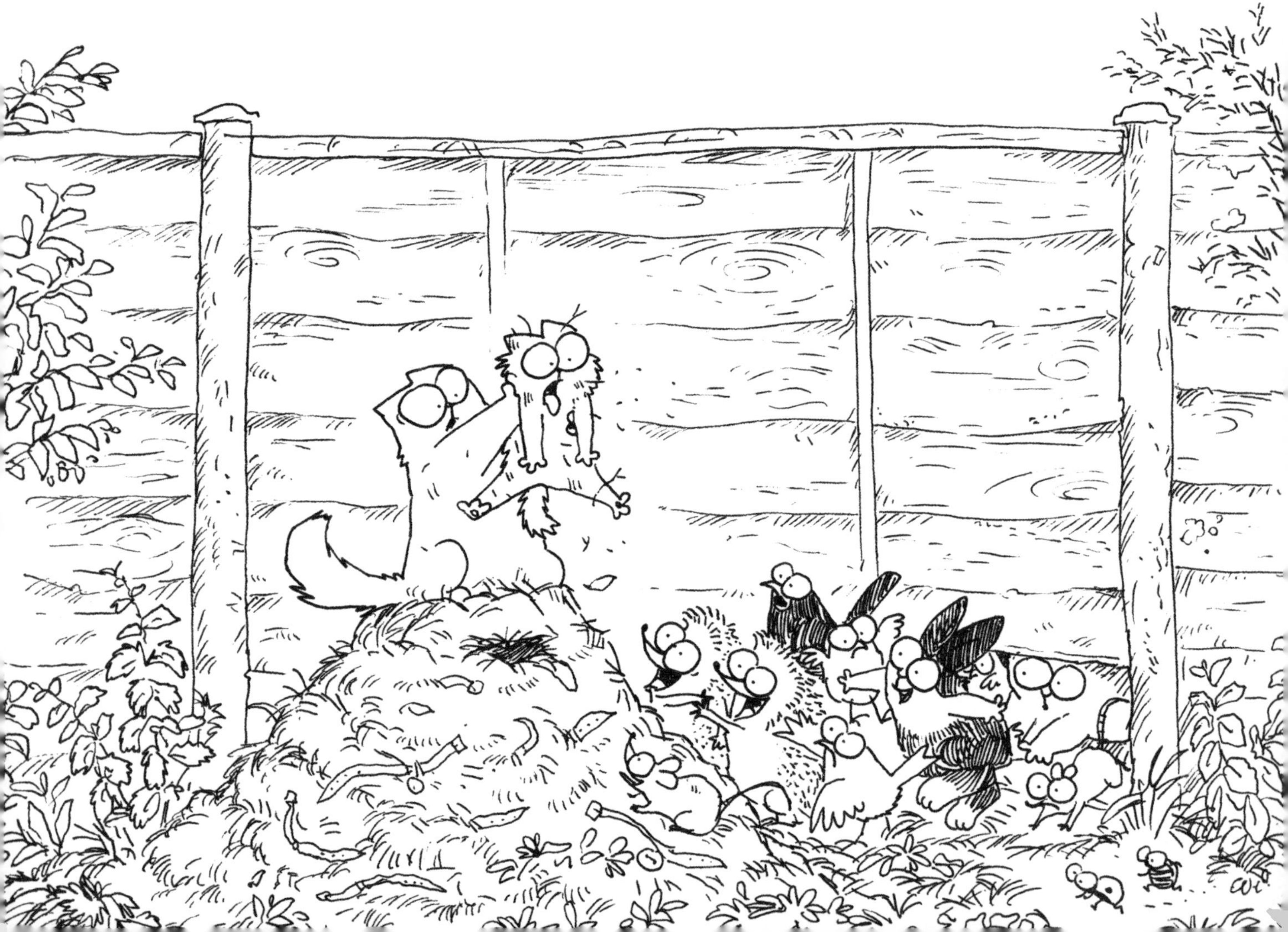

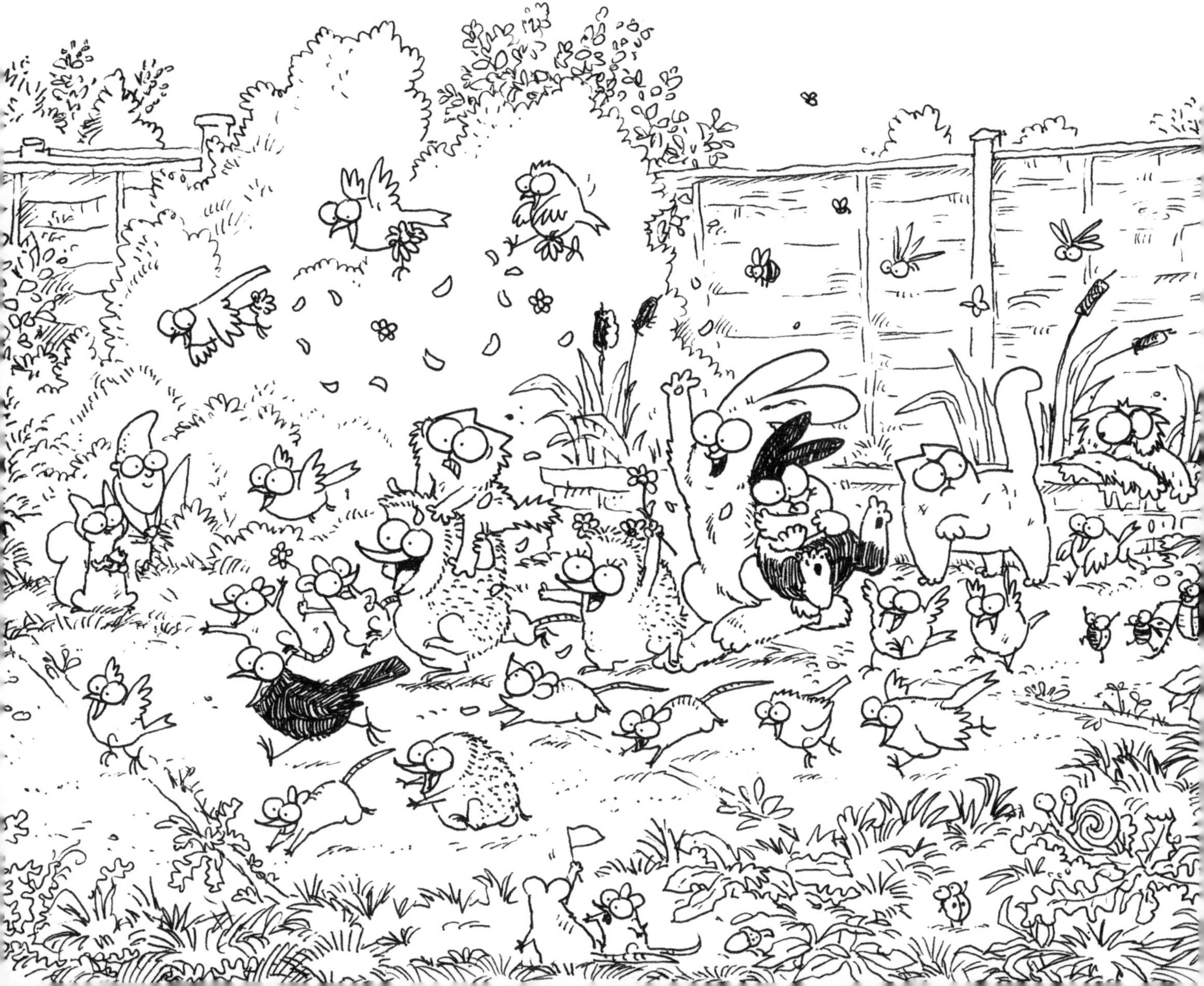

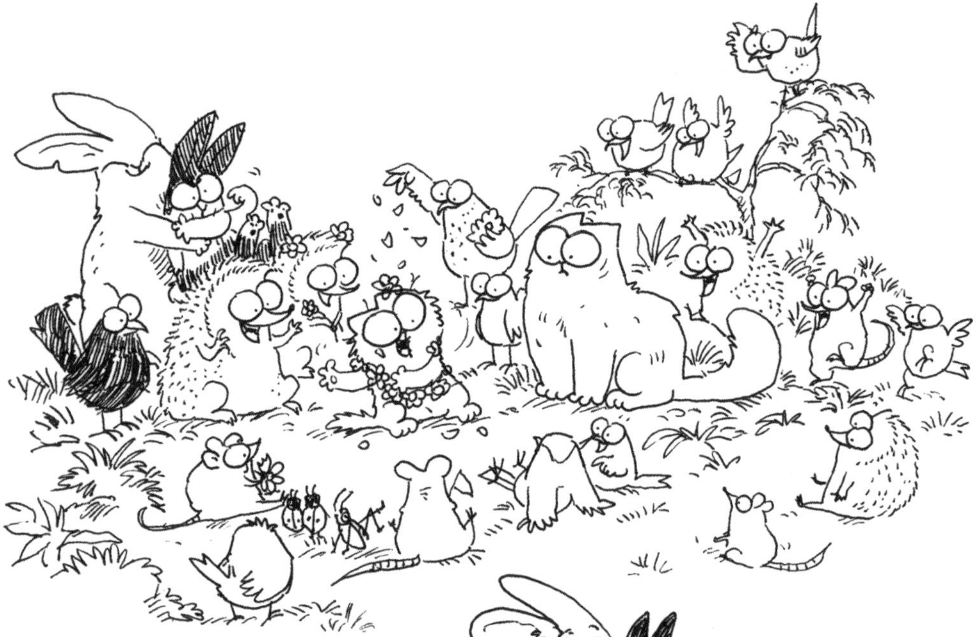

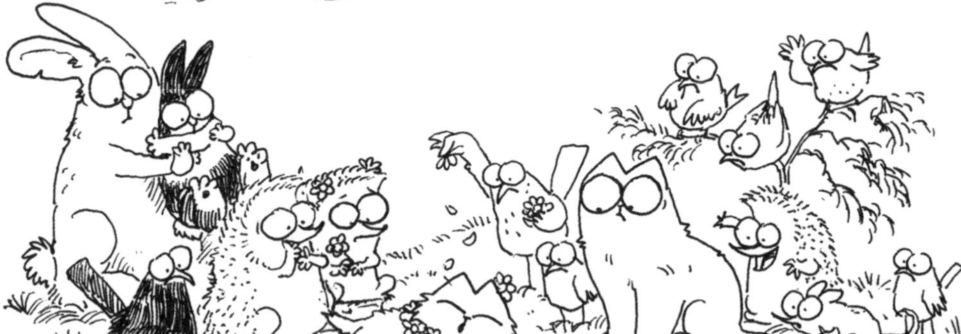

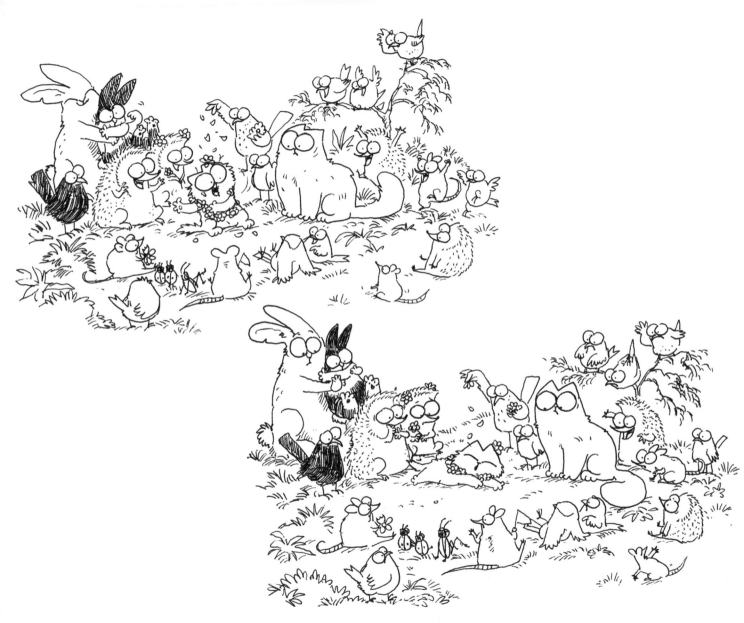

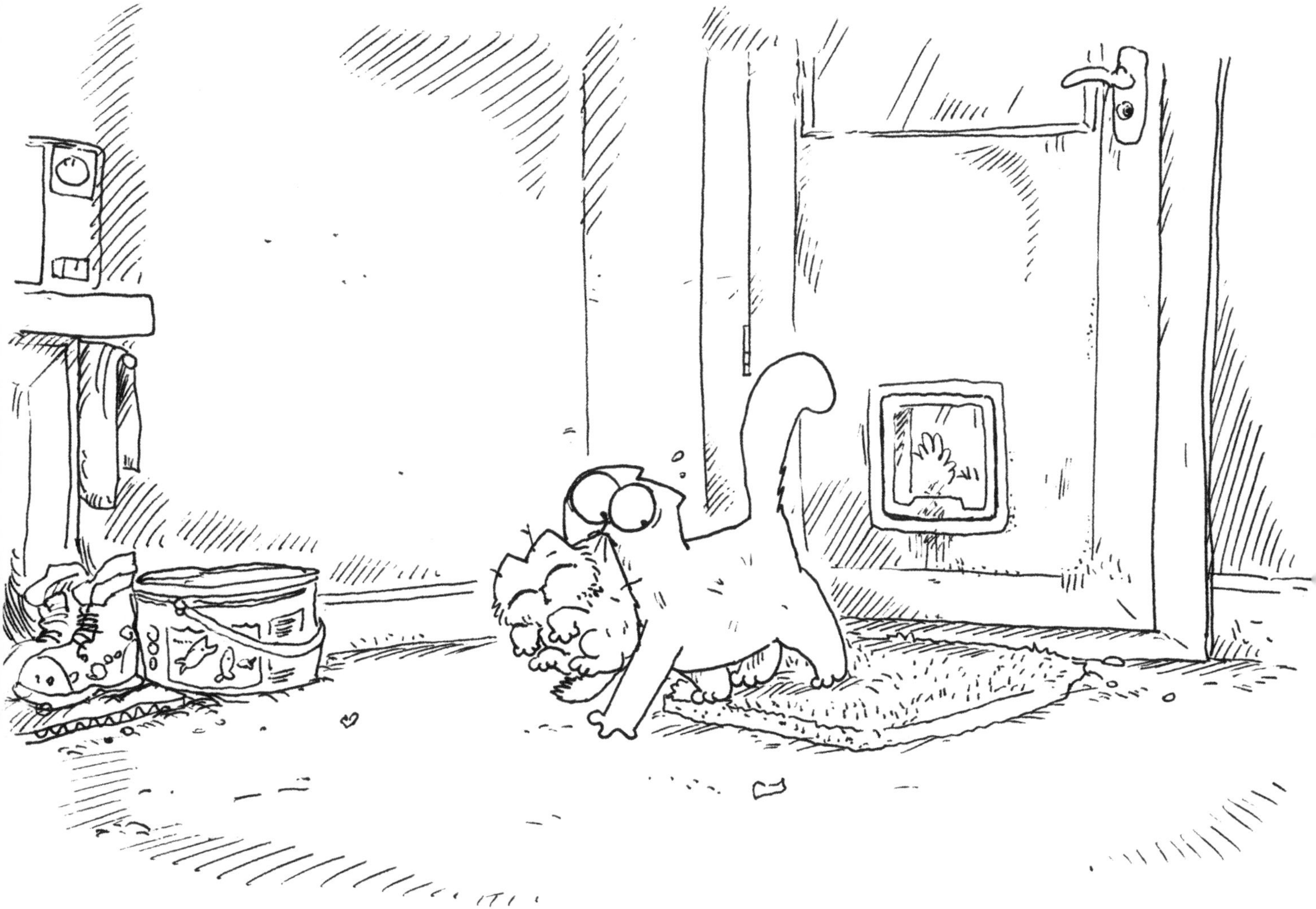

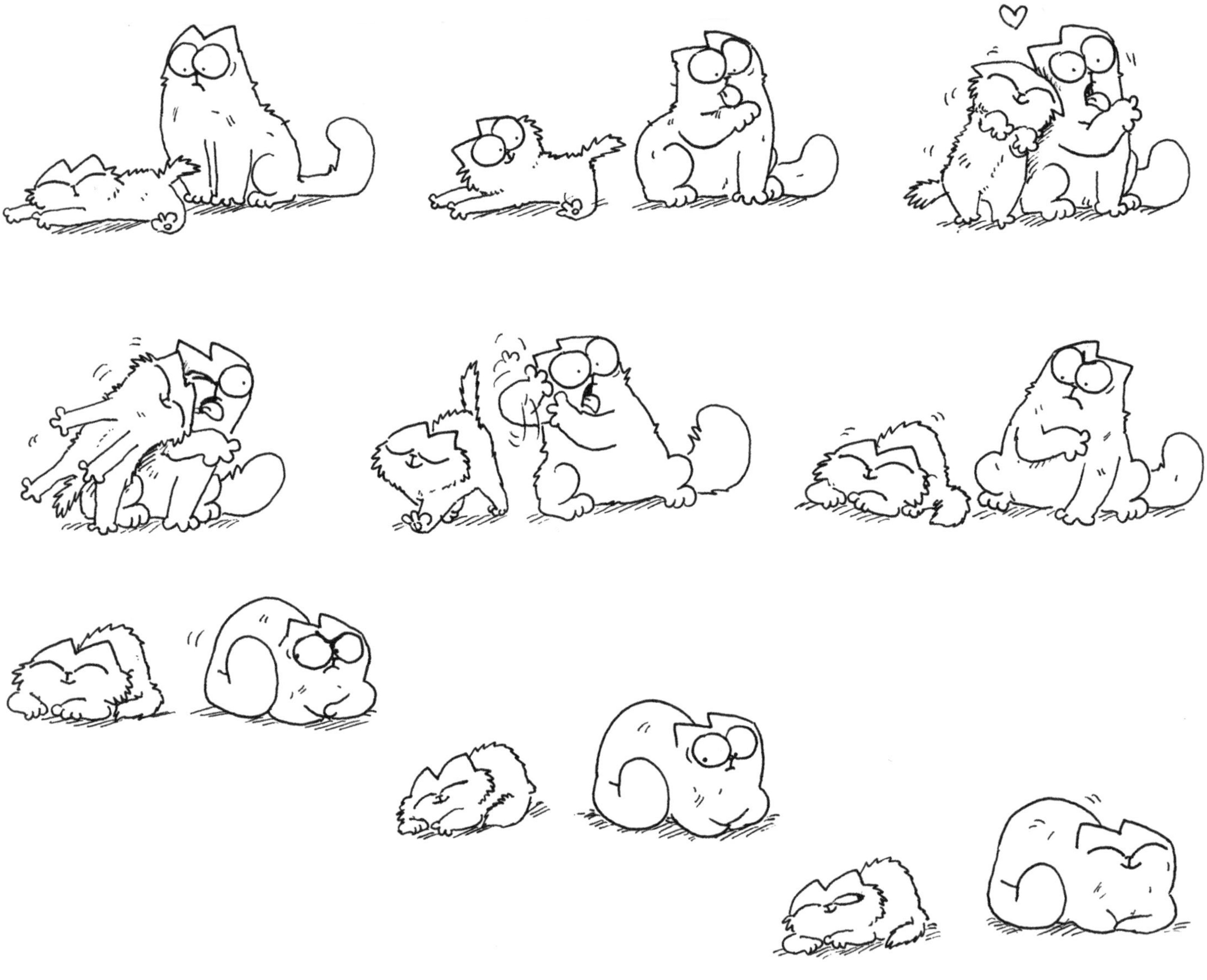

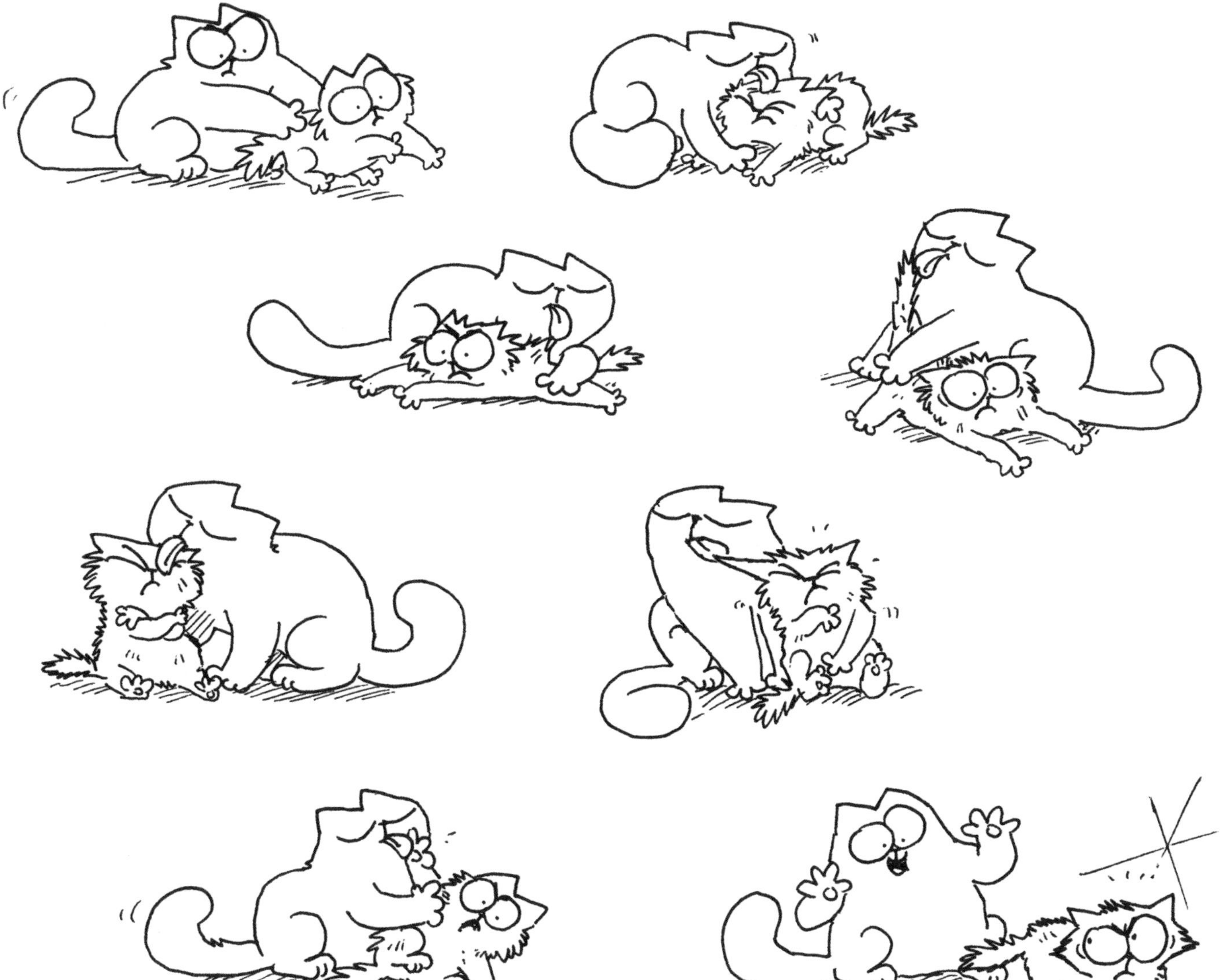

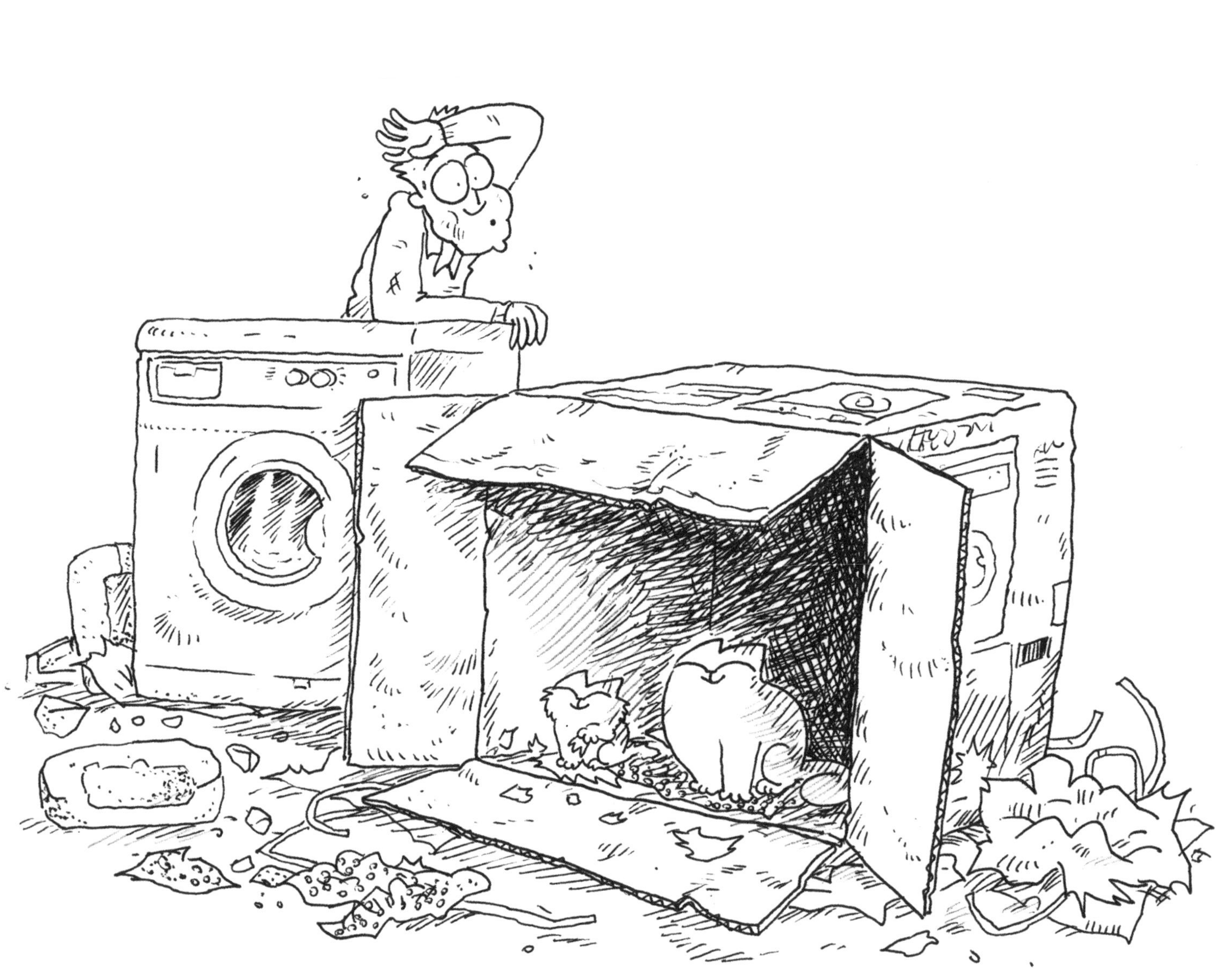

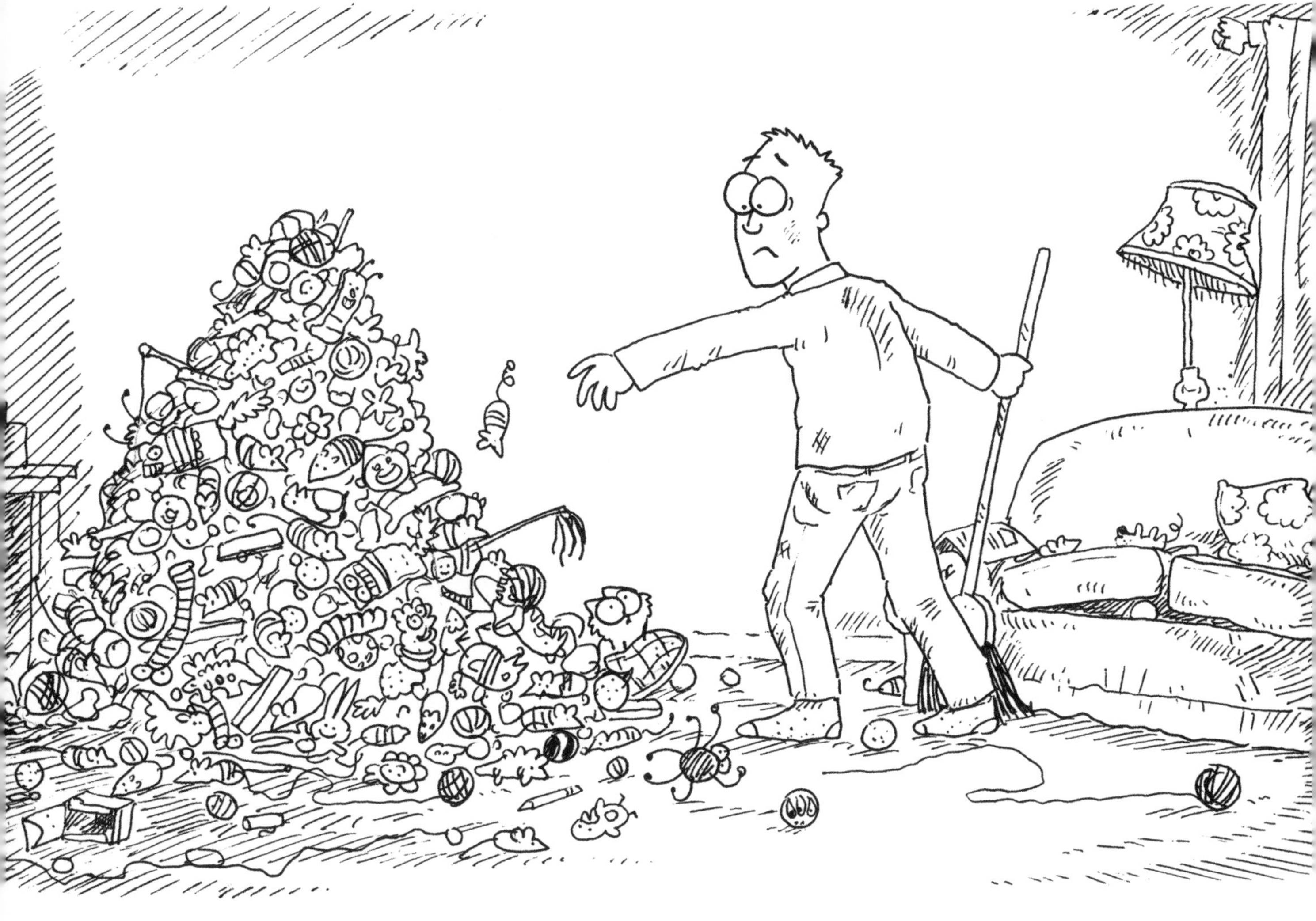

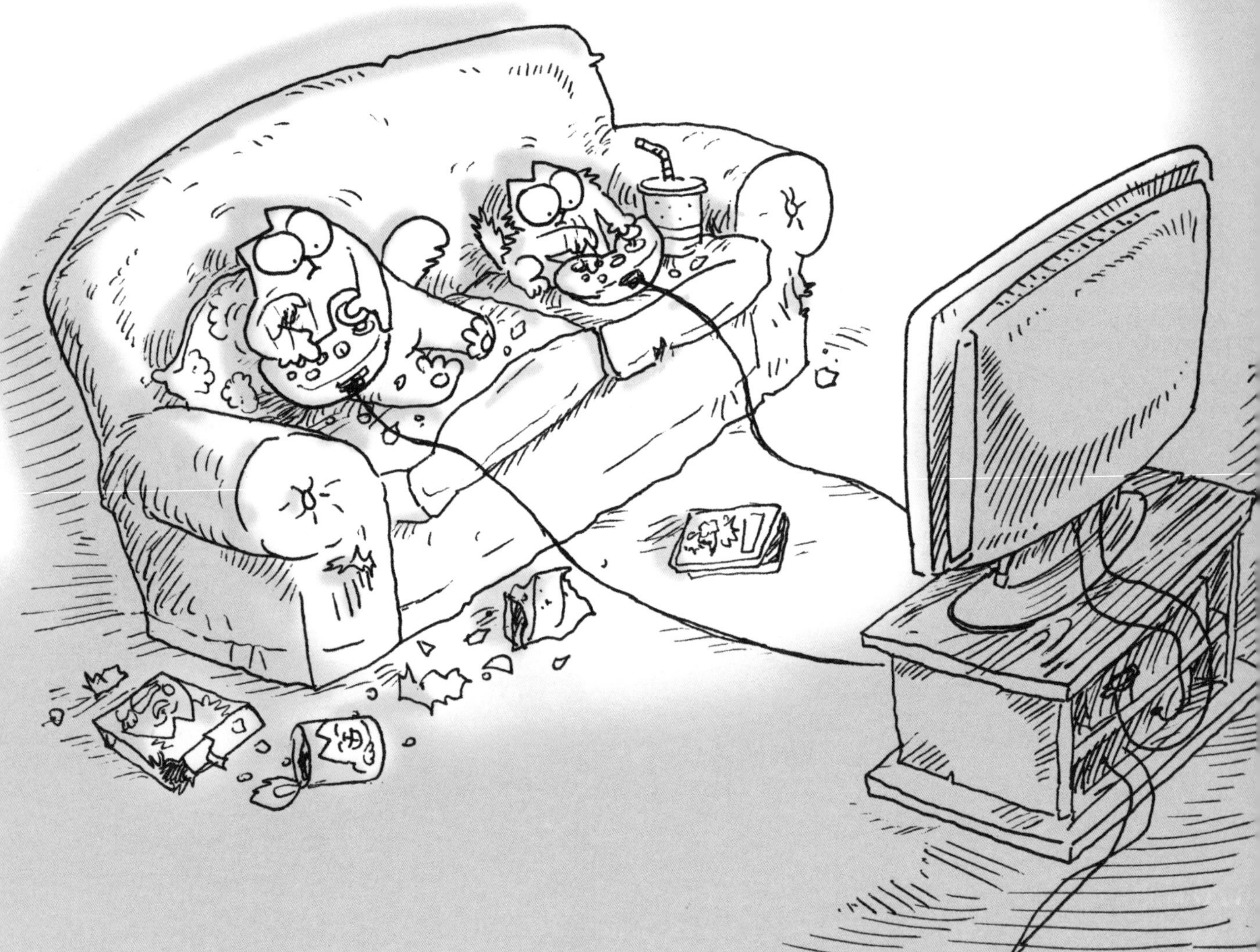

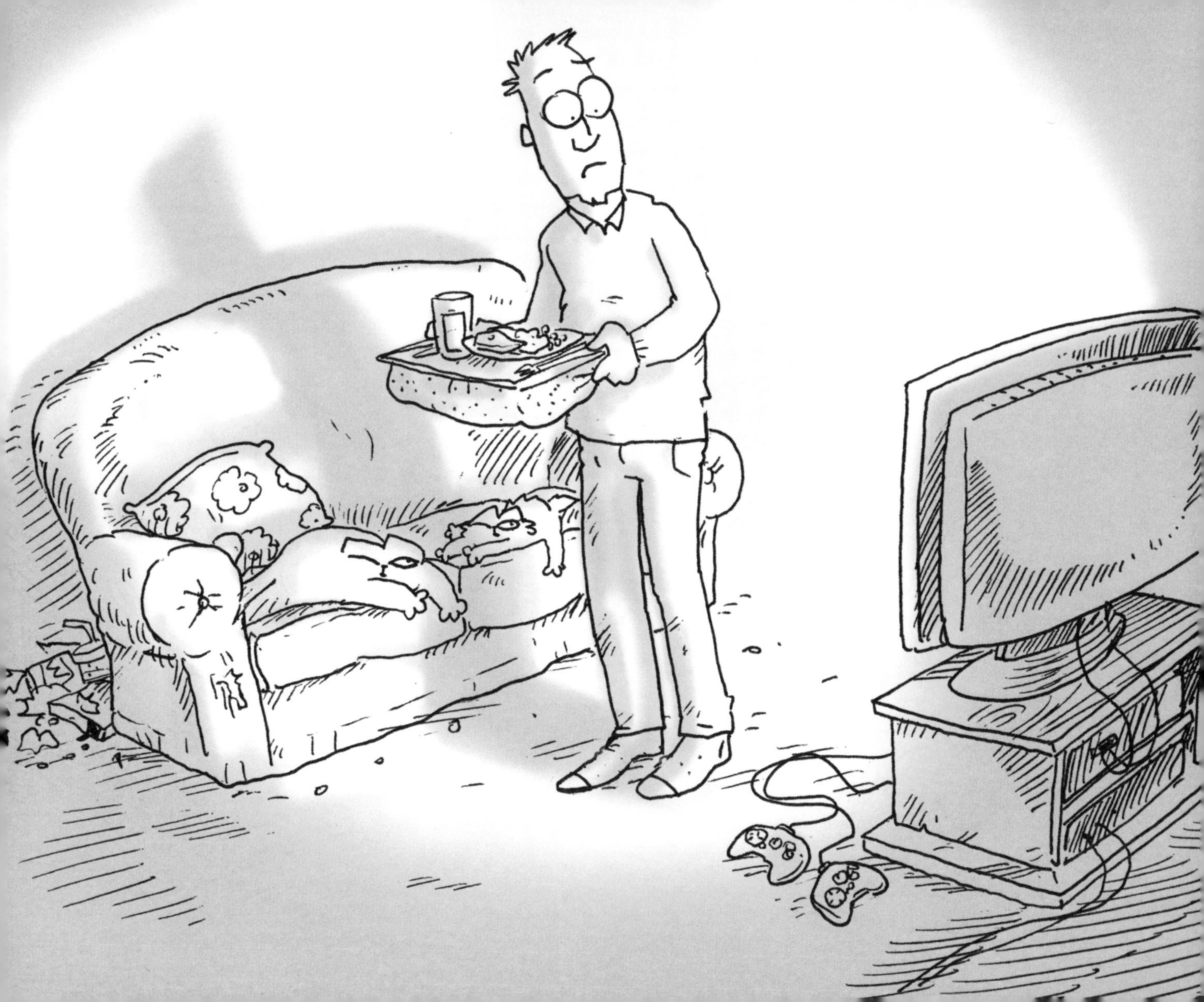

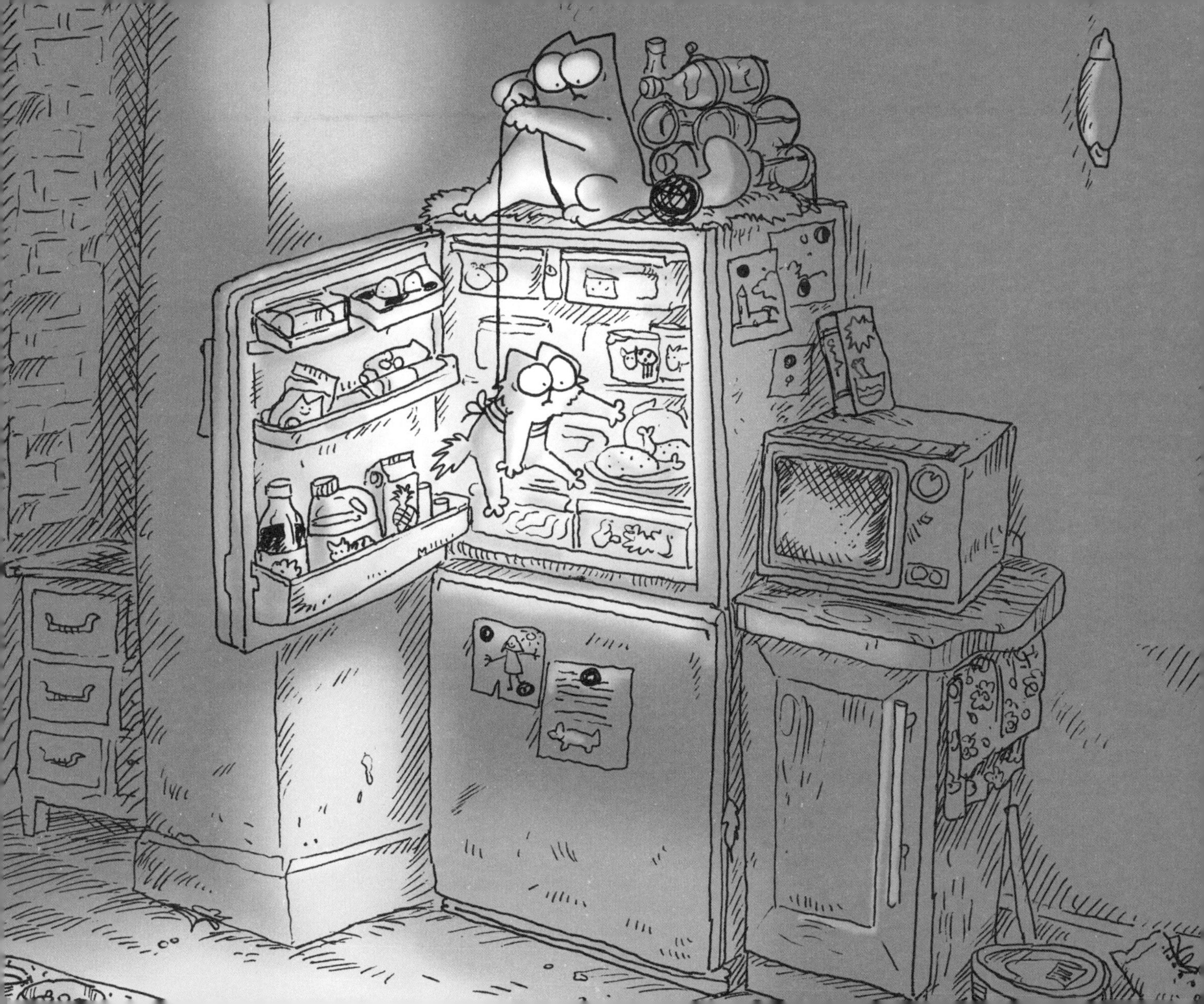

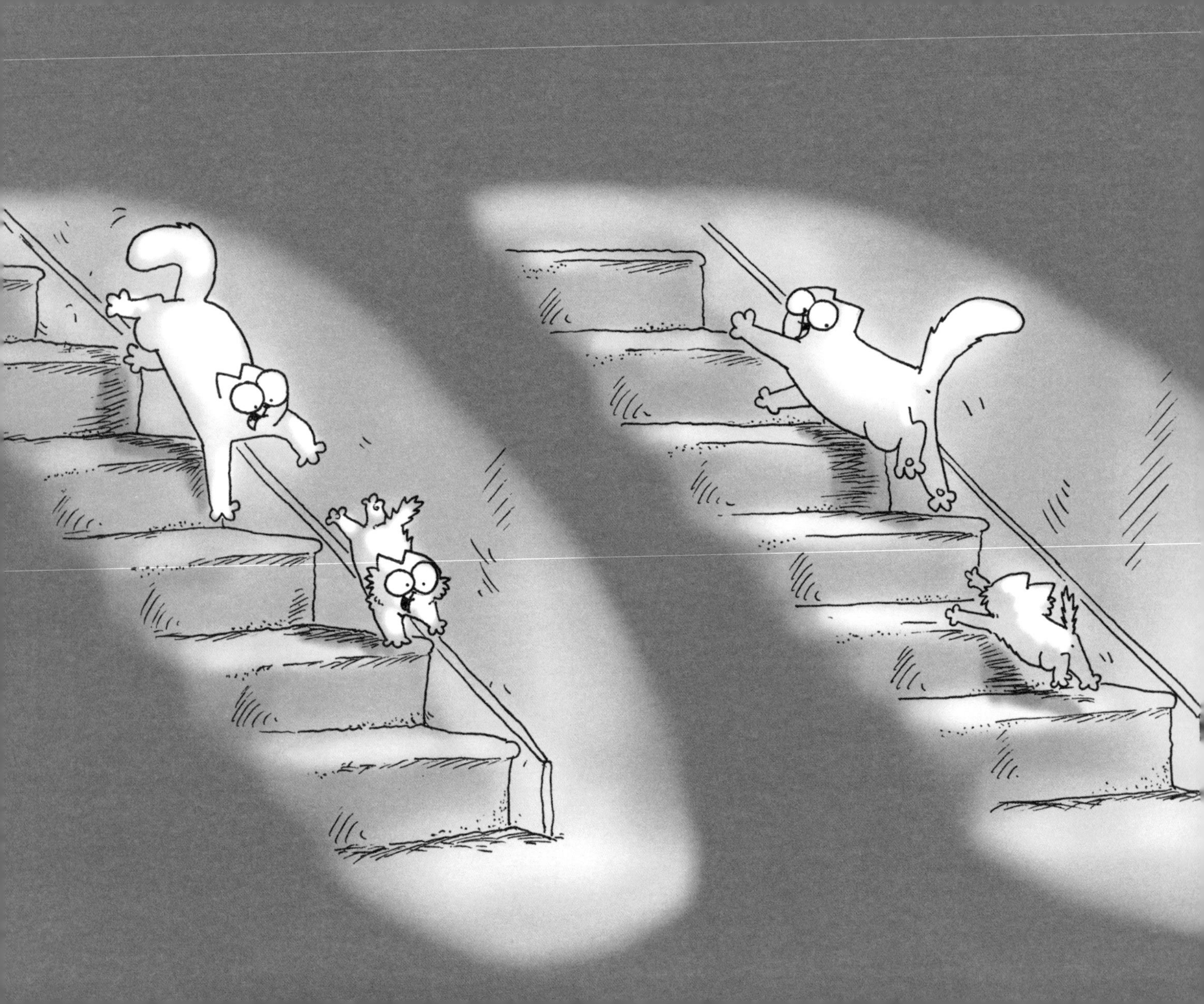

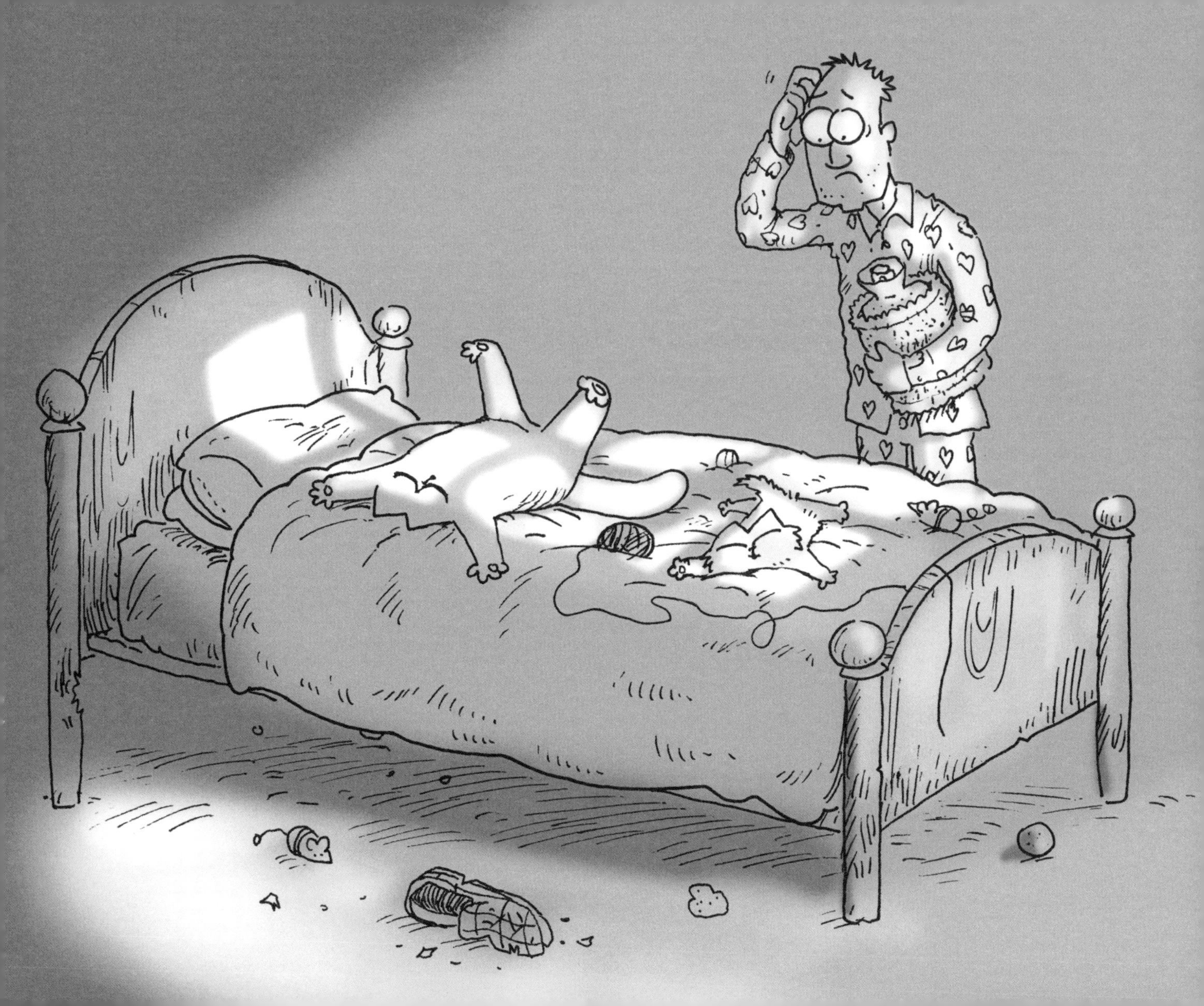

Acknowledgements

Everyone at Stray Cat Rescue for their ongoing work, Zoe Herbert-Jackson, Ross Walker, the Simon's Cat team, Mike Cook, Nigel Pay, Daniel Greaves, Mike Bell, Nick Davies and the Canongate team, Robert Kirby and Duncan Hayes at UA and, of course, my inspirational cats.

For all your Simon's Cat goodies,
check out the webshop at
www.simonscat.com

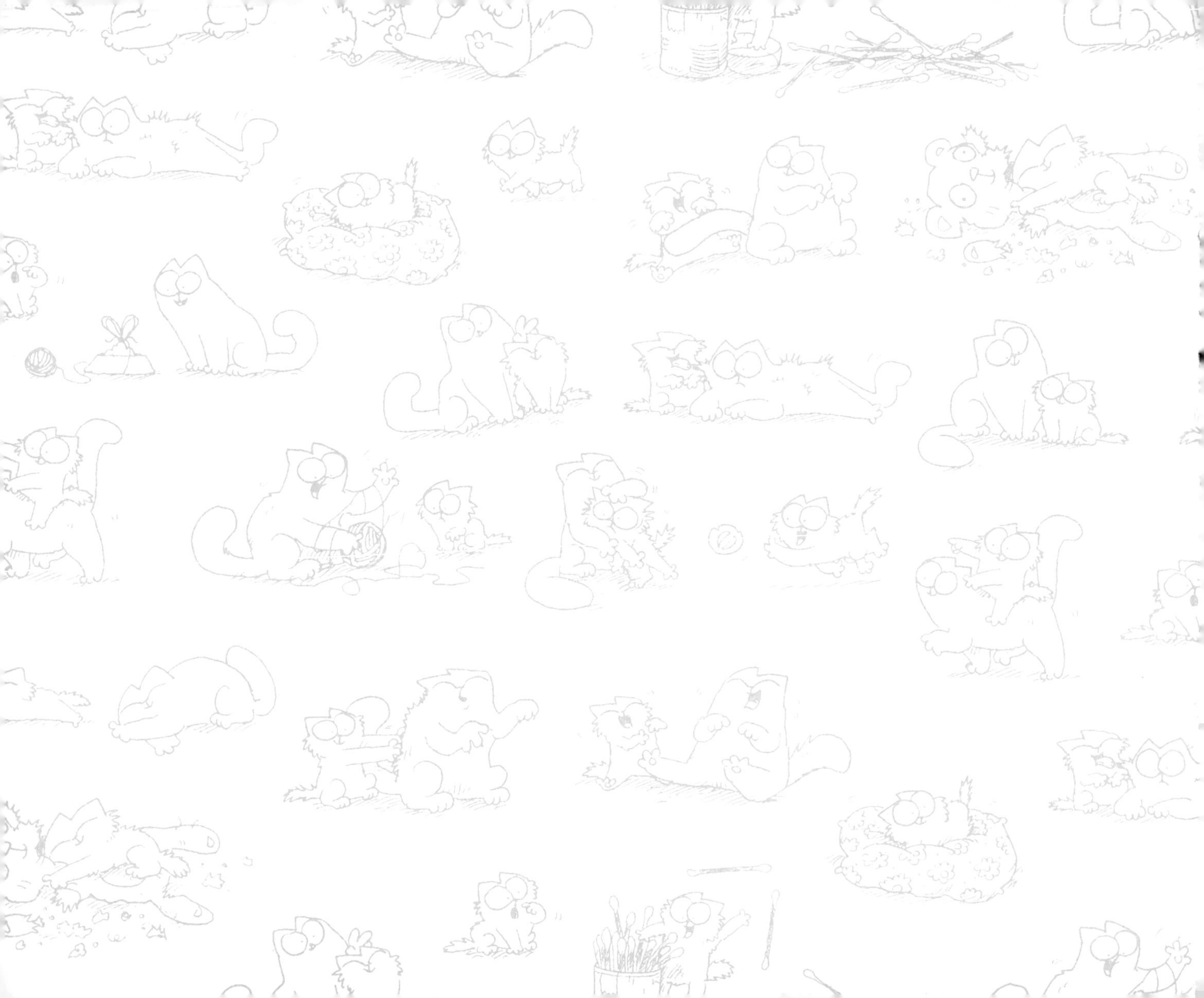